Collins
COBUILD

Key Words for IELTS

Book 2: IMPROVER

HarperCollins Publishers
Westerhill Road
Bishopbriggs
Glasgow
G64 2QT

First edition 2011

Reprint 10 9 8 7 6 5 4 3 2 1

© HarperCollins Publishers 2011

ISBN 978-0-00-736546-3

Collins ® is a registered trademark of
HarperCollins Publishers Limited

www.collinslanguage.com

A catalogue record for this book is
available from the British Library

Typeset by Davidson Publishing
Solutions, Glasgow

Printed in Great Britain by Clays Ltd,
St Ives plc

Editorial staff

Senior editor
Julie Moore

Project manager
Lisa Sutherland

Contributors
Sandra Anderson
Jamie Flockhart
Lucy Hollingworth
Virginia Klein
Claire Newton
Cerwyss O'Hare
Elizabeth Walter
Kate Wild

For the publishers
Lucy Cooper
Kerry Ferguson
Gavin Gray
Elaine Higgleton

Computing support
Thomas Callan

The publishers would like to thank
the following for their invaluable
contribution to the series:
Sharon Chalmers
Rachael Clarke
Jane Cursiter
Patrick Hubbuck
Martin Jenkins

contents

Introduction   4

Pronunciation guide   5

Guide to entries   6–7

Guide to grammatical labels   8

Word lists   9
  Sciences   10
  Social sciences   13
  Arts   17
  Multi-discipline   18
  Academic study   29
  Academic word list   30

Key words A–Z   37

Collins COBUILD KeyWords for IELTS: Book 2 Improver is the second in a series of three vocabulary books created for learners of English who plan to take the IELTS exam. *Book 2: Improver* covers the key words and phrases you need to master in order to achieve the IELTS score required by many universities and employers.

The first section of the book consists of **word lists** organized by subject and topic area. You can use these lists to help you **revise** sets of vocabulary or when preparing for writing tasks. The words are grouped into academic **subject areas**, such as Science and History, **common topics** such as social issues and the environment, as well as according to **functions**, such as talking about cause and effect or describing trends.

The second section of the book contains alphabetically ordered dictionary-style entries for **key words** and **phrases**. The vocabulary items have been chosen to fully prepare you for the kind of language found in the IELTS exam. The words and phrases regularly appear in the most **common IELTS topics**, and are clearly labelled by subject area. More formal vocabulary, including words from the **Academic Word List**, have also been included so that you can feel comfortable with the style of language used in formal, written contexts. You will find all the vocabulary you will need when working on IELTS-style writing tasks, such as data commentary and basic essays.

Each word is illustrated with **examples** of natural English taken from the Collins corpus and reflects the style of language used in IELTS texts. As well as definitions and examples, entries include additional information about **collocations** and **phrases**, as well as **usage notes** to help you put the vocabulary you have learnt into practice.

Words from the same root, for example, *analyse, analysis, analyst*, are shown together to help you make these vital **links** between words. By understanding how these words relate to each other, you will be able to vary the way you express your ideas, which will help improve your writing and speaking skills.

There are **synonyms** and **antonyms** at each entry to help you widen your range of vocabulary and create more variety in your writing style. The **Extend your vocabulary** boxes help you understand the differences between sets of similar words, so you can be sure that your English is accurate and natural.

We hope you enjoy preparing for IELTS using *Collins COBUILD KeyWords for IELTS*. Once you have mastered the vocabulary in Book 2, the words and phrases in Book 3 will help you to not only achieve the IELTS score you are aiming for, but equip you for success in the future.

We have used the International Phonetic Alphabet (IPA) to show how the words are pronounced.

IPA Symbols

Vowel Sounds

ɑː	calm, ah
æ	act, mass
aɪ	dive, cry
aɪə	fire, tyre
aʊ	out, down
aʊə	flour, sour
e	met, lend, pen
eɪ	say, weight
eə	fair, care
ɪ	fit, win
iː	seem, me
ɪə	near, beard
ɒ	lot, spot
eʊ	note, coat
ɔː	claw, more
ɔɪ	boy, joint
ʊ	could, stood
uː	you, use
ʊə	sure, pure
ɜː	turn, third
ʌ	fund, must
ə	the first vowel in about

Consonant Sounds

b	bed, rub
d	done, red
f	fit, if
g	good, dog
h	hat, horse
j	yellow, you
k	king, pick
l	lip, bill
m	mat, ram
n	not, tin
p	pay, lip
r	run, read
s	soon, bus
t	talk, bet
v	van, love
w	win, wool
x	loch
z	zoo, buzz
ʃ	ship, wish
ʒ	measure, leisure
ŋ	sing, working
tʃ	cheap, witch
θ	thin, myth
ð	then, bathe
dʒ	joy, bridge

Notes

Primary and secondary stress are shown by marks above and below the line, in front of the stressed syllable. For example, in the word *abbreviation*, /əˌbriːviˈeɪʃən/, the second syllable has secondary stress and the fourth syllable has primary stress.

We do not normally show pronunciations for compound words (words which are made up of more than one word). Pronunciations for the words that make up the compounds are usually found at their entries in other parts of the book. However, compound words do have stress markers.

6   guide to dictionary entries

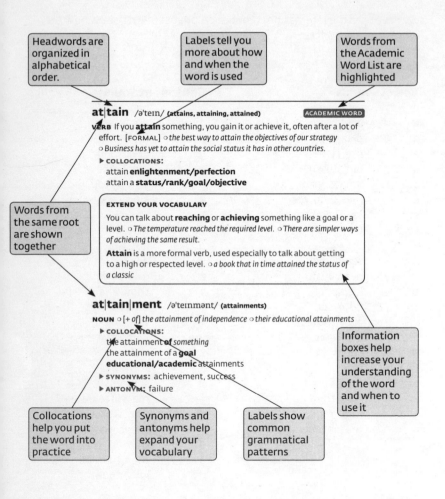

Headwords are organized in alphabetical order.

Labels tell you more about how and when the word is used

Words from the Academic Word List are highlighted

Words from the same root are shown together

at|tain /əˈteɪn/ **(attains, attaining, attained)**   ACADEMIC WORD

VERB If you **attain** something, you gain it or achieve it, often after a lot of effort. [FORMAL] ○ *the best way to attain the objectives of our strategy* ○ *Business has yet to attain the social status it has in other countries.*

▶ **COLLOCATIONS:**
attain **enlightenment/perfection**
attain a **status/rank/goal/objective**

EXTEND YOUR VOCABULARY

You can talk about **reaching** or **achieving** something like a goal or a level. ○ *The temperature reached the required level.* ○ *There are simpler ways of achieving the same result.*

Attain is a more formal verb, used especially to talk about getting to a high or respected level. ○ *a book that in time attained the status of a classic*

at|tain|ment /əˈteɪnmənt/ **(attainments)**

NOUN ○ [+ of] *the attainment of independence* ○ *their educational attainments*

▶ **COLLOCATIONS:**
the attainment **of** *something*
the attainment of a **goal**
educational/academic attainments
▶ **SYNONYMS:** achievement, success
▶ **ANTONYM:** failure

Information boxes help increase your understanding of the word and when to use it

Collocations help you put the word into practice

Synonyms and antonyms help expand your vocabulary

Labels show common grammatical patterns

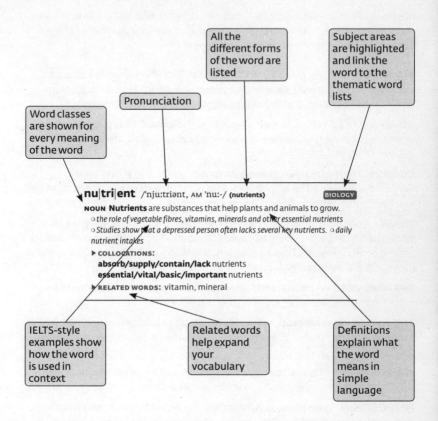

All the different forms of the word are listed

Subject areas are highlighted and link the word to the thematic word lists

Pronunciation

Word classes are shown for every meaning of the word

nu|tri|ent /'njuːtriənt, AM 'nuː-/ (nutrients) [BIOLOGY]

NOUN **Nutrients** are substances that help plants and animals to grow. ○ the role of vegetable fibres, vitamins, minerals and other essential nutrients ○ Studies show that a depressed person often lacks several key nutrients. ○ daily nutrient intakes

▶ COLLOCATIONS:
   absorb/supply/contain/lack nutrients
   essential/vital/basic/important nutrients
▶ RELATED WORDS: vitamin, mineral

IELTS-style examples show how the word is used in context

Related words help expand your vocabulary

Definitions explain what the word means in simple language

All the words in the dictionary section have grammar information given about them. For each word, its word class is shown after the headword. The sections below show more information about each word class.

ADJECTIVE　An adjective is a word that is used for telling you more about a person or thing. You would use an adjective to talk about appearance, colour, size, or other qualities, e.g. *He has been <u>absent</u> from his desk for two weeks.*

ADVERB　An adverb is a word that gives more information about when, how, or where something happens, e.g. *The costs of each part of the process can be measured fairly <u>accurately</u>.*

CONJUNCTION　A conjunction is a word such as *and, but, if,* and *since.* Conjunctions are used for linking two words or two parts of a sentence together, e.g. *Their system worked, <u>although</u> no one was sure how.*

NOUN　A noun is a word that refers to a person, a thing, or a quality. In this book, the label *noun* is given to all countable nouns. A countable noun is used for talking about things that can be counted, and that have both singular and plural forms, e.g. *She turned her <u>head</u> away, difficult financial <u>situations</u>.*

PHRASAL VERB　A phrasal verb consists of a verb and one or more particles, e.g. *All experiments were <u>carried out</u> by three psychologists.*

PHRASE　Phrases are groups of words which are used together and which have a meaning of their own, e.g. *Most schools are unwilling to cut down on staff <u>in order to</u> cut costs.*

PLURAL NOUN　A plural noun is always plural, and it is used with plural verbs, e.g. *He called the <u>emergency services</u> and they arrived within minutes.*

PREPOSITION　A preposition is a word such as *by, with,* or *from* which is always followed by a noun group or the *-ing* form of a verb, e.g. *The themes are repeated <u>throughout</u> the film.*

PRONOUN　A pronoun is a word that you use instead of a noun, when you do not need or want to name someone or something directly, e.g. *No one drug will suit everyone and sometimes <u>several</u> may have to be tried.*

UNCOUNTABLE NOUN　An uncountable noun is used for talking about things that are not normally counted, or that we do not think of as single items. Uncountable nouns do not have a plural form, and they are used with a singular verb, e.g. *The report has inevitably been greeted with <u>scepticism</u>.*

VERB　A verb is a word that is used for saying what someone or something does, or what happens to them, or to give information about them, e.g. *The exhibition <u>traces</u> the history of graphic design.*

Word lists

SCIENCES

General science

Scientific processes
circulate (verb)
  circulation (uncount)
emit (verb)
  emission (noun)
evaporate (verb)
  evaporation (uncount)
flow (verb, noun, uncount)
form (verb)
generate (verb)
  generation (uncount)
magnify (verb)
  magnification (uncount, noun)
rotate (verb)
vaporize (verb)

Scientific phenomena
current (noun)
movement (noun)
nuclear (adj)
phenomenon (noun)
power (uncount, verb)
pressure (uncount)
property (noun)
solar (adj)

Scientific research
device (noun)
equation (noun)
instrument (noun)
law (noun)
microscope (noun)
  microscopic (adj)
pioneer (noun, verb)
  pioneering (adj)
sample (noun)
satellite (noun)
specimen (noun)
trial (noun)

Substances
carbon (uncount)
carbon dioxide (uncount)
fluid (noun)
hydrogen (uncount)
material (noun, plural)
matter (uncount)

mineral (noun)
toxic (adj)
vapour (noun)

The environment
carbon footprint (noun)
carbon neutral (adj)
conserve (verb)
  conservation (uncount)
renewable (adj)

Pure sciences

Chemistry
element (noun)
formula (noun)
solution (noun)

Physics
attract (verb)
  attraction (noun)
circuit (noun)
gravity (uncount)
magnet (noun)
  magnetic (adj)
mass (adj, noun)
power (uncount, verb)
  powerful (adj)
  powerfully (adv)
pressure (uncount)
signal (noun)
volt (noun)
  voltage (noun)
wave (noun)

Applied sciences

Engineering
architecture (uncount)
  architectural (adj)
  architect (noun)
circuit (noun)
device (noun)
generate (verb)
  generation (uncount)
input (noun, verb)
mechanism (noun)

output (uncount)
plant (noun)
power (uncount, verb)
  powerful (adj)
  powerfully (adv)
volt (noun)
  voltage (noun)

IT
access (uncount, verb)
  accessible (adj)
data (uncount)
input (noun, verb)
network (noun)
output (uncount)
program (noun, verb)
retrieve (verb)
  retrieval (uncount)
telecommunications (uncount)
virus (noun)
  viral (adj)

Maths

Algebra
algebra (uncount)
equation (noun)
formula (noun)

Arithmetic
arithmetic (uncount)
cube (noun)
  cubic (adj)
digit (noun)
minus (conj, adj)
numeral (noun)
plus (conj, adj)
square (verb, noun)
sum (noun, ph verb)

Geometry
angle (noun)
circumference (uncount)
diameter (noun)
geometry (uncount)
perimeter (noun)
radius (noun)

Biology & medicine

Biology
bacteria (plural)
  bacterial (adj)
cell (noun)
germ (noun)
nerve (noun)
organism (noun)

evolve (verb)
  evolution (uncount, noun)
female (adj, noun)
hereditary (adj)
  heredity (uncount)
infant (noun)
  infancy (uncount)
inherit (verb)
instinct (noun)
  instinctive (adj)
male (adj, noun)
mature (verb)
sex (noun, uncount)
  sexual (adj)
sibling (noun)
territory (uncount)
  territorial (adj)
vision (uncount)

crop (noun)
ecology (uncount, noun)
  ecological (adj)
  ecologically (adv)
  ecologist (noun)

Health & medicine
calorie (noun)
hygiene (uncount)
  hygienic (adj)
life expectancy (uncount)
nutrition (uncount)
vision (uncount)

clinical (adj)
diagnose (verb)
  diagnosis (noun)
examine (verb)
  examination (noun)

screen (verb)
  screening (noun)
side-effect (noun)
surgery (uncount)
  surgeon (noun)
  surgical (adj)
  surgically (adv)

depression (noun)
disorder (noun)
fatal (adj)
  fatally (adv)
  fatality (noun)
infect (verb)
  infection (uncount, noun)
  infectious (adj)
mental (adj)
  mentally (adv)
recover (verb)
  recovery (noun)

Medical science
bacteria (plural)
  bacterial (adj)
cell (noun)
germ (noun)
hereditary (adj)
  heredity (uncount)
toxic (adj)
trial (noun)
virus (noun)
  viral (adj)

Geography

Human geography
developed (adj)
developing (adj)
ecology (uncount, noun)
  ecological (adj)
  ecologically (adv)
  ecologist (noun)

famine (uncount)
globe (noun)
  global (adj)
  globally (adv)
  globalization (uncount)

infrastructure (noun)
inhabitant (noun)
  inhabit (verb)
overseas (adj)
territory (uncount)
  territorial (adj)
Third World (noun)
urban (adj)
  urbanized (adj)

Physical geography
Celsius (adj)
centigrade (adj)
current (noun)
evaporate (verb)
  evaporation (uncount)
Fahrenheit (adj, uncount)
vapour (noun)
  vaporize (verb)

pole (noun)
  polar (adj)
tropics (plural)
  tropical (adj)

deposit (noun, verb)
erode (verb)
  erosion (uncount)
geology (uncount)
  geological (adj)
  geologist (noun)
mineral (noun)

Sociology

sociology (uncount)
sociological (adj)
sociologist (noun)

Social groups
advantaged (adj)
class (noun, verb)
emigrate (verb)
emigration (uncount)
emigrant (noun)
ethnic (adj)
ethnicity (uncount)
female (adj, noun)
gender (noun)
immigrate (verb)
immigration (uncount)
immigrant (noun)
male (adj, noun)
minority (noun)
race (noun)
racial (adj)
racist (adj, noun)
sex (noun, uncount)
sexual (adj)
stereotype (noun, verb)
stereotypical (adj)

The family
domestic (adj)
household (noun)
sibling (noun)
spouse (noun)

Social attitudes
attitude (noun)
moral (adj)
morally (adv)
norm (noun)
poll (noun, verb)

Social issues
abuse (uncount, noun, verb)
abuser (noun)
discriminate (verb)
discrimination (uncount)
exploit (verb)
exploitation (uncount)

famine (uncount)
hardship (noun)
illiterate (adj, noun)
life expectancy (uncount)
literate (adj)
literacy (uncount)
prejudice (noun)
prejudiced (adj)
prejudicial (adj)

Society & the state
aid (uncount, verb, noun)
censor (verb, noun)
censorship (uncount)
civil (adj)
depend (verb)
dependence (uncount)
dependent (adj)
welfare (uncount, adj)

Politics

Government & politics
civil (adj)
domestic (adj)
federal (adj)
federation (noun)
private (adj)
privately (adv)
privatize (verb)
privatization (noun)
public (adj)

candidate (noun)
candidacy (noun)
executive (noun)
ministry (noun)
parliament (noun)
parliamentary (adj)
administration (uncount, noun)
administrative (adj)
bureaucracy (uncount)
bureaucratic (adj)
elect (verb)
election (noun)
electorate (noun)
measures (noun)
poll (noun, verb)
scheme (noun)

Political issues
developed (adj)
developing (adj)
Third World (noun)

aid (uncount, verb, noun)
conflict (uncount, noun, verb)
corruption (uncount)
  corrupt (adj)
crisis (noun)
terrorist (noun)
  terrorism (uncount)

Political movements
abolish (verb)
  abolition (uncount)
activist (noun)
  activism (uncount)
censor (verb, noun)
  censorship (uncount)
movement (noun)
reform (noun, verb)
  reformer (noun)
revolution (noun)
  revolutionary (adj)
  revolutionize (verb)

Political systems & beliefs
capitalism (uncount)
  capitalist (adj, noun)
communism (uncount)
  communist (noun, adj)
conservative (adj)
democracy (uncount, noun)
  democratic (adj)
  democrat (noun)
ideal (noun)
  idealism (uncount)
  idealistic (adj)
left-wing (adj)
liberal (adj, noun)
radical (adj)
  radically (adv)
republic (noun)
  republican (adj, noun)
right-wing (adj)
socialism (uncount)
  socialist (adj, noun)

Business & economics

Business sectors
commerce (uncount)
  commercial (adj)
  commercially (adv)
insurance (uncount)
manufacture (verb)
  manufacturing (uncount)
  manufacturer (noun)

corporate (adj)
  corporation (noun)
industry (noun)
  industrial (adj)
institute (noun)
institution (noun)
multinational (adj, noun)
private (adj)
  privately (adv)
  privatize (verb)
  privatization (noun)
public (adj)
sector (noun)

Doing business
contract (noun)
demand (uncount)
licence (noun)
  license (verb)
regulate (verb)
  regulated (adj)
  regulator (noun)
  regulatory (adj)
resource (noun)
supply (verb, noun, uncount)

output (uncount)
plant (noun)

consume (verb)
  consumption (uncount)
  consumer (noun)

distribute (verb)
  distributed (adj)
  distribution (uncount, noun)
export (verb, noun)
  exportation (uncount)
goods (plural)
import (verb, uncount, noun)
  importation (uncount)
launch (verb, noun)
purchase (verb, noun)
retail (uncount)
  retailer (noun)
trade (uncount, verb)

Jobs & roles
analyst (noun)
architect (noun)
consultant (noun)
economist (noun)
editor (noun)
lecturer (noun)
psychologist (noun)
surgeon (noun)

candidate (noun)
consumer (noun)
executive (noun)
investor (noun)
manufacturer (noun)
regulator (noun)
retailer (noun)
spokesperson (noun)
volunteer (noun, verb)
workforce (noun)

The workplace
administration (uncount, noun)
  administrative (adj)
candidate (noun)
  candidacy (noun)
department (noun)
  departmental (adj)
labour (uncount)
occupation (noun, uncount)
  occupational (adj)
union (noun)
voluntary (adj)
  voluntarily (adv)
  volunteer (noun, verb)

workforce (noun)
workplace (noun)

Economics & finance
asset (noun, plural)
bankrupt (adj)
  bankruptcy (uncount)
capital (uncount)
capitalism (uncount)
  capitalist (adj, noun)
credit (uncount)
debt (noun, uncount)
demand (uncount)
deposit (noun, verb)
economy (noun)
  economic (adj)
  economical (adj)
  economically (adv)
  economics (uncount)
  economist (noun)
expenditure (uncount)
fee (noun)
fund (plural, verb)
  funding (uncount)
inflation (uncount)
interest (noun, uncount)
invest (verb)
  investment (uncount, noun)
  investor (noun)
mortgage (noun)
subsidy (noun)
  subsidize (verb)
sum (noun, ph verb)
supply (verb, noun, uncount)

Law

Law
accuse (verb)
  accusation (noun)
allege (verb)
  alleged (adj)
  allegedly (adv)
appeal (verb, noun)
commit (verb)
  commitment (noun)
  committed (adj)

SOCIAL SCIENCES

defend (verb)
  defence (noun)
  defendant (noun)
justice (uncount)
legislate (verb)
  legislation (uncount)
  legislative (adj)
offence (noun)
  offend (verb)
  offender (noun)
penalty (noun)
rule (verb)
sentence (noun, verb)
suspect (noun)
verdict (noun)

Education

grade (verb, noun)
illiterate (adj, noun)
literate (adj)
  literacy (uncount)

Academic study
academic (adj)
  academically (adv)
campus (noun)
department (noun)
  departmental (adj)
discipline (noun)
faculty (noun)
lecture (noun)
  lecturer (noun)
professor (noun)
scholarship (noun)
seminar (noun)
tutor (noun)
  tutorial (noun)
  tuition (uncount)

Academic qualifications
assess (verb)
  assessment (noun)
bachelor's degree (noun)
doctorate (noun)
  doctoral (adj)

master's degree (noun)
PhD (noun)
postgraduate (noun, adj)
thesis (noun)
undergraduate (noun)

Academic subjects
anthropology (uncount)
  anthropologist (noun)
archaeology (uncount)
  archaeological (adj)
  archaeologist (noun)
architecture (uncount)
  architectural (adj)
  architect (noun)
astronomy (uncount)
  astronomer (noun)
  astronomical (adj)
ecology (uncount, noun)
  ecological (adj)
  ecologically (adv)
  ecologist (noun)
economics (uncount)
  economist (noun)
geology (uncount)
  geological (adj)
  geologist (noun)
humanities (plural)
linguistic (adj, uncount)
  linguistically (adv)
  linguist (noun)
philosophy (uncount)
  philosopher (noun)
psychology (uncount)
  psychological (adj)
  psychologist (noun)
sociology (uncount)
  sociological (adj)
  sociologist (noun)
statistics (noun, uncount)
  statistician (noun)
theology (uncount)
  theological (adj)
  theologian (noun)

Art & literature

Art & design
abstract (adj)
architecture (uncount)
  architectural (adj)
  architect (noun)
classical (adj)
contemporary (adj)
style (noun)

Literature
excerpt (noun)
extract (noun)
playwright (noun)
plot (noun, verb)
prose (uncount)
verse (uncount)

The media
broadcast (noun, verb)
edit (verb)
  editor (noun)
  edition (noun)
mainstream (noun)
publish (verb)
  publication (uncount, noun)

Linguistics

Linguistics
express (verb)
  expression (noun)
gesture (noun)
glossary (noun)
illiterate (adj, noun)
linguistic (adj, uncount)
  linguistically (adv)
  linguist (noun)
literate (adj)
  literacy (uncount)
terminology (uncount)
text (noun)
  textual (adj)

History

History
archaeology (uncount)
  archaeological (adj)
  archaeologist (noun)
civilization (noun)
classical (adj)
classics (uncount)
contemporary (adj)
era (noun)
invade (verb)
  invasion (noun)
pioneer (noun, verb)
  pioneering (adj)
prehistoric (adj)
revolution (noun)
  revolutionary (adj)
  revolutionize (verb)

MULTI-DISCIPLINE

Actions & processes

conduct (verb)
function (noun, verb)
  functional (adj)
implement (verb)
  implementation (uncount)
insert (verb)
participate (verb)
  participation (uncount)
perform (verb)
  performance (noun)
practise (verb)
  practice (noun)
procedure (noun)
  procedural (adj)
react (verb)
  reaction (noun)
undertake (verb)
  undertaking (noun)

achieve (verb)
  achievement (noun)
address (verb)
challenge (noun, verb)
overcome (verb)
struggle (verb, noun)

consume (verb)
  consumption (uncount)
employ (verb)
utilize (verb)
  utilization (uncount)

acquire (verb)
  acquisition (noun, uncount)
adopt (verb)
  adoption (uncount)
gain (verb, noun)
gather (verb)
obtain (verb)
purchase (verb, noun)
retrieve (verb)
  retrieval (uncount)

provide (verb)
  provision (uncount)
release (verb, noun)

submit (verb)
  submission (noun)

assemble (verb)
  assembly (noun, uncount)
construct (verb)
  construction (uncount)
form (verb)
  formation (uncount, noun)
manufacture (verb)
  manufacturing (uncount)
produce (verb)

accompany (verb)
attach (verb)
  attachment (noun)
attend (verb)
  attendance (uncount, noun)
circulate (verb)
  circulation (uncount)
collapse (verb)
distribute (verb)
  distributed (adj)
  distribution (uncount, noun)
flow (verb, noun, uncount)
rotate (verb)
  rotation (noun)

commence (verb)
establish (verb)
  establishment (noun)
launch (verb, noun)
stimulate (verb)
  stimulation (uncount)

abandon (verb)
abolish (verb)
  abolition (uncount)
cease (verb)
complete (verb)
  completion (noun)
delay (verb, noun)
dispose of (ph verb)
  disposal (uncount)
disrupt (verb)
  disruption (noun)
  disruptive (adj)
eliminate (verb)
  elimination (uncount)

interfere (verb)
interference (uncount)
postpone (verb)
postponement (noun)
withdraw (verb)
withdrawal (noun, uncount)

dominate (verb)
dominant (adj)
exclude (verb)
excluding (prep)
exclusion (noun)
impose (verb)
imposition (uncount)
isolate (verb)
isolation (uncount)
isolated (adj)
prohibit (verb)
prohibition (uncount)
regulate (verb)
regulated (adj)
regulatory (adj)
restrict (verb)
restriction (noun)

co-ordinate (verb)
co-ordination (uncount)
ensure (verb)
guarantee (verb, noun)
motivate (verb)
motivation (uncount)
negotiate (verb)
promote (verb)
promotion (uncount)

demonstrate (verb)
demonstration (noun)
display (verb, noun)
disprove (verb)
represent (verb)
representative (adj)
reveal (verb)

detect (verb)
detection (uncount)
detector (noun)
diagnose (verb)
diagnosis (noun)

encounter (verb)
examine (verb)
examination (noun)
identify (verb)
identification (uncount)
inspect (verb)
inspection (noun)
investigate (verb)
investigation (noun)
monitor (verb, noun)
pursue (verb)
seek (verb)

allocate (verb)
allocation (noun)
assess (verb)
assessment (noun)
determine (verb)
determination (noun)
distinguish (verb)
elect (verb)
election (noun)
select (verb)
verify (verb)
verification (uncount)

arise (verb)
emerge (verb)
emergence (uncount)
occur (verb)
occurrence (noun)
undergo (verb)

ease (verb)
enhance (verb)
enhancement (noun)
strengthen (verb)

maintain (verb)
maintenance (uncount)
preserve (verb)
preservation (uncount)
remain (verb)
retain (verb)
retention (uncount)
sustain (verb)
sustainable (adj)
sustainability (uncount)

observe (verb)
  observation (uncount)
occupy (verb)
  occupant (noun)
possess (verb)
  possession (uncount, noun)
rely (verb)
  reliant (adj)
  reliance (uncount)
require (verb)
  requirement (noun)

apply (verb)
  application (noun)
attract (verb)
  attraction (noun)
expose (verb)
  exposure (uncount)
reserve (noun)
simulate (verb)
  simulation (noun)

Change

adapt (verb)
  adaptation (uncount)
  adaptable (adj)
  adaptability (uncount)
adjust (verb)
  adjustment (noun)
alter (verb)
  alteration (noun)
alternate (verb)
breakthrough (noun)
convert (verb)
  conversion (uncount)
develop (verb)
  development (noun)
  developmental (adj)
erode (verb)
  erosion (uncount)
evaporate (verb)
  evaporation (uncount)
evolve (verb)
  evolution (uncount, noun)
exchange (verb)
extend (verb)
  extension (uncount)

modify (verb)
  modification (noun)
reverse (verb, adj)
  reversal (noun)
revise (verb)
  revision (noun)
substitute (verb, noun)
  substitution (noun)
transfer (verb, noun, uncount)
transform (verb)
  transformation (noun)
vary (verb)
  variation (noun)
  variable (noun)

Mental processes

accept (verb)
  acceptable (adj)
  acceptance (noun, uncount)
analyse (verb)
  analysis (noun)
assume (verb)
  assumption (noun)
concentrate (verb)
  concentration (uncount, noun)
evaluate (verb)
  evaluation (noun)
  evaluative (adj)
intend (verb)
  intention (noun)
  intentional (adj)
perceive (verb)
  perception (noun)
  perceptible (adj)
  perceptibly (adv)
presume (verb)
reason (uncount)
  reasoning (uncount)
recognize (verb)
  recognition (uncount)
regard (verb)
tolerate (verb)
  tolerant (adj)
  tolerance (uncount)

Speech & reporting

agree (verb)
agreement (uncount)
approve (verb)
approval (uncount)
compromise (noun, verb)
confirm (verb)
confirmation (uncount)
co-operate (verb)
co-operation (uncount)
co-operative (adj)

consult (verb)
consultation (noun)
inquiry (noun)
request (verb, noun)
respond (verb)
response (noun)

contact (uncount, verb)
contribute (verb)
contribution (noun)
debate (noun, verb)
express (verb)
expression (noun)
inform (verb)

accuse (verb)
accusation (noun)
allege (verb)
alleged (adj)
allegedly (adv)
criticize (verb)
criticism (noun, uncount)
critical (adj)
critically (adv)
question (verb, noun)

contradict (verb)
contradiction (noun)
contradictory (adj)
controversy (noun)
controversial (adj)
controversially (adv)
deny (verb)
denial (noun, uncount)
dispute (noun, verb)

object (noun, verb)
objection (noun)
oppose (verb)
opposed (adj)
opposing (adj)
opposition (uncount, noun)
reject (verb)
rejection (uncount)

emphasis (noun)
emphasize (verb)
focus (verb, noun)
highlight (verb)
note (verb)
stress (verb, noun)
underline (verb)

define (verb)
definition (noun)
expand on/upon (ph verb)
following (adj, pron)
guideline (noun)
instruction (noun, plural)
simplify (verb)
simplification (noun)

predict (verb)
prediction (noun)
predictable (adj)
project (verb)
projection (noun)

argue (verb)
argument (noun)
claim (verb, noun)
declare (verb)
declaration (noun)
introduce (verb)
introduction (noun)
present (adj, verb)
presentation (noun)
propose (verb)
proposal (noun)
proposition (noun)
put forward (ph verb)
state (verb)
statement (noun)
suggest (verb)

chart (verb)
register (verb)
  registration (uncount)
survey (noun, verb)

according to (phrase)
mention (verb)
quote (verb, noun)
  quotation (noun)
refer (verb)
  reference (noun)
report (verb)
source (noun)

illustrate (verb)
  illustration (noun)
indicate (verb)
  indication (noun)
  indicator (noun)

compare (verb)
  comparison (noun)
conclude (verb)
  conclusion (noun)
contrast (noun, verb)
implication (noun)
imply (verb)
interpret (verb)
  interpretation (noun)

bear out (ph verb)
defend (verb)
justify (verb)
  justification (noun)
support (verb, uncount)

generalize (verb)
  generalization (noun)
overview (noun)
review (noun, verb)

Compare & contrast

advantage (noun, uncount)
compare (verb)
  comparison (noun)
contrast (noun, verb)

distinct (adj)
  distinction (noun)
  distinctive (adj)
  distinctively (adv)
equivalent (noun)
  equivalence (uncount)
identical (adj)
  identically (adv)
outweigh (verb)
vary (verb)
  variation (noun)
  variable (noun)

Cause & effect

aim (noun)
condition (noun)
  conditional (adj)
  conditionally (adv)
goal (noun)
origin (noun)
  originate (verb)
target (noun, verb)
trigger (verb, noun)

consequence (noun)
  consequently (adv)
follow (verb)
impact (noun, verb)
outcome (noun)
result (verb)
  resultant (adj)
therefore (adv)
thus (adv)

Connections

associated (adj)
concern (verb)
  concerned (adj)
  concerning (prep)
connected (adj)
  connection (noun)
correspond (verb)
  corresponding (adj)
in terms of (phrase)

reflect (verb)
reflection (noun)
regarding (prep)
relate (verb)
related (adj)
relation (noun)
respective (adj)
respectively (adv)
versus (prep)

indirect (adj)
indirectly (adv)
integrate (verb)
integration (uncount)
interested (adj)
joint (adj)
jointly (adv)
logic (uncount)
logical (adj)
logically (adv)
mutual (adj)
mutually (adv)
relevant (adj)
separate (verb)
separation (noun)

Trends

dramatic (adj)
dramatically (adv)
drastic (adj)
drastically (adv)
sharp (adj)
sharply (adv)
steady (adj)
steadily (adv)
steep (adj)
steeply (adv)

decline (verb, noun)
dip (verb, noun)
plummet (verb)
reduce (verb)
reduction (noun, uncount)

fluctuate (verb)
fluctuation (noun)
progress (uncount)
progression (noun)
progressive (adj, noun)
progressively (adv)
shift (verb, noun)
trend (noun)

exceed (verb)
excess (noun)
excessive (adj)
excessively (adv)
expand (verb)
expansion (uncount)
peak (noun, verb)
soar (verb)

Time

constant (noun)
continuous (adj)
continuously (adv)
seldom (adv)

forthcoming (adj)
long-term (adj, noun)
prospect (noun)
prospective (adj)

interval (noun)
phase (noun)

former (pron)
initial (adj)
initially (adv)
preliminary (adj)
prior (adj)
sequence (noun)
sequential (adj)
simultaneous (adj)
simultaneously (adv)
subsequent (adj)
subsequently (adv)
ultimate (adj)
ultimately (adv)

brief (adj)
briefly (adv)
pace (noun)
rapid (adj)
rapidly (adv)
rate (noun)

Methods

approach (verb, noun)
criterion (noun)
logic (uncount)
logical (adj)
logically (adv)
method (noun)
methodology (noun)
model (noun, verb)
strategy (noun)
strategic (adj)
style (noun)
subject (noun)
systematic (adj)
systematically (adv)
theory (noun)
theoretical (adj)

Groups & categories

category (noun)
categorize (verb)
characteristic (noun, adj)
class (noun, verb)
classify (verb)
classification (uncount)
component (noun)
compose (verb)
composition (uncount)
comprise (verb)
consist (verb)
field (noun)
grade (verb)
intermediate (adj)

Parts & features

aspect (noun)
feature (noun)
nature (noun)
property (noun)
quality (uncount, noun)
trait (noun)
value (uncount, verb, plural, noun)

body (noun)
fragment (noun, verb)
fragmentation (uncount)
layer (noun)
portion (noun)
sample (noun)
sector (noun)
segment (noun)
specimen (noun)
unit (noun)

Structures

base (noun, verb)
basis (noun)
foundation (noun)
fundamental (adj)
fundamentally (adv)

bond (noun)
format (noun)
framework (noun)
network (noun)
profile (noun)

Shapes & positions

angle (noun)
cone (noun)
cube (noun)
cubic (adj)
curve (noun, verb)
curved (adj)
cylinder (noun)
cylindrical (adj)
irregular (adj)

oval (adj)
solid (adj, noun)
sphere (noun)
spiral (noun, adj, verb)

diagonal (adj)
  diagonally (adv)
exterior (noun, adj)
external (adj)
  externally (adv)
horizontal (adj, noun)
  horizontally (adv)
interior (noun)
internal (adj)
  internally (adv)
neighbouring (adj)
overlap (verb)
parallel (adj)
position (noun)
surface (noun)
surroundings (plural)
vertical (adj)
  vertically (adv)

anticlockwise (adv, adj)
clockwise (adv)
cycle (noun)
destination (noun)
route (noun)

Size & amount

capacity (uncount, noun)
per cent (noun, adj, adv)
  percentage (noun)
proportion (noun)
quantity (noun)
  quantify (verb)
  quantifiable (adj)
ratio (noun)
scale (noun)

minimal (adj)
  minimally (adv)
minimum (adj, noun)
minority (noun)
shortage (noun)
infinite (adj)

majority (noun)
maximum (adj, noun)
multiple (adj)
numerous (adj)
substantial (adj)
  substantially (adv)
sufficient (adj)
  sufficiently (adv)

Measurements

acre (noun)
circumference (uncount)
cubic (adj)
diameter (noun)
dimension (noun, plural)
hectare (noun)
mass (adj, noun)
perimeter (noun)
radius (noun)
volume (noun)

approximate (adj, verb)
  approximately (adv)
narrow (adj, verb)
register (verb)
standard (noun, adj)
statistics (noun, uncount)
  statistical (adj)
  statistically (adv)

Types of people & groups of people

activist (noun)
critic (noun)
inhabitant (noun)
observer (noun)
occupant (noun)
participant (noun)
representative (adj)
spokesperson (noun)

body (noun)
electorate (noun)
panel (noun)
partnership (noun)

Ideas & beliefs

concept (noun)
notion (noun)
principle (noun)

attitude (noun)
ideal (noun)
  idealism (uncount)
  idealistic (adj)
insight (noun)
outlook (noun)
perspective (noun)
standpoint (noun)
viewpoint (noun)

favour (verb)

bias (noun, verb)
  biased (adj)
impartial (adj)
  impartiality (uncount)
  impartially (adv)
neutral (adj)
objective (noun, adj)
  objectively (adv)
partial (adj)
  partially (adv)
radical (adj)
  radically (adv)
rational (adj)
  rationally (adv)
subjective (adj)
  subjectively (adv)

Importance

centre (noun)
  central (adj)
chief (adj)
  chiefly (adv)
fundamental (adj)
  fundamentally (adv)
leading (adj)
notable (adj)
  notably (adv)

primary (adj)
  primarily (adv)
prime (adj)
principal (adj)
  principally (adv)
priority (noun)
  prioritize (verb)
  prioritization (uncount)
significant (adj)
  significantly (adv)
  significance (uncount)
vital (adj)
  vitally (adv)

insignificant (adj)
secondary (adj)

Certainty & probability

allegedly (adv)
apparently (adv)
feasible (adj)
  feasibility (uncount)
hypothetical (adj)
  hypothetically (adv)
inevitable (adj)
  inevitably (adv)
  inevitability (noun)
liable (adj)
  liability (uncount)
obligatory (adj)
option (noun)
  optional (adj)
potential (adj)
  potentially (adv)
probable (adj)
  probability (noun)
random (adj)
  randomly (adv)
realistic (adj)
  realistically (adv)
theoretical (adj)
undoubted (adj)
  undoubtedly (adv)

Degree

comparative (adj)
comparatively (adv)
considerable (adj)
considerably (adv)
definite (adj)
definitely (adv)
degree (noun)
extent (noun)
intense (adj)
intensely (adv)
intensity (uncount)
largely (adv)
moderate (adj)
moderately (adv)
precise (adj)
precisely (adv)
precision (uncount)
relative (adj)
relatively (adv)
severe (adj)
severely (adv)
severity (uncount)
specific (adj)
subtle (adj)
subtly (adv)
subtlety (noun, uncount)
universal (adj)
universally (adv)
virtual (adj)
virtually (adv)

Abstract qualities

absent (adj)
absence (noun)
abstract (adj)
accuracy (uncount)
adequacy (uncount)
ambiguity (noun)
anonymous (adj)
anonymity (uncount)
capability (noun)
concrete (adj)
consistency (uncount)

feasibility (uncount)
identity (noun)
objectivity (uncount)
relevance (uncount)
subjectivity (uncount)
validity (uncount)

Positive qualities

accurate (adj)
accurately (adv)
adequate (adj)
adequately (adv)
advantage (noun, uncount)
advantageous (adj)
appropriate (adj)
appropriately (adv)
capable (adj)
comprehensive (adj)
comprehensively (adv)
concise (adj)
concisely (adv)
consistent (adj)
consistently (adv)
innovative (adj)
pioneering (adj)
reasonable (adj)
reasonably (adv)
reliable (adj)
reliability (uncount)
satisfy (verb)
satisfactory (adj)
secure (adj)
securely (adv)
stable (adj)
stability (uncount)
straightforward (adj)
transparent (adj)
transparently (adv)
transparency (uncount)
unambiguous (adj)
unambiguously (adv)
valid (adj)
validity (uncount)
versatile (adj)
versatility (uncount)

Negative qualities

ambiguous (adj)
  ambiguously (adv)
harsh (adj)
  harshness (uncount)
inaccurate (adj)
  inaccurately (adv)
  inaccuracy (noun)
inadequate (adj)
  inadequately (adv)
inconsistent (adj)
inferior (adj)
insufficient (adj)
  insufficiently (adv)
invalid (adj)
irrelevant (adj)
overdue (adj)
strain (noun, verb, uncount)
stress (verb, noun)
tense (adj)
  tension (uncount)
unstable (adj)
vague (adj)
vulnerable (adj)
  vulnerability (noun)

Linking words

albeit (adv)
furthermore (adv)
in addition
  additionally (adv)
latter (pron, adj)
likewise (adv)
moreover (adv)
namely (adv)
nevertheless (adv)
respectively (adv)
thus (adv)
whereas (conj)
while (conj)
whilst (conj)

Studying

bachelor's degree (noun)
discipline (noun)
doctorate (noun)
  doctoral (adj)
master's degree (noun)
PhD (noun)
postgraduate (noun, adj)
scholarship (noun)
undergraduate (noun)

campus (noun)
department (noun)
  departmental (adj)
faculty (noun)

lecture (noun)
  lecturer (noun)
professor (noun)
seminar (noun)
tutor (noun)
  tutorial (noun)
  tuition (uncount)

Texts

appendix (noun)
assignment (noun)
contents (plural)
dissertation (noun)
glossary (noun)
index (noun)
journal (noun)
text (noun)
  textual (adj)

Graphs & charts

axis (noun)
bar chart (noun)
chart (noun, verb)
diagram (noun)
figure (noun)
flow chart (noun)
horizontal (adj, noun)
key (noun)
label (verb, noun)
pie chart (noun)
vertical (adj)

Academic writing

bracket (noun)
case study (noun)
conclude (verb)
  conclusion (noun)
define (verb)
  definition (noun)
draft (noun)
edit (verb)
  editor (noun)
  edition (noun)
hypothesis (noun)
i.e.
quote (verb, noun)
  quotation (noun)
refer (verb)
  reference (noun)
source (noun)
summary (noun)
  summarize (verb)
terminology (uncount)
thesis (noun)

abandon (verb)
abstract (adj)
academic (adj)
  academically (adv)
access (uncount, verb)
  accessible (adj)
accompany (verb)
accurate (adj)
  accurately (adv)
  accuracy (uncount)
achieve (verb)
  achievement (noun)
acquire (verb)
  acquisition (noun, uncount)
adapt (verb)
  adaptation (uncount)
  adaptable (adj)
  adaptability (uncount)
adequate (adj)
  adequately (adv)
  adequacy (uncount)
adjust (verb)
  adjustment (noun)
administration (uncount, noun)
  administrative (adj)
aid (uncount, verb, noun)
albeit (adv)
allocate (verb)
  allocation (noun)
alter (verb)
  alteration (noun)
ambiguous (adj)
  ambiguously (adv)
  ambiguity (noun)
analyse (verb)
  analysis (noun)
  analyst (noun)
apparently (adv)
appendix (noun)
approach (verb, noun)
appropriate (adj)
  appropriately (adv)
approximate (adj, verb)
  approximately (adv)
aspect (noun)
assemble (verb)
  assembly (noun, uncount)
assess (verb)
  assessment (noun)

assignment (noun)
assume (verb)
  assumption (noun)
attach (verb)
  attachment (noun)
attitude (noun)
automatic (adj)
  automatically (adv)
on someone's behalf (phrase)
bias (noun, verb)
  biased (adj)
bond (noun)
brief (adj)
  briefly (adv)
capable (adj)
  capability (noun)
capacity (uncount, noun)
category (noun)
  categorize (verb)
cease (verb)
challenge (noun, verb)
chart (noun, verb)
circumstances (plural)
civil (adj)
classical (adj)
collapse (verb)
commence (verb)
commit (verb)
  commitment (noun)
  committed (adj)
component (noun)
comprehensive (adj)
  comprehensively (adv)
comprise (verb)
concentrate (verb)
  concentration (uncount, noun)
concept (noun)
conclude (verb)
  conclusion (noun)
conduct (verb)
confirm (verb)
  confirmation (uncount)
conflict (uncount, noun, verb)
consequence (noun)
  consequently (adv)
considerable (adj)
  considerably (adv)
consist (verb)
consistent (adj)

consistently *(adv)*
consistency *(uncount)*
constant (noun)
construct (verb)
construction *(uncount)*
consult (verb)
consultation *(noun)*
consultant *(noun)*
consume (verb)
consumption *(uncount)*
consumer *(noun)*
contact (uncount, verb)
context (noun)
contract (noun)
contradict (verb)
contradiction *(noun)*
contradictory *(adj)*
contrary (adj)
contrast (noun, verb)
contribute (verb)
contribution *(noun)*
controversy (noun)
controversial *(adj)*
controversially *(adv)*
convention (noun)
conventional *(adj)*
conventionally *(adv)*
convert (verb)
conversion *(uncount)*
co-operate (verb)
co-operation *(uncount)*
co-operative *(adj)*
co-ordinate (verb)
co-ordination *(uncount)*
corporate (adj)
corporation *(noun)*
correspond (verb)
corresponding *(adj)*
credit (uncount)
criterion (noun)
cycle (noun)
data (uncount)
debate (noun, verb)
decline (verb, noun)
define (verb)
definition *(noun)*
definite (adj)
definitely *(adv)*
demonstrate (verb)

demonstration *(noun)*
deny (verb)
denial *(noun, uncount)*
depression (noun)
detect (verb)
detection *(uncount)*
detector *(noun)*
dimension (noun, plural)
discriminate (verb)
discrimination *(uncount)*
display (verb, noun)
dispose of (ph verb)
disposal *(uncount)*
distinct (adj)
distinction *(noun)*
distinctive *(adj)*
distinctively *(adv)*
distribute (verb)
distributed *(adj)*
distribution *(uncount, noun)*
domestic (adj)
dominate (verb)
dominant *(adj)*
draft (noun)
dramatic (adj)
dramatically *(adv)*
duration (uncount)
economy (noun)
economic *(adj)*
economical *(adj)*
economically *(adv)*
economics *(uncount)*
economist *(noun)*
edit (verb)
editor *(noun)*
edition *(noun)*
element (noun)
eliminate (verb)
elimination *(uncount)*
emerge (verb)
emergence *(uncount)*
emphasis (noun)
emphasize *(verb)*
encounter (verb)
enhance (verb)
enhancement *(noun)*
ensure (verb)
equation (noun)
equivalent (noun)

equivalence (uncount)
erode (verb)
  erosion (uncount)
establish (verb)
  establishment (noun)
ethnic (adj)
  ethnicity (uncount)
evaluate (verb)
  evaluation (noun)
  evaluative (adj)
evolve (verb)
  evolution (uncount, noun)
exceed (verb)
  excess (noun)
  excessive (adj)
  excessively (adv)
exclude (verb)
  excluding (prep)
  exclusion (noun)
expand (verb)
  expand on/upon (ph verb)
  expansion (uncount)
exploit (verb)
  exploitation (uncount)
export (verb, noun)
  exportation (uncount)
expose (verb)
  exposure (uncount)
external (adj)
  externally (adv)
extract (noun)
feature (noun)
federal (adj)
  federation (noun)
fee (noun)
finite (adj)
flexible (adj)
  flexibility (uncount)
fluctuate (verb)
  fluctuation (noun)
focus (verb, noun)
format (noun)
formula (noun)
forthcoming (adj)
foundation (noun)
framework (noun)
function (noun, verb)
  functional (adj)
fund (plural, verb)
  funding (uncount)

fundamental (adj)
  fundamentally (adv)
gender (noun)
generate (verb)
  generation (uncount)
globe (noun)
  global (adj)
  globally (adv)
  globalization (uncount)
goal (noun)
grade (verb, noun)
guarantee (verb, noun)
guideline (noun)
hence (adv)
highlight (verb)
hypothesis (noun)
  hypothetical (adj)
  hypothetically (adv)
identical (adj)
  identically (adv)
identify (verb)
  identification (uncount)
illustrate (verb)
  illustration (noun)
immigrate (verb)
  immigration (uncount)
  immigrant (noun)
impact (noun, verb)
implement (verb)
  implementation (uncount)
implication (noun)
imply (verb)
impose (verb)
  imposition (uncount)
index (noun)
indicate (verb)
  indication (noun)
  indicator (noun)
inevitable (adj)
  inevitably (adv)
  inevitability (noun)
infrastructure (noun)
initial (adj)
  initially (adv)
innovation (noun, uncount)
  innovative (adj)
input (noun, verb)
insert (verb)
insight (noun)

inspect (verb)
  inspection (noun)
instance (noun)
institute (noun)
institution (noun)
instruction (noun, plural)
integrate (verb)
  integration (uncount)
intense (adj)
  intensely (adv)
  intensity (uncount)
intermediate (adj)
internal (adj)
  internally (adv)
interpret (verb)
  interpretation (noun)
interval (noun)
invest (verb)
  investment (uncount, noun)
  investor (noun)
investigate (verb)
  investigation (noun)
irrelevant (adj)
isolate (verb)
  isolation (uncount)
  isolated (adj)
journal (noun)
justify (verb)
  justification (noun)
label (verb, noun)
labour (uncount)
layer (noun)
lecture (noun)
  lecturer (noun)
legislate (verb)
  legislation (uncount)
  legislative (adj)
liberal (adj, noun)
licence (noun)
  license (verb)
likewise (adv)
logic (uncount)
  logical (adj)
  logically (adv)
maintain (verb)
  maintenance (uncount)
majority (noun)
mature (verb)
mechanism (noun)

mental (adj)
  mentally (adv)
method (noun)
  methodology (noun)
minimal (adj)
  minimally (adv)
minimum (adj, noun)
ministry (noun)
minority (noun)
modify (verb)
  modification (noun)
monitor (verb, noun)
motivate (verb)
  motivation (uncount)
mutual (adj)
  mutually (adv)
network (noun)
neutral (adj)
nevertheless (adv)
norm (noun)
notion (noun)
nuclear (adj)
objective (noun, adj)
  objectively (adv)
  objectivity (uncount)
obtain (verb)
occupation (noun, uncount)
  occupational (adj)
occupy (verb)
  occupant (noun)
occur (verb)
  occurrence (noun)
ongoing (adj)
option (noun)
  optional (adj)
outcome (noun)
output (uncount)
overlap (verb)
overseas (adj)
panel (noun)
parallel (adj)
participate (verb)
  participation (uncount)
  participant (noun)
partnership (noun)
per cent (noun, adj, adv)
  percentage (noun)
perceive (verb)
  perception (noun)

perceptible *(adj)*
perceptibly (adv)
perspective *(noun)*
phase *(noun)*
phenomenon *(noun)*
philosophy *(uncount)*
philosopher (noun)
plus *(conj, adj)*
portion *(noun)*
potential *(adj)*
potentially (adv)
precise *(adj)*
precisely (adv)
precision (uncount)
predict *(verb)*
prediction (noun)
predictable (adj)
preliminary *(adj)*
presume *(verb)*
primary *(adj)*
primarily (adv)
prime *(adj)*
principal *(adj)*
principally (adv)
principle *(noun)*
prior *(adj)*
priority *(noun)*
prioritize (verb)
prioritization (noun)
procedure *(noun)*
procedural (adj)
prohibit *(verb)*
prohibition (uncount)
promote *(verb)*
promotion (uncount)
proportion *(noun)*
prospect *(noun)*
prospective (adj)
psychology *(uncount)*
psychological (adj)
psychologist (noun)
publish *(verb)*
publication (uncount, noun)
purchase *(verb, noun)*
pursue *(verb)*
quote *(verb, noun)*
quotation (noun)
radical *(adj)*
radically (adv)

random *(adj)*
randomly (adv)
ratio *(noun)*
rational *(adj)*
rationally (adv)
react *(verb)*
reaction (noun)
recover *(verb)*
recovery (noun)
register *(verb)*
registration (uncount)
regulate *(verb)*
regulated (adj)
regulator (noun)
regulatory (adj)
reject *(verb)*
rejection (uncount)
release *(verb, noun)*
relevant *(adj)*
relevance (uncount)
reliable *(adj)*
reliability (uncount)
reluctant *(adj)*
reluctantly (adv)
reluctance (uncount)
rely *(verb)*
reliant (adj)
reliance (uncount)
require *(verb)*
requirement (noun)
resource *(noun)*
respond *(verb)*
response (noun)
restrict *(verb)*
restriction (noun)
retain *(verb)*
retention (uncount)
reveal *(verb)*
reverse *(verb, adj)*
reversal (noun)
revise *(verb)*
revision (noun)
revolution *(noun)*
revolutionary (adj)
revolutionize (verb)
route *(noun)*
scheme *(noun)*
scope *(noun)*
sector *(noun)*

secure (adj)
  securely (adv)
seek (verb)
select (verb)
sequence (noun)
  sequential (adj)
sex (noun, uncount)
  sexual (adj)
shift (verb, noun)
significant (adj)
  significantly (adv)
  significance (uncount)
simulate (verb)
  simulation (noun)
somewhat (adv)
source (noun)
specific (adj)
stable (adj)
  stability (uncount)
  stabilize (verb)
statistics (noun, uncount)
  statistical (adj)
  statistically (adv)
  statistician (noun)
status (uncount)
straightforward (adj)
strategy (noun)
  strategic (adj)
stress (verb, noun)
style (noun)
submit (verb)
  submission (noun)
subsequent (adj)
  subsequently (adv)
subsidy (noun)
  subsidize (verb)
substitute (verb, noun)
  substitution (noun)
sufficient (adj)
  sufficiently (adv)
sum (noun, ph verb)
summary (noun)
  summarize (verb)
supplement (verb, noun)
  supplementary (adj)
survey (noun, verb)
sustain (verb)
  sustainable (adj)
  sustainability (uncount)

symbol (noun)
  symbolic (adj)
  symbolize (verb)
target (noun, verb)
tense (adj)
  tension (uncount)
text (noun)
  textual (adj)
theory (noun)
  theoretical (adj)
thesis (noun)
transfer (verb, noun, uncount)
transform (verb)
  transformation (noun)
trend (noun)
trigger (verb, noun)
ultimate (adj)
  ultimately (adv)
undergo (verb)
underlying (adj)
undertake (verb)
  undertaking (noun)
unique (adj)
  uniquely (adv)
utilize (verb)
  utilization (uncount)
valid (adj)
  validity (uncount)
vary (verb)
  variation (noun)
  variable (noun)
version (noun)
via (prep)
virtual (adj)
  virtually (adv)
visible (adj)
  visibly (adv)
vision (uncount)
visual (adj)
  visually (adv)
volume (noun)
voluntary (adj)
  voluntarily (adv)
  volunteer (noun, verb)
welfare (uncount, adj)
whereas (conj)
widespread (adj)

Key to grammatical labels used in word lists

adj	adjective
adv	adverb
conj	conjunction
noun	noun
phrase	phrases
ph verb	phrasal verb
plural	plural noun
prep	preposition
pron	pronoun
uncount	uncountable noun
verb	verb

Key Words
A–Z

Aa

aban|don /əˈbændən/

ACADEMIC WORD

(abandons, abandoning, abandoned)

1 VERB If you **abandon** a place, thing, or person, you leave the place, thing, or person permanently or for a long time, especially when you should not do so. ○ *He claimed that his parents had abandoned him.* ○ *The road is strewn with abandoned vehicles.*

▶ **COLLOCATIONS:**
abandon a **child/baby**
an abandoned **building/warehouse/mine/quarry/vehicle/car**
hastily/abruptly/temporarily abandon *someone/something*

▶ **SYNONYMS:** desert, leave

2 VERB If you **abandon** an activity or piece of work, you stop doing it before it is finished. ○ *The authorities have abandoned any attempt to distribute food.* ○ *The scheme's investors, fearful of bankruptcy, decided to abandon the project.*

▶ **COLLOCATIONS:**
abandon an **attempt/effort**
abandon a **project/plan/idea**

▶ **ANTONYMS:** continue, persevere

abol|ish /əˈbɒlɪʃ/ (abolishes, abolishing, abolished)

POLITICS

VERB If someone in authority **abolishes** a system or practice, they formally put an end to it. ○ *Parliament voted to abolish the death penalty.* ○ *ten years after slavery was formally abolished*

▶ **COLLOCATIONS:**
abolish **slavery/apartheid**
abolish **capital/corporal punishment**
abolish the **death penalty**
abolish **taxes/fees**
formally/officially/effectively abolish *something*
abolish *something* **altogether**

▶ **SYNONYMS:** eliminate, end

abo|li|tion /ˌæbəˈlɪʃən/

UNCOUNTABLE NOUN ○ [+ of] *the abolition of slavery in Brazil and the Caribbean* ○ [+ of] *a book advocating the abolition of capital punishment*

a

▶ **COLLOCATIONS:**
the abolition **of** something
the abolition of **slavery/apartheid**
the abolition of the **monarchy**
advocate/recommend/propose the abolition of something
demand/oppose the abolition of something

▶ **SYNONYM:** end

---

ab|sent /ˈæbsənt/

ADJECTIVE If someone or something is **absent from** a place or situation where they should be or where they usually are, they are not there. ○ [+ *from*] *Women are conspicuously absent from higher management.* ○ *Employees who are absent without a genuine reason should be disciplined.* ○ *Any soldier failing to report would be considered absent without leave.*

▶ **COLLOCATIONS:**
absent **from** somewhere/something
absent from a **list/agenda**
absent from **work/school**
conspicuously/noticeably/notably absent

▶ **PHRASE:** absent without leave

▶ **ANTONYM:** present

ab|sence /ˈæbsəns/ (absences)

1 NOUN Someone's **absence** from a place is the fact that they are not there. ○ *a bundle of letters which had arrived for me in my absence* ○ *the problem of high sickness absence in the public sector*

▶ **COLLOCATIONS:**
in someone's absence
a **lengthy/continued/four-year** absence
an **unexplained/unauthorized** absence
sickness/injury absence

▶ **ANTONYM:** presence

2 NOUN The **absence** of something from a place is the fact that it is not there or does not exist. ○ [+ *of*] *The presence or absence of clouds can have an important impact on heat transfer.* ○ [+ *of*] *In the absence of a will the courts decide who the guardian is.*

▶ **COLLOCATIONS:**
the absence **of** something
in the absence of something
the absence of **evidence/proof/information**
the absence of a **will/explanation/alternative**

▶ **SYNONYM:** lack

▶ **ANTONYM:** presence

ab|stract /ˈæbstrækt/ `ACADEMIC WORD` `ARTS`

1 **ADJECTIVE** An **abstract** idea or way of thinking is based on general ideas rather than on real things and events. ○ *abstract principles such as justice* ○ *Fractional dimension is an abstract concept that enables mathematicians to measure the complexity of an object.* ○ *the faculty of abstract reasoning*

▶ **COLLOCATIONS:**
   an abstract **concept/principle/notion**
   abstract **reasoning/thinking/thought**
   purely/highly abstract
▶ **SYNONYMS:** theoretical, conceptual
▶ **ANTONYMS:** actual, concrete

2 **ADJECTIVE** **Abstract** art makes use of shapes and patterns rather than showing people or things. ○ *a modern abstract painting* ○ *Pollock's great masterpiece of abstract expressionism*

▶ **COLLOCATIONS:**
   abstract **art/sculpture/expressionism**
   an abstract **painting/painter/pattern**
▶ **ANTONYM:** figurative

abuse (abuses, abusing, abused) `SOCIOLOGY`

> The noun is pronounced /əˈbjuːs/. The verb is pronounced /əˈbjuːz/.

1 **UNCOUNTABLE NOUN** **Abuse** of someone is cruel and violent treatment of them. ○ *investigation of alleged child abuse* ○ [+ *of*] *the systematic abuse of prisoners*

▶ **COLLOCATIONS:**
   abuse **of** *someone*
   abuse of a **child/minor/prisoner/detainee**
   sexual/physical/emotional/psychological/racial abuse
   systematic/alleged/widespread abuse
   an abuse **scandal/allegation/victim**
▶ **SYNONYMS:** violation, mistreatment

2 **NOUN** **Abuse** of something is the use of it in a wrong way or for a bad purpose. ○ [+ *of*] *What went on here was an abuse of power.* ○ *liver damage caused by disease, alcohol or drug abuse*

▶ **COLLOCATIONS:**
   abuse **of** *something*
   abuse of **power/trust**
   drug/alcohol/substance/steroid abuse
▶ **SYNONYM:** misuse

3 **VERB** If someone **is abused**, they are treated cruelly and violently. ○ *The report showed that up to one in four girls and one in seven boys are sexually abused.* ○ *guards routinely abused prisoners* ○ *those who work with abused children*

▶ COLLOCATIONS:
sexually/verbally/physically/racially abused
abuse a **child/boy/girl**
abuse a **prisoner/detainee**

▶ SYNONYMS: mistreat, violate

4 VERB If you **abuse** something, you use it in a wrong way or for a bad purpose. ○ *He showed how the rich and powerful can abuse their position.* ○ *teachers and coaches who abuse the trust they are given*

▶ COLLOCATIONS:
abuse **power/trust**
abuse a **position/privilege**
abuse **alcohol/drugs/substances**

▶ SYNONYM: exploit

abus|er /əˈbjuːzə/ (abusers)

1 NOUN An **abuser** is someone who treats a person cruelly and violently. ○ *a convicted child abuser*

▶ COLLOCATIONS:
a **child/sex** abuser
prosecute/convict an abuser
a **serial/alleged/suspected** abuser

▶ SYNONYM: molester

2 NOUN An **abuser** is someone who uses something in a wrong way or for a bad purpose. ○ *the treatment of alcohol and drug abusers*

▶ COLLOCATION: a **drug/substance/alcohol** abuser

▶ SYNONYMS: alcoholic, addict

aca|dem|ic /ˌækəˈdemɪk/ `ACADEMIC WORD` `EDUCATION`

1 ADJECTIVE Academic is used to describe things that relate to the work done in schools, colleges, and universities, especially work which involves studying and reasoning rather than practical or technical skills. ○ *Their academic standards are high.* ○ *the start of the last academic year* ○ *The author has settled for a more academic approach.*

2 ADJECTIVE Someone who is **academic** is good at studying. ○ *The system is failing most disastrously among less academic children.*

▶ COLLOCATIONS:
academic **standards/excellence/ability/freedom**
academic **research/work/staff/life**
an academic **qualification/achievement/career**
an academic **journal/institution/study/subject**
the academic **year**

▶ PHRASES:
academic and vocational
academic and professional

▶ SYNONYM: scholarly

aca|dem|ical|ly /ˌækəˈdemɪkli/

ADVERB ○ *He is academically gifted.* ○ *scholarships for those who excel academically*

▶ COLLOCATIONS:
academically **gifted/talented/bright/brilliant**
excel/succeed/perform/achieve academically
struggle academically

---

ac|cept /ækˈsept/ (accepts, accepting, accepted)

1 VERB If you **accept** something that you have been offered, you say yes to it or agree to take it. ○ *students who have accepted an offer of a university place* ○ *All those invited to next week's peace conference have accepted.*

▶ COLLOCATIONS:
accept a **gift/donation/offer/invitation**
gratefully/gladly/reluctantly accept **something**

▶ SYNONYMS: take, welcome

▶ ANTONYM: refuse

2 VERB If you **accept** an idea, statement, or fact, you believe that it is true or valid. ○ [+ as] *It is now accepted as fact that the brain and the immune system communicate.* ○ *a workforce generally accepted to have the best conditions in Europe*

▶ COLLOCATIONS:
accept something **as** something
accept something as **proof/evidence/fact**
generally/widely/internationally/commonly accepted
readily/reluctantly accept something

▶ SYNONYMS: acknowledge, recognize

▶ ANTONYMS: reject, dispute

USAGE: accept or except?

These words sound very similar and are easily confused, so be careful with their spelling.

Accept is a verb meaning to agree to or to believe something.
○ *the generally accepted meaning of the term*

Except is a conjunction used to introduce the only person or thing that something does not apply to. ○ *He remained in Sussex, except for war service, for the rest of his life.*

ac|cept|able /æk'septəbəl/

1 **ADJECTIVE** **Acceptable** activities and situations are those that most people approve of or consider to be normal. ○ [+ *for*] *It is becoming more acceptable for women to drink alcohol.* ○ *The air pollution exceeds most acceptable levels by 10 times or more.*

2 **ADJECTIVE** If something is **acceptable to** someone, they agree to consider it, use it, or allow it to happen. ○ [+ *to*] *They have thrashed out a compromise formula acceptable to Moscow.* ○ *They recently failed to negotiate a mutually acceptable new contract.*

▶ COLLOCATIONS:
acceptable **for/to** *someone*
socially/politically/morally acceptable
an acceptable **level/standard**
an acceptable **compromise/alternative/solution**
acceptable **behaviour**
find/consider/deem *something* acceptable

▶ SYNONYM: satisfactory

▶ ANTONYM: unacceptable

ac|cept|ance /æk'septəns/ (acceptances)

1 **NOUN** **Acceptance of** an offer or a proposal is the act of saying yes to it or agreeing to it. ○ [+ *of*] *The Party is being degraded by its acceptance of secret donations.* ○ *a letter of acceptance* ○ *his acceptance speech for the Nobel Peace Prize*

▶ COLLOCATIONS:
acceptance **of** *something*
acceptance of a **proposal/plan/offer/invitation**
an acceptance **speech/letter**

▶ ANTONYMS: rejection, refusal

2 **UNCOUNTABLE NOUN** If there is **acceptance** of an idea, most people believe or agree that it is true. ○ *a theory that is steadily gaining acceptance* ○ [+ *that*] *There was a general acceptance that the defence budget would shrink.*

▶ COLLOCATIONS:
gain/win acceptance
general/wide/widespread/growing acceptance
grudging/tacit/resigned acceptance

▶ SYNONYM: agreement

▶ ANTONYM: disagreement

ac|cess /'ækses/ (accesses, accessing, accessed) ACADEMIC WORD IT

1 **UNCOUNTABLE NOUN** If you have **access to** a building or other place, you are able or allowed to go into it. ○ *Fewer than one in ten secondary schools have wheelchair access.* ○ [+ *to*] *Scientists have only recently been able to gain access to the area.*

2 UNCOUNTABLE NOUN If you have **access to** something such as information or equipment, you have the opportunity or right to see it or use it. ○ [+ *to*] *a Code of Practice that would give patients right of access to their medical records* ○ *households with internet access*

a

▶ COLLOCATIONS:
access **to** *something/somewhere*
access to **information/funds**
gain/give/grant/allow/provide access
deny/restrict/block access
fast/high-speed/instant/easy/direct/free access
public/wheelchair access
internet/broadband/wireless access

▶ SYNONYMS: entry, entrance

3 VERB If you **access** something, especially information held on a computer, you succeed in finding or obtaining it. ○ *You've illegally accessed and misused confidential security files.* ○ *a service that allows users to access the internet on their phones*

▶ COLLOCATIONS:
access **data/information**
access the **internet**
access a **file/site/network/service**
instantly/easily/remotely/illegally access *something*

ac|ces|sible /æk'sesɪbəl/

1 ADJECTIVE If a place or building is **accessible to** people, it is easy for them to reach it or get into it. If an object is **accessible**, it is easy to reach. ○ [+ *to*] *The Centre is easily accessible to the general public.* ○ *The premises are wheelchair accessible.*

2 ADJECTIVE If something is **accessible to** people, they can easily use it or obtain it. ○ [+ *to*] *The legal aid system should be accessible to more people.* ○ *This device helps make virtual reality a more usable and accessible technology.*

▶ COLLOCATIONS:
accessible **to/for** *someone*
easily/readily/publicly accessible
wheelchair accessible
an accessible **area/location**
make *something* accessible

▶ ANTONYM: inaccessible

---

ac|com|pa|ny /ə'kʌmpəni/

ACADEMIC WORD

(accompanies, accompanying, accompanied)

1 VERB If you **accompany** someone, you go somewhere with them. [FORMAL] ○ *Ken agreed to accompany me on a trip to Africa.* ○ *The Prime Minister, accompanied by the governor, led the President up to the house.*

▶ **COLLOCATIONS:**
accompanied **by** *someone*
accompanied by a **bodyguard/adult/escort**
▶ **SYNONYM:** escort

2 VERB If one thing **accompanies** another, it happens or exists at the same time, or as a result of it. [FORMAL] ○ *This volume of essays was designed to accompany an exhibition in Cologne.* ○ *Wakefield's paper was accompanied by a critical commentary.*

▶ **COLLOCATIONS:**
accompanied **by** *something*
accompanied by a **photograph/caption/commentary**
accompany a **text/illustration/article**

ac|cord|ing to

> Pronounced /əˈkɔːdɪŋ tə/ before a consonant and /əˈkɔːdɪŋ tʊ/ before a vowel.

1 PHRASE If someone says that something is true **according to** a particular person, book, or other source of information, they are indicating where they got their information. ○ *Philip stayed at the hotel, according to Mr Hemming.* ○ *According to current theory, novae are close double stars.*

> **USAGE:** Reporting from sources
>
> The phrase **according to** is used in academic writing to introduce ideas from sources; other writers, researchers, studies, reports, etc. It can be used either before or after the reported idea. ○ *According to researchers, cases of the disease have been in people with a specific genetic characteristic.*
>
> You use either **according to** or a reporting verb, such as **argue, note, mention** etc. You cannot use **according to** followed by a reporting verb. ○ *Researchers note that cases of the disease have been in people with a specific genetic characteristic.*

2 PHRASE If something is done **according to** a particular set of principles, these principles are used as a basis for the way it is done. ○ *Coal is usually classified according to a scale of hardness and purity.* ○ *They must take their own decision according to their own legal advice.*
▶ **SYNONYM:** based on

3 PHRASE If something varies **according to** a changing factor, it varies in a way that is determined by this factor. ○ *Prices vary according to the quantity ordered.* ○ *The route that the boatmen choose varies according to the water level.*
▶ **SYNONYM:** depending on

ac|cu|rate /ˈækjʊrət/

ADJECTIVE **Accurate** information, measurements, and statistics are correct to a very detailed level. An **accurate** instrument is able to give you information of this kind. ○ *Accurate diagnosis is needed to guide appropriate treatment strategies.* ○ *a quick and accurate way of monitoring the amount of carbon dioxide in the air*

▸ **COLLOCATIONS:**
  reasonably/historically/scientifically/factually accurate
  accurate **information/figures**
  an accurate **description/measurement/diagnosis/prediction**
▸ **SYNONYMS:** precise, exact, correct
▸ **ANTONYMS:** inaccurate, incorrect

ac|cu|rate|ly /ˈækjʊrətli/

ADVERB ○ *The test can accurately predict what a bigger explosion would do.*
  ○ *The costs of each part of the process can be measured fairly accurately.*

▸ **COLLOCATIONS:**
  accurately **describe/measure/perceive** *something*
  determine/predict *something*
▸ **SYNONYMS:** precisely, exactly, correctly
▸ **ANTONYMS:** inaccurately, incorrectly

ac|cu|ra|cy /ˈækjʊrəsi/

UNCOUNTABLE NOUN ○ [+ *of*] *We cannot guarantee the accuracy of these figures.*
  ○ *weapons that could fire with accuracy at targets 3,000 yards away*

▸ **COLLOCATIONS:**
  the accuracy **of** *something*
  the accuracy of a **measurement/diagnosis/test**
  the accuracy of **information/figures**
  guarantee/ensure/measure accuracy
  historical/mathematical/unerring/pinpoint accuracy
  an accuracy **rate/level**
▸ **PHRASE:** speed and accuracy
▸ **SYNONYMS:** exactness, precision, correctness
▸ **ANTONYMS:** inaccuracy, vagueness

ac|cuse /əˈkjuːz/ (accuses, accusing, accused)

1 VERB If you **accuse** someone **of** doing something wrong or dishonest, you say or tell them that you believe that they did it. ○ [+ *of*] *Some middle-class Christian groups have been accused of turning their backs on the poor.* ○ [+ *of*] *Today, Rostov stands accused of extortion and racketeering.*

2 VERB If you **are accused of** a crime, a witness or someone in authority states or claims that you did it, and you may be formally charged with it and put on trial. ○ [+ of] *Her assistant was accused of theft and fraud by the police.* ○ [+ of] *All seven charges accused him of lying in his testimony.* ○ *the accused men*

▶ **COLLOCATIONS:**
accuse *someone* **of** *something*
accuse *someone* of **wrongdoing/murder/corruption**
a **critic/prosecutor/opponent/official** accuses *someone*
the **police** accuse *someone*
falsely/wrongly/unjustly accused

▶ **PHRASE:** stand accused

▶ **SYNONYMS:** blame, charge

ac|cu|sa|tion /ˌækjʊˈzeɪʃən/ (accusations)

NOUN ○ [+ of] *people who have made public accusations of rape* ○ [+ that] *The government denied the accusation that it was involved in the murders.*

▶ **COLLOCATIONS:**
an accusation **of** *something*
an accusation of **corruption/racism**
make/level/repeat an accusation
deny/reject an accusation
a **wild/false/unfounded/serious** accusation

▶ **SYNONYMS:** charge, allegation, complaint

---

achieve /əˈtʃiːv/ (achieves, achieving, achieved)   ACADEMIC WORD

VERB If you **achieve** a particular aim or effect, you succeed in doing it or causing it to happen, usually after a lot of effort. ○ *There are many who will work hard to achieve these goals.* ○ *We have achieved what we set out to do.*

▶ **COLLOCATIONS:**
achieve a **goal/objective/aim**
achieve **success/fame/independence/peace**
achieve *something* **easily/finally**
achieve **academically**

▶ **SYNONYMS:** accomplish, manage

▶ **ANTONYM:** fail

achieve|ment /əˈtʃiːvmənt/ (achievements)

NOUN ○ *Reaching this agreement so quickly was a great achievement.* ○ [+ of] *Only the achievement of these goals will bring lasting peace.*

▶ **COLLOCATIONS:**
achievement **of** *something*
achievement of a **goal/objective**
a **great/lifetime/crowning** achievement

a **sporting/academic/educational/artistic** achievement
celebrate/recognize an achievement
▶ SYNONYMS: accomplishment, success
▶ ANTONYM: failure

---

ac|quire /əˈkwaɪə/ (acquires, acquiring, acquired) `ACADEMIC WORD`

1 VERB If you **acquire** something, you buy or obtain it for yourself, or someone gives it to you. [FORMAL] ○ *General Motors acquired a 50% stake in Saab for about $400m.* ○ *efforts to acquire nuclear weapons*

2 VERB If you **acquire** something such as a skill or a habit, you learn it, or develop it through your daily life or experience. ○ *Their sleeping brains were continuing to process the newly acquired information.* ○ *Piaget was convinced that children acquire knowledge and abilities in stages.*

▶ COLLOCATIONS:
a **company/purchaser/shareholder** acquires *something*
acquire a **stake/share**
acquire **land/property/assets/wealth**
acquire a **skill/habit/reputation**
acquire **knowledge**
newly/recently acquired
▶ PHRASE: an acquired taste
▶ ANTONYM: lose
→ see note at **purchase**

EXTEND YOUR VOCABULARY

Get is a very common verb in everyday English. In formal academic writing, more specific verbs are often used.

If you get something by paying for it, you can use **buy**, **purchase** or **acquire**. Acquire is especially used to talk about businesses rather than individuals. ○ *The company acquired/purchased properties throughout Australia.*

You can use **acquire** or **obtain** when you get something in other ways, for example, by being given it.

acquire **assets/wealth/ownership/shares**
obtain **information/documents/copies/data/samples**

You can use **acquire**, **gain** or **develop** when you get a skill, a reputation, knowledge, etc, gradually over time.

acquire a **skill/reputation/knowledge/status/ability**
gain **confidence/acceptance/reputation/experience**
develop a **skill/strategy/relationship/reputation**

a

ac|qui|si|tion /ˌækwɪˈzɪʃən/ (acquisitions)

1 NOUN If a company or business person makes an **acquisition**, they buy another company or part of a company. ○ [+ of] *the acquisition of a profitable paper recycling company* ○ *the number of mergers and acquisitions made by Europe's 1,000 leading firms*

2 UNCOUNTABLE NOUN The **acquisition** of a skill or a particular type of knowledge is the process of learning it or developing it. ○ *the process of language acquisition* ○ [+ of] *the acquisition of basic skills*

▸ **COLLOCATIONS:**
the acquisition **of** *something*
the acquisition of **assets/land/property/skills**
land/language acquisition
make/finance/fund/propose/complete an acquisition
a **recent/planned/compulsory/further** acquisition
acquisition **costs/activity**

▸ **PHRASE:** mergers and acquisitions

▸ **SYNONYMS:** purchase, procurement, achievement, attainment

▸ **ANTONYMS:** sale, loss

---

acre /ˈeɪkə/ (acres)

NOUN An **acre** is an area of land measuring 4840 square yards or 4047 square metres. ○ [+ of] *The property is set in two acres of land.* ○ *a 15-acre cattle farm*

▸ **COLLOCATIONS:**
an acre **of** *something*
an acre of **land/parkland/farmland/woodland**

▸ **RELATED WORD:** hectare

---

ac|tiv|ist /ˈæktɪvɪst/ (activists)   `POLITICS`

NOUN An **activist** is a person who works to bring about political or social changes by campaigning in public or working for an organization.
○ *The police say they suspect the attack was carried out by animal rights activists.*

▸ **COLLOCATIONS:**
a **human rights/animal rights/peace/democracy** activist
an **anti-war/anti-abortion/anti-poverty** activist
a **political/environmental** activist
activists **protest/march/campaign**

▸ **SYNONYMS:** agitator, protester

ac|tiv|ism /ˈæktɪvɪzm/

UNCOUNTABLE NOUN Activism is the process of campaigning in public or working for an organization in order to bring about political or social change. ○ *He believed in political activism to achieve justice.*

▸ **COLLOCATION: political/social/environmental** activism

---

a|dapt /ə'dæpt/ (adapts, adapting, adapted)

1 VERB If you **adapt to** a new situation or **adapt yourself to** it, you change your ideas or behaviour in order to deal with it successfully. ○ [+ *to*] *We will have to be prepared to adapt to the change.* ○ [+ *to*] *They have had to adapt themselves to a war economy.*

▸ **COLLOCATIONS:**
adapt **to** *something*
adapt to **change**
adapt **readily/quickly**
difficulty/problems adapting to *something*

▸ **SYNONYMS:** adjust, acclimate, become accustomed

2 VERB If you **adapt** something, you change it to make it suitable for a new purpose or situation. ○ [+ *for*] *Shelves were built to adapt the library for use as an office.* ○ [+ *for*] *a specially adapted toilet for people with disabilities*

▸ **COLLOCATIONS:**
adapt *something* **for** *a purpose/someone*
specially/skilfully adapted
adapt a **technology/technique/method**

EXTEND YOUR VOCABULARY

Change is a very common verb in English. In formal academic writing, more specific verbs are often used.

Adapt and **customize** mean to change something to make it suitable for a particular purpose or situation. ○ *The software can be adapted/ customized to suit the user's needs.*

Modify and **alter** mean to change something slightly. **Modify** is often used to talk about making improvements. **Alter** often refers to changes that just happen naturally or over time. ○ *a slightly modified version of the design* ○ *Our experiences can actually alter the structure of the brain.*

---

ad|ap|ta|tion /ˌædæp'teɪʃən/

UNCOUNTABLE NOUN Adaptation is the act of changing something or changing your behaviour to make it suitable for a new purpose or situation. ○ *Most living creatures are capable of adaptation when compelled to do so.*

▸ **SYNONYMS:** adjustment, modification

adapt|able /ə'dæptəbəl/

ADJECTIVE If you describe a person or animal as **adaptable**, you mean that they are able to change their ideas or behaviour in order to deal with new situations. ○ *a more adaptable and skilled workforce* ○ *They are adaptable foragers that learn to survive on a wide range of food sources.*

▶ COLLOCATIONS:
highly/easily/infinitely/remarkably adaptable
an adaptable **workforce/creature/species**

▶ SYNONYM: flexible

▶ ANTONYMS: inflexible, rigid

adapt|abil|ity /əˌdæptəˈbɪlɪti/

UNCOUNTABLE NOUN ○ [+ *of*] *The adaptability of wool is one of its great attractions.*

▶ COLLOCATION: the adaptability **of** *something*

▶ SYNONYM: flexibility

▶ ANTONYM: inflexibility

---

ad|di|tion /əˈdɪʃən/ (additions)

1 PHRASE You use **in addition** when you want to mention another item connected with the subject you are discussing. ○ *Part-time English classes are offered. In addition, students can take classes in word-processing and computing.* ○ [+ *to*] *In addition to the 48 constellations known since ancient times, Bayer showed 12 new constellations.*

▶ COLLOCATION: in addition **to** *something*

▶ SYNONYMS: additionally, furthermore

2 NOUN An **addition to** something is a thing which is added to it. ○ [+ *to*] *This is a fine book; a worthy addition to the Cambridge Encyclopedia series.* ○ *This plywood addition helps to strengthen the structure.*

▶ COLLOCATIONS:
an addition **to** *something*
a **welcome/valuable/worthy/new/recent** addition

3 UNCOUNTABLE NOUN The **addition of** something is the fact that it is added to something else. ○ [+ *of*] *It was completely refurbished in 1987, with the addition of a picnic site.* ○ [+ *of*] *the addition of vitamin C to fruit juices*

▶ COLLOCATION: the addition **of** *something*

▶ ANTONYM: removal

ad|di|tion|al /əˈdɪʃənəl/

ADJECTIVE **Additional** things are extra things apart from the ones already present. ○ *Table 2 gives additional information about participants.* ○ *The insurer will also have to pay the additional costs of the trial.*

▶ COLLOCATIONS:
additional **costs/shares/information**
an additional **payment/contribution/expense**

▶ SYNONYMS: supplementary, extra

ad|di|tion|al|ly /əˈdɪʃənəli/

ADVERB You use **additionally** to introduce something extra such as an extra fact or reason. [FORMAL] ○ *You can pay bills over the Internet. Additionally, you can check your balance or order statements.*

▶ **SYNONYMS:** further, in addition

ad|dress /əˈdres/ (addresses, addressing, addressed)

VERB If you **address** a problem or task, you try to understand it or deal with it. ○ *Mr King sought to address those fears when he spoke at the meeting.* ○ *US policy has failed to adequately address this problem.*

▶ **COLLOCATIONS:**
  address a **problem/issue/concern/question**
  adequately/urgently/specifically/directly address *something*
▶ **ANTONYM:** avoid

ad|equate /ˈædɪkwət/ `ACADEMIC WORD`

ADJECTIVE If something is **adequate**, there is enough of it or it is good enough to be used or accepted. ○ *One in four people worldwide are without adequate homes.* ○ [+ to-inf] *The old methods weren't adequate to meet current needs.*

▶ **COLLOCATIONS:**
  adequate **for** *something*
  adequate for a **purpose/task/need**
  adequate **protection/provision/compensation/resources**
  perfectly/quite/barely/hardly adequate
▶ **SYNONYM:** sufficient
▶ **ANTONYM:** inadequate

ad|equate|ly /ˈædɪkwətli/

ADVERB ○ *Many students are not adequately prepared for higher education.* ○ *Traditional analysis methods cannot deal adequately with these highly complex systems.*

▶ **COLLOCATIONS:**
  respond/function adequately
  adequately **deal with** *something*
  adequately **trained/compensated/funded/protected/prepared**
▶ **SYNONYM:** sufficiently
▶ **ANTONYM:** inadequately

ad|equa|cy /ˈædɪkwəsi/

UNCOUNTABLE NOUN Adequacy is the quality of being good enough or great enough in amount to be acceptable. ○ [+ of] *Several studies point to a real cause for concern over the adequacy of the diet eaten by British children.*

► **COLLOCATIONS:**
the adequacy **of** *something*
assess/examine/evaluate the adequacy of *something*
► **SYNONYM:** sufficiency
► **ANTONYM:** inadequacy

---

ad|just /əˈdʒʌst/ (adjusts, adjusting, adjusted) `ACADEMIC WORD`

1 VERB When you **adjust to** a new situation, you get used to it by changing your behaviour or your ideas. ○ [+ to] *We are preparing our fighters to adjust themselves to civil society.* ○ [+ to] *I felt I had adjusted to the idea of being a mother very well.*

2 VERB If you **adjust** something, you change it so that it is more effective or appropriate. ○ *To attract investors, Panama has adjusted its tax and labour laws.* ○ *The clamp can be adjusted to fit any tyre size.* ○ *seasonally adjusted figures*

► **COLLOCATIONS:**
adjust **to** *something*
adjusted **for** *something*
adjusted for **inflation/height/age**
adjust **figures/rates**
adjust *something* to **reflect/fit** *something*
seasonally/periodically/automatically/manually adjusted
adjusted **accordingly**
► **SYNONYMS:** adapt, change, shift

ad|just|ment /əˈdʒʌstmənt/ (adjustments)

NOUN ○ [+ to] *Compensation could be made by adjustments to taxation.* ○ [+ for] *Investment is up by 5.7% after adjustment for inflation.* ○ [+ to] *A technician made an adjustment to a smoke machine at the back of the auditorium.*

► **COLLOCATIONS:**
an adjustment **to/in/for** *something*
adjustment for **inflation/age/height**
a **structural/seasonal/slight/minor** adjustment
make/require/need an adjustment
► **SYNONYMS:** adaptation, change

---

ad|min|is|tra|tion /ædˌmɪnɪˈstreɪʃən/ `ACADEMIC WORD` `POLITICS`
(administrations)

1 UNCOUNTABLE NOUN Administration is the range of activities connected with organizing and supervising the way that an organization or institution functions. ○ *Too much time is spent on administration.* ○ *a master's degree in business administration* ○ [+ of] *Standards in the administration of justice have degenerated.*

▶ **COLLOCATIONS:**
the administration **of** *something*
the administration of a **state/region/program**
business/university administration
an administration **fee/cost/official/policy**

▶ **SYNONYMS:** management, organization, regulation

2 NOUN You can refer to a country's government as **the administration**; used especially in the United States. ○ *O'Leary served in both the Ford and Carter administrations.* ○ *He urged the administration to come up with a credible package to reduce the budget deficit.*

▶ **COLLOCATIONS:**
the **previous/current/incoming** administration
the **Republican/Democrat** administration
the **Nixon/Clinton/Bush/Obama** administration

▶ **SYNONYM:** government

ad|min|is|tra|tive /ædˈmɪnɪstrətɪv, AM -streɪt-/

ADJECTIVE ○ *Other industries have had to sack managers to reduce administrative costs.* ○ *The project will have an administrative staff of 12.*

▶ **COLLOCATIONS:**
administrative **costs/expenses/staff/management**
an administrative **system/structure/procedure**
an administrative **assistant/officer**
an administrative **task/duty/error**

▶ **SYNONYMS:** bureaucratic, organizational, secretarial, clerical

adopt /əˈdɒpt/ (adopts, adopting, adopted)

VERB If you **adopt** a new attitude, plan, or way of behaving, you begin to have it. ○ *Parliament adopted a resolution calling for the complete withdrawal of troops.* ○ *Pupils should be helped to adopt a positive approach to the environment.*

▶ **COLLOCATIONS:**
adopt *something* **as** *something*
adopt *something* as a **policy/standard**
adopt a **stance/approach/attitude/strategy/tactic/policy**
unanimously/formally/widely adopted

▶ **SYNONYMS:** embrace, endorse, support, accept

adop|tion /əˈdɒpʃən/

UNCOUNTABLE NOUN ○ [+ *of*] *the adoption of Japanese management practices by British manufacturing* ○ [+ *of*] *the widespread adoption of renewable energy*

▶ **COLLOCATIONS:**
the adoption **of** *something*

the adoption of a **practice**
the adoption of **technology**
widespread/rapid/mass adoption

▶ **SYNONYMS:** acceptance, endorsement

---

ad|van|tage /æd'vɑːntɪdʒ, -'væn-/ (advantages)

1 NOUN An **advantage** is something that puts you in a better position than other people. ○ [+ over] *They are deliberately flouting the law in order to obtain an advantage over their competitors.* ○ [+ to] *A good crowd will be a definite advantage to me and the rest of the team.*

▶ **COLLOCATIONS:**
an advantage **over/to/for** *someone*
an advantage over **competitors/rivals/opponents**
an advantage to/for **employers/consumers/patients**
a **competitive/unfair/distinct/huge** advantage
enjoy/hold/have/obtain/secure/derive an advantage
confer/offer/provide an advantage

▶ **SYNONYMS:** aid, edge
▶ **ANTONYM:** disadvantage

2 UNCOUNTABLE NOUN Advantage is the state of being in a better position than others who are competing against you. ○ [+ over] *Men have created a social and economic position of advantage for themselves over women.*

▶ **COLLOCATION:** advantage **over** *someone*
▶ **SYNONYMS:** dominance, superiority, privilege
▶ **ANTONYM:** disadvantage

ad|van|taged /æd'vɑːntɪdʒd, -'væn-/

ADJECTIVE A person or place that is **advantaged** is in a better social or financial position than other people or places. ○ *Some cities are always going to be more advantaged.*

▶ **COLLOCATIONS:**
an advantaged **area/background/child/position**
socially/economically/financially advantaged
the **less** advantaged

▶ **SYNONYM:** privileged
▶ **ANTONYM:** disadvantaged

ad|van|ta|geous /ˌædvən'teɪdʒəs/

ADJECTIVE If something is **advantageous to** you, it is likely to benefit you. ○ [+ to] *Free exchange of goods was advantageous to all.* ○ *Coca-Cola enjoyed an extraordinarily advantageous market position during the early twentieth century.*

▶ **COLLOCATIONS:**
advantageous **to** *someone/something*
an advantageous **position/rate/condition**
mutually/economically/politically advantageous
▶ **SYNONYM:** favourable
▶ **ANTONYMS:** unfavourable, disadvantageous

agree /əˈgriː/ (agrees, agreeing, agreed)

VERB If one account of an event or one set of figures **agrees with** another, the two accounts or sets of figures are the same or are consistent with each other. ○ [+ with] *His second statement agrees with facts as stated by the other witnesses.* ○ [+ with] *The total of columns I and J should agree with the amount shown for income.*

▶ **COLLOCATION:** agree **with** *something*
▶ **SYNONYMS:** tally, correspond, match

agree|ment /əˈgriːmənt/

UNCOUNTABLE NOUN If there is **agreement** between two accounts of an event or two sets of figures, they are the same or are consistent with each other. ○ [+ with] *Many other surveys have produced results essentially in agreement with these figures.* ○ [+ between] *There is a measure of agreement between these accounts.*

▶ **COLLOCATIONS:**
in agreement
agreement **between** *things*
in agreement **with** *something*
▶ **SYNONYMS:** concurrence, correspondence

aid /eɪd/ (aids, aiding, aided) `ACADEMIC WORD` `SOCIAL SCIENCE`

1 UNCOUNTABLE NOUN Aid is money, equipment, or services that are provided for people, countries, or organizations who need them but cannot provide them for themselves. ○ [+ to] *regular flights carrying humanitarian aid to Cambodia* ○ *They have already pledged billions of dollars in aid.* ○ *food aid convoys*

▶ **COLLOCATIONS:**
aid **to/for** *someone*
provide/distribute/deliver aid
humanitarian/food/foreign/emergency aid
an aid **package/convoy/worker/agency**

2 VERB To **aid** a country, organization, or person means to provide them with money, equipment, or services that they need. ○ *U.S. efforts to aid Kurdish refugees* ○ *a charitable organization that has spent millions aiding pharmaceutical research*

a

3 VERB To **aid** someone means to help or assist them. [WRITTEN] ○ [+ *in*]
a software system to aid managers in advanced decision-making ○ *The hunt for her killer will continue, with police aided by the army and air force.*

▶ **COLLOCATIONS:**
aid *someone* **in** *something*
aided **by** *someone*

▶ **SYNONYMS:** help, assist

---

aim /eɪm/ (aims)

NOUN The **aim** of something that you do is the purpose for which you do it or the result that it is intended to achieve. ○ [+ *of*] *The main aim of the present study was to test Boklage's findings.* ○ *a research programme that has largely failed to achieve its principal aims*

▶ **COLLOCATIONS:**
the aim **of** *something*
the aim of a **project/exercise/chapter/study**
achieve/accomplish/state/pursue an aim
the **main/ultimate/primary** aim
a **stated/clear/long-term** aim

▶ **PHRASE:** aims and objectives

> **EXTEND YOUR VOCABULARY**
>
> The **purpose** of something is your reason for doing it. The **aim** of something is what you hope to achieve. ○ *The main purpose of the visit was to attend the conference.* ○ *The aim of the project is to encourage kids to write and read using internet technology.*
>
> You can also talk about your **goals** or **objectives**. These are usually more specific results that you hope to achieve at the end of something. ○ *the goal of a 40% reduction in waste* ○ *The main objectives are to provide a quicker response in emergencies.*

---

al|be|it /ɔːlˈbiːɪt/   ACADEMIC WORD

ADVERB You use **albeit** to introduce a fact or comment which reduces the force or significance of what you have just said. [FORMAL] ○ *Charles's letter was indeed published, albeit in a somewhat abbreviated form.* ○ *A growing body of evidence, albeit circumstantial, links aluminium with Alzheimer's disease.*

---

al|ge|bra /ˈældʒɪbrə/   MATHS

UNCOUNTABLE NOUN **Algebra** is a type of mathematics in which letters are used to represent possible quantities. ○ *a textbook on linear algebra*

▶ COLLOCATIONS:
elementary/advanced/linear algebra
an algebra **textbook/class**

---

al‖lege /əˈledʒ/ (alleges, alleging, alleged)   LAW

VERB If you **allege that** something bad is true, you say it but do not prove it.
[FORMAL] ○ [+ that] *She alleged that there was rampant drug use among the male members of the group.* ○ [+ to-inf] *The accused is alleged to have killed a man.*
○ [+ that] *It was alleged that the restaurant discriminated against black customers.*
▶ COLLOCATIONS:
allege a **violation/breach/infringement**
allege **fraud/misconduct/abuse**
a **lawsuit/prosecutor** alleges *something*
▶ ANTONYM: deny

> **ACADEMIC WRITING: Careful language**
>
> **Allege** is used in a legal context to show that a crime has not yet been proved in court. ○ *Police allege the vehicle contained several weapons.*
>
> You can also use **allege** and **claim** in academic writing to report that someone has said something that has not been proved, especially to show that you do not completely agree with the idea or opinion. ○ *Critics alleged the company had misled employees.* ○ *Campaigners claim that the animals are mistreated.*

al‖leged /əˈledʒd/

ADJECTIVE An **alleged** fact has been stated but has not been proved to be true.
[FORMAL] ○ *They have begun a hunger strike in protest at the alleged beating.*
○ *a list of alleged war criminals*
▶ COLLOCATIONS:
an alleged **offence/incident/plot/violation**
an alleged **victim/accomplice**
▶ SYNONYMS: supposed, stated

al‖leg‖ed‖ly /əˈledʒɪdli/

ADVERB ○ *His van allegedly struck the two as they were crossing a street.*
▶ SYNONYM: supposedly

---

al‖lo‖cate /ˈæləkeɪt/ (allocates, allocating, allocated)   ACADEMIC WORD

VERB If one item or share of something **is allocated to** a particular person or **for** a particular purpose, it is given to that person or used for that purpose.
○ [+ to] *Tickets are limited and will be allocated to those who apply first.* ○ [+ for] *The 1985 federal budget allocated $7.3 billion for development programmes.*

▶ **COLLOCATIONS:**
allocate *something* **for/to** *something/someone*
allocate **money/funding/resources/tickets/seats**
randomly/automatically allocate *something*

▶ **SYNONYMS:** assign, allot

al|lo|ca|tion /ˌæləˈkeɪʃən/ (allocations)

NOUN ○ [+ *for*] *The aid allocation for Pakistan was still under review.* ○ *Town planning and land allocation had to be coordinated.* ○ [+ *of*] *greater efficiency in the allocation of resources*

▶ **COLLOCATIONS:**
the allocation **of** *something*
the allocation of **resources/funds/shares/responsibility**
asset/resource/aid/land/budget/ticket allocation

▶ **SYNONYM:** distribution

al|ter /ˈɔːltə/ (alters, altering, altered)   `ACADEMIC WORD`

VERB If something **alters** or if you **alter** it, it changes. ○ *Little had altered in the village.* ○ *attempts to genetically alter the caffeine content of coffee plants*

→ see note at **adapt**

▶ **COLLOCATIONS:**
alter the **course/outcome** of *something*
alter the **composition/balance/structure** of *something*
alter the **facts/perceptions/wording**
radically/fundamentally/structurally/genetically alter *something*

▶ **SYNONYMS:** change, adapt

al|tera|tion /ˌɔːltəˈreɪʃən/ (alterations)

NOUN An **alteration** is a change in or to something. ○ [+ *to*] *Making some simple alterations to your diet will make you feel fitter.* ○ [+ *in*] *an alteration in hormone balance which causes blood sugar levels to fall*

▶ **COLLOCATIONS:**
an alteration **in/of/to** *something*
make/propose an alteration
require/undergo alteration
a **structural/genetic** alteration
a **minor/major/necessary/significant** alteration

▶ **SYNONYM:** change

al|ter|nate /ˈɔːltəneɪt/ (alternates, alternating, alternated)

VERB When you **alternate** two things, you keep using one then the other. When one thing **alternates with** another, the first regularly occurs after the other. ○ [+ with] *a mental disorder characterized by distinct periods of elevated mood alternating with periods of depression* ○ [+ with] *The band alternated romantic love songs with bouncy dance numbers.*

▶ **COLLOCATIONS:**
   alternate **with** *something*
   alternate **between** *things*

---

am|bigu|ous /æmˈbɪgjʊəs/

ADJECTIVE If you describe something as **ambiguous**, you mean that it is unclear or confusing because it can be understood in more than one way. ○ *This agreement is very ambiguous and open to various interpretations.* ○ *The Foreign Secretary's remarks clarify an ambiguous statement issued earlier this week.*

▶ **COLLOCATIONS:**
   deliberately/somewhat/highly ambiguous
   remain/seem ambiguous
   an ambiguous **relationship/position/result/phrase/statement**
   ambiguous **language/wording**
▶ **SYNONYMS:** vague, unclear, obscure
▶ **ANTONYMS:** clear, unambiguous

am|bigu|ous|ly /æmˈbɪgjʊəsli/

ADVERB ○ *an ambiguously worded document* ○ *Zaire's national conference on democracy ended ambiguously.*

▶ **SYNONYMS:** unclearly, uncertainly
▶ **ANTONYM:** unambiguously

am|bi|gu|ity /ˌæmbɪˈgjuːɪti/ (ambiguities)

NOUN If you say that there is **ambiguity** in something, you mean that it is unclear or confusing, or it can be understood in more than one way. ○ [+ about] *There is considerable ambiguity about what this part of the agreement actually means.* ○ [+ of] *the ambiguities of language*

▶ **COLLOCATIONS:**
   ambiguity **in/of/about** *something*
   clarify/resolve/remove ambiguity
   deliberate/legal/textual ambiguity
▶ **SYNONYM:** vagueness
▶ **ANTONYM:** clarity

---

ana|lyse /ˈænəlaɪz/ (analyses, analysing, analysed)

1 VERB If you **analyse** something, you consider it carefully or use statistical methods in order to fully understand it. [in AM, use **analyze**] ○ *McCarthy was asked to analyse the data from the first phase of trials of the vaccine.* ○ [+ what] *This book teaches you how to analyse what is causing the stress in your life.*

2 VERB If you **analyse** something, you examine it using scientific methods in order to find out what it consists of. [in AM, use **analyze**] ○ *Thompson and her colleagues analysed the samples using the antibody test.* ○ *They had their tablets analysed to find out whether they were getting the real drug or not.*

▶ **COLLOCATIONS:**
   analyse **data/statistics/results/trends**
   analyse a **sample**
   analyse *something* **critically/carefully/scientifically**

▶ **SYNONYMS:** examine, study, inspect, investigate

analy|sis /əˈnælɪsɪs/ **(analyses)**

NOUN ○ *The main results of the analysis are summarized below.* ○ [+ of] *This involves mathematical analysis of data from astronomy.* ○ [+ of] *an analysis of President Bush's domestic policy*

▶ **COLLOCATIONS:**
   analysis **of** *something*
   analysis of **data/samples**
   undertake/conduct/perform an analysis
   a **statistical/technical/chemical/forensic/scientific** analysis
   a **detailed/thorough/comparative/objective** analysis
   analyses **indicate/show/suggest** *something*

▶ **SYNONYMS:** examination, study, investigation, inspection

ana|lyst /ˈænəlɪst/ **(analysts)**

NOUN An **analyst** is a person whose job is to analyse a subject and give opinions about it. ○ *Political analysts have warned of a resurgence of violence.* ○ *Analysts are predicting total sales for the year to reach 500 million.*

▶ **COLLOCATIONS:**
   a **political/news** analyst
   a **securities/market/industry** analyst
   analysts **survey/predict/expect/forecast** *things*

---

an|gle /ˈæŋgəl/ **(angles)**   MATHS   SCIENCE

NOUN An **angle** is the difference in direction between two lines or surfaces. Angles are measured in degrees. ○ *The boat is now leaning at a 30 degree angle.*

▶ **COLLOCATION:** a **90-degree/45-degree/acute** angle

---

anony|mous /əˈnɒnɪməs/

ADJECTIVE If you remain **anonymous** when you do something, you do not let people know that you were the person who did it. ○ *You can remain anonymous if you wish.* ○ *anonymous phone calls*

▸ COLLOCATIONS:
   remain anonymous
   an anonymous **phone call/caller/letter/donor**
▸ SYNONYMS: unknown, unidentified, unnamed
▸ ANTONYMS: named, known

ano|nym|ity /ˌænʊˈnɪmɪti/

UNCOUNTABLE NOUN ○ *Both mother and daughter, who have requested anonymity, are doing fine.* ○ *The system offers participants complete anonymity.*
▸ COLLOCATIONS:
   request/grant/preserve anonymity
   complete/strict/total/relative anonymity
▸ SYNONYM: confidentiality

an|thro|pol|ogy /ˌænθrəˈpɒlədʒi/   SOCIAL SCIENCE

UNCOUNTABLE NOUN **Anthropology** is the scientific study of people, society, and culture. ○ *a leading scholar of cultural anthropology*
▸ COLLOCATIONS:
   an anthropology **professor/student/department**
   cultural/social/physical/applied anthropology

an|thro|polo|gist /ˌænθrəˈpɒlədʒɪst/ (anthropologists)

NOUN ○ *an anthropologist who had been in China for three years*
▸ COLLOCATION: a **cultural/social/forensic/renowned** anthropologist

anti|clock|wise /ˌæntiˈklɒkwaɪz/ also **anti-clockwise**

ADVERB If something is moving **anticlockwise**, it is moving in the opposite direction to the direction in which the hands of a clock move. [BRIT; in AM, use **counterclockwise**] ○ *The cutters are opened by turning the knob anticlockwise.*

• **Anticlockwise** is also an adjective. ○ *As seen from above the Sun's north pole, the planets orbit the Sun in an anticlockwise direction.*
▸ ANTONYM: clockwise

ap|par|ent|ly /əˈpærəntli/   ACADEMIC WORD

ADVERB You use **apparently** to refer to something that seems to be true, although you are not sure whether it is or not. ○ *The recent deterioration has been caused by an apparently endless recession.*
▸ COLLOCATION: apparently **random/unrelated/healthy/unaware**
▸ SYNONYMS: seemingly, ostensibly

a

> **ACADEMIC WRITING: Careful language**
>
> In academic writing, you try not to present as facts things you do not
> have clear evidence for. You often use adverbs to show how certain (or
> not) you are about something.
>
> **Apparently** and **seemingly** show that you are describing what seems
> to be true, based on your impression of the situation, but without clear
> evidence.
>
> **Reportedly**, **allegedly** and **ostensibly** show that something is based
> on what other people or sources say, but that you have doubts about.

ap|peal /ə'piːl/ (appeals, appealing, appealed)   LAW

1 **VERB** If you **appeal to** someone in authority against a decision, you formally
ask them to change it. In British English, you **appeal against** something. In
American English, you **appeal** something. ○ [+ against] *He said they would
appeal against the decision.* ○ *We intend to appeal the verdict.* ○ [+ to] *Maguire has
appealed to the Supreme Court to stop her extradition.*

  ▶ **COLLOCATIONS:**
   appeal **against** *something*
   appeal **to** *someone*
   appeal a **ruling/verdict/sentence/decision**
   appeal **successfully/unsuccessfully**

2 **NOUN** An **appeal** is a formal request for a decision to be changed.
   ○ [+ against] *Mr Russell has lodged a formal appeal against his dismissal.* ○ *The jury
agreed with her, but she lost the case on appeal.*

  ▶ **COLLOCATIONS:**
   on appeal
   an appeal **against** *something*
   an appeal against a **conviction/decision/ban**
   lodge/file/dismiss/reject an appeal

  ▶ **SYNONYM:** request

ap|pen|dix /ə'pendɪks/ (appendices)   ACADEMIC STUDY   ACADEMIC WORD

NOUN An **appendix to** a book is extra information that is placed after the end
of the main text. ○ *An additional 6 percent was spent in active recreation
(see appendix 7.1).*

> **ACADEMIC WRITING: Parts of a text**
>
> Academic texts, including books, reports and other academic papers, are
> usually organized in the same way. They start with a table of **contents**
> showing the chapters or sections the text is divided into.

Then after the main text, there is a list of **references**, also called a **bibliography**, listing sources referred to in the text.

There may be a number of **appendices** showing information or data that is too long or detailed to include in the main text, but which a reader can refer to if they are interested. In the example above, appendix 7.1 will probably show more detailed statistics.

At the end of academic books there is usually an **index** showing key words and topics and the page numbers to help you find information in the book.

---

ap|ply /əˈplaɪ/ (applies, applying, applied)

1 VERB If something such as a rule or a remark **applies to** a person or in a situation, it is relevant to the person or the situation. ○ [+ to] *The convention does not apply to us.* ○ *The rule applies where a person owns stock in a corporation.*

2 VERB If you **apply** something such as a rule, system, or skill, you use it in a situation or activity. ○ *These psychologists are applying psychological principles in order to improve the effectiveness of industrial organizations.* ○ [+ to] *His project is concerned with applying the technology to practical business problems.*

▶ COLLOCATIONS:
apply **to** someone/something
a **rule/principle/condition** applies
apply a **principle/technique/rule/criterion**

▶ SYNONYMS: pertain, be relevant, use

ap|pli|ca|tion /ˌæplɪˈkeɪʃən/ (applications)

NOUN The **application of** a rule or piece of knowledge is the use of it in a particular situation. ○ [+ of] *Students learned the practical application of the theory they had learned in the classroom.* ○ [+ to] *The book provides a succinct outline of artificial intelligence and its application to robotics.*

▶ COLLOCATIONS:
the application **of** something
something's application **to** something
the application of a **principle/theory/rule**
the application of **technology**
a **practical/commercial/clinical/specific** application

▶ SYNONYMS: use, relevance

---

ap|proach /əˈprəʊtʃ/ ACADEMIC WORD
(approaches, approaching, approached)

1 VERB When you **approach** a task, problem, or situation in a particular way, you deal with it or think about it in that way. ○ *The Bank has approached the issue in a practical way.* ○ *Employers are interested in how you approach problems.*

▶ **COLLOCATION:** approach a **task/issue/problem**

▶ **SYNONYMS:** tackle, address

2 NOUN Your **approach to** a task, problem, or situation is the way you deal with it or think about it. ○ [+ *to*] *We will be exploring different approaches to gathering information.* ○ *The programme adopts a multidisciplinary approach.*

▶ **COLLOCATIONS:**
an approach **to** *something*
adopt/take/prefer an approach
a **pragmatic/cautious/different/innovative** approach

▶ **SYNONYMS:** methodology, procedure, technique

---

ap|pro|pri|ate /əˈprəʊpriət/

ADJECTIVE Something that is **appropriate** is suitable or acceptable for a particular situation. ○ [+ *to*] *Dress neatly and attractively in an outfit appropriate to the job.* ○ *The teacher can then take appropriate action.*

▶ **COLLOCATIONS:**
appropriate **to/for** *something*
appropriate to/for a **purpose/occasion/task**
appropriate **action/treatment/punishment**
an appropriate **measure/response**
deem/consider *something* appropriate
wholly/entirely/perfectly/highly appropriate

▶ **SYNONYMS:** suitable, acceptable

▶ **ANTONYM:** inappropriate

ap|pro|pri|ate|ly /əˈprəʊpriətli/

ADVERB ○ *Dress appropriately and ask intelligent questions.* ○ *It's entitled, appropriately enough, 'Art for the Nation'.*

▶ **COLLOCATIONS:**
respond/act/dress/behave appropriately
appropriately **named/titled**

▶ **SYNONYMS:** suitably, acceptably

▶ **ANTONYM:** inappropriately

---

ap|prove /əˈpruːv/ (approves, approving, approved)

VERB If someone in a position of authority **approves** a plan or idea, they formally agree to it and say that it can happen. ○ *The Russian Parliament has approved a program of radical economic reforms.* ○ *MPs approved the Bill by a majority of 97.*

▶ **COLLOCATIONS:**
approve a **plan/bill/measure/proposal/request**
approved by **parliament/voters**
approved by a **committee/board/majority**

unanimously/formally/officially approved
▶ SYNONYMS: sanction, authorize, allow
▶ ANTONYMS: reject, veto

ap|prov|al /əˈpruːvəl/

UNCOUNTABLE NOUN **Approval** is a formal or official statement that something is acceptable. ○ [+ of] *The testing and approval of new drugs will be speeded up.* ○ [+ of] *The initiative is awaiting the approval of the medical research ethics committee.*
▶ COLLOCATIONS:
  the approval **of** something
  the approval **of/from** someone
  seek/obtain/await/gain/grant approval
  subject to/pending approval
  formal/final/regulatory approval
▶ SYNONYM: authorization

ap|proxi|mate `ACADEMIC WORD`
(approximates, approximating, approximated)

> The adjective is pronounced /əˈprɒksɪmət/. The verb is pronounced /əˈprɒksɪmeɪt/.

1 ADJECTIVE An **approximate** number, time, or position is close to the correct number, time, or position, but is not exact. ○ *The approximate cost varies from around £150 to £250.* ○ *The times are approximate only.*
▶ COLLOCATIONS:
  an approximate **cost/value/price/age/height/size**
  an approximate **guide/definition/location**
▶ SYNONYM: rough
▶ ANTONYMS: exact, precise

2 VERB If something **approximates to** something else, it is similar to it but is not exactly the same. ○ [+ to] *Something approximating to a fair outcome will be ensured.* ○ *By about 6 weeks of age, most babies begin to show something approximating a day/night sleeping pattern.*
▶ COLLOCATIONS:
  approximate **to** something
  closely/roughly approximate

ap|proxi|mate|ly /əˈprɒksɪmətli/

ADVERB ○ *Approximately $150 million is to be spent on improvements.* ○ *Each session lasted approximately 30 to 40 minutes.*
▶ SYNONYMS: roughly, about, around
▶ ANTONYMS: exactly, precisely

ar|chae|ol|ogy /ˌɑːkiˈɒlədʒi/ also **archeology** `HISTORY`

UNCOUNTABLE NOUN Archaeology is the study of the societies and peoples of the past by examining the remains of their buildings, tools, and other objects. ○ *an archaeology professor at Florida State University*

▶ **COLLOCATIONS:**
   an archaeology **student/professor/lecturer/department**
   maritime/biblical/industrial/classical archaeology

ar|chaeo|logi|cal /ˌɑːkiəˈlɒdʒɪkəl/

ADJECTIVE ○ *one of the region's most important archaeological sites* ○ *The earliest archaeological evidence for dingoes in Australia is 3500 years old.*

▶ **COLLOCATIONS:**
   an archaeological **site/dig/excavation/find**
   archaeological **treasure/evidence/remains**

ar|chae|olo|gist /ˌɑːkiˈɒlədʒɪst/ (archaeologists)

NOUN An **archaeologist** is a person whose job is to study societies and peoples of the past by examining the remains of their buildings, tools, and other objects. ○ *The archaeologists found a house built around 300 BC, with a basement and attic.*

▶ **COLLOCATION:** archaeologists **discover/find/unearth/excavate** things

---

archi|tec|ture /ˈɑːkɪtektʃə/ `ARTS` `ENGINEERING`

UNCOUNTABLE NOUN Architecture is the art of planning, designing, and constructing buildings. ○ *He studied classical architecture and design in Rome.*

▶ **COLLOCATION: Gothic/Victorian/modern** architecture
▶ **PHRASE:** architecture and design
▶ **SYNONYMS:** design, planning

archi|tec|tur|al /ˌɑːkɪˈtektʃərəl/

ADJECTIVE ○ *Italy's architectural heritage* ○ *the unique architectural style of the town*
▶ **COLLOCATION:** the architectural **heritage/style/design**

archi|tect /ˈɑːkɪtekt/ (architects)

NOUN An **architect** is a person who designs buildings.

▶ **COLLOCATIONS:**
   an architect **designs/builds** things
   a **renowned/modernist/chief** architect

---

ar|gue /ˈɑːgjuː/ (argues, arguing, argued)

1 VERB If you **argue that** something is true, you state it and give the reasons why you think it is true. ○ [+ that] *Mawby and Gill argue that there are four areas*

in which victims' rights need strengthening. ○ [+ that] It could be argued that incentives should not be necessary.

▶ **COLLOCATIONS:**
analysts/critics/officials/opponents argue *something*
argue **convincingly**

▶ **SYNONYM:** claim

2 VERB If you **argue for** something, you say why you agree with it, in order to persuade people that it is right. If you **argue against** something, you say why you disagree with it, in order to persuade people that it is wrong.
○ [+ against] *The report argues against tax increases.* ○ [+ for] *I argued the case for an independent central bank.*

▶ **COLLOCATION:** argue **for/against** *something*

ar|gu|ment /ˈɑːgjʊmənt/ (arguments)

NOUN An **argument** is a statement or set of statements that you use in order to try to convince people that your opinion about something is correct.
○ [+ for] *There's a strong argument for lowering the price.* ○ [+ against] *The doctors have set out their arguments against the proposals.*

→ see note at **thesis**

▶ **COLLOCATIONS:**
an argument **for/against** *something*
an argument **in favour of** *something*
someone's **main/basic/general** argument
put forward/advance/present an argument
a **strong/powerful/persuasive/compelling** argument

▶ **PHRASES:**
a line of argument
both sides of an argument

▶ **SYNONYMS:** statement, case, reasoning

---

arise /əˈraɪz/ (arises, arising, arose, arisen)

VERB If a situation or problem **arises**, it begins to exist or people start to become aware of it. ○ *if a problem arises later in the pregnancy* ○ *The birds also attack crops when the opportunity arises.*

→ see note at **occur**

▶ **COLLOCATIONS:**
a **problem/need/opportunity/question/situation** arises
arise **as a result of** *something*

▶ **SYNONYM:** occur

a

arith|me|tic /əˈrɪθmɪtɪk/ MATHS

UNCOUNTABLE NOUN **Arithmetic** is the part of mathematics that is concerned with the addition, subtraction, multiplication, and division of numbers.
○ *teaching the basics of reading, writing and arithmetic* ○ *an arithmetic test*

▶ **COLLOCATIONS:**
  do/teach arithmetic
  simple/mental arithmetic
  an arithmetic **book/problem**

▶ **PHRASE:** reading, writing and arithmetic

ar|ti|fi|cial /ˌɑːtɪˈfɪʃəl/

ADJECTIVE **Artificial** objects, materials, or processes do not occur naturally and are created by human beings, for example using science or technology.
○ *a wholefood diet free from artificial additives, colours and flavours* ○ *The city is dotted with small lakes, natural and artificial.*

▶ **COLLOCATIONS:**
  an artificial **limb/leg/heart**
  an artificial **sweetener/additive/flavouring/fertilizer**
  an artificial **lake/surface**
  somewhat/wholly/highly/totally artificial

▶ **PHRASE:** artificial intelligence

▶ **SYNONYMS:** synthetic, man-made

▶ **ANTONYM:** natural

ar|ti|fi|cial|ly /ˌɑːtɪˈfɪʃəli/

ADVERB ○ *artificially sweetened lemonade* ○ *drugs which artificially reduce heart rate*

▶ **COLLOCATIONS:**
  induce/create something artificially
  artificially **coloured/sweetened/enhanced**

as|pect /ˈæspekt/ (aspects) ACADEMIC WORD

NOUN An **aspect** of something is one of the parts of its character or nature.
○ [+ *of*] *Climate and weather affect every aspect of our lives.* ○ [+ *of*] *a framework covering different aspects of telecommunications and information technology*

▶ **COLLOCATIONS:**
  an aspect **of** something
  an aspect of **life/culture/society/nature**
  every aspect
  various/all/different/other aspects
  a **positive/negative/important/key** aspect
  a **financial/spiritual/technical** aspect

cover/examine/explore an aspect
▶ SYNONYMS: angle, feature

---

as|sem|ble /ə'sembəl/ ACADEMIC WORD
(assembles, assembling, assembled)

1 VERB When people **assemble** or when someone **assembles** them, they come together in a group, usually for a particular purpose such as a meeting. ○ *There wasn't even a convenient place for students to assemble between classes.* ○ [+ in] *Thousands of people assembled in a stadium in Thokoza.* ○ *He has assembled a team of experts.*

▶ COLLOCATIONS:
assemble **in/at** *somewhere*
assemble **for** *something*
assemble for a **meeting/ceremony/occasion**
a **crowd/team** assembles
delegates/guests/workers assemble

▶ SYNONYMS: gather, meet, congregate

2 VERB To **assemble** something means to collect it together or to fit the different parts of it together. ○ *He is assembling evidence concerning a murder.* ○ *a firm which assembles components into a finished product*

▶ COLLOCATIONS:
hastily/hurriedly assemble *something*
assemble a **collection/array/fleet**
assemble a **bomb/kit**

▶ ANTONYMS: disassemble, dismantle

as|sem|bly /ə'sembli/ **(assemblies)**

1 NOUN An **assembly** is a large group of people who meet regularly to make decisions or laws for a particular region or country. ○ *the campaign for the first free election to the National Assembly*

▶ COLLOCATIONS:
elect/convene/dissolve an assembly
a **regional/national/legislative** assembly

2 UNCOUNTABLE NOUN The **assembly** of a machine, device, or object is the process of fitting its different parts together. ○ [+ of] *For the rest of the day, he worked on the assembly of an explosive device.* ○ *car assembly plants*

▶ COLLOCATIONS:
the assembly **of** *something*
an assembly **plant/line**
assembly **instructions**

▶ SYNONYMS: construction, manufacture

a

as|sess /əˈses/ (assesses, assessing, assessed) `ACADEMIC WORD` `EDUCATION`

VERB When you **assess** a person, thing, or situation, you consider them in order to make a judgment about them. ○ *Our correspondent has been assessing the impact of the sanctions.* ○ *The test was to assess aptitude rather than academic achievement.* ○ *[+ whether] It would be a matter of assessing whether she was well enough to travel.*

▶ **COLLOCATIONS:**
  assess the **damage/impact/risk/progress**
  assess a **situation**
  assess **objectively/independently/accurately/properly**

▶ **SYNONYMS:** evaluate, judge, test

as|sess|ment /əˈsesmənt/ (assessments)

NOUN ○ *[+ of] There is little assessment of the damage to the natural environment.* ○ *Everything from course learning materials to final assessment is completed via the Web.* ○ *[+ by] He was remanded to a mental hospital for assessment by doctors.*

▶ **COLLOCATIONS:**
  assessment **of** something
  assessment **by** someone
  assessment of a **situation**
  risk/damage assessment
  undergo/conduct/complete an assessment
  a **frank/objective/accurate/detailed** assessment
  a **blunt/gloomy/initial/preliminary** assessment
  a **psychiatric/psychological/environmental** assessment

▶ **SYNONYMS:** evaluation, test, appraisal

as|set /ˈæset/ (assets) `BUSINESS`

1 NOUN Something or someone that is an **asset** is considered useful or helps a person or organization to be successful. ○ *[+ of] Her leadership qualities were the greatest asset of the Conservative Party.* ○ *His Republican credentials made him an asset.*

▶ **COLLOCATIONS:**
  an asset **of** something
  a **valuable/great** asset

▶ **SYNONYMS:** distinction, advantage

2 PLURAL NOUN The **assets** of a company or a person are all the things that they own. ○ *[+ of] By the end of 1989 the group had assets of 3.5 billion francs.* ○ *Some tried to sell assets to pay the debts back.*

▶ **COLLOCATIONS:**
  assets **of** £x
  the assets of a **company/corporation/estate**

net/total/average assets
valuable/tangible assets
acquire/purchase/sell assets
value/invest/freeze assets
▶ SYNONYMS: possessions, property, capital
▶ ANTONYM: liability

---

as|sign|ment /əˈsaɪnmənt/   [ACADEMIC WORD] [ACADEMIC STUDY]
(assignments)

NOUN An **assignment** is a task or piece of work that you are given to do, especially as part of your job or studies. ○ *The assessment for the course involves written assignments and practical tests.* ○ *His first overseas assignment was in Ghana.*
▶ COLLOCATIONS:
  a **writing/written/work/homework** assignment
  a **special/overseas** assignment
  a **tough/challenging/temporary** assignment
▶ SYNONYMS: coursework, test, task, job

---

as|so|ci|at|ed /əˈsəʊsieɪtɪd/

ADJECTIVE If one thing is **associated with** another, the two things are connected with each other. ○ [+ with] *These symptoms are particularly associated with migraine headaches.* ○ [+ with] *Marie Curie's name is still associated with science funding.*
▶ COLLOCATIONS:
  associated **with** *something*
  closely associated
▶ SYNONYMS: linked, connected, related
▶ ANTONYM: unrelated

---

as|sume /əˈsjuːm, AM əˈsuːm/   [ACADEMIC WORD]
(assumes, assuming, assumed)

VERB If you **assume that** something is true, you imagine that it is true, sometimes wrongly. ○ [+ that] *It is a misconception to assume that the two continents are similar.* ○ [+ to-inf] *If mistakes occurred, they were assumed to be the fault of the commander on the spot.*
▶ COLLOCATIONS:
  wrongly/mistakenly/automatically/safely assume *something*
  widely assumed
▶ SYNONYMS: presume, expect
▶ ANTONYM: doubt

as|sump|tion /əˈsʌmpʃən/ (assumptions)

NOUN If you make an **assumption that** something is true or will happen, you accept that it is true or will happen, often without any real proof. ○ *Dr Subroto questioned the scientific assumption on which the global warming theory is based.* ○ [+ *of*] *Economists are working on the assumption of an interest rate cut.*

▶ COLLOCATIONS:
   on an assumption
   an assumption **of** *something*
   an assumption of **superiority/risk/guilt**
   make/challenge/question an assumption
   an **underlying/implicit** assumption

▶ SYNONYMS: presumption, premise, supposition

as|trono|my /əˈstrɒnəmi/   SCIENCE

UNCOUNTABLE NOUN **Astronomy** is the scientific study of the stars, planets, and other natural objects in space. ○ *a 10-day astronomy mission*

▶ COLLOCATIONS:
   an astronomy **professor/enthusiast/mission**
   planetary/optical/theoretical/modern astronomy

as|tro|nomi|cal /ˌæstrəˈnɒmɪkəl/

ADJECTIVE ○ *the British Astronomical Association* ○ *an alternative method of astronomical observation*

▶ COLLOCATIONS:
   an astronomical **observation/discovery**
   an astronomical **observatory/telescope/instrument**

as|trono|mer /əˈstrɒnəmə/ (astronomers)

NOUN An **astronomer** is a scientist who studies the stars, planets, and other natural objects in space. ○ *William Herschel, the eminent astronomer who discovered the planet Uranus*

at|tach /əˈtætʃ/ (attaches, attaching, attached)   ACADEMIC WORD

1 VERB If you **attach** something **to** an object, you join it or fasten it to the object. ○ [+ *to*] *The gadget can be attached to any vertical surface.* ○ *For further information, please contact us on the attached form.*

2 VERB In computing, if you **attach** a file **to** a message that you send to someone, you send it with the message but separate from it. ○ [+ *to*] *It is possible to attach executable program files to e-mail.*

▶ COLLOCATIONS:
   attach *something* **to** *something*

attach a **rope/wire/cord/device**
attach a **file/chart/form**
firmly/securely/permanently/physically attach *something*

▶ **SYNONYM:** connect
▶ **ANTONYM:** detach

at|tach|ment /əˈtætʃmənt/ (attachments)

1 NOUN An **attachment** is a device that can be fixed onto a machine in order to enable it to do different jobs. ○ [+ *for*] *Some models come with attachments for dusting.*

▶ **COLLOCATIONS:**
an attachment **for** *something*
a **camera/hose/shower** attachment

▶ **SYNONYMS:** fixture, fitting, part

2 NOUN An **attachment** is a document or file that is added to another document or an email ○ [+ *to*] *Justice Fitzgerald included a 120-page discussion paper as an attachment to the annual report.* ○ *When you send an e-mail you can also send a sound or graphic file as an attachment.*

▶ **COLLOCATIONS:**
an attachment **to** *something*
send *something* **as** an attachment
open an attachment

▶ **SYNONYMS:** appendix, supplement

---

at|tend /əˈtend/ (attends, attending, attended)

1 VERB If you **attend** a meeting or other event, you are present at it. ○ *Thousands of people attended the funeral.* ○ *The meeting will be attended by finance ministers from many countries.*

▶ **COLLOCATIONS:**
attended **by** *someone*
attend a **meeting/conference/summit/funeral**
delegates/guests/representatives attend *something*
sparsely/poorly/well attended

▶ **ANTONYM:** miss

2 VERB If you **attend** an institution such as a school, college, or church, you go there regularly. ○ *Numbers for international students attending FE colleges show an increase of more than 21% over the previous year's figures.*

▶ **COLLOCATIONS:**
attend a **school/university/college**
students/pupils/children attend *something*
attend **regularly/rarely**

at|tend|ance /əˈtendəns/ (attendances)

1 UNCOUNTABLE NOUN Someone's **attendance** at an event or an institution is the fact that they are present at the event or go regularly to the institution. ○ [+ *at*] *Her attendance at school was sporadic.* ○ *Church attendance continues to decline.*

2 NOUN The **attendance** at an event is the number of people who are present at it. ○ *Average weekly cinema attendance in February was 2.41 million.* ○ *This year attendances were 28% lower than forecast.*

▶ **COLLOCATIONS:**
  attendance **at** *something*
  attendance at a **meeting/conference/event**
  attendance at **school/church**
  compulsory/mandatory attendance
  average/total/weekly attendance
  an attendance **rate/figure/record**
  boost/increase attendance

▶ **SYNONYM:** presence
▶ **ANTONYM:** absence

at|ti|tude /ˈætɪtjuːd, AM -tuːd/ (attitudes) `ACADEMIC WORD`

NOUN Your **attitude to** something is the way that you think and feel about it, especially when this shows in the way you behave. ○ [+ *towards*] *the general change in attitude towards people with disabilities.* ○ [+ *to*] *Being unemployed produces negative attitudes to work.* ○ *prevailing cultural attitudes*

▶ **COLLOCATIONS:**
  an attitude **to/towards/about** *something*
  adopt/maintain/change an attitude
  a **negative/positive/hostile** attitude
  a **progressive/liberal/prevailing** attitude

▶ **SYNONYMS:** outlook, opinion, point of view

at|tract /əˈtrækt/ (attracts, attracting, attracted) `PHYSICS`

VERB If one object **attracts** another object, it causes the second object to move towards it. ○ [+ *to*] *Anything with strong gravity attracts other things to it.* ○ [+ *to*] *streams of charged particles which are magnetically attracted to the poles of the earth*

▶ **COLLOCATION:** attract *something* **to** *something*
▶ **ANTONYM:** repel

at|trac|tion /əˈtrækʃən/ (attractions)

NOUN ○ *The Arctic exerts a magnetic attraction even in the Antipodes.* ○ [+ *for*] *Each particle has a strong force of attraction for the particles around it.*

► **COLLOCATIONS:**
an attraction **to/for** *something*
a **strong/magnetic** attraction
► **ANTONYM:** repulsion

auto|mat|ic /ˌɔːtəˈmætɪk/ `ACADEMIC WORD`

ADJECTIVE An **automatic** machine or device is one which has controls that enable it to perform a task without needing to be constantly operated by a person. **Automatic** methods and processes involve the use of such machines. ○ *Modern trains have automatic doors.*
► **COLLOCATIONS:**
an automatic **weapon/rifle/machine/gearbox**
fully/virtually automatic
► **SYNONYMS:** automated, mechanical
► **ANTONYM:** manual

auto|mati|cal|ly /ˌɔːtəˈmætɪkli/

ADVERB ○ *Messages are automatically scanned for viruses.* ○ *When the intake blocked, the engines automatically shut down.*
► **ANTONYM:** manually

axis /ˈæksɪs/ (axes) `ACADEMIC STUDY`

NOUN An **axis** of a graph is one of the two lines on which the scales of measurement are marked. ○ *These points are shown along the horizontal axis in Figure 6.1.*
► **COLLOCATIONS:**
an axis **of** *something*
the **horizontal/vertical** axis

> **ACADEMIC WRITING: Describing graphs and charts**
>
> When you describe a graph, you refer to the line along the bottom of the graph as the **horizontal axis** and the line down the side of the graph as the **vertical axis**. ○ *The vertical axis shows the level of the students' knowledge and the horizontal axis shows the length of the course in weeks.*
>
> The **key** to a graph, chart or diagram helps you to understand what the different parts of it mean. For example, a **key** for a chart might show you that the figures for girls are shown in red and in blue for boys.
>
> A diagram is often **labelled** to show you what the different parts are.

Bb

bach|elor's de|gree
/ˈbætʃələz dɪˌgriː/ **(bachelor's degrees)**

`EDUCATION` `ACADEMIC STUDY`

N-COUNT A **bachelor's degree** is a first degree awarded by universities.
○ [+ in] *He received his bachelor's degree in computer science at Brown University in 1976.* ○ [+ in] *Lab positions require a bachelor's degree, preferably in biology.*

▶ **COLLOCATIONS:**
a bachelor's degree **in** *something*
a bachelor's degree in **history/French/philosophy**
study for a bachelor's degree
obtain/get/receive/earn a bachelor's degree

▶ **SYNONYM:** undergraduate degree

▶ **RELATED WORD:** master's degree

> **USAGE:** Academic qualifications
>
> There are two main types of **bachelor's degree**; a **bachelor of arts**, a **BA**, in subjects like history, languages, etc. and a **bachelor of science**, a **BSc**.
>
> A second university degree is usually called a **master's degree**. Again, the main types are a **master of arts**, an **MA**, and a **master of science**, an **MSc**.

bac|te|ria /bækˈtɪəriə/

`BIOLOGY` `MEDICINE`

PLURAL NOUN Bacteria are very small organisms. Some bacteria can cause disease. ○ *Chlorine is added to kill bacteria.* ○ *The viruses and bacteria of most diseases are in the air around us every day.*

▶ **COLLOCATIONS:**
bacteria **kill/infect/invade/destroy** *something*
bacteria **spread/multiply/thrive**
harmful/deadly/resistant bacteria

▶ **RELATED WORD:** virus

bac|te|rial /bækˈtɪəriəl/

ADJECTIVE ○ *Cholera is a bacterial infection.*

▶ **COLLOCATION:** bacterial **infection/contamination**

▶ **RELATED WORD:** viral

b

bal|ance /ˈbæləns/ (balances, balancing, balanced)

1 VERB If you **balance** one thing **with** something different, each of the things has the same strength or importance. ○ *The state has got to find some way to balance these two needs.* ○ [+ with] *If your main occupation is using your brain, balance this with exercise.*

▶ COLLOCATIONS:
balance *something* **with** *something*
evenly/finely/carefully balanced

2 NOUN A **balance** is a situation in which all the different parts are equal in strength or importance. ○ [+ between] *We are for ever trying to achieve a balance between two opposites.* ○ [+ of] *a way to ensure that people get the right balance of foods* ○ [+ of] *the ecological balance of the forest*

▶ COLLOCATIONS:
a balance **between** *things*
the balance **of** *something*
find/achieve/strike/maintain/restore a balance
redress/tip/upset/shift the balance
a **perfect/right/healthy/delicate/fine** balance

▶ PHRASE: balance of power

▶ SYNONYM: equilibrium

bank|rupt /ˈbæŋkrʌpt/   BUSINESS

ADJECTIVE People or organizations that go **bankrupt** do not have enough money to pay their debts. ○ *If the firm cannot sell its products, it will go bankrupt.* ○ *He was declared bankrupt after failing to pay a £114m loan guarantee.*

▶ COLLOCATIONS:
go/become bankrupt
be **declared** bankrupt

▶ SYNONYM: insolvent

▶ ANTONYM: solvent

bank|rupt|cy /ˈbæŋkrʌptsi/

UNCOUNTABLE NOUN ○ *It is the second airline in two months to file for bankruptcy.* ○ *Many established firms were facing bankruptcy.*

▶ COLLOCATIONS:
face/file for/avoid/declare bankruptcy
bankruptcy **law/proceedings/protection**

▶ SYNONYM: insolvency

▶ ANTONYM: solvency

bar chart /ˈbɑː tʃɑːt/ (bar charts)

NOUN A **bar chart** is a graph which uses parallel rectangular shapes to represent changes in the size, value, or rate of something or to compare the amount of something relating to a number of different countries or groups. [mainly BRIT; in AM, use **bar graph**] ○ *The bar chart below shows the huge growth of U.K. car exports over the past few years.*

▶ COLLOCATIONS:
   a bar chart **shows/illustrates/reflects** *something*
   a bar chart **compares** *things*

ACADEMIC WRITING: Charts and graphs

There are several ways to show information visually. A **graph** shows how two sets of numbers or measurements relate to each other. It has two axes - a line along the bottom and down the left side - and one or more lines plotted across the graph showing a trend.

Chart is a general word to describe information shown visually. A **bar chart** shows numbers represented by rectangular bars next to each other. A **pie chart** shows amounts represented by sections of a circle. A **flow chart** shows the steps in a process represented by shapes joined by arrows.

A **diagram** is a simple picture showing how something works. ○ *as shown in the diagram of a mechanical fuel pump*

In academic writing, all charts, graphs and diagrams can be referred to as **figures**. In a long academic text, the **figures** are usually labelled with numbers so that they can be referred to in the text. ○ *the movement of plates that form the Earth's crust (see figure 2.5)*

---

base /beɪs/ (bases, basing, based)

1 NOUN The **base** of something is its lowest edge, part, or surface. ○ [+ *of*] *The surgeon placed catheters through the veins and arteries near the base of the head.* ○ [+ *of*] *the base of a 20cm deep round tin* ○ *The rock was very smooth at the base.*

▶ COLLOCATIONS:
   the base **of** *something*
   a **square/round/broad/narrow** base

▶ SYNONYMS: bottom, foot

▶ ANTONYM: top

2 VERB If you **base** one thing **on** another thing, the first thing develops from the second thing. ○ [+ *on*] *He based his conclusions on the evidence he had.* ○ [+ *on*] *Selection decisions are seldom based on test data alone.*

▶ COLLOCATIONS:
   base *something* **on/upon** *something*

base a **decision/estimate/conclusion** on *something*
base a **finding/prediction/judgement/argument** on *something*
largely/loosely/solely/broadly based on *something*
▶ SYNONYMS: build, found

ba|sis /ˈbeɪsɪs/ (bases)

NOUN If something is done **on** a particular **basis**, it is done according to that method, system, or principle. ○ *We're going to be meeting there on a regular basis.* ○ *They want all groups to be treated on an equal basis.* ○ *These judges dealt with questions of law on a day-to-day basis.*

▶ COLLOCATIONS:
on a *particular* basis
on a **regular/individual/equal** basis
on a **part-time/voluntary/temporary** basis
on a **daily/weekly/monthly/permanent** basis
a **case-by-case/day-to-day/pro rata** basis
a **first-come-first-served/need-to-know** basis
▶ SYNONYMS: method, system, footing, principle

bear out /beə ˈaʊt/ (bears out, bearing out, bore out, borne out)

PHRASAL VERB If someone or something **bears** a person **out** or **bears out** what that person is saying, they support what that person is saying. ○ *Recent studies have borne out claims that certain perfumes can bring about profound psychological changes.* ○ *Her theories have been borne out by several research studies.*

▶ COLLOCATIONS:
a **fact/point/theory/diagnosis** is borne out
a **claim/assertion/opinion** is borne out
▶ SYNONYMS: confirm, support
▶ ANTONYMS: refute, disprove

be|half /bɪˈhɑːf, -ˈhæf/ ACADEMIC WORD

PHRASE If you do something **on** someone's **behalf**, you do it for that person as their representative. The form **in** someone's **behalf** is also used, mainly in American English. ○ *She made an emotional public appeal on her son's behalf.* ○ [+ *of*] *Secret Service officer Robin Thompson spoke on behalf of his colleagues.*

▶ COLLOCATIONS:
on/in *someone's* behalf
on behalf **of** *someone*
on behalf of a **client/constituent**
on behalf of the **victim/plaintiff/defendant**
▶ SYNONYMS: interest, sake, part

bias /baɪəs/ **(biases, biasing, biased)**   `ACADEMIC WORD`

1 NOUN Bias is a tendency to prefer one person or thing to another, and to favour that person or thing. ○ [+ *against*] *Bias against women permeates every level of the judicial system.* ○ *There were fierce attacks on the BBC for alleged political bias.*

2 NOUN Bias is a concern with or interest in one thing more than others. ○ [+ *towards*] *The Department has a strong bias towards neuroscience.*

▶ **COLLOCATIONS:**
   bias **against/towards** something
   show/display/perceive/allege bias
   eliminate/avoid bias
   political/racial/cultural/gender bias

▶ **SYNONYMS:** prejudice, favour

3 VERB To **bias** someone means to influence them in favour of a particular choice. ○ *We mustn't allow it to bias our teaching.*

bi|ased /baɪəst/

ADJECTIVE ○ [+ *against*] *He seemed a bit biased against women in my opinion.* ○ [+ *towards*] *University funding was tremendously biased towards scientists.* ○ *examples of inaccurate and biased reporting* ○ *politically biased allegations*

▶ **COLLOCATIONS:**
   biased **against** someone/something
   biased **in favour of/towards** someone/something
   biased **reporting/coverage/research/advice**
   a biased **opinion/sample/referee/judge**
   racially/culturally/politically biased
   heavily biased

▶ **SYNONYM:** prejudiced

▶ **ANTONYM:** impartial

body /ˈbɒdi/ **(bodies)**

1 NOUN A **body** is an organized group of people who deal with something officially. ○ *the Chairman of the policemen's representative body, the Police Federation* ○ *the main trade union body, COSATU, Congress of South African Trade Unions*

▶ **COLLOCATIONS:**
   the **ruling/governing** body
   a **regulatory/advisory/professional** body
   a **legislative/statutory/public/international/independent** body
   a body **represents** someone
   the body **responsible for** something

▶ **SYNONYM:** organization

2 NOUN The body of something such as a building or a document is the main part of it or the largest part of it. ○ [+ of] *The main body of the church had been turned into a massive television studio.* ○ [+ of] *Give an introduction, followed by the body of the material, then a brief summary.*

▶ COLLOCATIONS:
the body **of** something
the body of the **work/material**

▶ SYNONYM: bulk

---

bond /bɒnd/ (bonds) `ACADEMIC WORD`

1 NOUN A **bond between** people is a strong feeling of friendship, love, or shared beliefs and experiences that unites them. ○ [+ between] *The experience created a very special bond between us.* ○ [+ that] *the bond that linked them*

2 NOUN A **bond between** people or groups is a close connection that they have with each other, for example because they have a special agreement. ○ [+ between] *the strong bond between church and nation* ○ [+ with] *The republic is successfully breaking its bonds with Moscow.*

▶ COLLOCATIONS:
a bond **between** people
a bond **with** someone/something
a bond **of** something
a bond of **affection/friendship/trust/love**
forge/strengthen a bond
a **strong/healthy** bond

▶ SYNONYMS: tie, connection, link, attachment

3 NOUN A **bond** between two things is the way in which they stick to one another or are joined in some way. ○ [+ with] *The glue may not create a bond with some plastics.* ○ [+ between] *The molecule contains four carbon atoms arranged in a ring with a triple bond between two of them.*

▶ COLLOCATIONS:
a bond **with** something
a bond **between** things
a bond between **atoms**
a **strong/weak** bond

▶ SYNONYM: attachment

---

brack|et /ˈbrækɪt/ (brackets) `ACADEMIC STUDY`

NOUN If you say that someone or something is in a particular **bracket**, you mean that they come within a particular range, for example a range of incomes, ages, or prices. ○ *a 33% top tax rate on everyone in these high-income brackets* ○ *Do you fall outside that age bracket?*

▶ COLLOCATION: a **tax/income/age/price** bracket

▶ SYNONYMS: range, sector

---

break|through /ˈbreɪkθruː/ (breakthroughs)

NOUN A **breakthrough** is an important development or achievement. ○ [+ in] *The company looks poised to make a significant breakthrough in China.* ○ *The breakthrough came hours before a U.N. deadline.*

▶ COLLOCATIONS:
a breakthrough **in** *something*
a breakthrough in **technology/research**
make/achieve/represent/produce/expect a breakthrough
a **possible/major/significant/imminent** breakthrough
a **technological/scientific** breakthrough

▶ SYNONYMS: development, achievement, advance

▶ ANTONYM: setback

---

brief /briːf/ (briefer, briefest)   `ACADEMIC WORD`

ADJECTIVE Something that is **brief** lasts for only a short time, or does not contain too many details. ○ *She once made a brief appearance on television.* ○ *During her brief reign, Mary had over 300 of her own subjects burnt alive.* ○ *a systematic yet brief history of Sufism*

▶ COLLOCATIONS:
a brief **appearance/conversation/speech**
a brief **pause/period/respite/visit**
a brief **statement/description/history/report**
relatively/mercifully brief

▶ SYNONYMS: fleeting, short, concise

▶ ANTONYM: lengthy

brief|ly /ˈbriːfli/

ADVERB ○ *There are four basic alternatives; they are described briefly below.* ○ *Briefly, no less than nine of our agents have passed information to us.*

▶ COLLOCATION: **appear/speak/describe/pause** briefly

---

broad|cast /ˈbrɔːdkɑːst, -kæst/ (broadcasts, broadcasting)   `MEDIA`

> The form **broadcast** is used in the present tense and is also the past tense and past participle of the verb.

1 NOUN A **broadcast** is a programme, performance, or speech on the radio or on television. ○ [+ on] *In a broadcast on state radio the government announced that it was willing to resume peace negotiations.* ○ [+ of] *the first live television broadcast of a presidential news conference*

▶ **COLLOCATIONS:**
a broadcast **on/of** *something*
a broadcast **from** *somewhere*
a broadcast on **television/radio**
a **radio/television/digital** broadcast
a **news/outside/live/national** broadcast
watch/listen to/hear/record a broadcast
▶ **SYNONYMS:** programme, transmission

2 VERB To **broadcast** a programme means to send it out by radio waves, so that it can be heard on the radio or seen on television. ○ *[+ on] The concert will be broadcast live on television and radio.*

▶ **COLLOCATIONS:**
broadcast **on** *something*
broadcast on **television/radio**
broadcast **live**
broadcast a **message/programme/image**
a broadcasting **network**
▶ **SYNONYMS:** transmit, relay

---

bu|reau|cra|cy /bjʊˈrɒkrəsi/

POLITICS

UNCOUNTABLE NOUN Bureaucracy refers to all the rules and procedures followed by government departments and similar organizations, especially when you think that these are complicated and cause long delays. ○ *People usually complain about having to deal with too much bureaucracy.*

▶ **COLLOCATIONS:**
state/government bureaucracy
cut/create bureaucracy
excessive/unnecessary bureaucracy
▶ **SYNONYMS:** red tape, regulations, administration

bu|reau|crat|ic /ˌbjʊərəˈkrætɪk/

ADJECTIVE Bureaucratic means involving complicated rules and procedures which can cause long delays. ○ *Diplomats believe that bureaucratic delays are inevitable.* ○ *The department has become a bureaucratic nightmare.*

Cc

calo|rie /ˈkæləri/ (calories)

NOUN **Calories** are units used to measure the energy value of food. People who are on diets try to eat food that does not contain many calories. ○ *A glass of wine does have quite a lot of calories.* ○ *calorie controlled diets*

▶ **COLLOCATIONS:**
  burn/consume/eat/contain calories
  calorie **controlled**
  low-/high- calorie
  calorie **restriction/intake/count/content**

▶ **SYNONYM:** energy

cam|pus /ˈkæmpəs/ (campuses)

NOUN A **campus** is an area of land that contains the main buildings of a university or college. ○ *during a rally at the campus* ○ *Private automobiles are not allowed on campus.*

▶ **COLLOCATIONS:**
  on campus
  main/university/college/school campus
  a campus **visit/newspaper/bookstore/library**

▶ **SYNONYM:** grounds

can|di|date /ˈkændɪdeɪt, -dət/ (candidates)

NOUN A **candidate** is someone who is being considered for a position, for example someone who is running in an election or applying for a job. ○ *The Democratic candidate is still leading in the polls.* ○ *[+ for] He is a candidate for the office of Governor.* ○ *We all spoke to them and John emerged as the best candidate.*

▶ **COLLOCATIONS:**
  a candidate **for** *something*
  a candidate for the **post/presidency/seat/leadership**
  a candidate **stands/runs/wins/applies**
  a **presidential/parliamentary/mayoral** candidate
  a **potential/independent/liberal** candidate
  elect/choose/support a candidate
  interview/favour/consider a candidate
  a candidate **list**

▶ **SYNONYMS:** applicant, contender, nominee

can|di|da|cy /ˈkændɪdəsi/ (candidacies)

NOUN Someone's **candidacy** is their position of being a candidate in an
election. ○ [+ for] *Today he is formally announcing his candidacy for President.*
○ *Mr Hart's presidential candidacy was soon at an end.*

▶ **COLLOCATIONS:**
   someone's candidacy **for** something
   someone's candidacy for the **presidency/leadership/post**
   someone's candidacy for **governor**
   the **presidential** candidacy

▶ **SYNONYM:** candidature

ca|pable /ˈkeɪpəbəl/   ACADEMIC WORD

ADJECTIVE If a person or thing is **capable of** doing something, they have the
ability to do it. ○ [+ of] *He appeared hardly capable of conducting a coherent
conversation.* ○ [+ of] *The kitchen is capable of catering for several hundred people.*
○ [+ of] *a man capable of murder*

▶ **COLLOCATIONS:**
   capable **of** something
   capable of **cruelty/greatness**
   look/seem/prove capable
   perfectly/physically/fully capable

▶ **SYNONYM:** able
▶ **ANTONYM:** incapable

ca|pa|bil|ity /ˌkeɪpəˈbɪlɪti/ (capabilities)

NOUN If you have the **capability** or the **capabilities** to do something, you
have the ability or the qualities that are necessary to do it. ○ *People experience
differences in physical and mental capability depending on the time of day.* ○ *The
standards set four years ago in Seoul will be far below the athletes' capabilities now.*

▶ **COLLOCATIONS:**
   collaborative/technological/technical capability
   organizational/analytical/intellectual capability
   wireless/processing/manufacturing capability

▶ **SYNONYMS:** ability, functionality
▶ **ANTONYM:** inability

ca|pac|ity /kəˈpæsɪti/ (capacities)   ACADEMIC WORD

1 UNCOUNTABLE NOUN The **capacity** of something such as a factory, industry,
or region is the quantity of things that it can produce or deliver with the
equipment or resources that are available. ○ [+ in] *the amount of spare capacity
in the economy* ○ *Bread factories are working at full capacity.*

2 NOUN The **capacity** of a piece of equipment or a building is its size, power, or volume. ○ [+ of] *an aircraft with a bomb-carrying capacity of 454 kg* ○ *a feature which gave the vehicles a much greater fuel capacity than other trucks* ○ [+ of] *Each stadium had a seating capacity of about 50,000.*

▶ **COLLOCATIONS:**
   capacity **in/of** something
   increase/reduce/limit something's capacity
   spare/full capacity
   a **limited/excess** capacity
   production/storage/generating/fuel capacity
   a **crowd/audience/building/stadium** capacity
▶ **PHRASE:** filled to capacity
▶ **SYNONYMS:** ability, size

---

capi|tal /ˈkæpɪtəl/   BUSINESS ECONOMICS

1 UNCOUNTABLE NOUN Capital is a large sum of money which you use to start a business, or which you invest in order to make more money. ○ *Companies are having difficulty in raising capital.* ○ *A large amount of capital is invested in all these branches.*

2 UNCOUNTABLE NOUN You can use **capital** to refer to buildings or machinery which are necessary to produce goods or to make companies more efficient, but which do not make money directly. ○ *capital equipment that could have served to increase production* ○ *capital investment*

3 UNCOUNTABLE NOUN Capital is the part of an amount of money borrowed or invested which does not include interest. ○ *With a conventional repayment mortgage, the repayments consist of both capital and interest.* ○ [+ on] *pay off the capital on your interest-only mortgage*

▶ **COLLOCATIONS:**
   the capital **on** something
   venture/share capital
   capital **gain/appreciation/expenditure/spending**
   capital **repayment/investment/equipment**
   raise/attract/invest capital
   repay/pay off the capital

---

capi|tal|ism /ˈkæpɪtəlɪzəm/   POLITICS ECONOMICS

UNCOUNTABLE NOUN Capitalism is an economic and political system in which property, business, and industry are owned by private individuals and not by the state. ○ *the return of capitalism to Hungary* ○ *the headlong rush towards global capitalism*

▶ COLLOCATIONS:
global/industrial/western/modern capitalism
free-market capitalism
▶ SYNONYMS: private enterprise, free enterprise
▶ RELATED WORDS: socialism, communism

capi|tal|ist /ˈkæpɪtəlɪst/ (capitalists)

1 ADJECTIVE A **capitalist** country or system supports or is based on the principles of capitalism. ○ *I'm a strong believer in the capitalist system.*
○ *capitalist economic theory*

▶ COLLOCATIONS:
a capitalist **system/society/economy/democracy**
a capitalist **enterprise/theory**

2 NOUN A **capitalist** is someone who believes in and supports the principles of capitalism. ○ *relations between capitalists and workers*

car|bon /ˈkɑːbən/   SCIENCE

UNCOUNTABLE NOUN **Carbon** is a chemical element that diamonds and coal are made up of. ○ *Carbon is the basic building unit of all these compounds.*
○ *Carbohydrates contain only carbon, hydrogen and oxygen.*

▶ COLLOCATIONS:
carbon **dating**
a carbon **atom/compound**

car|bon di|ox|ide /ˌkɑːbən daɪˈɒksaɪd/   SCIENCE

UNCOUNTABLE NOUN **Carbon dioxide** is a gas. It is produced by animals and people breathing out, and by chemical reactions. ○ *Plants absorb carbon dioxide from the air and moisture from the soil.* ○ *Scientists say carbon dioxide and other "greenhouse gases" trap heat in the atmosphere.*

▶ COLLOCATIONS:
carbon dioxide **gas**
carbon dioxide **production/emissions/levels**
the carbon dioxide **content/balance**
absorb/release/give off carbon dioxide
emit/produce carbon dioxide

car|bon foot|print /ˌkɑːbən ˈfʊtprɪnt/   SCIENCE

NOUN Your **carbon footprint** is a measure of the amount of carbon dioxide released into the atmosphere by your activities over a particular period.
○ *We all need to look for ways to reduce our carbon footprint.* ○ [+ of] *the carbon footprint of fossil fuelled power plants*

▶ COLLOCATIONS:
the carbon footprint **of** something
reduce/calculate your carbon footprint

---

car|bon neu|tral /ˌkɑːbən ˈnjuːtrəl, ᴀᴍ ˈnuːt-/ `SCIENCE`

ADJECTIVE A **carbon neutral** lifestyle, company, or activity does not cause an increase in the overall amount of carbon dioxide in the atmosphere. ○ *You can make your flights carbon neutral by planting trees to make up for the greenhouse gas emissions.* ○ *They offer members advice on how to become a "carbon neutral citizen".*

▶ COLLOCATIONS:
go carbon neutral
a carbon neutral **citizen/product/lifestyle/company**

---

case study /ˈkeɪs stʌdi/ (case studies) `ACADEMIC STUDY`

NOUN A **case study** is a written account that gives detailed information about a person, group, or thing and their development over a period of time. ○ [+ of] *a large case study of malaria in West African children* ○ *We need also to explain the findings from our case studies.*

▶ COLLOCATIONS:
a case study **of** something
make/present a case study
a case study **shows/covers/suggests** something
a **historical/clinical/critical** case study

---

cat|ego|ry /ˈkætɪgri, ᴀᴍ -gɔːri/ (categories) `ACADEMIC WORD`

NOUN If people or things are divided into **categories**, they are divided into groups in such a way that the members of each group are similar to each other in some way. ○ [+ of] *This book clearly falls into the category of fictionalised autobiography.* ○ *The tables were organised into six different categories.*

▶ COLLOCATIONS:
a category **of** something
in/into a category
fall into a category
a **different/broad/general** category
a **product** category

▶ SYNONYMS: class, classification

cat|ego|rize /ˈkætɪgəraɪz/ (categorizes, categorizing, categorized)

VERB If you **categorize** people or things, you divide them into sets or you say which set they belong to. [in ʙʀɪᴛ, also use **categorise**] ○ *Lindsay, like his films, is hard to categorise.* ○ [+ as] *Make a list of your child's toys and then categorise them as sociable or antisocial.* ○ [V-ing] *new ways of categorizing information*

C

▶ **COLLOCATIONS:**
categorize *something* **as** *something*
hard/difficult to categorize
▶ **SYNONYM:** classify

---

cease /siːs/ (ceases, ceasing, ceased) `ACADEMIC WORD`

1 VERB If something **ceases**, it stops happening or existing. [FORMAL] ○ *At one o'clock the rain ceased.* ○ *Six years on, his February depressions have ceased.*

2 VERB If you **cease to** do something, you stop doing it. [FORMAL] ○ [+ to-inf] *A brain deprived of oxygen ceases to function within a few minutes.* ○ [+ to-inf] *The Church has almost ceased to exist in Albania.*

3 VERB If you **cease** something, you stop it happening or working. [FORMAL] ○ *The Tundra Times ceased publication this week.* ○ [+ v-ing] *A small number of firms have ceased trading.*

▶ **COLLOCATIONS:**
hostilities cease
cease an **activity**
cease **production/operations/trading**
cease **immediately/abruptly/altogether**
cease to **exist/function/operate**

▶ **ANTONYM:** begin

> **EXTEND YOUR VOCABULARY**
>
> In everyday English, you often say that something **stops**, **ends** or **finishes**. ○ *soon after the fighting stopped/ended* ○ *The meeting finished/ ended just after 6.*
>
> In more formal academic writing, you can say that someone **ceases** an activity, especially a business activity.
>
> > cease **production/activity/operations/trading** ○ *The country's second largest airline ceased operations.*
>
> You can say that a process which people take part in **concludes** to mean that it comes to an end.
>
> > a **meeting/conference/trial/competition** concludes ○ *The hearing is expected to conclude tomorrow.*

---

cell /sel/ (cells) `BIOLOGY` `MEDICINE`

NOUN A **cell** is the smallest part of an animal or plant that is able to function independently. Every animal or plant is made up of millions of cells. ○ *Those cells divide and give many other different types of cells.* ○ *blood cells* ○ *Soap destroys the cell walls of bacteria.*

▶ **COLLOCATIONS:**
a **stem/blood/cancerous/normal** cell
the cell **wall/membrane**
a cell **divides**
a cell **contains/produces/lines/secretes** something

Celsius /'selsiəs/ SCIENCE GEOGRAPHY

ADJECTIVE Celsius is a scale for measuring temperature, in which water
freezes at 0 degrees and boils at 100 degrees. It is represented by the symbol
°C. ○ *Highest temperatures 11° Celsius, that's 52° Fahrenheit.* ○ *an increase of just
one degree Celsius in core body temperature*

▶ **COLLOCATION: degrees** Celsius
▶ **SYNONYM:** centigrade

---

cen|sor /'sensə/ **(censors, censoring, censored)** POLITICS SOCIOLOGY

1 VERB If someone in authority **censors** letters or the media, they officially
examine them and cut out any parts that they consider unacceptable ○ *The
military-backed government has heavily censored the news.* ○ *ITV companies tend
to censor bad language in feature films.*

▶ **COLLOCATIONS:**
a censored **version/letter**
censor the **mail/content/material/language**
heavily censored
▶ **SYNONYM:** cut

2 NOUN A **censor** is a person who has been officially appointed to examine
letters or the media and to cut out any parts that are regarded as
unacceptable. ○ *The report was cleared by the American military censors.* ○ *the
British Board of Film Censors*

▶ **COLLOCATION:** a **military/film** censor

cen|sor|ship /'sensəʃɪp/

UNCOUNTABLE NOUN Censorship is the censoring of books, plays, films, or
reports, especially by government officials, because they are considered
immoral or secret in some way. ○ *The government today announced that press
censorship was being lifted.* ○ *constant battles over censorship and the limits of
good taste*

▶ **COLLOCATIONS:**
press/military censorship
strict/government/state censorship

cen|ti|grade /'sentɪgreɪd/   SCIENCE GEOGRAPHY

ADJECTIVE Centigrade is a scale for measuring temperature, in which water freezes at o degrees and boils at 100 degrees. It is represented by the symbol °C. ○ *daytime temperatures of up to forty degrees centigrade*

▶ **COLLOCATION: degrees** centigrade

▶ **SYNONYM:** Celsius

cen|tre /'sentə/ (centres)

NOUN If something or someone is at the **centre of** a situation, they are the most important thing or person involved. [in AM, use **center**] ○ [+ *of*] *the man at the centre of the controversy* ○ [+ *of*] *At the centre of the inquiry has been concern for the pensioners involved.*

▶ **COLLOCATIONS:**
  the centre **of** *something*
  at the centre
  at the centre of a **controversy/row/scandal**
  at the centre of a **dispute/debate**
  the centre of **attention**

▶ **SYNONYMS:** middle, heart

▶ **ANTONYM:** edge

cen|tral /'sentrəl/

ADJECTIVE The **central** person or thing in a particular situation is the most important one. ○ [+ *to*] *Black dance music has been central to mainstream pop since the early '6os.* ○ *a central part of their culture*

▶ **COLLOCATIONS:**
  central **to** *something*
  a central **part/character/role/figure/theme**
  remain central

▶ **SYNONYMS:** main, chief, key

▶ **ANTONYM:** unimportant

chal|lenge /'tʃælɪndʒ/   ACADEMIC WORD
(challenges, challenging, challenged)

1 NOUN A **challenge** is something new and difficult which requires great effort and determination. ○ *I like a big challenge and they don't come much bigger than this.* ○ *The new government's first challenge is the economy.*

2 NOUN A **challenge to** something is a questioning of its truth or value. A **challenge to** someone is a questioning of their authority. ○ [+ *to*] *The demonstrators have now made a direct challenge to the authority of the government.* ○ [+ *to*] *Paranormal dreams pose a challenge to current scientific conceptions.*

▶ **COLLOCATIONS:**
a challenge **to** *something*
present/pose/accept/face/meet a challenge
a **serious/real/major/great** challenge
a **legal** challenge
▶ **SYNONYMS:** question, test, confrontation

3 VERB If you **challenge** ideas or people, you question their truth, value, or authority. ○ *Democratic leaders have challenged the president to sign the bill.* ○ *[+ on] I challenged him on the hypocrisy of his political attitudes.*

▶ **COLLOCATIONS:**
challenge *someone* **on/about** *something*
challenge a **notion/assumption/decision**
successfully/seriously challenge *something*
▶ **SYNONYM:** question

---

char|ac|ter|is|tic /ˌkærɪktəˈrɪstɪk/ **(characteristics)**

1 NOUN The **characteristics** of a person or thing are the qualities or features that belong to them and make them recognizable. ○ *[+ of] Genes determine the characteristics of every living thing.* ○ *their physical characteristics*

▶ **COLLOCATIONS:**
the characteristics **of** *someone/something*
a **defining/distinguishing** characteristic
a **shared/unique** characteristic
a **physical/fundamental/essential** characteristic
▶ **SYNONYMS:** feature, trait

2 ADJECTIVE A quality or feature that is **characteristic of** someone or something is one which is often seen in them and seems typical of them. ○ *[+ of] the absence of strife between the generations that was so characteristic of such societies* ○ *Nehru responded with characteristic generosity.*

▶ **COLLOCATIONS:**
characteristic **of** *someone/something*
characteristic **greed/modesty/wit**
▶ **SYNONYM:** typical
▶ **ANTONYM:** uncharacteristic

---

chart /tʃɑːt/ **(charts, charting, charted)** ACADEMIC STUDY ACADEMIC WORD

1 NOUN A **chart** is a diagram, picture, or graph which is intended to make information easier to understand. ○ *Male unemployment was 14.2%, compared with 5.8% for women (see chart on next page).* ○ *The chart below shows our top 10 choices.*

→ see note at **bar chart**

▶ **COLLOCATIONS:**
a **bar/flow/pie** chart
a chart **shows/illustrates/suggests** something
▶ **SYNONYMS:** diagram, graph

2 VERB If you **chart** the development or progress of something, you observe it and record or show it. You can also say that a report or graph **charts** the development or progress of something. ○ *One GP has charted a dramatic rise in local childhood asthma since the M25 was built nearby.* ○ *This magnificent show charts his meteoric rise from 'small town' country singer to top international Rock idol.*

▶ **COLLOCATIONS:**
chart something's **course/progress**
chart something's **rise/decline**
▶ **SYNONYM:** record

chief /tʃiːf/

ADJECTIVE The **chief** cause, part, or member of something is the most important one. ○ *Financial stress is well established as a chief reason for divorce.* ○ *The job went to one of his chief rivals.*

▶ **COLLOCATION:** the chief **reason/cause**
▶ **SYNONYMS:** main, major, key, principal
▶ **ANTONYMS:** minor, unimportant

chief|ly /ˈtʃiːfli/

ADVERB You use **chiefly** to indicate that a particular reason, emotion, method, or feature is the main or most important one. ○ *He joined the consular service, chiefly because this was one of the few job vacancies.* ○ *His response to attacks on his work was chiefly bewilderment.*

▶ **COLLOCATION:** chiefly **responsible**
▶ **PHRASE:** chiefly because
▶ **SYNONYMS:** mainly, primarily

cir|cuit /ˈsɜːkɪt/ (circuits) `ENGINEERING` `PHYSICS`

NOUN An electrical **circuit** is a complete route which an electric current can flow around. ○ *Any attempts to cut through the cabling will break the electrical circuit.* ○ *[+ within] the thin metal connections that make up the circuits within a microprocessor*

▶ **COLLOCATIONS:**
a circuit **in/within** something
a **closed-/short-** circuit
an **electronic/electrical** circuit
break/overload/connect a circuit
a circuit **board/breaker**

cir|cu|late /'sɜːkjʊleɪt/ (circulates, circulating, circulated)

VERB When something **circulates**, it moves easily and freely within a closed place or system. ○ [+ via] *a virus which circulates via the bloodstream* ○ [+ through] *the sound of water circulating through pipes*

▶ **COLLOCATIONS:**
circulate **around/via/through** *something*
blood/water/air circulates

▶ **SYNONYM:** flow

cir|cu|la|tion /ˌsɜːkjʊ'leɪʃən/

UNCOUNTABLE NOUN ○ [+ of] *The north pole is warmer than the south and the circulation of air around it is less well contained.* ○ [+ of] *the principle of free circulation of goods*

▶ **COLLOCATIONS:**
the circulation **of** *something*
the circulation of **blood/air/goods/money**

▶ **SYNONYM:** flow

cir|cum|fer|ence /sə'kʌmfrəns, -fərəns/ `MATHS`

UNCOUNTABLE NOUN The **circumference** of a circle, place, or round object is the distance around its edge. ○ *a scientist calculating the Earth's circumference* ○ *The island is 3.5 km in circumference.*

▶ **COLLOCATIONS:**
the circumference **of** *something*
in circumference
measure the circumference

cir|cum|stances /'sɜːkəmstænsɪz/ `ACADEMIC WORD`

PLURAL NOUN The **circumstances** of a particular situation are the conditions which affect what happens. ○ *Recent opinion polls show that 60 percent favor abortion under certain circumstances.* ○ [+ of] *The strategy was too dangerous in the explosive circumstances of the times.* ○ *I wish we could have met under happier circumstances.*

▶ **COLLOCATIONS:**
the circumstances **of** *something*
under *particular* circumstances
certain/similar/different/exceptional circumstances

▶ **SYNONYM:** conditions

civ|il /'sɪvəl/ `ACADEMIC WORD` `POLITICS` `SOCIOLOGY`

ADJECTIVE You use **civil** to describe things that relate to the people of a country and their rights and activities, often in contrast with the armed forces. ○ *civil unrest* ○ *the U.S. civil aviation industry* ○ *a United Nations covenant on civil and political rights*

▶ **COLLOCATIONS:**
the civil **service**
a civil **servant**
civil **society/law/liberties/rights**
civil **war/unrest/disobedience**
civil **aviation**

---

civi|li|za|tion /ˌsɪvɪlaɪˈzeɪʃən/ (civilizations)   [HISTORY]

NOUN A **civilization** is a human society with its own social organization and culture. [in BRIT, also use **civilisation**] ○ [+ *of*] *The ancient civilizations of Central and Latin America were founded upon corn.* ○ *It seemed to him that western civilization was in grave economic and cultural danger.*

▶ **COLLOCATIONS:**
the civilizations **of** somewhere
western civilization
an **ancient/modern** civilization
▶ **SYNONYM:** society

---

claim /kleɪm/ (claims, claiming, claimed)

1 VERB If you say that someone **claims that** something is true, you mean they say that it is true but you are not sure whether or not they are telling the truth. ○ [+ *that*] *He claimed that it was all a conspiracy against him.* ○ [+ *to-inf*] *A man claiming to be a journalist threatened to reveal details about her private life.* ○ *He claims a 70 to 80 per cent success rate.*

→ see note at **allege**
▶ **COLLOCATION:** claim **falsely/rightly/wrongly/repeatedly**
▶ **SYNONYMS:** maintain, assert, allege

2 NOUN A **claim** is something which someone says which they cannot prove and which may be false. ○ [+ *that*] *He repeated his claim that the people of Trinidad and Tobago backed his action.* ○ [+ *that*] *He rejected claims that he had affairs with six women.*

▶ **COLLOCATIONS:**
reject/investigate a claim
a **true/false** claim
▶ **SYNONYMS:** allegation, assertion

---

class /klɑːs, klæs/ (classes, classing, classed)   [SOCIOLOGY] [SCIENCE]

1 NOUN Class refers to the division of people in a society into groups according to their social status. ○ *the relationship between social classes* ○ *What it will do is* *create a whole new ruling class.* ○ *the characteristics of the British class structure*

▶ COLLOCATIONS:
  social/middle/upper/working class
  the **educated/professional/governing/ruling** classes
  class **distinction/structure**

▶ PHRASE: class and gender

▶ SYNONYM: caste

2 NOUN A **class of** things is a group of them with similar characteristics.
  ○ [+ of] *Harbour staff noticed that measurements given for the same class of boats often varied.* ○ [+ of] *the division of the stars into six classes of brightness*

▶ COLLOCATIONS:
  a class **of** *things*
  a class of **drugs/shares/securities**

▶ SYNONYMS: type, sort, kind

3 VERB If someone or something **is classed as** a particular thing, they are regarded as belonging to that group of things. ○ [+ as] *Since the birds interbreed they cannot be classed as different species.* ○ [+ as] *I class myself as an ordinary working person.* ○ [+ as] *Malaysia wants to send back refugees classed as economic migrants.*

▶ COLLOCATIONS:
  class *someone/something* **as** *something*
  class *someone* as **sensitive/overweight**
  officially class *someone/something*

▶ SYNONYMS: classify, categorize

---

clas|si|cal /ˈklæsɪkəl/ ACADEMIC WORD ARTS HISTORY

1 ADJECTIVE You use **classical** to describe something that is traditional in form, style, or content. ○ *Fokine did not change the steps of classical ballet; instead he found new ways of using them.* ○ *the scientific attitude of Smith and earlier classical economists*

▶ COLLOCATIONS:
  classical **music/ballet**
  classical **tradition**

▶ ANTONYM: modern

2 ADJECTIVE Classical is used to describe things which relate to the ancient Greek or Roman civilizations. ○ *the healers of ancient Egypt and classical Greece* ○ *It's a technological achievement that is unrivalled in the classical world.* ○ *classical architecture*

▶ COLLOCATIONS:
  classical **architecture/mythology/civilization**
  the classical **world**

clas|sics /ˈklæsɪks/ `HISTORY`

UNCOUNTABLE NOUN Classics is the study of the ancient Greek and Roman civilizations, especially their languages, literature, and philosophy. ○ *a Classics degree* ○ *He was a classics major and he could read Latin as if it were English.*

clas|si|fy /ˈklæsɪfaɪ/ (classifies, classifying, classified)

VERB To **classify** things means to divide them into groups or types so that things with similar characteristics are in the same group. ○ [+ *into*] *It is necessary initially to classify the headaches into certain types.* ○ *Rocks can be classified according to their mode of origin.* ○ [+ *as*] *The coroner immediately classified his death as a suicide.*

▶ **COLLOCATIONS:**
classify *something* **as/according to** *something*
classify *something* **into** *things*
classify *something* into **categories/types**
classify *something* **officially/wrongly/correctly**

▶ **SYNONYMS:** categorize, sort

clas|si|fi|ca|tion /ˌklæsɪfɪˈkeɪʃən/

UNCOUNTABLE NOUN ○ [+ *of*] *the arbitrary classification of knowledge into fields of study* ○ *the British Board of Film Classification*

▶ **COLLOCATIONS:**
the classification **of** *something*
the classification of **diseases/drugs/organisms**
a classification **system**

▶ **SYNONYM:** categorization

clini|cal /ˈklɪnɪkəl/ `MEDICINE`

ADJECTIVE Clinical means involving or relating to the direct medical treatment or testing of patients. ○ *The first clinical trials were expected to begin next year.* ○ *a clinical psychologist* ○ *the clinical after-effects of the accident*

▶ **COLLOCATIONS:**
a clinical **trial/psychologist/study**
clinical **practice**

clock|wise /ˈklɒkwaɪz/

ADVERB When something is moving **clockwise**, it is moving in a circle in the same direction as the hands on a clock. ○ [+ *around*] *He told the children to start moving clockwise around the room.* ○ [+ *around*] *In the southern hemisphere winds rotate clockwise around the center of the cyclone.*

▶ **COLLOCATION:** clockwise **around** *something*
▶ **ANTONYMS:** anti-clockwise, counterclockwise

col|lapse /kə'læps/ (collapses, collapsing, collapsed) [ACADEMIC WORD]

1 VERB If a building or other structure **collapses**, it falls down very suddenly. ○ *A section of the Bay Bridge had collapsed.* ○ [V-ing] *Most of the deaths were caused by landslides and collapsing buildings.*

▶ **COLLOCATION:** a **building/tower/roof/wall** collapses

2 VERB If something, for example a system or institution, **collapses**, it fails or comes to an end completely and suddenly. ○ [+ under] *His business empire collapsed under a massive burden of debt.* ○ [V-ing] *The rural people have been impoverished by a collapsing economy.*

▶ **COLLOCATIONS:**
collapse **under** *something*
a **regime/economy/system** collapses

▶ **SYNONYM:** fail

com|mence /kə'mens/ [ACADEMIC WORD]
(commences, commencing, commenced)

VERB When something **commences** or you **commence** it, it begins. [FORMAL] ○ [+ at] *The academic year commences at the beginning of October.* ○ *They commenced a systematic search.* ○ *The company commenced work on its expansion project in 1994-95.*

▶ **COLLOCATIONS:**
commence **at/in/on** *a time*
commence **proceedings/operations/work**

EXTEND YOUR VOCABULARY

In everyday English, you often say that something **starts** or **begins**. ○ *What time do classes start/begin in the morning?*

Commence is used in more formal writing. ○ *Course times: Courses commence at 10.00 am.*

In formal writing, you also say that something **emerges** or **originates** to talk about its start in a historical context. You use **emerge** to talk about something becoming known for the first time, especially gradually. You use **originate** to talk about where or how something first started. ○ *The virus first emerged in China's Guangdong province in November 2002.* ○ *The concept originated in Germany in the 1960s.*

---

com|merce /'kɒmɜːs/ [BUSINESS]

UNCOUNTABLE NOUN Commerce is the activities and procedures involved in buying and selling things. ○ *They have made their fortunes from industry and commerce.* ○ *The online commerce market is new, rapidly evolving and intensely competitive.*

▶ COLLOCATIONS:
regulate/affect commerce
obstruct/disrupt/facilitate/promote commerce
electronic/online/internet commerce
global/international/foreigncommerce
▶ SYNONYM: trade

com|mer|cial /kə'mɜːʃəl/

1 ADJECTIVE Commercial means involving or relating to the buying and selling of goods. ○ *Docklands in its heyday was a major centre of industrial and commercial activity.* ○ *Attacks were reported on police, vehicles and commercial premises.*

2 ADJECTIVE Commercial organizations and activities are concerned with making money or profits, rather than, for example, with scientific research or providing a public service. ○ *Conservationists in Chile are concerned over the effect of commercial exploitation of forests.* ○ *Whether the project will be a commercial success is still uncertain.*

▶ COLLOCATIONS:
increasingly/purely commercial
a commercial **interest/property/use**
a commercial **venture/enterprise/activity/success**
commercial **premises**
▶ SYNONYM: business

com|mer|cial|ly /kə'mɜːʃəli/

ADVERB ○ *British Aerospace reckon that the plane will be commercially viable if 400 can be sold.* ○ *Insulin is produced commercially from animals.* ○ *Designers are becoming more commercially minded.*

▶ COLLOCATIONS:
commercially **available/viable/sensitive/successful**
use/sell/exploit *something* commerically
grow/produce *something* commercially

---

com|mit /kə'mɪt/ (commits, committing, committed) `ACADEMIC WORD` `LAW`

1 VERB If someone **commits** a crime or a sin, they do something illegal or bad. ○ *I have never committed any crime.* ○ *This is a man who has committed murder.*
▶ COLLOCATION: commit a **crime/offence/atrocity/murder**

2 VERB If you **commit** money or resources **to** something, you decide to use them for a particular purpose. ○ [+ to] *They called on Western nations to commit more money to the poorest nations.* ○ [+ for] *The government had committed billions of pounds for a programme to reduce acid rain.*

▶ COLLOCATIONS:
commit *something* **to/for** *something*
commit **time/money/troops**

▶ SYNONYMS: give, pledge

3 VERB If you **commit yourself to** something, you say that you will definitely do it. ○ [+ to] *I would advise people to think very carefully about committing themselves to working Sundays.* ○ [+ to] *You don't have to commit to anything over the phone.*

▶ COLLOCATIONS:
commit **to** *something*
fully/totally commit to *something*

▶ SYNONYM: promise

com|mit|ment /kə'mɪtmənt/ (commitments)

NOUN If you make a **commitment to** do something, you promise that you will do it. [FORMAL] ○ *We made a commitment to keep working together.* ○ [+ to] *They made a commitment to peace.*

▶ COLLOCATIONS:
a commitment **to** *something*
make/honour a commitment
a **long-term/lifelong/long-standing/ongoing** commitment
a **financial/emotional/work/family** commitment

▶ SYNONYMS: pledge, promise

com|mit|ted /kə'mɪtɪd/

ADJECTIVE ○ [+ to] *He said the government remained committed to peace.* ○ *a committed socialist*

▶ COLLOCATIONS:
committed **to** *something*
fully/deeply committed
a committed **campaigner/socialist/environmentalist**

---

com|mun|ism /'kɒmjʊnɪzəm/ also Communism   POLITICS

UNCOUNTABLE NOUN **Communism** is the political belief that all people are equal and that workers should control the means of producing things. ○ *Liberals agree with the assumption that communism is evil and should be fought.*

▶ COLLOCATIONS:
Soviet/Chinese/international communism
communism **collapsed/fell**

▶ SYNONYM: socialism
▶ ANTONYM: capitalism

com|mun|ist /ˈkɒmjʊnɪst/ (communists)

1 NOUN A **communist** is someone who believes in communism. ○ *I became a communist out of resistance to fascism.*

▸ **COLLOCATION:** a **former/hardline** communist

2 ADJECTIVE Communist means relating to communism. ○ *the Communist Party* ○ *the history of the communist leaders in the USSR*

▸ **COLLOCATIONS:**
the communist **party/regime/government/state**
a communist **leader**
communist **rule**

com|para|tive /kəmˈpærətɪv/

1 ADJECTIVE You use **comparative** to show that your description of something is accurate only when it is compared to something else, or to what is usual. ○ *those who manage to reach comparative safety* ○ *The task was accomplished with comparative ease.*

▸ **COLLOCATIONS:**
a comparative **advantage**
comparative **ease/safety**

▸ **SYNONYM:** relative

2 ADJECTIVE A **comparative** study is a study that involves the comparison of two or more things of the same kind. ○ *a comparative study of the dietary practices of people from various regions of India* ○ *a professor of English and comparative literature*

▸ **COLLOCATIONS:**
a comparative **study/analysis**
comparative **literature/religion**

com|para|tive|ly /kəmˈpærətɪvli/

ADVERB ○ *a comparatively small nation* ○ *children who find it comparatively easy to make and keep friends*

▸ **COLLOCATIONS:**
comparatively **little/small**
comparatively **rare/modest/mild/inexpensive**

com|pare /kəmˈpeə/ (compares, comparing, compared)

VERB When you **compare** things, you consider them and discover the differences or similarities between them. ○ *Compare the two illustrations in Fig 60.* ○ [+ with] *Was it fair to compare independent schools with state schools?* ○ [+ to] *Note how smooth the skin of the upper arm is, then compare it to the skin on the elbow.*

▶ **COLLOCATION:** compare *something* **with/to** *something*

▶ **PHRASES:**
compare and contrast
compared with the average

com|pari|son /kəm'pærɪsən/ (comparisons)

NOUN When you make a **comparison**, you consider two or more things and discover the differences between them. ○ [+ *of*] *a comparison of the British and German economies* ○ [+ *between*] *Its recommendations are based on detailed comparisons between the public and private sectors.* ○ *There are no previous statistics for comparison.*

▶ **COLLOCATIONS:**
a comparison **of/between** *things*
in/by comparison
make/draw a comparison
invite/bear comparison
a **difficult/unfair/valid** comparison
a **direct/inevitable** comparison

---

com|plete /kəm'pliːt/ (completes, completing, completed)

1 VERB If you **complete** something, you finish doing, making, or producing it. ○ *Peter Mayle has just completed his first novel.* ○ *the rush to get the stadiums completed on time*

2 VERB If you **complete** something, you do all of it. ○ *She completed her degree in two years.* ○ *This book took years to complete.*

▶ **COLLOCATIONS:**
complete a **deal/purchase/task/project/journey**
complete a **course/degree**
successfully completed

▶ **SYNONYM:** finish

3 VERB If you **complete** a form or questionnaire, you write the answers or information asked for in it. ○ *Simply complete the coupon below.* ○ *We ask candidates to complete a psychometric questionnaire.*

▶ **COLLOCATION:** complete a **questionnaire/form/survey**

▶ **SYNONYMS:** fill in, fill out

com|ple|tion /kəm'pliːʃən/ (completions)

NOUN ○ *The project is nearing completion.* ○ *House completions for the year should be up from 1,841 to 2,200.*

▶ **COLLOCATIONS:**
near/approach completion
completion **date/rate**

com|po|nent /kəm'pəʊnənt/ (components) `ACADEMIC WORD`

NOUN The **components** of something are the parts that it is made of. ○ [+ of] *Enriched uranium is a key component of a nuclear weapon.* ○ *The management plan has four main components.* ○ *automotive component suppliers to motor manufacturers*

▶ **COLLOCATIONS:**
  a component **of** *something*
  manufacture/supply components
  a **key/major/main** component
  a **vital/essential/critical** component
  a **software/hardware/electronic/electrical** component

com|pose /kəm'pəʊz/ (composes, composing, composed)

VERB The things that something **is composed of** are its parts or members. The separate things that **compose** something are the parts or members that form it. ○ [+ of] *The force would be composed of troops from NATO countries.* ○ *Protein molecules compose all the complex working parts of living cells.* ○ [+ of] *They agreed to form a council composed of leaders of the rival factions.*

→ see note at **comprise**

▶ **COLLOCATIONS:**
  composed **of** *something*
  mainly/largely/entirely composed of *something*

com|po|si|tion /ˌkɒmpə'zɪʃən/

UNCOUNTABLE NOUN When you talk about the **composition** of something, you are referring to the way in which its various parts are put together and arranged. ○ [+ of] *Television has transformed the size and composition of the audience at sporting occasions.* ○ *Forests vary greatly in composition from one part of the country to another.*

▶ **COLLOCATIONS:**
  the composition **of** *something*
  change/study/alter/determine *something's* composition
  something's **exact/chemical/racial** composition

com|pre|hen|sive /ˌkɒmprɪ'hensɪv/ `ACADEMIC WORD`

ADJECTIVE Something that is **comprehensive** includes everything that is needed or relevant. ○ *The Rough Guide to Nepal is a comprehensive guide to the region.* ○ *The first step involves a comprehensive analysis of the job.* ○ *a comprehensive investigation*

▶ **COLLOCATIONS:**
  a comprehensive **review/survey**
  a comprehensive **plan/strategy/approach**
  a comprehensive **package/range/collection**

> ▸ **SYNONYMS:** full, thorough, complete
> ▸ **ANTONYMS:** partial, limited

com|pre|hen|sive|ly /ˌkɒmprɪˈhensɪvli/

ADVERB ○ *This section is not intended to comprehensively cover all possible infectious conditions relating to fatigue.* ○ *the book is comprehensively illustrated*

> ▸ **COLLOCATION: cover/deal with** *something* comprehensively
> ▸ **SYNONYMS:** fully, thoroughly, completely
> ▸ **ANTONYM:** partially

---

com|prise /kəmˈpraɪz/ (comprises, comprising, comprised) `ACADEMIC WORD`

VERB If you say that something **comprises** or **is comprised of** a number of things or people, you mean it has them as its parts or members. [FORMAL] ○ *The exhibition comprises 50 oils and watercolours.* ○ *[+ of] The Coordinating Group is currently comprised of representatives from 73 financial institutions.*

> ▸ **COLLOCATIONS:**
> be comprised **of** *people/things*
> comprise *x* **per cent** of *something*
> a **consortium/committee/panel** comprises *people*
> a **collection/range/exhibition** comprises *things*
> comprised **mainly/mostly/largely**

> **EXTEND YOUR VOCABULARY**
>
> You can use **comprise**, **consist of**, **be composed of** and **constitute** to talk about all the people or things that form a whole. Be careful about the subjects and objects of the different verbs. You can say that the whole **comprises**, **is comprised of**, **consists of** or **is composed of** several parts. ○ *The $10 million complex comprises 27 luxury apartments.* ○ *The cornea consists of three layers of cells.* ○ *The infrastructure is composed of four fundamental subunits.*
>
> You can also say that several parts **comprise** or **constitute** the whole. ○ *Shia Arabs constitute the majority of the population in Bahrain and Lebanon, and comprise nearly 20 per cent of the population of Saudi Arabia.*
>
> You can use **contain** and **include** to talk about some of the people or parts that form a whole. ○ *Many modern adhesives contain chemicals that are harmful.* ○ *The art collection includes an impressive Pre-Raphaelite section.*

---

com|pro|mise /ˈkɒmprəmaɪz/
(compromises, compromising, compromised)

1 NOUN A **compromise** is a situation in which people accept something slightly different from what they really want, because of circumstances or

because they are considering the wishes of other people. ○ [+ *between*]
*Encourage your child to reach a compromise between what he wants and what you
want.* ○ *Every side makes compromises and concessions in order to reach an
agreement.* ○ *The government's policy of compromise is not universally popular.*

▶ COLLOCATIONS:
a compromise **between** *things/people*
reach/find a compromise
a **possible/necessary/likely/reasonable** compromise
a compromise **plan/deal/agreement/proposal/solution**
a compromise **candidate/bill**

▶ SYNONYMS: agreement, settlement

▶ ANTONYM: disagreement

2 VERB If you **compromise with** someone, you reach an agreement with
them in which you both give up something that you originally wanted. You
can also say that two people or groups **compromise**. ○ [+ *over*] *The
government has compromised with its critics over monetary policies.* ○ [+ *on*] *Israel
had originally wanted $1 billion in aid, but compromised on the $650 million.*

▶ COLLOCATIONS:
compromise **over/on** *something*
compromise **with** *someone*

▶ SYNONYM: concede

---

con|cen|trate /ˈkɒnsəntreɪt/   `ACADEMIC WORD`
(concentrates, concentrating, concentrated)

1 VERB If you **concentrate on** something, you give all your attention, effort,
and resources to it. ○ [+ *on*] *It was up to him to concentrate on his studies.* ○ *The
Party should concentrate resources at local rather than national level.* ○ *At work you
need to be able to concentrate.*

▶ COLLOCATIONS:
concentrate **on** *something*
concentrate **resources/power/effort**
concentrate **hard**

▶ SYNONYM: focus

2 VERB If something **is concentrated in** an area, it is all there rather than being
spread around. ○ [+ *in*] *Italy's industrial districts are concentrated in its northern
regions.* ○ [+ *in*] *Most development has been concentrated in and around cities.*

▶ COLLOCATIONS:
concentrated **in** *places*
geographically concentrated

▶ SYNONYMS: gather, collect

▶ ANTONYMS: scatter, spread

con|cen|tra|tion /ˌkɒnsənˈtreɪʃən/ (concentrations)

1 **UNCOUNTABLE NOUN** **Concentration** on something involves giving all your attention, effort, and resources to it. ○ *Neal kept interrupting, breaking my concentration.* ○ *[+ on] Changing needs led to a concentration on electricity generation.*

▶ **COLLOCATIONS:**
a concentration **on** *something*
lose/require/need/aid concentration
intense concentration
a concentration **level/span/lapse**

2 **NOUN** A **concentration of** something is a large amount of it or large numbers of it in a small area. ○ *[+ of] The area has one of the world's greatest concentrations of wildlife.* ○ *[+ of] There's been too much concentration of power in the hands of central authorities.*

▶ **COLLOCATIONS:**
a concentration **of** *something*
a concentration of **power/wealth**
a **high/low/dense/heavy** concentration

3 **NOUN** The **concentration of** a substance is the proportion of essential ingredients or substances in it. ○ *[+ of] pH is a measure of the concentration of free hydrogen atoms in a solution.* ○ *Global ozone concentrations had dropped over the last decade.*

▶ **COLLOCATIONS:**
the concentration **of** *something*
a **high/low** concentration
concentration **levels**

---

con|cept /ˈkɒnsept/ (concepts) `ACADEMIC WORD`

NOUN A **concept** is an idea or abstract principle. ○ *[+ of] She added that the concept of arranged marriages is misunderstood in the west.* ○ *basic legal concepts*

▶ **COLLOCATIONS:**
the concept **of** *something*
the concept of **freedom/democracy/justice**
understand/introduce/explain a concept
a **basic/original/abstract/simple/key/underlying** concept
a **marketing/design** concept

> **EXTEND YOUR VOCABULARY**
>
> You use **idea** to talk about anything that exists in people's minds; a plan, a suggestion, a belief, an opinion, etc.
>
> You can use **concept** and **notion** to talk about abstract ideas especially as part of academic thinking. A **notion** is often a belief or an understanding. ○ *Christaller develops his theory using four key concepts.* ○ *The judge rejected the notion of the 'victimless' crime.*

con|cern /kən'sɜːn/ (concerns, concerning, concerned)

1 VERB If something such as a book or a piece of information **concerns** a particular subject, it is about that subject. ○ *The bulk of the book concerns Sandy's two middle-aged children.* ○ *The proceedings concern the fraudulent offer and sale of over $2.1 billion in municipal securities.*

▶ SYNONYMS: cover, relate to

2 VERB If a situation, event, or activity **concerns** you, it affects or involves you. ○ *It doesn't concern you at all.* ○ *There are interesting political dimensions to these two duties, but they do not concern us here.*

▶ COLLOCATION: a **matter/issue/question** concerns *someone*

3 PHRASE You can say **as far as** something **is concerned** to indicate the subject that you are talking about. ○ *As far as starting a family is concerned, the trend is for women having their children later in life.* ○ *It's clear that orthodox medicine doesn't have all the answers where cancer is concerned.*

▶ SYNONYMS: regarding, as regards, in relation to

con|cerned /kən'sɜːnd/

ADJECTIVE ○ [+ with] *Randolph's work was exclusively concerned with the effects of pollution on health.* ○ *It's a very stressful situation for everyone concerned.*

▶ COLLOCATIONS:
concerned **in/with** *something*
primarily/particularly concerned with something
everyone concerned
the **person/people** concerned

▶ SYNONYMS: related, involved

con|cern|ing /kən'sɜːnɪŋ/

PREPOSITION You use **concerning** to indicate what a question or piece of information is about. [FORMAL] ○ *a large body of research concerning the relationship between anger and health* ○ *various questions concerning pollution and the environment*

▶ SYNONYMS: regarding, about

con|cise /kən'saɪs/

ADJECTIVE Something that is **concise** says everything that is necessary without using any unnecessary words. ○ *Burton's text is concise and informative.* ○ *Whatever you are writing make sure you are clear, concise, and accurate.*

▶ COLLOCATIONS:
a concise **summary/history/description/statement**
a concise **introduction/explanation/guide**

▶ PHRASE: clear and concise

▶ SYNONYMS: brief, succinct

con|cise|ly /kənˈsaɪsli/

ADVERB ○ He delivered his report clearly and concisely. ○ the art of writing concisely and elegantly

▸ **COLLOCATION:** concisely **express/outline/summarize** something

▸ **PHRASE:** clearly and concisely

---

con|clude /kənˈkluːd/ `ACADEMIC WORD` `ACADEMIC STUDY`
(concludes, concluding, concluded)

1 VERB If you **conclude that** something is true, you decide that it is true using the facts you know as a basis. ○ [+ that] Larry had concluded that he had no choice but to accept Paul's words as the truth. ○ [+ from] So what can we conclude from this debate?

▸ **COLLOCATIONS:**
conclude something **from** something
researchers/investigators/experts conclude
reasonably/reluctantly/unanimously/rightly conclude

▸ **SYNONYMS:** decide, judge

2 VERB When you **conclude**, you say the last thing that you are going to say. [FORMAL] ○ 'It's a waste of time,' he concluded. ○ I would like to conclude by saying that I do enjoy your magazine.

▸ **SYNONYMS:** end, close, finish

▸ **ANTONYM:** begin

→ see note at **cease**

con|clu|sion /kənˈkluːʒən/ **(conclusions)**

1 NOUN When you come to a **conclusion**, you decide that something is true after you have thought about it carefully and have considered all the relevant facts. ○ [+ that] Over the years I've come to the conclusion that she's a very great musician. ○ I have tried to give some idea of how I feel – other people will no doubt draw their own conclusions.

▸ **COLLOCATIONS:**
come to/draw/reach a conclusion
a **clear/obvious/foregone/inescapable** conclusion

▸ **SYNONYMS:** decision, opinion

2 NOUN The **conclusion** of a piece of academic writing is its last section. ○ The function of the essay's conclusion is to restate the main argument. ○ Your essay lacks only two paragraphs now: the introduction and the conclusion.

▸ **COLLOCATION:** the conclusion **of** something

▸ **RELATED WORD:** introduction

3 PHRASE You say **in conclusion** to indicate that what you are about to say is the last thing that you want to say. ○ *In conclusion, walking is a cheap, safe, enjoyable and readily available form of exercise.*

---

con|crete /ˈkɒŋkriːt/

1 ADJECTIVE You use **concrete** to indicate that something is definite and specific. ○ *He had no concrete evidence.* ○ *There were no concrete proposals on the table.*

▶ **COLLOCATION:** concrete **evidence/proof**

▶ **SYNONYMS:** specific, precise, definite

▶ **ANTONYM:** vague

2 ADJECTIVE A **concrete** object is a real, physical object. ○ *using concrete objects to teach addition and subtraction* ○ *Did we want to discuss abstract or concrete matters?*

▶ **COLLOCATION:** a concrete **object**

▶ **SYNONYMS:** real, material, actual

▶ **ANTONYM:** abstract

---

con|di|tion /kənˈdɪʃən/ (conditions)

NOUN A **condition** is something which must happen or be done in order for something else to be possible, especially when this is written into a contract or law. ○ [+ *for*] *economic targets set as a condition for loan payments* ○ [+ *of*] *terms and conditions of employment* ○ *Egypt had agreed to a summit subject to certain conditions.*

▶ **COLLOCATIONS:**
   a condition **for/of** *something*
   impose/attach/set a condition
   meet/satisfy/fulfil/breach a condition

▶ **SYNONYM:** requirement

con|di|tion|al /kənˈdɪʃənəl/

ADJECTIVE If a situation or agreement is **conditional on** something, it will only happen or continue if this thing happens. ○ [+ *on*] *Their support is conditional on his proposals meeting their approval.* ○ *as soon as your conditional offer has been accepted*

▶ **COLLOCATIONS:**
   conditional **on** *something*
   a conditional **offer/bid/deal/sale**
   conditional **approval/support/agreement**
   a conditional **discharge/sentence/ceasefire**
   highly conditional

▶ **SYNONYMS:** dependent, qualified

▶ **ANTONYM:** unconditional

con|di|tion|al|ly /kənˈdɪʃənəli/

ADVERB ○ *Mr Smith has conditionally agreed to buy a shareholding in the club.*
○ *Although William conditionally accepted the offer, he disagreed with its principles.*

▸ **COLLOCATIONS:**
conditionally **discharged/released**
conditionally **approved/agreed/accepted**

▸ **ANTONYM:** unconditionally

con|duct /kənˈdʌkt/ (conducts, conducting, conducted) `ACADEMIC WORD`

VERB When you **conduct** an activity or task, you organize it and carry it out.
○ *I decided to conduct an experiment.* ○ *He said they were conducting a campaign against democrats across the country.*

▸ **COLLOCATIONS:**
conduct **business/research**
conduct a **test/experiment/study**
conduct a **poll/survey/review/interview**
conduct a **search/investigation**

▸ **SYNONYMS:** run, direct, manage, organize

cone /kəʊn/ (cones)

NOUN A **cone** is a shape with a circular base and smooth curved sides ending in a point at the top. ○ [+ *of*] *A cone of light shone from a downlighter on to the desk.* ○ *The steady stream of sand falls to form a cone.*

con|firm /kənˈfɜːm/ (confirms, confirming, confirmed) `ACADEMIC WORD`

1 VERB If something **confirms** what you believe, suspect, or fear, it shows that it is definitely true. ○ [+ *that*] *X-rays have confirmed that he has not broken any bones.* ○ *These new statistics confirm our worst fears about the depth of the recession.* ○ [+ *wh*] *This confirms what I suspected all along.*

2 VERB If you **confirm** something that has been stated or suggested, you say that it is true because you know about it. ○ [+ *that*] *The spokesman confirmed that the area was now in rebel hands.* ○ [+ *wh*] *He confirmed what had long been feared.*

▸ **COLLOCATIONS:**
confirm a **report/diagnosis/finding**
confirm a **rumour/fear/suspicion/impression**
confirm *something's* **existence/presence/identity**
independently/officially confirmed

▸ **ANTONYMS:** deny, contradict

ACADEMIC WRITING: Describing supporting evidence.

In academic writing, you often need to provide evidence for ideas and arguments. There are several verbs you use to talk about giving evidence.

You can say that someone or something **confirms** or **supports** an idea. ○ *This theory has now been confirmed by the latest studies in genetics.* ○ *His findings supported the view that heredity determines intelligence.*

You can use **justify** to talk about giving reasons to prove why something is reasonable or necessary. ○ *There was adequate evidence justifying the initial decision.*

You can use **verify** to talk about checking that something is true or correct. ○ *It was not possible to independently verify the claim.*

con|fir|ma|tion /ˌkɒnfəˈmeɪʃən/

UNCOUNTABLE NOUN ○ [+ of] *They took her resignation from Bendix as confirmation of their suspicions.* ○ *She glanced over at James for confirmation.*

▶ **COLLOCATIONS:**
confirmation **of** something
receive/need/get/await/provide confirmation
written/official/independent confirmation
further/final confirmation

▶ **SYNONYMS:** proof, affirmation
▶ **ANTONYM:** denial

con|flict (conflicts, conflicting, conflicted) `ACADEMIC WORD` `POLITICS`

The noun is pronounced /ˈkɒnflɪkt/. The verb is pronounced /kənˈflɪkt/.

1 UNCOUNTABLE NOUN Conflict is serious disagreement and argument about something important. ○ *You must be sure to deal with any conflict immediately.* ○ [+ with] *Employees already are in conflict with management over job cuts.* ○ *The two companies came into conflict.*

▶ **COLLOCATIONS:**
conflict **with** someone
resolve/settle conflict
conflict **arises/exists**

▶ **SYNONYM:** disagreement
▶ **ANTONYM:** agreement

2 NOUN Conflict is fighting between countries or groups of people. [WRITTEN] ○ *talks aimed at ending four decades of conflict* ○ *The National Security Council has met to discuss ways of preventing a military conflict.*

▶ **COLLOCATIONS:**

end/settle/prevent/avoid conflict

a conflict **begins/erupts**

a **bloody/armed/violent/bitter** conflict

a **military/civil** conflict

a conflict **zone**

▶ **SYNONYMS:** hostility, fighting

▶ **ANTONYM:** peace

3 VERB If two beliefs, ideas, or interests **conflict**, they are very different.
○ *Personal ethics and professional ethics sometimes conflict.* ○ *three powers with conflicting interests*

▶ **COLLOCATIONS:**

conflicting **reports/claims/accounts/messages**

conflicting **interests/signals/feelings/views**

directly/potentially conflict

▶ **SYNONYM:** clash

---

con|nect|ed /kəˈnektɪd/

ADJECTIVE If one thing is **connected with** another, there is a link or relationship between them. ○ [+ with] *Have you ever had any skin problems connected with exposure to the sun?* ○ [+ to] *The dispute is not directly connected to the negotiations.*

▶ **COLLOCATIONS:**

connected **with/to** something

closely/directly connected

▶ **SYNONYMS:** linked, associated

▶ **ANTONYM:** unconnected

con|nec|tion /kəˈnekʃən/ (connections)

NOUN A **connection** is a relationship between two things, people, or groups. [in BRIT, also use **connexion**] ○ [+ between] *There was no evidence of a connection between BSE and the brain diseases recently confirmed in cats.* ○ [+ with] *The police say he had no connection with the security forces.* ○ [+ to] *He has denied any connection to the bombing.*

▶ **COLLOCATIONS:**

a connection **between** things

a connection **with/to** something

make/establish/suggest/deny/maintain a connection

a **clear/obvious/direct** connection

a **close/strong/important** connection

▶ **SYNONYMS:** relationship, link, association

con|se|quence /ˈkɒnsɪkwens/ (consequences) ACADEMIC WORD

1 NOUN The **consequences of** something are the results or effects of it.
○ [+ of] *Her lawyer said she understood the consequences of her actions and was prepared to go to jail.* ○ [+ for] *An economic crisis may have tremendous consequences for our global security.*

▶ **COLLOCATIONS:**
a consequence **of** something
the consequences **for** someone/something
the consequences of **war/action/failure**
the consequences for the **economy/future/region**
suffer/face/accept/consider/understand the consequences
serious/severe/tragic consequences
likely/unintended consequences
health/tax consequences

▶ **SYNONYM:** result

2 PHRASE If one thing happens and then another thing happens **in consequence** or **as a consequence**, the second thing happens as a result of the first. ○ *His death was totally unexpected and, in consequence, no plans had been made for his replacement.* ○ [+ of] *people who are suffering and dying as a consequence of cigarette smoking*

▶ **PHRASE:** in consequence/as a consequence of something

con|se|quent|ly /ˈkɒnsɪkwentli/

ADVERB Consequently means as a result. [FORMAL] ○ *They said that Freud had not understood women and consequently belittled them.* ○ *Apprehension and stress had made him depressed and consequently irritable with his family.*

▶ **SYNONYMS:** as a result, thus

con|serva|tive /kənˈsɜːvətɪv/ POLITICS

1 ADJECTIVE A **Conservative** politician or voter is a member of or votes for the Conservative Party in Britain. ○ *Most Conservative MPs appear happy with the government's reassurances.* ○ *disenchanted Conservative voters*

▶ **COLLOCATIONS:**
a Conservative **voter/MP**
the Conservative **Party**

▶ **SYNONYM:** Tory

2 ADJECTIVE Someone who is **conservative** has right-wing views. ○ *counties whose citizens invariably support the most conservative candidate in any election* ○ *the mood of America is turning back to the conservative views of the Ronald Reagan era*

3 ADJECTIVE Someone who is **conservative** or has **conservative** ideas is unwilling to accept changes and new ideas. ○ *People tend to be more aggressive when they're young and more conservative as they get older.* ○ *a narrow conservative approach to child care*

▶ **COLLOCATIONS:**
  a conservative **politician/activist/commentator**
  a conservative **view/approach/agenda**
  fiscally/socially/politically conservative
  deeply conservative

▶ **SYNONYMS:** right-wing, traditionalist, conventional, reactionary

▶ **ANTONYMS:** left-wing, radical

---

con|serve /kən'sɜːv/ **(conserves, conserving, conserved)**　　SCIENCE

1 VERB If you **conserve** a supply of something, you use it carefully so that it lasts for a long time. ○ *The republic's factories have closed for the weekend to conserve energy.* ○ *we must abandon our wasteful ways and conserve resources*

2 VERB To **conserve** something means to protect it from harm, loss, or change. ○ *aid to help developing countries conserve their forests* ○ *the body responsible for conserving historic buildings*

▶ **COLLOCATIONS:**
  conserve **water/electricity/power/fuel**
  conserve **energy/resources/heat/wildlife**
  conserve a **forest/building/habitat**
  conserve the **environment**

▶ **SYNONYMS:** save, protect, preserve

▶ **ANTONYM:** waste

con|ser|va|tion /ˌkɒnsə'veɪʃən/

1 UNCOUNTABLE NOUN **Conservation** is saving and protecting the environment. ○ *elephant conservation* ○ *tree-planting and other conservation projects*

2 UNCOUNTABLE NOUN The **conservation** of a supply of something is the careful use of it so that it lasts for a long time. ○ *projects aimed at promoting energy conservation* ○ *[+ of] rules concerning the conservation of fishery resources*

▶ **COLLOCATIONS:**
  the conservation **of** something
  the conservation of **energy/resources**
  promote/encourage conservation
  environmental/marine/urban conservation
  wildlife/nature/water conservation
  a conservation **measure/effort/project**
  a conservation **officer/group/movement/area**

con|sid|er|able /kən'sɪdərəbəl/ `ACADEMIC WORD`

ADJECTIVE Considerable means great in amount or degree. [FORMAL] ○ *Other studies found considerable evidence to support this finding.* ○ *Doing it properly makes considerable demands on our time.* ○ *Vets' fees can be considerable.*

▶ **COLLOCATIONS:**
a considerable **amount**
considerable **influence/pressure/demands**
considerable **skill/success**

▶ **SYNONYMS:** substantial, large

con|sid|er|ably /kən'sɪdərəbli/

ADVERB ○ *Children vary considerably in the rate at which they learn.* ○ *In the past ethical standards have often been considerably lower.*

▶ **COLLOCATIONS:**
considerably **more/less/higher/lower**
vary/differ/improve considerably

▶ **SYNONYM:** significantly

con|sist /kən'sɪst/ **(consists, consisting, consisted)** `ACADEMIC WORD`

VERB Something that **consists of** particular things or people is formed from them. ○ [+ *of*] *Breakfast consisted of porridge served with butter.* ○ [+ *of*] *Her crew consisted of children from Devon and Cornwall.*

→ see note at **comprise**

▶ **COLLOCATIONS:**
consist **of** *things/people*
consist **mainly/entirely/primarily**
consist **mostly/largely/only**

▶ **SYNONYM:** comprise

con|sist|ent /kən'sɪstənt/ `ACADEMIC WORD`

1 ADJECTIVE Someone who is **consistent** always behaves in the same way, has the same attitudes towards people or things, or achieves the same level of success in something. ○ *Becker has never been the most consistent of players anyway.* ○ *his consistent support of free trade* ○ *a consistent character with a major thematic function*

▶ **COLLOCATION:** a consistent **player/performer**
▶ **SYNONYM:** reliable
▶ **ANTONYMS:** inconsistent, erratic

2 ADJECTIVE If one fact or idea is **consistent with** another, they do not contradict each other. ○ [+ *with*] *This result is consistent with the findings of Garnett & Tobin.* ○ [+ *with*] *New goals are not always consistent with the existing policies.*

▶ **COLLOCATIONS:**
consistent **with** *something*
consistent with a **finding/hypothesis**
entirely/fairly/broadly/remarkably consistent
▶ **SYNONYM:** compatible
▶ **ANTONYMS:** inconsistent, incompatible

con|sist|ent|ly /kənˈsɪstəntli/

ADVERB ○ *It's something I have consistently denied.* ○ *Jones and Armstrong maintain a consistently high standard.*
▶ **COLLOCATION:** consistently **deny/argue/oppose/maintain/refuse/fail**
▶ **SYNONYM:** constantly
▶ **ANTONYM:** inconsistently

con|sist|en|cy /kənˈsɪstənsi/

UNCOUNTABLE NOUN ○ *He scores goals with remarkable consistency.* ○ [+ *in*] *There's always a lack of consistency in matters of foreign policy.* ○ [+ *of*] *We need to interview them several times to test the consistency of their statements.*
▶ **COLLOCATIONS:**
consistency **in** *something*
the consistency **of** *something*
ensure/maintain/show/lack consistency
remarkable/absolute consistency
▶ **SYNONYMS:** reliability, agreement
▶ **ANTONYM:** inconsistency

---

con|stant /ˈkɒnstənt/ (constants)   ACADEMIC WORD

NOUN A **constant** is a thing or value that always stays the same. ○ *Two significant constants have been found in a number of research studies.* ○ [+ *of*] *Here perhaps we confront a constant of human nature.*
▶ **ANTONYM:** variable

---

con|struct /kənˈstrʌkt/   ACADEMIC WORD
(constructs, constructing, constructed)

1 VERB If you **construct** something such as a building, road, or machine, you build it or make it. ○ *The French constructed a series of fortresses from Dunkirk on the Channel coast to Douai.* ○ [+ *from*] *The boxes should be constructed from rough-sawn timber.*

2 VERB If you **construct** something such as an idea, a piece of writing, or a system, you create it by putting different parts together. ○ *He eventually constructed a business empire which ran to Thailand and Singapore.* ○ [+ *from*]

The novel is constructed from a series of on-the-spot reports. ○ *using carefully-constructed tests*

▶ **COLLOCATIONS:**
construct *something* **from/of/out of** *something*
specially/carefully constructed

▶ **SYNONYMS:** create, design, build

con|struc|tion /kənˈstrʌkʃən/

1 **UNCOUNTABLE NOUN** **Construction** is the building of things such as houses, factories, roads, and bridges. ○ *the only nuclear power station under construction in Britain* ○ *the downturn in the construction industry* ○ *a job in construction*

2 **UNCOUNTABLE NOUN** The **construction** of something such as a vehicle or machine is the making of it. ○ [+ of] *companies who have long experience in the construction of those types of equipment* ○ *the finest wood for boat construction*

▶ **COLLOCATIONS:**
the construction **of** *something*
under construction
the construction **industry**
a construction **worker/company/site/project**
road/highway/housing construction
begin/complete/halt/finance/fund construction

▶ **ANTONYM:** demolition

---

con|sult /kənˈsʌlt/ (consults, consulting, consulted) `ACADEMIC WORD`

1 **VERB** If you **consult** an expert or someone senior to you or **consult with** them, you ask them for their opinion and advice about what you should do or their permission to do something. ○ *Consult your doctor about how much exercise you should attempt.* ○ [+ with] *He needed to consult with an attorney.* ○ *If you are in any doubt, consult a financial adviser.*

2 **VERB** If a person or group of people **consults with** other people or **consults** them, they talk and exchange ideas and opinions about what they might decide to do. ○ [+ with] *After consulting with her manager she decided to take on the part.* ○ *The two countries will have to consult their allies.* ○ *The umpires consulted quickly.*

▶ **COLLOCATIONS:**
consult **with** *someone*
consult a **doctor/solicitor/lawyer/specialist/adviser/expert**

▶ **SYNONYM:** confer

con|sul|ta|tion /ˌkɒnsəl'teɪʃən/ (consultations)

NOUN A **consultation**, or a **consultation with** someone is a meeting which is held to discuss something. **Consultation** is discussion about something. ○ [+ with] *The plans were drawn up in consultation with the World Health Organisation.* ○ [+ with] *A personal diet plan is devised after a consultation with a nutritionist.*

▶ COLLOCATIONS:
a consultation **with** someone
in consultation with someone
hold/launch/conduct a consultation
public/extensive/further/initial consultation
a consultation **process/period/exercise**

▶ SYNONYMS: discussion, meeting, deliberation

con|sult|ant /kən'sʌltənt/ (consultants)

NOUN A **consultant** is a person who gives expert advice to a person or organization on a particular subject. [+ to] ○ *a team of management consultants sent in to reorganise the department*

▶ COLLOCATIONS:
a consultant **to** someone/something
pay/hire a consultant
a **senior/independent/outside** consultant
a **technical/environmental/marketing/design** consultant
a **management/recruitment/property/security** consultant
a consultant's **report**

▶ SYNONYMS: specialist, adviser

---

con|sume /kən'sjuːm, AM -'suːm/   ACADEMIC WORD   BUSINESS
(consumes, consuming, consumed)

1 VERB If you **consume** something, you eat or drink it. [FORMAL] ○ *Many people experienced a drop in their cholesterol levels when they consumed oat bran.*

▶ SYNONYMS: eat, drink

2 VERB To **consume** an amount of fuel, energy, or time means to use it up. ○ *Some of the most efficient refrigerators consume 70 percent less electricity than traditional models.*

▶ COLLOCATIONS:
consume *an amount* **of** *something*
consume *an amount* of **time/energy**

con|sump|tion /kən'sʌmpʃən/

1 UNCOUNTABLE NOUN The **consumption** of fuel or natural resources is the amount of them that is used or the act of using them. ○ *a reduction in fuel* *consumption in the U.S.* ○ [+ *of*] *a tax on the consumption of non-renewable energy resources*

▶ COLLOCATIONS:
consumption **of** *something*
consumption of **fuel/energy/power**

2 UNCOUNTABLE NOUN The **consumption** of food or drink is the act of eating or drinking something, or the amount that is eaten or drunk. [FORMAL]
○ *Most of the wine was unfit for human consumption.* ○ [+ *of*] *The average daily consumption of fruit and vegetables is around 200 grams.* ○ *Excessive alcohol consumption is clearly bad.*

▶ COLLOCATIONS:
alcohol/sugar consumption
excessive/daily/high/low consumption

3 UNCOUNTABLE NOUN **Consumption** is the act of buying and using things.
○ [+ *of*] *the production and consumption of goods and services*

▶ COLLOCATIONS:
the consumption of **goods/services**
reduce/increase/cut consumption
consumption **rises/increases/falls**

con|sum|er /kən'sjuːmə, AM -'suː-/ **(consumers)**

NOUN A **consumer** is a person who buys things or uses services. ○ *claims that tobacco companies failed to warn consumers about the dangers of smoking* ○ *improving public services and consumer rights*

▶ COLLOCATIONS:
a consumer **wants/demands/buys** *something*
the **average/individual** consumer
electricity/gas/energy consumers
consumer **confidence/spending/protection**
consumer **goods**

▶ SYNONYMS: buyer, user, customer

con|tact /'kɒntækt/ **(contacts, contacting, contacted)** `ACADEMIC WORD`

1 UNCOUNTABLE NOUN **Contact** involves meeting or communicating with someone, especially regularly. ○ [+ *with*] *Opposition leaders are denying any contact with the government in Kabul.* ○ [+ *between*] *He forbade contact between directors and executives outside his presence.*

▶ COLLOCATIONS:
contact **with/between** *people*
maintain/establish contact
direct/close/regular/human/social contact
eye/radio/telephone contact

a contact **number/address**

▶ **PHRASES:**
make/have contact with someone
lose contact with someone

▶ **SYNONYM:** communication

2 VERB If you **contact** someone, you telephone them, write to them, or go to see them in order to tell or ask them something. ○ *Contact the Tourist Information Bureau for further details.* ○ *His client was on holiday and couldn't be contacted.*

▶ **COLLOCATIONS:**
contact the **police/authorities**
contact *someone* **immediately**

▶ **SYNONYM:** communicate with

3 UNCOUNTABLE NOUN When people or things are in **contact**, they are touching each other. ○ [+ with] *They compared how these organisms behaved when left in contact with different materials.* ○ *There was no physical contact.* ○ *This shows where the foot and shoe are in contact.*

▶ **COLLOCATIONS:**
in contact
in contact **with** *something/someone*
direct/physical/sexual contact

---

con|tem|po|rary /kən'tempərəri, AM -pəreri/ `ARTS` `HISTORY`

1 ADJECTIVE Contemporary things are modern and relate to the present time. ○ *one of the finest collections of contemporary art in the country* ○ *Only the names are ancient; the characters are modern and contemporary.*

▶ **COLLOCATIONS:**
contemporary **art/music/design/society/culture**
contemporary **artist/composer**

▶ **SYNONYMS:** modern, present-day, current

▶ **ANTONYM:** old-fashioned

2 ADJECTIVE Contemporary people or things were alive or happened at the same time as something else you are talking about. ○ *drawing upon official records and the reports of contemporary witnesses* ○ *He was easily recognised from contemporary paintings.*

---

con|tents /'kɒntents/ `ACADEMIC STUDY`

PLURAL NOUN The **contents** of a book are its different chapters and sections, usually shown in a list at the beginning of the book. ○ *There is no initial list of contents.* ○ *I ran my eye down the contents page of the poetry volume.*

→ see note at **appendix**

▶ **COLLOCATIONS:**
   a **table/list** of contents
   a contents **page**
▶ **SYNONYMS:** index, chapters

---

con|text /ˈkɒntekst/ (contexts)   `ACADEMIC WORD`

1 NOUN The **context of** an idea or event is the general situation that relates
to it, and which helps it to be understood. ○ [+ *of*] *We are doing this work in the
context of reforms in the economic, social and cultural spheres.* ○ *the historical
context in which Chaucer wrote* ○ *This is the context in which President Chirac must
decide his policy.*

2 NOUN The **context** of a word, sentence, or text consists of the words,
sentences, or text before and after it which help to make its meaning clear.
○ *Without a context, I would have assumed it was written by a man.* ○ [+ *of*]
a neutral remark which, in the context of the article, sounded condemnatory

▶ **COLLOCATIONS:**
   the context **of** *something*
   the context of a **debate/discussion**
   a **historical/social/cultural/political** context
   broad/wide/proper context
▶ **SYNONYMS:** circumstances, conditions, situation, background

3 PHRASE If something is seen **in context** or if it is put **into context**, it is
considered together with all the factors that relate to it. ○ *Taxation is not
popular in principle, merely acceptable in context.* ○ [+ *of*] *It is important that we
put Jesus into the context of history.*

▶ **COLLOCATIONS:**
   in/into the context of *something*
   in/into context
▶ **ANTONYM:** out of context

---

con|tinu|ous /kənˈtɪnjʊəs/

ADJECTIVE A **continuous** process or event continues for a period of time
without stopping. ○ *Residents report that they heard continuous gunfire.*
○ *a record of five years' continuous employment* ○ *a continuous stream of electromagnetic signals*

▶ **COLLOCATIONS:**
   continuous **improvement/employment/assessment**
   a continuous **stream/loop**
▶ **SYNONYMS:** unbroken, constant, uninterrupted
▶ **ANTONYM:** occasional

con|tinu|ous|ly /kənˈtɪnjʊəsli/

ADVERB ○ *The civil war has raged almost continuously since 1976.* ○ *It is the oldest continuously-inhabited city in America.*

▶ **COLLOCATIONS:**
  run/operate/work continuously
  monitor/update/improve *something* continuously
▶ **SYNONYM:** constantly
▶ **ANTONYM:** occasionally

---

con|tract /ˈkɒntrækt/ (contracts)   `ACADEMIC WORD` `BUSINESS`

NOUN A **contract** is a legal agreement, usually between two companies or between an employer and employee, which involves doing work for a stated sum of money. ○ [+ for] *The company won a prestigious contract for work on Europe's tallest building.* ○ [+ with] *He was given a seven-year contract with an annual salary of $150,000.*

▶ **COLLOCATIONS:**
  a contract **for** *something*
  a contract **with** *someone*
  win/give/award/offer/sign a contract
  a contract **worth** *an amount*
  a **one-year/long-term/new** contract
  a **recording/maintenance/employment** contract
▶ **SYNONYMS:** commission, agreement

---

contra|dict /ˌkɒntrəˈdɪkt/   `ACADEMIC WORD`
(contradicts, contradicting, contradicted)

VERB If one statement or piece of evidence **contradicts** another, the first one makes the second one appear to be wrong. ○ *Her version contradicted the Government's claim that they were shot after being challenged.* ○ *The result seems to contradict a major U.S. study reported last November.* ○ *Often his conclusions flatly contradicted orthodox medical opinion.*

→ see note at **criticize**

▶ **COLLOCATIONS:**
  contradict a **belief/claim/statement**
  directly/flatly contradict *something*

contra|dic|tion /ˌkɒntrəˈdɪkʃən/ (contradictions)

NOUN If you describe an aspect of a situation as a **contradiction**, you mean that it is completely different from other aspects, and so makes the situation confused or difficult to understand. ○ [+ between] *In my opinion, there is no contradiction between the two types of treatment.* ○ [+ of] *The performance seemed* to me unpardonable, a contradiction of all that the Olympics is supposed to be. ○ [+ in] *There are various contradictions in the evidence.*

▶ **COLLOCATIONS:**
a contradiction **between** *things*
a contradiction **of/in** *something*
an **apparent** contradiction

▶ **SYNONYMS:** inconsistency, conflict

contra|dic|tory /ˌkɒntrəˈdɪktəri, AM -tɔːri/

ADJECTIVE If two or more facts, ideas, or statements are **contradictory**, they state or imply that opposite things are true. ○ *Customs officials have made a series of contradictory statements about the equipment.* ○ *advice that sometimes is contradictory and confusing*

▶ **COLLOCATIONS:**
a contradictory **statement/message**
contradictory **evidence/testimony**
apparently contradictory

▶ **SYNONYMS:** inconsistent, conflicting, incompatible

---

con|tra|ry /ˈkɒntrəri, AM -treri/ ▐ ACADEMIC WORD ▌

1 ADJECTIVE Ideas, attitudes, or reactions that are **contrary to** each other are completely different from each other. ○ [+ to] *This view is contrary to the aims of critical social research for a number of reasons.* ○ *Several of those present had contrary information.* ○ *people with contrary interests*

▶ **COLLOCATIONS:**
contrary **to** *something*
run/seem contrary to *something*
a contrary **view/opinion/direction**
contrary **evidence/information**

▶ **SYNONYMS:** opposite, different, opposing

2 PHRASE If you say that something is true **contrary to** other people's beliefs or opinions, you are emphasizing that it is true and that they are wrong. ○ *Contrary to popular belief, moderate exercise actually decreases your appetite.* ○ *Contrary to its popular definition, Shamanism is not a religion: there is no dogma here.*

> **USAGE:** Phrases
>
> **Contrary** is used in a number of common phrases. These are used in different contexts with particular meanings and should not be confused.
>
> **Contrary to** is used to emphasize that one idea or opinion is completely different from and often opposite to another. ○ *His views run contrary to the majority of people in this country.*

c

You can use **on the contrary** to introduce a positive statement that confirms a previous negative statement. ○ *A newly-published paper revealed that the blind white fish was not unknown to science. On the contrary, it had been discovered in 1937.*

You do not use **on the contrary** to introduce a situation that contrasts with one you have just described. In this context, you can use **on the other hand** or **in contrast**. ○ *In Australia white psychologists have grown up in a society where the emphasis is on the individual. In contrast, in Aboriginal society the emphasis is on the community.*

con|trast (contrasts, contrasting, contrasted)   ACADEMIC WORD

The noun is pronounced /ˈkɒntrɑːst, -træst/.
The verb is pronounced /kənˈtrɑːst, -ˈtræst/.

1 NOUN A **contrast** is a great difference between two or more things which is clear when you compare them. ○ [+ between] *the contrast between town and country* ○ [+ in] *The two visitors provided a startling contrast in appearance.*

▶ COLLOCATIONS:
a contrast **between** *things*
a contrast **in** *something*
a **stark/sharp/marked/striking/dramatic** contrast

2 PHRASE You say **by contrast** or **in contrast**, or **in contrast to** something, to show that you are mentioning a very different situation from the one you have just mentioned. ○ *The private sector, by contrast, has plenty of money to spend.* ○ *In contrast, the lives of girls in well-to-do families were often very sheltered.* ○ *In contrast to similar services in France and Germany, Intercity rolling stock is very rarely idle.*

3 PHRASE If one thing is **in contrast to** another, it is very different from it. ○ [+ to] *His public statements have always been in marked contrast to those of his son.*

4 VERB If you **contrast** one thing **with** another, you point out or consider the differences between those things. ○ [+ with] *She contrasted the situation then with the present crisis.* ○ *In this section we contrast four possible broad approaches.*

▶ COLLOCATIONS:
contrast *something* **with** *something*
contrast a **view/approach** with *something*

5 VERB If one thing **contrasts with** another, it is very different from it. ○ [+ with] *Johnson's easy charm contrasted sharply with the prickliness of his boss.* ○ [V-ing] *Paint the wall in a contrasting colour.*

▶ COLLOCATIONS:
contrast **with** *something*

a **colour/style** contrasts with *something*
contrast **sharply/starkly**

▶ SYNONYM: differ

---

con|trib|ute /kənˈtrɪbjuːt/   ACADEMIC WORD
(contributes, contributing, contributed)

1 VERB If you **contribute to** something, you say or do things to help to make it successful. ○ [+ to] *The three sons also contribute to the family business.* ○ [+ to] *He believes he has something to contribute to a discussion concerning the uprising.*

2 VERB If something **contributes to** an event or situation, it is one of the causes of it. ○ [+ to] *The report says design faults in both the vessels contributed to the tragedy.* ○ [V-ing] *Stress, both human and mechanical, may also be a contributing factor.*

▶ COLLOCATIONS:
contribute **to** *something*
a contributing **factor**
contribute **greatly/directly/significantly/substantially**

con|tri|bu|tion /ˌkɒntrɪˈbjuːʃən/ (contributions)

NOUN If you make a **contribution to** something, you do something to help make it successful or to produce it. ○ [+ to] *American economists have made important contributions to the field of financial and corporate economics.* ○ [+ to] *He was awarded a prize for his contribution to world peace.*

▶ COLLOCATIONS:
a contribution **to** *something*
make a contribution
a **significant/outstanding/major/positive** contribution

---

con|tro|ver|sy /ˈkɒntrəvɜːsi, kənˈtrɒvəsi/   ACADEMIC WORD
(controversies)

NOUN **Controversy** is a lot of discussion and argument about something, often involving strong feelings of anger or disapproval. ○ *The proposed cuts have caused considerable controversy.* ○ [+ over] *a fierce political controversy over human rights abuses*

▶ COLLOCATIONS:
a controversy **over/about/surrounding** *something*
considerable/political controversy
cause/spark controversy

▶ SYNONYMS: argument, discussion, debate
▶ ANTONYM: agreement

c

con|tro|ver|sial /ˌkɒntrəˈvɜːʃəl/

ADJECTIVE ○ *Immigration is a controversial issue in many countries.* ○ *The changes are bound to be controversial.* ○ *the controversial 19th century politician Charles Parnell*

▶ COLLOCATIONS:
a controversial **decision/plan/proposal/issue/figure**
prove controversial
highly controversial

con|tro|ver|sial|ly /ˌkɒntrəˈvɜːʃəli/

ADVERB ○ *More controversially, he claims that these higher profits cover the cost of finding fresh talent.* ○ *the issues she controversially espoused*

---

con|ven|tion /kənˈvenʃən/ (conventions)　ACADEMIC WORD

1 NOUN A **convention** is a way of behaving that is considered to be correct or polite by most people in a society. ○ [+ that] *It's just a social convention that men don't wear skirts.* ○ *Despite her wish to defy convention, she had become pregnant and married at 21.*

▶ COLLOCATIONS:
a **social** convention
defy convention

▶ SYNONYMS: custom, tradition, protocol

2 NOUN In art, literature, or the theatre, a **convention** is a traditional method or style. ○ [+ of] *We go offstage and come back for the convention of the encore.* ○ [+ of] *the stylistic conventions of Egyptian art*

▶ COLLOCATION: the conventions **of** something

3 NOUN A **convention** is an official agreement between countries or groups of people. ○ [+ on] *the U.N. convention on climate change* ○ *the Geneva convention*

▶ COLLOCATIONS:
a convention **on** something
a convention on **human rights/climate change**
sign a convention

▶ SYNONYMS: agreement, treaty

con|ven|tion|al /kənˈvenʃənəl/

1 ADJECTIVE Someone who is **conventional** has behaviour or opinions that are ordinary and normal. ○ *a respectable married woman with conventional opinions* ○ *this close, fairly conventional English family*

2 ADJECTIVE A **conventional** method or product is one that is usually used or that has been in use for a long time. ○ *These discs hold more than 400 times as much information as a conventional computer floppy disk.*

▶ COLLOCATIONS:
conventional **wisdom/thinking/treatment/methods**
conventional **forces/weapons**
▶ SYNONYMS: standard, traditional
▶ ANTONYM: unconventional

con|ven|tion|al|ly /kən'venʃənəli/

ADVERB ○ *People still wore their hair short and dressed conventionally.* ○ *Organically-grown produce does not differ greatly in appearance from conventionally-grown crops.*
▶ COLLOCATION: **dress/behave** conventionally
▶ SYNONYM: traditionally

---

con|vert /kən'vɜːt/ (converts, converting, converted) ACADEMIC WORD

1 VERB If one thing **is converted** or **converts into** another, it is changed into a different form. ○ [+ *into*] *The signal will be converted into digital code.* ○ [+ *into*] *naturally occurring substances which the body can convert into vitamins* ○ [+ *to*] *Spreadsheet data is automatically converted to a table.*

2 VERB If you **convert** a quantity **from** one system of measurement **to** another, you calculate what the quantity is in the second system. ○ [+ *to*] *Converting metric measurements to U.S. equivalents is easy.*
▶ COLLOCATION: convert **from** *something* **to/into** *something*
▶ SYNONYMS: change, transform, alter

con|ver|sion /kən'vɜːʃən/ (conversions)

UNCOUNTABLE NOUN ○ [+ *of*] *the conversion of disused rail lines into cycle routes* ○ *A loft conversion can add considerably to the value of a house.*
▶ COLLOCATIONS:
the conversion **of** *something*
the conversion of *something* **into** *something*
a **loft/basement/barn** conversion
▶ SYNONYMS: adaptation, modification, alteration, transformation

---

co-operate /kəʊ'ɒpəreɪt/ ACADEMIC WORD
(co-operates, co-operating, co-operated) also **cooperate**

VERB If you **co-operate with** someone, you work with them or help them for a particular purpose. You can also say that two people **co-operate**.
○ [+ *with*] *The U.N. had been co-operating with the State Department on a plan to find countries willing to take the refugees.* ○ [+ *in*] *It was agreed that the two leaders should co-operate in a joint enterprise.* ○ *The French and British are co-operating more closely than they have for years.*

> ▶ COLLOCATIONS:
> co-operate **with** someone
> co-operate **in** something
> co-operate **fully**
> ▶ SYNONYM: collaborate
> ▶ ANTONYM: conflict

co-operation /kəʊˌɒpəˈreɪʃən/

UNCOUNTABLE NOUN ○ [+ with] *A deal with Japan could indeed open the door to economic co-operation with East Asia.* ○ [+ by] *Scientists claimed there had been a lack of co-operation by food manufacturers.* ○ *The patient's co-operation is of course essential.*

> ▶ COLLOCATIONS:
> co-operation **with/by** someone
> **require/increase/strengthen** co-operation
> **economic/regional/international** co-operation
> **close/full** co-operation
> ▶ SYNONYMS: teamwork, collaboration
> ▶ ANTONYM: opposition

co-operative /kəʊˈɒpərətɪv/ also **cooperative**

ADJECTIVE ○ *The President said the visit would develop friendly and co-operative relations between the two countries.* ○ *a contented and co-operative workforce*

> ▶ COLLOCATION: a co-operative **approach/effort/relationship**
> ▶ SYNONYMS: helpful, obliging, supportive
> ▶ ANTONYM: unco-operative

---

co-ordinate /kəʊˈɔːdɪneɪt/ ACADEMIC WORD
(co-ordinates, co-ordinating, co-ordinated) also **coordinate**

VERB If you **co-ordinate** an activity, you organize the various people and things involved in it. ○ *Government officials visited the earthquake zone to co-ordinate the relief effort.* ○ *the setting up of an advisory committee to co-ordinate police work*

> ▶ COLLOCATIONS:
> a co-ordinated **effort/response/approach**
> a co-ordinated **operation/activity/action/attack**
> **centrally/nationally/closely/carefully** co-ordinated
> ▶ SYNONYMS: organize, synchronize

co-ordination /kəʊˌɔːdɪˈneɪʃən/

UNCOUNTABLE NOUN ○ [+ between] *the lack of co-ordination between the civilian and military authorities* ○ [+ of] *the co-ordination of economic policy* ○ [+ of]

Co-ordination of planning was to be the responsibility of the Group Marketing Director.

▶ **COLLOCATIONS:**
co-ordination **between** *people*
co-ordination **of** *something*
poor/close/good co-ordination
physical/hand-eye co-ordination

▶ **SYNONYMS:** organization, synchronization

cor|po|rate /ˈkɔːprət/ `ACADEMIC WORD` `BUSINESS`

ADJECTIVE Corporate means relating to business corporations or to a particular business corporation. ○ *top U.S. corporate executives* ○ *the U.K. corporate sector* ○ *a corporate lawyer* ○ *This established a strong corporate image.*

▶ **COLLOCATIONS:**
corporate **finance/business**
a corporate **lawyer/executive/image/body**

cor|po|ra|tion /ˌkɔːpəˈreɪʃən/ **(corporations)**

NOUN A **corporation** is a large business or company. ○ *multi-national corporations* ○ *the Seiko Corporation*

▶ **COLLOCATIONS:**
a **giant/major** corporation
a **multinational/foreign/private/global** corporation
corporation **tax/law**

▶ **SYNONYMS:** business, firm, company, organization

cor|re|spond /ˌkɒrɪˈspɒnd, AM ˌkɔːr-/ `ACADEMIC WORD`
(corresponds, corresponding, corresponded)

VERB If one thing **corresponds to** another, there is a close similarity or connection between them. You can also say that two things **correspond**. ○ [+ to] *All buttons and switches were clearly numbered to correspond to the chart on the wall.* ○ [+ with] *A 22 per cent increase in car travel corresponds with a 19 per cent drop in cycle mileage per person.* ○ *The two maps of London correspond closely.*

▶ **COLLOCATIONS:**
correspond **to/with** *something*
findings/numbers/figures correspond
correspond **exactly/closely/roughly**

▶ **SYNONYMS:** match, relate to

▶ **ANTONYM:** differ

cor|re|spond|ing /ˌkɒrɪˈspɒndɪŋ, AM ˌkɔːr-/

ADJECTIVE ○ *March and April sales this year were up 8 per cent on the corresponding* period in 1992. ○ [+ to] *Older types of meter show the reading on a series of dials, corresponding to different powers of 10.*

▶ COLLOCATIONS:
corresponding **to** *something*
a corresponding **figure/period**
a corresponding **increase/decrease**

▶ SYNONYMS: equivalent, matching, related

cor|rup|tion /kəˈrʌpʃən/ `POLITICS`

UNCOUNTABLE NOUN **Corruption** is dishonesty and illegal behaviour by people in positions of authority or power. ○ *The President faces 54 charges of corruption and tax evasion.* ○ *Distribution of food throughout the country is being hampered by inefficiency and corruption.* ○ *bribery and corruption*

▶ COLLOCATIONS:
expose/tackle/fight/investigate corruption
alleged/widespread/political/corporate corruption
police/government corruption
a corruption **scandal/charge/allegation/trial/case**

▶ SYNONYMS: dishonesty, fraud

cor|rupt /kəˈrʌpt/

ADJECTIVE Someone who is **corrupt** behaves in a way that is morally wrong, especially by doing dishonest or illegal things in return for money or power. ○ *to save the nation from corrupt politicians of both parties* ○ *corrupt police officers* ○ *He had accused three opposition members of corrupt practices.*

▶ COLLOCATIONS:
a corrupt **politician/official/regime**
corrupt **practices/conduct**

▶ SYNONYMS: dishonest, unscrupulous
▶ ANTONYMS: honest, scrupulous

cred|it /ˈkredɪt/ `ACADEMIC WORD` `BUSINESS`

UNCOUNTABLE NOUN If you are allowed **credit**, you are allowed to pay for goods or services several weeks or months after you have received them. ○ *The group can't get credit to buy farming machinery.* ○ *You can ask a dealer for a discount whether you pay cash or buy on credit.*

▶ COLLOCATIONS:
on credit
buy/get *something* on credit
interest-free credit
credit **card/rating**

cri|sis /ˈkraɪsɪs/ (crises) POLITICS

NOUN A **crisis** is a situation in which something or someone is affected by one or more very serious problems. ○ *Natural disasters have obviously contributed to the continent's economic crisis.* ○ *children's illnesses or other family crises* ○ *someone to turn to in moments of crisis*

▶ COLLOCATIONS:
   a **political/economic/humanitarian/financial** crisis
   a crisis **begins/deepens**
   a **severe** crisis
   a **hostage/energy/health/cash** crisis
   resolve/face a crisis
   crisis **talks/management**
   a crisis **point/situation/meeting**
▶ SYNONYM: emergency

cri|teri|on /kraɪˈtɪəriən/ (criteria) ACADEMIC WORD

NOUN A **criterion** is a factor on which you judge or decide something. ○ [+ *for*] *The most important criterion for entry is that applicants must design and make their own work.* ○ *British defence policy had to meet three criteria if it was to succeed.*

▶ COLLOCATIONS:
   the criteria **for** *something*
   meet the criteria
   economic/selection/inclusion/strict criteria
▶ SYNONYMS: standard, rule

> **USAGE:** Plural form
>
> The plural noun, **criteria**, is the most common form, because you often talk about a number of **criteria**. Remember that the correct singular form is **criterion**.

criti|cize /ˈkrɪtɪsaɪz/ (criticizes, criticizing, criticized)

VERB If you **criticize** someone or something, you express your disapproval of them by saying what you think is wrong with them. [in BRIT, also use **criticise**] ○ *Human rights groups are criticizing the decision.* ○ [+ *for*] *The regime has been harshly criticized for human rights violations.*

▶ COLLOCATIONS:
   criticize *someone* **for** *something*
   criticize the **government/administration/president**
   criticize a **decision/policy/proposal**
   sharply/harshly/strongly/widely criticized
▶ ANTONYMS: praise, support

> **ACADEMIC WRITING: Reporting disagreement**
>
> There are a number of reporting verbs used to show disagreement. You can say that a person or group **criticizes** or **condemns** someone else or their ideas, decisions or actions. **Condemn** is a much stronger word and usually expresses strong moral disapproval. ○ *This study has been widely criticized.* ○ *In a statement, the leadership condemned the bombings.*
>
> You can also say that someone **questions** or **doubts** an idea or the findings of research or that they **raise questions/doubts** about it. ○ *Some economists question the validity of these results.* ○ *A recent study raises doubts about the safety of such workers.*
>
> You can say that evidence or the findings of research **contradict** or **disprove** another idea or piece of research; that is, they show the opposite. ○ *Their findings contradict the claim that children are more adaptable to adversity.* ○ *The fossil helped to disprove the theory that the early large Australian carnivores were all reptilian.*

criti|cism /ˈkrɪtɪsɪzəm/ (criticisms)

1 NOUN Criticism is the action of expressing disapproval of something or someone. A **criticism** is a statement that expresses disapproval. ○ *This policy had repeatedly come under strong criticism on Capitol Hill.* ○ [+ of] *unfair criticism of his tactics* ○ [+ that] *The criticism that the English do not truly care about their children was often voiced.*

▶ **COLLOCATIONS:**
criticism **of** someone/something
draw/attract/face/reject criticism
strong/public/valid/unfair criticism
harsh/widespread/heavy/sharp criticism

▶ **SYNONYM:** disapproval

▶ **ANTONYM:** praise

2 UNCOUNTABLE NOUN Criticism is a serious examination and judgment of something such as a book or play. ○ *She has published more than 20 books including novels, poetry and literary criticism.* ○ *academic film criticism*

▶ **COLLOCATION: literary/film** criticism

crit|ic /ˈkrɪtɪk/ (critics)

1 NOUN A **critic** is a person who writes about and expresses opinions about things such as books, films, music, or art. ○ *Mather was film critic on the Daily Telegraph for many years.* ○ *The New York critics had praised her performance.*

▶ **COLLOCATIONS:**
a **film/theatre** critic
a **music/entertainment/art** critic

▶ **SYNONYM:** reviewer

2 NOUN Someone who is a **critic** of a person or system disapproves of them and criticizes them publicly. ○ [+ of] *He became a fierce critic of the tobacco industry.* ○ *Her critics accused her of caring only about success.*

▶ **COLLOCATIONS:**
a critic **of** someone/something
a critic of a **government/policy/war**
a **harsh/vocal/outspoken/fierce** critic

criti|cal /ˈkrɪtɪkəl/

1 ADJECTIVE To be **critical of** someone or something means to criticize them. ○ [+ of] *His report is highly critical of the trial judge.* ○ *He has apologised for critical remarks he made about the referee.*

▶ **COLLOCATIONS:**
critical **of** someone/something
critical of a **government/regime/policy/decision**
highly critical

▶ **SYNONYM:** disapproving

▶ **ANTONYM:** complimentary

2 ADJECTIVE A **critical** approach to something involves examining and judging it carefully. ○ *We need to become critical text-readers.* ○ *Marx's work was more than a critical study of capitalist production.* ○ *the critical analysis of political ideas*

▶ **COLLOCATION:** a critical **analysis/report/study**

▶ **SYNONYM:** analytical

▶ **ANTONYM:** undiscriminating

criti|cal|ly /ˈkrɪtɪkli/

ADVERB ○ *She spoke critically of Lara.* ○ *Wyman watched them critically.*

▶ **COLLOCATIONS:**
examine/evaluate/think/look critically
speak/respond critically
critically **acclaimed**

---

crop /krɒp/ (crops) `BIOLOGY`

NOUN **Crops** are plants such as wheat and potatoes that are grown in large quantities for food. ○ *Rice farmers here still plant and harvest their crops by hand.* ○ *The main crop is wheat and this is grown even on the very steep slopes.*

▶ **COLLOCATIONS:**
grow/plant/harvest a crop
a **bumper/cotton/grain** crop
crop **rotation/failure/production**

cube /kjuːb/ (cubes)　　　　　　　　　　　MATHS

1 NOUN A **cube** is a solid object with six square surfaces which are all the same size. ○ *cold water with ice cubes in it* ○ *The cabinet is shaped like a cube.*

2 NOUN The cube of a number is another number that is produced by multiplying the first number by itself twice. For example, the cube of 2 is 8. ○ [+ *of*] *the volume of the cell increases proportionally to the cube of its radius*
▶ **COLLOCATION:** the cube **of** *something*

cu|bic /ˈkjuːbɪk/

ADJECTIVE Cubic is used in front of units of length to form units of volume such as 'cubic metre' and 'cubic foot'. ○ *3 billion cubic metres of soil*
▶ **COLLOCATION:** a cubic **foot/metre**

cur|rent /ˈkʌrənt, AM ˈkɜːr-/ (currents)　　GEOGRAPHY SCIENCE

1 NOUN A **current** is a steady and continuous flowing movement of some of the water in a river, lake, or sea. ○ [+ *of*] *The ocean currents of the tropical Pacific travel from east to west.* ○ *The couple were swept away by the strong current.*

2 NOUN A **current** is a steady flowing movement of air. ○ [+ *of*] *a current of cool air* ○ *the spores are very light and can be wafted by the slightest air current*

3 NOUN An electric **current** is a flow of electricity through a wire or circuit. ○ *A powerful electric current is passed through a piece of graphite.* ○ [+ *of*] *the current of electricity from the stun gun*
▶ **COLLOCATIONS:**
　a current **of** *something*
　a current of **air/electricity**
　a **strong/ocean** current

curve /kɜːv/ (curves, curving, curved)

1 NOUN A **curve** is a smooth, gradually bending line, for example part of the edge of a circle. ○ [+ *of*] *the curve of his lips* ○ [+ *in*] *a curve in the road*
▶ **COLLOCATIONS:**
　a curve **of/in** *something*
　a **downward/upward** curve
▶ **SYNONYMS:** bend, arch

2 VERB If something **curves**, or if someone or something **curves** it, it has the shape of a curve. ○ *Her spine curved.* ○ *The track curved away below him.* ○ [V-*ing*] *a knife with a slightly curving blade* ○ *A small, unobtrusive smile curved the cook's thin lips.*

curved /kɜːvd/

ADJECTIVE ○ *a small, curved staircase* ○ *the curved lines of the chairs*

▶ **COLLOCATIONS:**
a curved **wall/staircase**
gently/slightly/elegantly/gracefully curved

▶ **SYNONYM:** bent

cy|cle /ˈsaɪkəl/ (cycles)

ACADEMIC WORD

NOUN A **cycle** is a series of events or processes that is repeated again and again, always in the same order. ○ [+ *of*] *the life cycle of the plant* ○ *The figures marked the final low point of the present economic cycle.* ○ [+ *of*] *They must break out of the cycle of violence.*

▶ **COLLOCATIONS:**
a cycle **of** *something*
a cycle of **violence/poverty**
break/complete the cycle
a **life/menstrual/economic/business** cycle

cyl|in|der /ˈsɪlɪndə/ (cylinders)

NOUN A **cylinder** is an object with flat circular ends and long straight sides. ○ [+ *of*] *a cylinder of foam.* ○ *It was recorded on a wax cylinder.*

▶ **COLLOCATIONS:**
a cylinder **of** *something*
a cylinder of **gas/oxygen/foam**

cy|lin|dri|cal /sɪˈlɪndrɪkəl/

ADJECTIVE Something that is **cylindrical** is in the shape of a cylinder. ○ *a cylindrical aluminium container* ○ *It is cylindrical in shape.*

Dd

da|ta /ˈdeɪtə/ ACADEMIC WORD IT

1 **UNCOUNTABLE NOUN** You can refer to information as **data**, especially when it is in the form of facts or statistics that you can analyse. ○ [+ *from*] *The study was based on data from 2,100 women.*

2 **UNCOUNTABLE NOUN** **Data** is information that can be stored and used by a computer program. ○ *You can compress huge amounts of data on to a CD-ROM.*

▶ **COLLOCATIONS:**
data **from** *people/things*
store/collect/collate/analyse/delete data
raw/primary data
data **protection/collection/transmission**
data **suggest/show/indicate** *things*

▶ **SYNONYMS:** information, figures, statistics

> **USAGE:** Plural or uncountable noun
>
> In British English, **data** is usually an uncountable noun and it is followed by a singular verb. ○ **This data shows** *that over the past century sea level rose at about 2 millimetres per year.*
>
> In technical or formal British English, **data** is more often used as a plural noun, followed by a plural verb. ○ **These data show** *that over the past century sea level rose at about 2 millimetres per year.*
>
> In American English, **data** is usually a plural noun.
>
> **Datum** is sometimes used as the singular form of **data**.

de|bate /dɪˈbeɪt/ (debates, debating, debated) ACADEMIC WORD

1 **NOUN** A **debate** is a discussion about a subject on which people have different views. ○ *An intense debate is going on within the Israeli government.* ○ [+ *about*] *There has been a lot of debate among scholars about this.*

▶ **COLLOCATIONS:**
a debate **on/over/about/within** *something*
a debate on a **subject/issue**
a **heated/lively/intense/ongoing** debate
a **televised/public/political** debate

spark/provoke/trigger a debate

▶ SYNONYMS: discussion, argument

2 VERB If people **debate** a topic, they discuss it fairly formally, putting forward different views. ○ *The United Nations Security Council will debate the issue today.* ○ *[+ whether] Scholars have debated whether or not Yagenta became a convert.*

▶ COLLOCATIONS:
debate *something* **with** *someone*
scholars/historians/scientists debate
debate a **matter/topic/issue**
hotly debated

▶ SYNONYMS: discuss, argue

---

debt /det/ (debts)

BUSINESS ECONOMICS

1 NOUN A **debt** is a sum of money that you owe someone. ○ *consumers struggling to repay outstanding debts* ○ *reducing the country's $18 billion foreign debt*

2 UNCOUNTABLE NOUN **Debt** is the state of owing money. ○ *Debt is a main reason for stress.* ○ *He was already deeply in debt through gambling losses.*

▶ COLLOCATIONS:
a debt **of** £x
in debt
owe/incur/repay/pay off a debt
foreign/long-term/outstanding/crippling debt
gambling/household/mortgage/credit-card debts
debt **repayment/relief/burden**

▶ SYNONYM: deficit

▶ ANTONYMS: profit, surplus

---

de|clare /dɪˈkleə/ (declares, declaring, declared)

VERB If you **declare** something, you state officially and formally that it exists or is the case. ○ *The government is ready to declare a permanent ceasefire.* ○ *His lawyers are confident that the judges will declare Mr Stevens innocent.* ○ *The U.N. has declared it to be a safe zone.*

▶ COLLOCATIONS:
declare a **ceasefire/truce/emergency**
declare **war**
declare *something* **unsafe/illegal/invalid**
declare *someone* **dead/bankrupt**
officially/formally/publicly declare

▶ SYNONYMS: assert, state, pronounce

dec|la|ra|tion /ˌdekləˈreɪʃən/ (declarations)

NOUN A **declaration** is an official announcement or statement. ○ *They will sign the declaration tomorrow.* ○ *[+ of] the issues arising from their declaration of independence*

▶ **COLLOCATIONS:**
a declaration **of** something
a declaration of **war/independence/sovereignty**
sign/issue/draft a declaration

▶ **SYNONYMS:** announcement, pronouncement, statement

---

de|cline /dɪˈklaɪn/ (declines, declining, declined)   `ACADEMIC WORD`

1 VERB If something **declines**, it becomes less in quantity, importance, or strength. ○ *[+ from] The number of staff has declined from 217,000 to 114,000.* ○ *Hourly output by workers declined 1.3% in the first quarter.* ○ *[V-ing] a declining birth rate*

▶ **COLLOCATIONS:**
decline **from** x **to** y
decline **by** x
decline **in** something
decline in **value/importance/popularity**
steadily/rapidly/sharply decline

2 NOUN If there is a **decline in** something, it becomes less in quantity, importance, or quality. ○ *[+ in] The reasons for the apparent decline in fertility are unclear.* ○ *Rome's decline in the fifth century* ○ *The first signs of economic decline became visible.*

▶ **COLLOCATIONS:**
a decline **in** something
a decline in **value/sales/revenue/population/fertility**
experience/suffer/report/reverse a decline
a **market/economic/population** decline
a **steep/sharp/rapid/gradual** decline

EXTEND YOUR VOCABULARY

You use **decrease** or **reduce** to talk about things becoming less in size or intensity.

decrease/reduce the **amount/risk/likelihood/incidence**
You use **decline** to talk about something becoming less in size, importance or quality, often in a way that is considered negative.
sales/revenues/exports decline
popularity/attendance/output declines

de|fend /dɪˈfend/ (defends, defending, defended) `LAW`

VERB When a lawyer **defends** a person who has been accused of something, the lawyer argues on their behalf in a court of law that the charges are not true. ○ *a lawyer who defended political prisoners during the military regime* ○ [+ *against*] *He has hired a lawyer to defend him against the allegations.*

▶ **COLLOCATIONS:**
  defend *someone* **against** *something*
  defend *someone* against a **charge/allegation/lawsuit**

▶ **ANTONYM:** prosecute

de|fence /dɪˈfens/ (defences)

> The spelling **defense** is used in American English.

1 NOUN In a court of law, an accused person's **defence** is the process of presenting evidence in their favour. ○ *He has insisted on conducting his own defence.*

2 NOUN **The defence** is the case that is presented by a lawyer in a trial for the person who has been accused of a crime. You can also refer to this person's lawyers as **the defence**. ○ *The defence was that the records of the interviews were fabricated by the police.* ○ *The defence pleaded insanity.*

▶ **COLLOCATIONS:**
  the defence **argues/claims/alleges** *something*
  conduct *someone's* defence
  a defence **lawyer/barrister/attorney**

▶ **ANTONYM:** prosecution

de|fend|ant /dɪˈfendənt/ (defendants)

NOUN A **defendant** is a person who has been accused of breaking the law and is being tried in court. ○ *All six defendants pleaded not guilty to the charges.*

▶ **COLLOCATIONS:**
  convict/sentence/acquit a defendant
  a defendant **pleads/denies/admits** *something*

▶ **SYNONYMS:** accused, suspect

de|fine /dɪˈfaɪn/ `ACADEMIC STUDY` `ACADEMIC WORD`
(defines, defining, defined)

1 VERB If you **define** something, you show, describe, or state clearly what it is and what its limits are, or what it is like. ○ [+ *what*] *We were unable to define what exactly was wrong with him.* ○ *a musical era when genres were less narrowly defined*

2 VERB If you **define** a word or expression, you explain its meaning, for example in a dictionary. ○ [+ *as*] *Collins English Dictionary defines a workaholic as 'a person obsessively addicted to work'.*

▶ **COLLOCATIONS:**
define *something* **as/in terms of** *something*
define a **term/concept**
a **rule/law** defines *something*
clearly/narrowly/broadly defined

▶ **SYNONYMS:** explain, expound, interpret

defi|ni|tion /ˌdefɪˈnɪʃən/ (definitions)

NOUN A **definition** is a statement giving the meaning of a word or expression, especially in a dictionary. ○ [+ of] *There is no general agreement on a standard definition of intelligence.* ○ *Human perception is highly imperfect and by definition subjective.*

▶ **COLLOCATIONS:**
by definition
a definition **of** *something*
a **dictionary/textbook/legal** definition
a **precise/broad/narrow/clear** definition
broaden/clarify/propose/change a definition

▶ **SYNONYMS:** explanation, interpretation

defi|nite /ˈdefɪnɪt/   `ACADEMIC WORD`

1 ADJECTIVE If something such as a decision or an arrangement is **definite**, it is firm and clear, and unlikely to be changed. ○ *It's too soon to give a definite answer.* ○ *She made no definite plans for her future.*

2 ADJECTIVE **Definite** evidence or information is true, rather than being someone's opinion or guess. ○ *We didn't have any definite proof.* ○ *There is no definite conclusion that can be reached from these studies.* ○ *The police had nothing definite against her.*

3 ADJECTIVE You use **definite** to emphasize the strength of your opinion or belief. ○ *There has already been a definite improvement.* ○ *That's a very definite possibility.*

▶ **COLLOCATIONS:**
definite **proof/evidence**
a definite **answer/conclusion/diagnosis**
a definite **advantage/possibility/improvement**

▶ **SYNONYMS:** certain, definitive, conclusive, real
▶ **ANTONYMS:** uncertain, inconclusive, inexact

defi|nite|ly /ˈdefɪnɪtli/

ADVERB You use **definitely** to emphasize that something is the case, or to emphasize the strength of your intention or opinion. ○ *I'm definitely going to get in touch with these people.* ○ *While intra-region trade in Asia has definitely* *improved, the pace of recovery in individual economies has been uneven.*

▶ SYNONYM: certainly
▶ ANTONYM: possibly

---

de|gree /dɪˈgriː/ (degrees)

1 NOUN You use **degree** to indicate the extent to which something happens or is the case, or the amount which something is felt. ○ [+ of] *These man-made barriers will ensure a very high degree of protection.* ○ [+ of] *Politicians have used television with varying degrees of success.*

▶ COLLOCATIONS:
  a degree **of** something
  a degree of **certainty/accuracy/autonomy/flexibility**
  a **varying/high** degree

▶ SYNONYMS: amount, extent

2 PHRASE You use expressions such as **to some degree**, **to a large degree**, or **to a certain degree** in order to indicate that something is partly true, but not entirely true. ○ *These statements are, to some degree, all correct.* ○ *It is impossible to make these points without generalising to a certain degree.*

▶ SYNONYM: to some extent

3 PHRASE You use expressions such as **to what degree** and **to the degree that** when you are discussing how true a statement is, or in what ways it is true. ○ *To what degree would you say you had control over things that went on?* ○ *The valves may scar and thicken to the degree that they may fail to open completely or close properly.*

▶ SYNONYMS: to what extent, to the extent that

---

de|lay /dɪˈleɪ/ (delays, delaying, delayed)

1 VERB If you **delay** doing something, you do not do it immediately or at the planned or expected time, but you leave it until later. ○ *The disclosures forced it to delay publication of its annual report.*

2 VERB To **delay** someone or something means to make them late or to slow them down. ○ *The therapy is known to delay the onset of osteoporosis.* ○ *Various set-backs and problems delayed production.*

▶ COLLOCATIONS:
  delay the **onset/start** of something
  delay the **implementation/introduction** of something
  delay a **decision/announcement/delivery**
  delay **publication/production**
  delay **indefinitely**

▶ SYNONYMS: postpone, slow
▶ ANTONYMS: expedite, hasten

3 NOUN If there is a **delay**, something does not happen until later than planned or expected. ○ [+ in] *The delay in the implementation of the law has dismayed businesses.* ○ *Although the tests have caused some delay, flights should be back to normal soon.*

▶ **COLLOCATIONS:**
a delay **in** *something*
a delay in **payment/implementation/completion**
a **flight/traffic** delay
cause/experience/avoid a delay
a **lengthy/further/unnecessary/bureaucratic/slight** delay

▶ **SYNONYM:** setback

de|mand /dɪˈmɑːnd, -ˈmænd/ BUSINESS ECONOMICS

UNCOUNTABLE NOUN If you refer to **demand**, or to the **demand for** something, you are referring to how many people want to have it, do it, or buy it. ○ *Another flight would be arranged if sufficient demand arose.* ○ [+ for] *Demand for coal is down.*

▶ **COLLOCATIONS:**
demand **for** *something*
demand for **goods/electricity/housing**
domestic/global demand
high/strong/sluggish/growing demand
stimulate/boost/fuel/create/reduce/dampen demand
meet/satisfy demand
demand **soars/slows/grows**
demand **exceeds/outstrips** *something*

▶ **PHRASE:** supply and demand
▶ **ANTONYM:** supply

de|moc|ra|cy /dɪˈmɒkrəsi/ (democracies) POLITICS

1 UNCOUNTABLE NOUN Democracy is a system of government in which people choose their rulers by voting for them in elections. ○ *the spread of democracy in Eastern Europe* ○ *the pro-democracy movement*

2 NOUN A **democracy** is a country in which the people choose their government by voting for it. ○ *The new democracies face tough challenges.*

▶ **COLLOCATIONS:**
restore/promote/establish/undermine democracy
multi-party/parliamentary/representative democracy
Western democracy

▶ **PHRASE:** freedom and democracy

demo|crat|ic /ˌdeməˈkrætɪk/

1 ADJECTIVE A **democratic** country, government, or political system is governed by representatives who are elected by the people. ○ *Bolivia returned to democratic rule in 1982, after a series of military governments.* ○ *the country's first democratic elections*

2 ADJECTIVE Something that is **democratic** is based on the idea that everyone should have equal rights and should be involved in making important decisions. ○ *Education is the basis of a democratic society.*

▶ **COLLOCATIONS:**
   a democratic **society/process/election/ideal**
   democratic **reform**
   truly/fully/newly democratic

▶ **SYNONYMS:** egalitarian, representative

▶ **ANTONYM:** totalitarian

demo|crat /ˈdeməkræt/ (democrats)

1 NOUN A **Democrat** is a member or supporter of a particular political party which has the word 'democrat' or 'democratic' in its title, for example the Democratic Party in the United States. ○ *a senior Christian Democrat* ○ *Congressman Tom Downey is a Democrat from New York.*

2 NOUN A **democrat** is a person who believes in the ideals of democracy, personal freedom, and equality. ○ *This is the time for democrats and not dictators.*

---

dem|on|strate /ˈdemənstreɪt/   ACADEMIC WORD
(demonstrates, demonstrating, demonstrated)

1 VERB To **demonstrate** a fact means to make it clear to people. ○ *The study also demonstrated a direct link between obesity and mortality.* ○ [+ *that*] *His experiments demonstrated that plants alter their shape at night.* ○ [+ *to*] *They are anxious to demonstrate to the voters that they have practical policies.*

2 VERB If you **demonstrate** something, you show people how it works or how to do it. ○ *The BBC has just successfully demonstrated a new digital radio transmission system.* ○ [+ *to*] *He flew the prototype to West Raynham to demonstrate it to a group of senior officers.*

▶ **COLLOCATIONS:**
   demonstrate *something* **to** *someone*
   a **study/experiment** demonstrates *something*
   amply/conclusively/convincingly/clearly demonstrate

▶ **SYNONYMS:** show, prove, display

▶ **ANTONYMS:** refute, disprove

dem|on|stra|tion /ˌdemənˈstreɪʃən/ (demonstrations)

1 NOUN A **demonstration** of something is a talk by someone who shows you how to do it or how it works. ○ *a cookery demonstration* ○ [+ *of*] *demonstrations of new products*

2 NOUN A **demonstration of** a fact or situation is a clear proof of it. ○ [+ *of*] *This is a clear demonstration of how technology has changed.*

▶ COLLOCATIONS:
a demonstration **of** something
a demonstration of **support/power/unity/commitment**
a **practical/hands-on** demonstration

▶ SYNONYMS: explanation, proof

---

deny /dɪˈnaɪ/ (denies, denying, denied)　　ACADEMIC WORD

VERB When you **deny** something, you state that it is not true. ○ *Official advice denies the existence of any link between the MMR vaccine and autism.* ○ [+ *that*] *The government has denied that there was a plot to assassinate the president.* ○ [+ *v-ing*] *They all denied ever having seen her.*

▶ COLLOCATIONS:
deny a **claim/allegation/charge/suggestion**
deny **murdering/killing/assaulting** someone
vehemently/strenuously/categorically deny something

▶ SYNONYM: refute
▶ ANTONYMS: admit, confirm

de|ni|al /dɪˈnaɪəl/ (denials)

NOUN A **denial** of something is a statement that it is not true, does not exist, or did not happen. ○ *Despite official denials, the rumours still persist.* ○ [+ *of*] *The archbishop has issued a vigorous denial of these allegations.*

▶ COLLOCATIONS:
a denial **of** something
a denial of **wrongdoing/involvement**
a **categorical/vehement/official** denial
issue a denial

▶ ANTONYM: confirmation

---

de|part|ment　　ACADEMIC STUDY　BUSINESS　EDUCATION
/dɪˈpɑːtmənt/ (departments)

NOUN A **department** is one of the sections in an organization such as a government, business, or university. ○ [+ *of*] *the U.S. Department of Health* ○ *He moved to the sales department.* ○ *the geography department of Moscow University*

▶ COLLOCATIONS:
  a department **of** *something*
  a department of **medicine/biology/agriculture**
  a **sales/finance/planning/personnel** department
  a **fire/police/health/state/government** department
▶ SYNONYMS: section, division

de|part|men|tal /ˌdiːpɑːtˈmentəl/

ADJECTIVE **Departmental** is used to describe the activities, responsibilities, or possessions of a department in a government, company, or other organization. ○ *cuts in departmental budgets*

▶ COLLOCATIONS:
  a departmental **head/budget**
  departmental **spending**

---

de|pend /dɪˈpend/ (depends, depending, depended)

VERB If you **depend on** someone or something, you need them in order to be able to survive physically, financially, or emotionally. ○ [+ *on*] *a modest port town whose livelihood depends on the shipping industry* ○ [+ *on*] *Butterfly survival depends on complex interactions between biological and physical factors in the environment.*

▶ COLLOCATIONS:
  depend **on/upon** *something/someone*
  something's **success/future** depends on *something*
▶ SYNONYM: rely

de|pend|ent /dɪˈpendənt/

ADJECTIVE To be **dependent on** something or someone means to need them in order to succeed or be able to survive. ○ [+ *on*] *The local economy is overwhelmingly dependent on oil and gas extraction.* ○ *Just 26 per cent of households are married couples with dependent children.*

▶ COLLOCATIONS:
  dependent **on/upon** *something/someone*
  dependent on/upon **aid/exports/tourism**
  heavily/totally/entirely dependent
  financially/economically/chemically dependent
▶ SYNONYM: reliant
▶ ANTONYM: independent

de|pend|ence /dɪˈpendəns/

UNCOUNTABLE NOUN Your **dependence on** something or someone is your need for them in order to succeed or be able to survive. ○ [+ *on*] *the city's* *traditional dependence on tourism* ○ [+ on] *Nottingham's efforts to encourage cycle use and reduce dependence on the car*

▶ COLLOCATIONS:

dependence **on** *something/someone*

dependence on **oil/tourism/aid/drugs**

physical/emotional/psychological dependence

economic/financial/mutual dependence

heavy/excessive/continued/growing dependence

reduce/lessen/increase dependence

▶ SYNONYM: reliance

▶ ANTONYM: independence

---

de|pos|it /dɪˈpɒzɪt/　　　　GEOGRAPHY ECONOMICS
(deposits, depositing, deposited)

1 NOUN A **deposit** is a sum of money which is part of the full price of something, and which you pay when you agree to buy it. ○ *A £50 deposit is required when ordering, and the balance is due upon delivery.*

▶ COLLOCATIONS:

a deposit **of** £x

require/request/pay/refund a deposit

▶ SYNONYM: security

2 NOUN A **deposit** is a sum of money which is in a bank account or savings account, especially a sum which will be left there for some time. ○ *Bank customers are able to make deposits and withdraw money from automatic teller machines.*

▶ COLLOCATIONS:

a **bank** deposit

a deposit **slip/account**

make a deposit

▶ ANTONYM: withdrawal

3 NOUN A **deposit** is an amount of a substance that has been left somewhere as a result of a chemical or geological process. ○ *After 10 minutes the surplus material is washed away and any remaining deposit examined with ultra violet light.* ○ [+ of] *underground deposits of gold and diamonds*

▶ COLLOCATIONS:

a deposit **of** *something*

a **mineral/nickel/gold/peat/glacial** deposit

a **fatty/calcium** deposit

▶ SYNONYMS: sediment, silt

4 VERB If a substance **is deposited** somewhere, it is left there as a result of a chemical or geological process. ○ *The phosphate was deposited by the decay of marine microorganisms.*

▸ **COLLOCATIONS:**
deposited **by** *something*
sediment/silt is deposited
a **layer/mineral** is deposited

---

de|pres|sion /dɪ'preʃən/ (depressions) `ACADEMIC WORD` `MEDICINE`

NOUN Depression is a mental state in which you are sad and feel that you
cannot enjoy anything, because your situation is so difficult and unpleasant.
○ *Mr Thomas was suffering from depression.* ○ *Any prolonged or
severe depression should receive professional treatment.*

▸ **COLLOCATIONS:**
suffer from/cause/treat/alleviate depression
severe/chronic/deep/mild depression
post-natal/clinical/manic depression

▸ **SYNONYMS:** despair, melancholy

---

des|ti|na|tion /ˌdestɪ'neɪʃən/ (destinations)

NOUN The **destination** of someone or something is the place to which they
are going or being sent. ○ *Spain is still our most popular holiday destination.*
○ *Only half of the emergency supplies have reached their destination.*

▸ **COLLOCATIONS:**
a **tourist/holiday/travel/popular/favourite** destination
a **final/ultimate** destination

▸ **ANTONYM:** origin

---

de|tect /dɪ'tekt/ (detects, detecting, detected) `ACADEMIC WORD`

VERB To **detect** something means to find it or discover that it is present
somewhere by using equipment or making an investigation. ○ *a sensitive
piece of equipment used to detect radiation* ○ *Most skin cancers can be cured if
detected and treated early.*

▸ **COLLOCATIONS:**
detect a **virus/abnormality/tumour**
detect **cancer/radiation**
detect a **trace/signal/sign**
a **sensor/radar/test** detects *things*

▸ **SYNONYMS:** discover, reveal
▸ **ANTONYMS:** miss, overlook

de|tec|tion /dɪ'tekʃən/

UNCOUNTABLE NOUN Detection is the act of noticing or sensing something.
○ [+ *of*] *the early detection of breast cancer*

d

▶ **COLLOCATIONS:**
the detection **of** *something*
early detection
radar/radiation/cancer/fraud detection
a detection **device/method/system**
▶ **PHRASE:** detection and prevention
▶ **SYNONYM:** discovery

de|tec|tor /dɪˈtektə/ (detectors)

NOUN A **detector** is an instrument which is used to discover that something is present somewhere, or to measure how much of something there is. ○ *an airport metal detector* ○ *fire alarms and smoke detectors* ○ *infra-red motion detectors*
▶ **COLLOCATION:** a **metal/smoke/radiation/motion** detector

de|ter|mine /dɪˈtɜːmɪn/ (determines, determining, determined)

1 VERB If a particular factor **determines** the nature of a thing or event, it causes it to be of a particular kind. [FORMAL] ○ *IQ is strongly determined by genetic factors.* ○ [+ whether] *What determines whether you are a career success or a failure?*
▶ **COLLOCATIONS:**
determined **by** *something*
determine *something's* **outcome/fate/future/value**
genetically/biologically determined
▶ **SYNONYMS:** dictate, decide

2 VERB To **determine** a fact means to discover it as a result of investigation. [FORMAL] ○ [+ what] *The investigation will determine what really happened.* ○ *Testing needs to be done to determine the long-term effects on humans.* ○ [+ that] *Science has determined that the risk is very small.*
▶ **COLLOCATIONS:**
determine the **cause/extent** of *something*
determine **precisely/conclusively/exactly**
▶ **SYNONYMS:** identify, discover, ascertain

de|ter|mi|na|tion /dɪˌtɜːmɪˈneɪʃən/

NOUN ○ *the gene which is responsible for male sex determination* ○ [+ of] *a tool which can be used to help in the determination of a pay structure*

de|vel|op /dɪˈveləp/ (develops, developing, developed)

1 VERB When something **develops**, it grows or changes over a period of time and usually becomes more advanced, complete, or severe. ○ *It's hard to say at* *this stage how the market will develop.* ○ *[+ into] These clashes could develop into open warfare.* ○ *[V-ing] Society begins to have an impact on the developing child.*

2 VERB If you say that a country **develops**, you mean that it changes from being a poor agricultural country to being a rich industrial country.

3 VERB If you **develop** a business or industry, or if it **develops**, it becomes bigger and more successful. ○ *She won a grant to develop her own business.* ○ *Over the last few years tourism here has developed considerably.*

▸ **COLLOCATIONS:**
develop **into** *something*
a **child/baby/foetus/brain** develops
a **country/nation/company** develops
develop **rapidly/gradually/slowly**
highly/fully/newly developed

▸ **SYNONYMS:** build, grow, expand

→ see note at **acquire**

de|vel|op|ment /dɪˈveləpmənt/ (developments)

NOUN ○ *[+ of] an ideal system for studying the development of the embryo* ○ *Education is central to a country's economic development.*

▸ **COLLOCATIONS:**
the development **of** *something*
the development of **technology/weapons/products**
a **recent/future** development
economic/commercial/industrial/sustainable development
promote/encourage/monitor development
a development **programme/project**

▸ **PHRASE:** research and development

▸ **SYNONYMS:** growth, expansion

de|vel|op|men|tal /dɪˌveləpˈmentəl/

ADJECTIVE **Developmental** means relating to the development of someone or something. ○ *the emotional, educational, and developmental needs of the child* ○ *adults with developmental disabilities*

▸ **COLLOCATION:** a developmental **stage/disorder/disability**

---

de|vel|oped /dɪˈveləpt/ `GEOGRAPHY` `POLITICS`

ADJECTIVE If you talk about **developed** countries or the **developed** world, you mean the countries or the parts of the world that are wealthy and have many industries. ○ *The developed nations have to recognize the growing gap between rich and poor around the world.* ○ *This scarcity is inevitable in less developed countries.*

d

▶ **COLLOCATIONS:**
the developed **world**
a developed **nation/country/society/economy/market**
▶ **SYNONYMS:** prosperous, industrialized
▶ **ANTONYM:** undeveloped

---

de|vel|op|ing /dɪ'veləpɪŋ/ GEOGRAPHY POLITICS

ADJECTIVE If you talk about **developing** countries or the **developing** world, you mean the countries or the parts of the world that are poor and have few industries. ○ *In the developing world cigarette consumption is increasing.* ○ *Income disparities between industrial and developing countries will continue to grow.*

▶ **COLLOCATIONS:**
the developing **world**
a developing **nation/country**
▶ **SYNONYMS:** emergent, Third World

---

de|vice /dɪ'vaɪs/ **(devices)** ENGINEERING SCIENCE

NOUN A **device** is an object that has been invented for a particular purpose, for example for recording or measuring something. ○ [+ *that*] *an electronic device that protects your vehicle 24 hours a day* ○ *An explosive device had been left inside a container.*

▶ **COLLOCATIONS:**
a **mechanical/electronic/nuclear/explosive** device
a **hand-held/wireless/portable/storage** device
a **communication/safety/medical/tracking** device
use/install/attach a device
▶ **SYNONYMS:** machine, instrument, gadget

---

di|ag|nose /'daɪəgnəʊz, AM -nəʊs/ MEDICINE
(diagnoses, diagnosing, diagnosed)

VERB If someone or something **is diagnosed as** having a particular illness or problem, their illness or problem is identified. If an illness or problem **is diagnosed**, it is identified. ○ [+ *with*] *Almost a million people are diagnosed with colon cancer each year.* ○ [+ *as*] *In 1894 her illness was diagnosed as cancer.*

▶ **COLLOCATIONS:**
someone is diagnosed **with** *something*
someone/something is diagnosed **as** *something*
diagnosed with **cancer/diabetes/leukaemia**
diagnosed with a **disorder/disease/tumour**
diagnosed as **epileptic/diabetic**

di|ag|no|sis /ˌdaɪəg'nəʊsɪs/ (diagnoses)

NOUN **Diagnosis** is the discovery and naming of what is wrong with someone who is ill or with something that is not working properly. ○ *I need to have a second test to confirm the diagnosis.* ○ [+ *of*] *The technique could allow earlier and more accurate diagnosis of conditions ranging from ME to Alzheimer's disease.*

▶ COLLOCATIONS:
  a diagnosis **of** something
  a diagnosis of **cancer/schizophrenia/autism**
  make/confirm/give a diagnosis
  a **correct/accurate/inaccurate/initial/early** diagnosis

▶ RELATED WORD: prognosis

di|ago|nal /daɪ'ægənəl/

ADJECTIVE A **diagonal** line or movement goes in a sloping direction, for example, from one corner of a square across to the opposite corner.
  ○ *a pattern of diagonal lines*

di|ago|nal|ly /daɪ'ægənəli/

ADVERB ○ *Tsunamis initiated in South American areas approach the U.S. West Coast diagonally.* ○ [+ *opposite*] *He was seated diagonally opposite her.*

▶ COLLOCATIONS:
  diagonally **opposite** someone/something
  diagonally **across** something
  run diagonally
  cut/slice something diagonally

dia|gram /'daɪəgræm/ (diagrams)   `ACADEMIC STUDY` `MATHS`

NOUN A **diagram** is a simple drawing which consists mainly of lines and is used, for example, to explain how a machine works. ○ *Each tube enters the muscle wall of the uterus (see diagram on page 20).*

→ see note at **bar chart**

▶ COLLOCATIONS:
  a diagram **illustrates/shows** something
  draw a diagram
  a **schematic/explanatory/simple/complex** diagram

▶ SYNONYM: illustration

▶ RELATED WORD: graph

di|am|eter /daɪ'æmɪtə/ (diameters)   `MATHS`

NOUN The **diameter** of a round object is the length of a straight line that can be drawn across it, passing through the middle of it. ○ [+ *of*] *a tube less than* *a fifth of the diameter of a human hair* ○ *a length of 22-mm diameter steel pipe*

▶ **COLLOCATIONS:**
a diameter **of** *x cm*
x cm **in** diameter

▶ **RELATED WORDS:** radius, circumference

---

dig|it /ˈdɪdʒɪt/ (digits) [MATHS]

NOUN A **digit** is a written symbol for any of the ten numbers from 0 to 9. ○ *Her telephone number differs from mine by one digit.* ○ *Inflation is still in double digits.*

▶ **COLLOCATIONS:**
a **single** digit
binary/double/triple digits

▶ **SYNONYMS:** number, figure

---

di|lem|ma /daɪˈlemə, AM dɪl-/ (dilemmas)

NOUN A **dilemma** is a difficult situation in which you have to choose between two or more alternatives. ○ *Many Muslim women face the terrible dilemma of having to choose between employment and their Islamic garb.* ○ *The issue raises a moral dilemma.*

▶ **COLLOCATIONS:**
pose/raise/face/solve a dilemma
a **moral/ethical/policy/workplace** dilemma

▶ **SYNONYMS:** difficulty, problem, predicament

---

di|men|sion /daɪˈmenʃən, dɪm-/ (dimensions) [ACADEMIC WORD]

1 NOUN A particular **dimension** of something is a particular aspect of it.
○ [+ to] *There is a political dimension to the accusations.* ○ [+ to] *This adds a new dimension to our work.*

▶ **COLLOCATIONS:**
a dimension **of/to** *something*
a **moral/spiritual** dimension
a **different/important/added/extra** dimension
bring/add a dimension

▶ **SYNONYM:** aspect

2 NOUN A **dimension** is a measurement such as length, width, or height. If you talk about the **dimensions** of an object or place, you are referring to its size and proportions. ○ [+ of] *Drilling will continue on the site to assess the dimensions of the new oilfield.* ○ [+ of] *the grandiose dimensions of the building*

▶ **SYNONYMS:** scale, size, extent, measurement

dip /dɪp/ (dips, dipping, dipped)

VERB If the amount or level of something **dips**, it becomes smaller or lower, usually only for a short period of time. ○ [+ to] *Unemployment dipped to 6.9 per cent last month.* ○ *The president became more cautious as his popularity dipped.*

▶ COLLOCATIONS:
dip **below/to** x
dip **steeply/sharply/alarmingly**
temperatures/shares/ratings dip

▶ ANTONYM: rise

- **Dip** is also a noun. ○ [+ in] *the current dip in farm spending*

▶ COLLOCATIONS:
a dip **in** *something*
a dip in **profits/sales/revenue/confidence**

▶ ANTONYM: rise

EXTEND YOUR VOCABULARY

You use **drop** and **fall** to talk about a number, rate or level becoming less. ○ *Property prices have dropped/fallen considerably in the last three years.*

You can use **dip** to talk about something dropping slightly for a short period of time. ○ *The company's shares dipped initially, but ended the day little changed.*

You can use **plummet** to talk about something dropping very suddenly and dramatically. ○ *Prices plummeted by as much as 50 per cent.*

---

dis|ci|pline /ˈdɪsɪplɪn/ (disciplines) `ACADEMIC STUDY` `EDUCATION`

NOUN A **discipline** is a particular area of study, especially a subject of study in a college or university. [FORMAL] ○ *We're looking for people from a wide range of disciplines.* ○ *the study of economics as an academic discipline*

▶ SYNONYMS: subject, area, speciality

---

dis|crimi|nate /dɪsˈkrɪmɪneɪt/ `ACADEMIC WORD` `SOCIOLOGY`
(discriminates, discriminating, discriminated)

VERB To **discriminate against** a group of people or **in favour of** a group of people means to unfairly treat them worse or better than other groups. ○ [+ against] *They believe the law discriminates against women.* ○ [+ in favour of] *legislation which would discriminate in favour of racial minorities*

▶ COLLOCATIONS:
discriminate **against/in favour of** *someone*
unlawfully/unfairly/racially/systematically discriminate

dis|crimi|na|tion /dɪsˌkrɪmɪˈneɪʃən/

UNCOUNTABLE NOUN **Discrimination** is the practice of treating one person or group of people less fairly or less well than other people or groups. ○ *exempt from sex discrimination laws* ○ *[+ against] discrimination against immigrants* ○ *measures to counteract racial discrimination*

▶ **COLLOCATIONS:**
discrimination **against** someone
racial/age/employee discrimination
sex/gender discrimination
blatant/unlawful/positive discrimination
a discrimination **lawsuit/complaint/claim/law**

▶ **SYNONYMS:** prejudice, bias, unfairness, inequality

▶ **ANTONYMS:** fairness, equality

dis|or|der /ˌdɪsˈɔːdə/ (disorders) `MEDICINE`

NOUN A **disorder** is a problem or illness which affects someone's mind or body. ○ *a rare nerve disorder that can cause paralysis of the arms*

▶ **COLLOCATIONS:**
a **mental/psychiatric/stress/personality/eating** disorder
a **bowel/kidney/brain** disorder
inherit/diagnose/treat/suffer from a disorder

▶ **SYNONYMS:** complaint, illness

dis|play /dɪsˈpleɪ/ (displays, displaying, displayed) `ACADEMIC WORD`

VERB If you **display** a characteristic, quality, or emotion, you behave in a way which shows that you have it. ○ *Researchers have found that women can display symptoms of a heart attack up to a month in advance.* ○ *He has displayed remarkable courage in his efforts to reform the party.*

▶ **COLLOCATIONS:**
display a **symptom/sign/attitude/tendency**
display a **lack** of something
display **emotion/talent/courage**

▶ **SYNONYM:** show

▶ **ANTONYM:** hide

• **Display** is also a noun. ○ *[+ of] a public display of unity*

▶ **COLLOCATIONS:**
a display **of** something
a display of **emotion/affection/unity/solidarity**

▶ **SYNONYM:** show

dis|pose of /dɪsˈpəʊz əv, STRONG ɒv, AM ʌv/ ・ ACADEMIC WORD
(disposes of, disposing of, disposed of)

PHRASAL VERB If you **dispose of** something that you no longer want or need,
you throw it away. ○ *the safest means of disposing of nuclear waste* ○ *Engine oil
cannot be disposed of down drains.*

▶ **COLLOCATIONS:**
　dispose of **waste/rubbish/sewage**
　safely/illegally/easily dispose of *something*
▶ **ANTONYM:** keep

dis|pos|al /dɪsˈpəʊzəl/

UNCOUNTABLE NOUN Disposal is the act of getting rid of something that is no
longer wanted or needed. ○ [+ *of*] *methods for the permanent disposal of
radioactive wastes* ○ *waste disposal sites*

▶ **COLLOCATIONS:**
　the disposal **of** *something*
　the disposal of **waste/sewage/chemicals**
　waste/garbage/sewage/bomb disposal
　a disposal **site/expert**
▶ **SYNONYMS:** discarding, dumping

---

dis|prove /dɪsˈpruːv/ **(disproves, disproving, disproved, disproven)**

VERB To **disprove** an idea, belief, or theory means to show that it is not true.
○ *The statistics to prove or disprove his hypothesis will take years to collect.*
○ *opinion pieces claiming to disprove the global-warming theory*

→ see note at **criticize**
▶ **COLLOCATION:** disprove a **theory/myth/claim/belief**
▶ **SYNONYM:** refute
▶ **ANTONYM:** prove

---

dis|pute /dɪsˈpjuːt/ **(disputes, disputing, disputed)**

1 NOUN A **dispute** is an argument or disagreement between people or
groups. ○ [+ *with*] *They have won previous pay disputes with the government.*
○ [+ *between*] *a bitter dispute between the European Community and the United
States over subsidies to farmers*

▶ **COLLOCATIONS:**
　a dispute **over** *something*
　a dispute **with** *someone*
　a dispute **between** *groups*
　a **pay/custody/border** dispute

settle/resolve/solve/end/win a dispute
a **bitter/ongoing/long-running** dispute
▶ **SYNONYMS:** argument, disagreement, debate
▶ **ANTONYM:** agreement

2 VERB If you **dispute** a fact, statement, or theory, you say that it is incorrect
or untrue. ○ *He disputed the allegations.* ○ *[+ that] No one disputes that vitamin C
is of great value in the treatment of scurvy.* ○ *[+ whether] Some economists disputed
whether consumer spending is as strong as the figures suggest.*
▶ **COLLOCATIONS:**
dispute a **claim/assertion/allegation**
dispute **figures/facts**
hotly/vigorously/bitterly disputed
▶ **SYNONYMS:** argue, contest, refute

dis|rupt /dɪsˈrʌpt/ (disrupts, disrupting, disrupted)

VERB If someone or something **disrupts** an event, system, or process, they
cause difficulties that prevent it from continuing or operating in a normal
way. ○ *Anti-war protesters disrupted the debate.* ○ *The drought has severely
disrupted agricultural production.*
▶ **COLLOCATIONS:**
disrupt **supplies/production/traffic/proceedings**
severely/seriously disrupt *something*
▶ **SYNONYM:** interrupt

dis|rup|tion /dɪsˈrʌpʃən/ (disruptions)

NOUN ○ *[+ to] The strike is expected to cause delays and disruption to flights from
Britain.* ○ *[+ in] A stroke is the result of a disruption in the blood supply to the brain.*
▶ **COLLOCATIONS:**
a disruption **to/in/of** *something*
a disruption in/of **supply/production/activity**
cause/avoid/minimize disruption
severe/widespread disruption
▶ **SYNONYM:** interruption

dis|rup|tive /dɪˈsrʌptɪv/

ADJECTIVE ○ *Alcohol can produce violent, disruptive behavior.* ○ *[+ to] The process of
implementing these changes can be very disruptive to a small company.*
▶ **COLLOCATIONS:**
disruptive **to** *someone/something*
a disruptive **pupil/student/passenger/protest**
a disruptive **influence/effect**
highly/hugely/potentially disruptive
▶ **ANTONYMS:** stabilising, calming

---

dis|ser|ta|tion /ˌdɪsə'teɪʃən/ **(dissertations)** `ACADEMIC WORD`

NOUN A **dissertation** is a long formal piece of writing on a particular subject, especially for a university degree. ○ [+ on] *He is currently writing a dissertation on the Somali civil war.* ○ *For his doctoral dissertation he investigated fossil land snails.*

▶ **COLLOCATIONS:**
　a dissertation **on** *something*
　write/complete a dissertation
　a **doctoral/PhD/unpublished** dissertation

▶ **SYNONYM:** thesis

---

dis|tinct /dɪ'stɪŋkt/ `ACADEMIC WORD`

ADJECTIVE If something is **distinct from** something else of the same type, it is different or separate from it. ○ [+ from] *Engineering and technology are disciplines distinct from one another and from science.* ○ *This book is divided into two distinct parts.*

▶ **COLLOCATIONS:**
　distinct **from** *something*
　a distinct **category/type/species/entity**

▶ **SYNONYMS:** separate, discrete, diverse
▶ **ANTONYM:** connected

dis|tinc|tion /dɪ'stɪŋkʃən/ **(distinctions)**

NOUN A **distinction between** similar things is a difference. ○ [+ between] *There are obvious distinctions between the two wine-making areas.* ○ [+ between] *We have drawn an important distinction between the market value and the intrinsic value of a firm.*

▶ **COLLOCATIONS:**
　a distinction **between** *things*
　draw/make a distinction
　a **clear/sharp/subtle** distinction

▶ **SYNONYMS:** difference, differentiation, separation

dis|tinc|tive /dɪ'stɪŋktɪv/

ADJECTIVE Something that is **distinctive** has a special quality or feature which makes it easily recognizable and different from other things of the same type. ○ *the distinctive odour of chlorine* ○ *Thompson's distinctive prose style*

▶ **COLLOCATIONS:**
　a distinctive **style/characteristic/feature**
　a distinctive **flavour/aroma/voice**
　highly/visually distinctive

▶ **SYNONYMS:** unique, characteristic, idiosyncratic

dis|tinc|tive|ly /dɪˈstɪŋktɪvli/

ADVERB ○ the distinctively fragrant taste of elderflowers
▶ SYNONYM: uniquely

---

dis|tin|guish /dɪˈstɪŋgwɪʃ/ (distinguishes, distinguishing, distinguished)

VERB If you can **distinguish** one thing **from** another or **distinguish between** two things, you can see or understand how they are different. ○ [+ from] *Asteroids are distinguished from meteorites in terms of their visibility.* ○ [+ between] *Research suggests that babies learn to see by distinguishing between areas of light and dark.*

▶ COLLOCATIONS:
distinguish **between** things
distinguish *something* **from** *something*
reliably/easily/clearly distinguish

▶ SYNONYM: differentiate

---

dis|trib|ute /dɪˈstrɪbjuːt, ˈdɪstrɪbjuːt/ `ACADEMIC WORD` `BUSINESS`
(distributes, distributing, distributed)

1 VERB If you **distribute** things, you hand them or deliver them to a number of people. ○ *Students shouted slogans and distributed leaflets.* ○ [+ to] *Soldiers are working to distribute food to the refugees.* ○ [+ among] *Profits are distributed among the policyholders.*

2 VERB When a company **distributes** goods, it supplies them to the shops or businesses that sell them. ○ *We didn't understand how difficult it was to distribute a national paper.* ○ *firms that manufacture and distribute DVDs*

▶ COLLOCATIONS:
distribute *something* **to/among** *people*
distribute **leaflets/flyers/pamphlets/copies/aid/food**

▶ SYNONYMS: disseminate, issue
▶ ANTONYM: collect

dis|trib|ut|ed /dɪˈstrɪbjuːtɪd/

ADJECTIVE If things are **distributed** throughout an area, object, or group, they exist throughout it. ○ [+ throughout] *These cells are widely distributed throughout the body.* ○ [+ in] *Distant galaxies are not as evenly distributed in space as theory predicts.*

▶ COLLOCATIONS:
distributed **throughout/in** *something/somewhere*
evenly/equitably/widely/unevenly/randomly distributed

▶ SYNONYM: spread

dis|tri|bu|tion /ˌdɪstrɪˈbjuːʃən/ (distributions)

1 UNCOUNTABLE NOUN The **distribution** of things involves giving or delivering them to a number of people or places. ○ [+ of] *the council which controls the distribution of foreign aid* ○ *emergency food distribution*

2 NOUN The **distribution** of something is how much of it there is in each place or at each time, or how much of it each person has. ○ [+ of] *a more equitable distribution of wealth* ○ [+ of] *the geographical distribution of parasitic diseases such as malaria*

▶ **COLLOCATIONS:**
the distribution **of** *something*
the distribution of **wealth/income/aid/resources**
rigid/unequal/equitable distribution
income/capital/cash/food distribution
a distribution **channel/system/network**

▶ **SYNONYMS:** allocation, dissemination, spread

▶ **ANTONYM:** collection

---

doc|tor|ate /ˈdɒktərət/ (doctorates)   EDUCATION   ACADEMIC STUDY

NOUN A **doctorate** is the highest degree awarded by a university. ○ [+ in] *He obtained his doctorate in Social Psychology.*

▶ **COLLOCATIONS:**
a doctorate **in** *something*
a doctorate in **physics/sociology/linguistics**
award/earn/receive a doctorate
an **honorary** doctorate

▶ **SYNONYMS:** PhD, higher degree

doc|tor|al /ˈdɒktərəl/

ADJECTIVE A **doctoral** thesis or piece of research is written or done in order to obtain a doctor's degree. ○ *a doctoral student in mathematics*

▶ **COLLOCATIONS:**
a doctoral **thesis/dissertation/student/degree**
doctoral **research**

▶ **SYNONYM:** postgraduate

---

do|mes|tic /dəˈmestɪk/   ACADEMIC WORD   POLITICS   SOCIOLOGY

1 ADJECTIVE Domestic political activities, events, and situations happen or exist within one particular country. ○ *over 100 domestic flights a day to 15 U.K. destinations* ○ *sales in the domestic market*

▶ **COLLOCATIONS:**
domestic **politics/demand/production/competition**
the domestic **market/economy**
a domestic **issue/flight**

▶ **SYNONYM:** internal

▶ **ANTONYMS:** foreign, international

2 ADJECTIVE Domestic means relating to or concerned with the home and family. ○ *a plan for sharing domestic chores* ○ *the sale of furniture and domestic appliances* ○ *victims of domestic violence*

▶ **COLLOCATIONS:**
a domestic **chore/servant/appliance**
domestic **violence**

▶ **SYNONYM:** household

▶ **ANTONYM:** industrial

---

domi|nate /ˈdɒmɪneɪt/ ACADEMIC WORD
(dominates, dominating, dominated)

VERB To **dominate** a situation means to be the most powerful or important person or thing in it. ○ *Microsoft's products dominate the global market for computer operating systems.* ○ *countries where life is dominated by war*

▶ **COLLOCATIONS:**
dominated **by** *someone/something*
dominate a **conversation/discussion**
dominate a **market/campaign/agenda**

▶ **SYNONYMS:** lead, overshadow, govern

domi|nant /ˈdɒmɪnənt/

ADJECTIVE Someone or something that is **dominant** is more powerful, successful, influential, or noticeable than other people or things. ○ *a change which would maintain his party's dominant position in Scotland* ○ *She was a dominant figure in the French film industry.*

▶ **COLLOCATIONS:**
a dominant **theme/ideology/feature**
a dominant **position/role/culture**
politically/economically/socially/overwhelmingly dominant

▶ **SYNONYMS:** pre-eminent, leading, powerful

▶ **ANTONYMS:** inferior, subordinate

---

draft /drɑːft, dræft/ **(drafts)** ACADEMIC WORD ACADEMIC STUDY

NOUN A **draft** is an early version of a piece of writing. ○ *a draft report from a major U.S. university* ○ [+ *of*] *a final draft of an essay*

▶ **COLLOCATIONS:**
a draft **of** *something*
a draft of a **paper/manuscript/chapter/essay**
a draft **report/bill/document**
a **rough/first/final** draft
write/type/prepare/compose/revise a draft

▶ **SYNONYM:** version

---

dra|mat|ic /drəˈmætɪk/ `ACADEMIC WORD`

ADJECTIVE A **dramatic** change or event happens suddenly and is very noticeable and surprising. ○ *A fifth year of drought is expected to have dramatic effects on the California economy.* ○ *This policy has led to a dramatic increase in our prison populations.*

▶ **COLLOCATIONS:**
a dramatic **effect/impact/change/shift/improvement**
a dramatic **increase/rise/decrease/decline/fall**

▶ **SYNONYMS:** sudden, striking

▶ **ANTONYM:** gradual

dra|mati|cal|ly /drəˈmætɪkli/

ADVERB ○ *At speeds above 50mph, serious injuries dramatically increase.*
○ *the construction of a dam which will dramatically alter the landscape*

▶ **COLLOCATIONS:**
increase/rise/vary/grow dramatically
change/alter/reduce/improve *something* dramatically

▶ **SYNONYMS:** suddenly, strikingly

▶ **ANTONYM:** gradually

> **EXTEND YOUR VOCABULARY**
>
> There are a range of different adjectives and adverbs you can use to describe changes and trends. You use **dramatic/dramatically** to describe a big change that happens very suddenly. ○ *a dramatic shift in public opinion*
>
> You can use **rapid/rapidly** to emphasize that something changes very quickly. ○ *a rapidly growing population*
>
> You can use **significant/significantly**, **noteable/notably** or **marked/markedly** to describe a change that is big enough to be important or to have an effect. ○ *Birth rates have dropped significantly over the past 30 years.* ○ *a marked improvement in standards of living*
>
> You can describe a sudden increase or decrease, especially as shown on a graph, as **sharp** or **steep**. ○ *a sharp/steep rise in unemployment*

dras|tic /ˈdræstɪk/

1 ADJECTIVE If you have to take **drastic** action in order to solve a problem, you have to do something extreme and basic to solve it. ○ *Drastic measures are needed to clean up the profession.* ○ *He's not going to do anything drastic about economic policy.*

2 ADJECTIVE A **drastic** change is a very great change. ○ *a drastic reduction in the numbers of people dying*

▶ **COLLOCATIONS:**
drastic **measures/steps/cutbacks/action**
a drastic **change/reduction/decline**
▶ **SYNONYMS:** radical, severe, extreme
▶ **ANTONYM:** slight

dras|ti|cal|ly /ˈdræstɪkli/

ADVERB ○ *As a result, services have been drastically reduced.*

▶ **COLLOCATIONS:**
drastically **reduced/altered/cut/changed**
drop/decline/improve drastically
▶ **SYNONYMS:** radically, severely, extremely
▶ **ANTONYM:** slightly

du|ra|tion /djʊˈreɪʃən, AM dʊr-/ ACADEMIC WORD

UNCOUNTABLE NOUN The **duration of** an event or state is the time during which it happens or exists. ○ [+ of] *The result was an increase in the average duration of prison sentences.* ○ *Courses are of two years' duration.*

▶ **COLLOCATIONS:**
the duration **of** *something*
the duration of a **war**
x **hours'/minutes'/years'** duration
a **long/short/average/maximum** duration
▶ **SYNONYMS:** extent, period, term

Ee

ease /iːz/ (eases, easing, eased)

VERB If something unpleasant **eases** or if you **ease** it, it is reduced in degree, speed, or intensity. ○ *Tensions had eased.* ○ *I gave him some brandy to ease the pain.* ○ [V-ing] *editorials calling for the easing of sanctions*

▶ **COLLOCATIONS:**
   tension/pain/pressure/concern eases
   a **burden/restriction/crisis** eases
   ease **sanctions**
   greatly/considerably/gently/slightly eased

▶ **SYNONYMS:** reduce, diminish, relax

▶ **ANTONYM:** increase

ecol|ogy /ɪˈkɒlədʒi/ (ecologies)   BIOLOGY GEOGRAPHY

UNCOUNTABLE NOUN Ecology is the study of the relationships between plants, animals, people, and their environment, and the balances between these relationships. ○ *a senior lecturer in ecology* ○ *a growing interest in conservation and ecology*

eco|logi|cal /ˌiːkəˈlɒdʒɪkəl/

ADJECTIVE ○ *Large dams have harmed Siberia's delicate ecological balance.* ○ *ecological disasters, such as the destruction of rainforest*

▶ **COLLOCATIONS:**
   an ecological **disaster/catastrophe**
   the ecological **balance**

▶ **SYNONYM:** environmental

eco|logi|cal|ly /ˌiːkəˈlɒdʒɪkli/

ADVERB ○ *Running is economical and ecologically sound.*

▶ **COLLOCATIONS:**
   ecologically **sound/sustainable/friendly/responsible**
   ecologically **sensitive/aware**

▶ **SYNONYM:** environmentally

ecolo|gist /ɪˈkɒlədʒɪst/ (ecologists)

NOUN An **ecologist** is a person who studies ecology. ○ *Ecologists argue that the benefits of treating sewage with disinfectants are doubtful.*

econo|my /ɪˈkɒnəmi/

ACADEMIC WORD BUSINESS ECONOMICS

(economies)

NOUN An **economy** is the system according to which the money, industry, and trade of a country or region are organized. ○ *Zimbabwe boasts Africa's most industrialized economy.* ○ *the rate at which the U.S. economy grows*

▶ COLLOCATIONS:

the **local/global/national/rural/industrial** economy

a **booming/strong/sluggish/weak** economy

an economy **grows/shrinks**

eco|nom|ic /ˌiːkəˈnɒmɪk, ˌek-/

ADJECTIVE Economic means concerned with the organization of the money, industry, and trade of a country, region, or society. ○ *Poland's radical economic reforms* ○ *The pace of economic growth is picking up.*

▶ COLLOCATIONS:

economic **growth/recovery/development**

economic **reform/policy/activity/aid**

an economic **downturn/crisis/slowdown**

the economic **situation/impact**

an economic **adviser**

▶ SYNONYMS: financial, monetary

eco|nomi|cal /ˌiːkəˈnɒmɪkəl, ˌek-/

ADJECTIVE Something that is **economical** does not require a lot of money to operate. For example a car that only uses a small amount of petrol is **economical**. ○ *the most economical method of extracting essential oils from plant materials*

▶ COLLOCATION: an economical **method/solution/alternative/option**

▶ PHRASE: efficient and economical

▶ SYNONYMS: cost-effective, inexpensive

▶ ANTONYMS: uneconomical, expensive, wasteful

> **USAGE: economic** or **economical**?
>
> Be careful not to confuse these two adjectives. **Economic** describes something related to the economy. ○ *the government's economic policies*
>
> Something that is **economical** is cost-effective. ○ *the most effective and economical use of resources*

eco|nomi|cal|ly /ˌiːkəˈnɒmɪkli, ˌek-/

ADVERB ○ *an economically depressed area* ○ *Small English orchards can hardly compete economically with larger French ones.*

▶ **COLLOCATIONS:**
prosper/benefit/grow/survive economically
suffer/struggle/develop economically
economically **viable/feasible/sustainable**
economically **dependent/disadvantaged/depressed/inefficient**

eco|nom|ics /ˌiːkəˈnɒmɪks, ˌek-/

1 **UNCOUNTABLE NOUN** **Economics** is the study of the way in which money, industry, and trade are organized in a society. ○ *He gained a first class Honours degree in economics.* ○ *having previously studied economics and fine art*

▶ **COLLOCATION:** an economics **professor/degree/department**

▶ **PHRASE:** economics and politics

2 **UNCOUNTABLE NOUN** The **economics** of a society or industry is the system of organizing money and trade in it. ○ *a radical free-market economics policy* ○ [+ of] *the economics of the third world*

▶ **COLLOCATIONS:**
the economics **of** *somewhere/something*
the economics of **industry/business**
Keynesian/classical/experimental/free-market economics
development/market economics
an economics **correspondent/editor/policy**

▶ **SYNONYM:** finance

econo|mist /ɪˈkɒnəmɪst/ (economists)

NOUN An **economist** is a person who studies, teaches, or writes about economics. ○ *the chief economist of the World Bank* ○ *few economists expect to see a rise this year*

▶ **COLLOCATIONS:**
a **leading/chief/senior** economist
market/health economists
economists **say/believe/expect/predict/forecast/warn**

---

edit /ˈedɪt/ (edits, editing, edited) `ACADEMIC STUDY` `ACADEMIC WORD` `MEDIA`

1 **VERB** If you **edit** a text such as an article or a book, you correct and adapt it so that it is suitable for publishing. ○ *The majority of contracts give the publisher the right to edit a book after it's done.* ○ *an edited version of the speech*

2 **VERB** If you **edit** a book or a series of books, you collect several pieces of writing by different authors and prepare them for publishing. ○ *This collection of essays is edited by Ellen Knight.* ○ *She has edited the media studies quarterly, Screen.*

▶ **COLLOCATIONS:**
edited **by** *someone*
heavily/carefully edited

an edited **version/extract**
edit a **magazine/book/journal/collection/anthology**
▶ **SYNONYMS:** revise, correct
▶ **RELATED WORD:** proofread

edi|tor /'edɪtə/ (editors)

NOUN An **editor** is a person who collects pieces of writing by different authors and prepares them for publication in a book or a series of books. ○ [+ *of*] *Michael Rosen is the editor of the anthology.* ○ *Editor's Introduction to the British edition*

▶ **COLLOCATIONS:**
an editor **of** *something*
an editor's **decision/note**
a **managing/commissioning** editor

ACADEMIC WRITING: Abbreviations in reference lists

A number of abbreviations are commonly used in reference lists and bibliographies.

Ed. is the abbreviation for the **editor** of a book which is a collection of pieces by different writers. The plural form is **eds.**. ○ *Smith, J. and Jones, M (eds.) 2004 Issues in Global English*

Vol. is the abbreviation for **volume** where a book or journal is one of a number published with the same title. ○ *Modern Language Journal Vol. 4* The usual abbreviation for **page** is **p.** and for **pages** is **pp.** ○ *See Lewis 2008 pp.251-255*

---

edi|tion /ɪ'dɪʃən/ (editions)

NOUN An **edition** is a particular version of a book, magazine, or newspaper that is printed at one time. ○ *A paperback edition is now available at bookshops.* ○ [+ *of*] *They brought out a special edition of The Skulker.*

▶ **COLLOCATIONS:**
an edition **of** *something*
a **special/new/limited/revised** edition
the **first/second/latest** edition
a **print/online/electronic** edition
a **collector's/paperback/hardback** edition

---

elect /ɪ'lekt/ (elects, electing, elected)   POLITICS

VERB When people **elect** someone, they choose that person to represent them, by voting for them. ○ *The people of the Philippines have voted to elect a new president.* ○ *Manchester College elected him Principal in 1956.* ○ [+ *as*]

The country is about to take a radical departure by electing a woman as its new president.

▶ COLLOCATIONS:
elect *someone* **as** *something*
elect a **president/government/leader/official**

elec|tion /ɪˈlekʃən/ (elections)

NOUN ○ *the first fully free elections for more than fifty years* ○ *The final election results will be announced on Friday.*

▶ COLLOCATIONS:
a **general/presidential/local/national** election
hold/call/win/lose an election
an election **campaign/victory**
election **results**

elec|tor|ate /ɪˈlektərət/ (electorates)

NOUN The **electorate** of a country or area is all the people in it who have the right to vote in an election. ○ *He has the backing of almost a quarter of the electorate.* ○ *the Maltese electorate*

▶ COLLOCATIONS:
convince/divide/split the electorate
the electorate **vote/decide**

▶ SYNONYM: voters

el|ement /ˈelɪmənt/ (elements)   ACADEMIC WORD   CHEMISTRY

1 NOUN The different **elements** of a situation, activity, or process are the different parts of it. ○ [+ of] *The exchange of prisoners of war was one of the key elements of the U.N.'s peace plan.* ○ [+ of] *The plot has all the elements not only of romance but of high drama.*

▶ COLLOCATIONS:
an element **of** *something*
an element of **surprise/truth/luck/danger/uncertainty/risk**
contain/include/add an element
a **key/important/essential/main/vital/basic** element
certain/core elements

▶ SYNONYMS: part, constituent, component

2 NOUN An **element** is a substance such as gold, oxygen, or carbon that consists of only one type of atom. ○ *an essential trace element for animals and man* ○ *the minerals and elements in sea water*

▶ COLLOCATION: a **trace/chemical/radioactive** element

▶ RELATED WORD: compound

eli|gible /ˈelɪdʒɪbəl/

ADJECTIVE Someone who is **eligible to** do something is qualified or able to do it, for example because they are old enough. ○ [+ to-inf] *Almost half the population are eligible to vote in today's election.* ○ [+ for] *You could be eligible for a university scholarship.*

▶ **COLLOCATIONS:**
eligible **for** *something*
eligible for **parole/release/compensation/assistance**
eligible for a **grant/refund/bonus/benefit**
eligible to **vote/apply/enter/play/participate/compete**
automatically/potentially/currently eligible
an eligible **voter/employee/patient**

▶ **SYNONYMS:** entitled, qualified

▶ **ANTONYM:** ineligible

eli|gibil|ity /ˌelɪdʒəˈbɪlɪti/

UNCOUNTABLE NOUN ○ [+ for] *The rules covering eligibility for benefits changed in the 1980s.* ○ *Each worker must meet various eligibility requirements.*

▶ **COLLOCATIONS:**
eligibility **for** *something*
eligibility for **credit/benefit/parole**
an eligibility **requirement/criterion/rule**
determine/establish *someone's* eligibility

▶ **ANTONYM:** ineligibility

---

elimi|nate /ɪˈlɪmɪneɪt/ (eliminates, eliminating, eliminated) `ACADEMIC WORD`

VERB To **eliminate** something, especially something you do not want or need, means to remove it completely. [FORMAL] ○ *The Sex Discrimination Act has not eliminated discrimination in employment.* ○ [+ from] *If you think you may be allergic to a food or drink, eliminate it from your diet.*

▶ **COLLOCATIONS:**
eliminate *something* **from** *something*
eliminate a **need/risk/requirement/deficit/threat/possibility**
eliminate **waste**
effectively eliminate *something*

▶ **SYNONYMS:** remove, abolish

elimi|na|tion /ɪˌlɪmɪˈneɪʃən/

UNCOUNTABLE NOUN ○ [+ of] *the prohibition and elimination of chemical weapons* ○ [+ of] *complete elimination of halitosis is usually possible*

▶ **COLLOCATIONS:**
the elimination **of** *something*

the elimination of **weapons/discrimination/waste**
the elimination of **subsidies/taxes/poverty**
▶ SYNONYMS: removal, abolition, eradication

---

emerge /ɪˈmɜːdʒ/ (emerges, emerging, emerged)   `ACADEMIC WORD`

1 VERB To **emerge** means to come out from an enclosed or dark space such as
a room or a vehicle, or from a position where you could not be seen.
○ [+ from] *like a butterfly emerging from a chrysalis* ○ [V-ing] *holes made by the
emerging adult beetle*

▶ COLLOCATIONS:
emerge **from** *somewhere*
emerge from **obscurity/hibernation/darkness**
emerge from a **chrysalis/cocoon**
▶ SYNONYM: appear
▶ ANTONYM: disappear

2 VERB If a fact or result **emerges** from a period of thought, discussion, or
investigation, it becomes known as a result of it. ○ *the growing corruption that
has emerged in the past few years* ○ [+ that] *It soon emerged that neither the July nor
August mortgage repayment had been collected.*

▶ COLLOCATIONS:
details emerge
evidence emerges
a **pattern/picture** emerges

3 VERB If someone or something **emerges as** a particular thing, they become
recognized as that thing. ○ [+ as] *Vietnam has emerged as the world's third-
biggest rice exporter.* ○ *New leaders have emerged.*

▶ COLLOCATIONS:
emerge **as** *something*
emerge as a **favourite/victor/winner/candidate/contender**
→ see note at **commence**

emer|gence /ɪˈmɜːdʒəns/

UNCOUNTABLE NOUN The **emergence of** something is the process or event of
its coming into existence. ○ [+ of] *the emergence of new democracies in East and
Central Europe* ○ [+ of] *measures that help to prevent the emergence of future
generations of terrorists*

▶ COLLOCATIONS:
the emergence **of** *something*
the **sudden/recent/gradual/rapid** emergence
prevent the emergence of *something*
▶ SYNONYMS: arrival, surfacing, rise, appearance

emi|grate /ˈemɪɡreɪt/ (emigrates, emigrating, emigrated)

VERB If you **emigrate**, you leave your own country to live in another country.
○ [+ to] He emigrated to Belgium. ○ [+ from] The family emigrated from England to Canada in 1924. ○ They planned to emigrate.

▶ **COLLOCATION:** emigrate **from/to** somewhere
▶ **SYNONYMS:** move, relocate, migrate
▶ **RELATED WORD:** immigrate

emi|gra|tion /ˌemɪˈɡreɪʃən/

UNCOUNTABLE NOUN ○ [+ of] the huge emigration of workers to the West ○ The Spanish Civil War provoked another wave of emigration.

▶ **COLLOCATIONS:**
the emigration **of** people
halt/stop/allow/encourage/force/increase emigration
mass/illegal/free/massive emigration
emigration **law/policy**
▶ **SYNONYMS:** departure, migration
▶ **RELATED WORD:** immigration

emi|grant /ˈemɪɡrənt/ (emigrants)

NOUN An **emigrant** is a person who has left their own country to live in another country. ○ the departure of emigrants to America

▶ **COLLOCATIONS:**
a **Jewish/Irish** emigrant
a **prospective/would-be** emigrant
▶ **RELATED WORD:** immigrant

> **EXTEND YOUR VOCABULARY**
>
> You use **emigrate/emigration/emigrant** when you are talking about people leaving a country. ○ thousands of Irish emigrants who left Ireland after the 1846-49 famine
>
> You use **immigrate/immigration/immigrant** when you are talking about people coming into a country. ○ a decrease in the levels of illegal immigration into the US
>
> You can use **migrate/migration/migrant** to talk more generally about the movement of people or animals from place to place. ○ Many of the city's construction workers are migrants from the countryside. ○ the spring migration of the snow geese

emit /ɪˈmɪt/ (emits, emitting, emitted) `SCIENCE`

VERB If something **emits** heat, light, gas, or a smell, it produces it and sends it out by means of a physical or chemical process. [FORMAL] ○ The new device *emits a powerful circular column of light.* ○ *the amount of carbon dioxide emitted*

▶ COLLOCATIONS:
emit **radiation**
emit a **signal/ray/pollutant/particle**
a **plant/engine/phone** emits *something*

▶ SYNONYM: release

emis|sion /ɪ'mɪʃən/ (emissions)

NOUN An **emission of** something such as gas or radiation is the release of it into the atmosphere. [FORMAL] ○ [+ *of*] *The emission of gases such as carbon dioxide should be stabilised.* ○ [+ *from*] *Sulfur emissions from steel mills become acid rain.*

▶ COLLOCATIONS:
the emission **of/from** *something*
the emission of **gas/radiation/chemicals**
reduce/cut/limit/control emissions
harmful/toxic/CO2/greenhouse-gas emissions
global/industrial emissions
emission **reduction/control/standards/levels**

▶ SYNONYMS: release, leakage

em|pha|sis /'emfəsɪs/ (emphases) `ACADEMIC WORD`

NOUN **Emphasis** is special or extra importance that is given to an activity or to a part or aspect of something. ○ [+ *on*] *Too much emphasis is placed on research.* ○ [+ *on*] *Grant puts a special emphasis on weather in his paintings.*

▶ COLLOCATIONS:
an emphasis **on** *something*
place/put/add emphasis
great/particular emphasis
heavy/strong/special emphasis

▶ SYNONYMS: importance, attention, weight

em|pha|size /'emfəsaɪz/ (emphasizes, emphasizing, emphasized)

VERB To **emphasize** something means to indicate that it is particularly important or true, or to draw special attention to it. [in BRIT, also use **emphasise**] ○ [+ *that*] *But it's also been emphasized that no major policy changes can be expected.* ○ [+ *how*] *Discuss pollution with your child, emphasizing how nice a clean street, lawn, or park looks.*

▶ COLLOCATIONS:
emphasize the **importance/need**
repeatedly/strongly emphasize *something*

▶ PHRASE: cannot emphasize enough

▶ SYNONYM: stress

em|ploy /ɪmˈplɔɪ/ (employs, employing, employed)

VERB If you **employ** certain methods, materials, or expressions, you use them. ○ *the vocabulary that she employs* ○ [+ *in*] *the approaches and methods employed in the study*

▶ **COLLOCATIONS:**
employ something **in/as** something
employ a **technique/method/strategy**

▶ **SYNONYMS:** use, utilize

en|coun|ter /ɪnˈkaʊntə/　ACADEMIC WORD
(encounters, encountering, encountered)

VERB If you **encounter** problems or difficulties, you experience them. ○ *Every day of our lives we encounter stresses of one kind or another.* ○ *Environmental problems they found in Poland were among the worst they encountered.*

▶ **COLLOCATIONS:**
encounter **resistance/opposition**
encounter a **difficulty/problem**

▶ **SYNONYMS:** meet, experience, face

en|hance /ɪnˈhɑːns, -ˈhæns/　ACADEMIC WORD
(enhances, enhancing, enhanced)

VERB To **enhance** something means to improve its value, quality, or attractiveness. ○ *They'll be keen to enhance their reputation abroad.* ○ *The superb sets are enhanced by Bobby Crossman's marvellous costumes.*

▶ **COLLOCATIONS:**
enhanced **by** something
enhance the **quality/value/performance** of something
enhance someone's **reputation**
digitally/surgically/further enhance something

▶ **SYNONYMS:** improve, enrich

en|hance|ment /ɪnˈhɑːnsmənt, -ˈhæns-/ (enhancements)

NOUN The **enhancement of** something is the improvement of it in relation to its value, quality, or attractiveness. [FORMAL] ○ [+ *of*] *Music is merely an enhancement to the power of her words.* ○ [+ *of*] *the enhancement of the human condition*

▶ **COLLOCATIONS:**
the enhancement **of** something
minor/cosmetic enhancement
productivity/performance/security enhancement
image/breast/career enhancement

▶ **SYNONYM:** improvement

en|sure /ɪnˈʃʊə/ (ensures, ensuring, ensured) `ACADEMIC WORD`

VERB To **ensure** something, or to **ensure that** something happens, means to make certain that it happens. [FORMAL] ○ [+ that] *Britain's negotiators had ensured that the treaty was a significant change in direction.* ○ [+ that] *Ensure that it is written into your contract.*

▶ COLLOCATIONS:
ensure the **safety/survival/stability/success** of *something*
ensure **fairness/accuracy/integrity**

▶ SYNONYM: guarantee

equa|tion /ɪˈkweɪʒən/ (equations) `ACADEMIC WORD` `MATHS` `SCIENCE`

NOUN An **equation** is a mathematical statement saying that two amounts or values are the same, for example 6x4=12x2. ○ *He solved complex equations in his head.*

▶ COLLOCATIONS:
solve an equation
a **mathematical/simple** equation

▶ SYNONYM: formula

equiva|lent /ɪˈkwɪvələnt/ (equivalents) `ACADEMIC WORD`

NOUN If one amount or value is **the equivalent of** another, they are the same.
○ [+ of] *The equivalent of two tablespoons of polyunsaturated oils is ample each day.*
○ [+ of] *Even the cheapest car costs the equivalent of 70 years' salary for a government worker.*

▶ COLLOCATIONS:
the equivalent **of** something
the equivalent of a **pound/pint**
a **modern/modern-day** equivalent
a **cinematic/literary/musical/visual** equivalent
the **male/female** equivalent

▶ SYNONYM: equal

equiva|lence /ɪˈkwɪvələns/

UNCOUNTABLE NOUN If there is **equivalence** between two things, they have the same use, function, size, or value. ○ [+ of] *the equivalence of science and rationality* ○ [+ between] *The effect is a moral equivalence between the two.*

▶ COLLOCATION: equivalence **of/between** things
▶ SYNONYM: equality

era /ˈɪərə/ (eras) `HISTORY`

NOUN You can refer to a period of history or a long period of time as an **era** when you want to draw attention to a particular feature or quality that it has. ○ *the nuclear era* ○ [+ of] *It was an era of austerity.*

e

▸ COLLOCATIONS:
an era **of** *something*
enter/mark/end an era
an era **dawns**
a **new/modern/golden** era
an era of **peace/co-operation/prosperity**
▸ SYNONYMS: age, time, period

---

erode /ɪˈrəʊd/ **(erodes, eroding, eroded)** [ACADEMIC WORD] [GEOGRAPHY]

VERB If rock or soil **erodes** or **is eroded** by the weather, sea, or wind, it cracks and breaks so that it is gradually destroyed. ○ *By 1980, Miami beach had all but totally eroded.* ○ *Once exposed, soil is quickly eroded by wind and rain.*

▸ COLLOCATIONS:
eroded **by** *something*
a **cliff/coastline** is eroded
soil/rock is eroded
steadily/gradually/seriously eroded
▸ SYNONYMS: disintegrate, crumble

ero|sion /ɪˈrəʊʒən/

UNCOUNTABLE NOUN ○ *As their roots are strong and penetrating, they prevent erosion.* ○ *[+ of] erosion of the river valleys* ○ *soil erosion*

▸ COLLOCATIONS:
erosion **of** *something*
erosion of **soil**
coastal/beach erosion
prevent/cause erosion
▸ SYNONYMS: disintegration, weathering

---

es|tab|lish /ɪˈstæblɪʃ/ **(establishes, establishing, established)** [ACADEMIC WORD]

1 VERB If someone **establishes** something such as an organization, a type of activity, or a set of rules, they create it or introduce it in such a way that it is likely to last for a long time. ○ *The U.N. has established detailed criteria for who should be allowed to vote.* ○ *The School was established in 1989 by an Italian professor.*

→ see note at **launch**
▸ SYNONYM: found

2 VERB If you **establish that** something is true, you discover facts that show that it is definitely true. [FORMAL] ○ *[+ that] Medical tests established that she was not their own child.* ○ *[+ how] It will be essential to establish how the money is being spent.* ○ *An autopsy was being done to establish the cause of death.*

▶ **COLLOCATIONS:**
establish a **link/relationship**
firmly/quickly establish *something*
▶ **SYNONYMS:** ascertain, prove, confirm

es|tab|lish|ment /ɪˈstæblɪʃmənt/ **(establishments)**

1 NOUN The **establishment of** an organization or system is the act of creating it or beginning it. [FORMAL] ○ [+ *of*] *His ideas influenced the establishment of National Portrait Galleries in London and Edinburgh.* ○ [+ *of*] *the establishment of diplomatic relations*

▶ **COLLOCATIONS:**
the establishment **of** *something*
announce/support/propose/oppose the establishment
the establishment of a **state**
the establishment of **relations**
▶ **SYNONYMS:** creation, formation

2 NOUN An **establishment** is a shop, business, or organization occupying a particular building or place. [FORMAL] ○ *a scientific research establishment* ○ *shops and other commercial establishments*

▶ **COLLOCATIONS:**
a **political/medical/educational** establishment
a **literary/scientific/religious** establishment
▶ **SYNONYMS:** office, building

---

eth|nic /ˈeθnɪk/ `ACADEMIC WORD`

ADJECTIVE **Ethnic** means connected with or relating to different racial or cultural groups of people. ○ *a survey of Britain's ethnic minorities* ○ *ethnic tensions*

▶ **COLLOCATIONS:**
an ethnic **minority/group/community**
ethnic **cleansing/conflict/violence/tensions**

eth|nic|ity /eθˈnɪsɪti/

UNCOUNTABLE NOUN **Ethnicity** is the state or fact of belonging to a particular ethnic group. ○ *He said his ethnicity had not been important to him.* ○ *a dozen boys of mixed ethnicity*

---

evalu|ate /ɪˈvæljʊeɪt/ `ACADEMIC WORD`
(evaluates, evaluating, evaluated)

VERB If you **evaluate** something or someone, you consider them in order to make a judgment about them, for example about how good or bad they are. ○ *They will first send in trained nurses to evaluate the needs of the individual situation.* ○ *The market situation is difficult to evaluate.* ○ [+ *how*] *we evaluate how well we do something*

▶ COLLOCATIONS:

evaluate a **situation/impact/risk**

evaluate the **effectiveness** of *something*

evaluate the **performance** of *someone*

carefully evaluate *something*

▶ SYNONYMS: assess, analyze

evalu|ation /ɪˌvæljʊˈeɪʃən/ (evaluations)

NOUN ○ [+ of] *the opinions and evaluations of college supervisors* ○ *Evaluation is standard practice for all training arranged through the school.*

▶ COLLOCATIONS:

evaluation **of** *something*

undergo/provide evaluation

performance/job/psychiatric/psychological evaluation

thorough/careful/formal evaluation

evaluation **process/team/system/report**

▶ SYNONYMS: analysis, appraisal, assessment, review

evalu|ative /ɪˈvæljʊətɪv/

ADJECTIVE [FORMAL] ○ *ten years of evaluative research* ○ *The professor rightly states the need for longer-term evaluative studies.*

▶ COLLOCATION: evaluative **criteria/procedures**

evapo|rate /ɪˈvæpəreɪt/   GEOGRAPHY SCIENCE
(evaporates, evaporating, evaporated)

VERB When a liquid **evaporates**, or **is evaporated**, it changes from a liquid state to a gas, because its temperature has increased. ○ *The water is evaporated by the sun.* ○ [+ into] *prevent the pungent oils from evaporating into the air*

▶ COLLOCATIONS:

evaporate **by/in/into** *something*

evaporate in/into the **sunlight/heat/air/atmosphere**

water/moisture/liquid/sweat evaporates

evapo|ra|tion /ɪˌvæpəˈreɪʃən/

UNCOUNTABLE NOUN ○ [+ from] *High temperatures also result in high evaporation from the plants.* ○ [+ of] *the evaporation of the sweat on the skin*

▶ COLLOCATIONS:

evaporation **of/from** *something*

evaporation of **sweat/moisture/liquid**

evaporation from the **ocean/soil/surface**

water/moisture evaporation

prevent/reduce/increase evaporation

▶ PHRASE: evaporation and condensation

evolve /ɪ'vɒlv/ (evolves, evolving, evolved) `ACADEMIC WORD` `BIOLOGY`

1 VERB When animals or plants **evolve**, they gradually change and develop into different forms. ○ *The bright plumage of many male birds has evolved to attract females.* ○ [+ from] *Maize evolved from a wild grass in Mexico.* ○ [+ into] *when amphibians evolved into reptiles*

2 VERB If something **evolves** or you **evolve** it, it gradually develops over a period of time into something different and usually more advanced. ○ [+ into] *a tiny airline which eventually evolved into Pakistan International Airlines* ○ [+ from] *Popular music evolved from folk songs.* ○ *As medical knowledge evolves, beliefs change.*

▶ **COLLOCATIONS:**
evolve **from/into** something
evolve **over** time
culture/language/society/technology evolves
humans/organisms/species evolve
rapidly/constantly/gradually/slowly evolve

▶ **SYNONYMS:** develop, adapt

evo|lu|tion /ˌiːvə'luːʃən, ˌev-/

UNCOUNTABLE NOUN ○ [+ of] *the evolution of plants and animals.* ○ *the theory of evolution by natural selection* ○ [+ of] *a crucial period in the evolution of modern physics*

▶ **COLLOCATIONS:**
the evolution **of** something
human/natural/biological evolution
evolution **theory**

▶ **PHRASE:** evolution by natural selection

▶ **SYNONYM:** development

ex|am|ine /ɪg'zæmɪn/ (examines, examining, examined) `MEDICINE`

1 VERB If you **examine** something, you look at it carefully. ○ *He examined her passport and stamped it.* ○ *Forensic scientists are examining the bombers' car.*

▶ **COLLOCATIONS:**
examine **evidence**
a **scientist/investigator/expert** examines something
examine **forensically/closely**

▶ **SYNONYMS:** study, inspect

2 VERB If a doctor **examines** you, he or she looks at your body, feels it, or does simple tests in order to check how healthy you are. ○ *Another doctor examined her and could still find nothing wrong.*

▶ COLLOCATIONS:
a **doctor/psychiatrist/specialist** examines *someone*
examine a **patient**
examine *someone* **carefully**

3 VERB If an idea, proposal, or plan **is examined**, it is considered very
carefully. ○ *I have given the matter much thought, examining all the possible
alternatives.* ○ *The plans will be examined by E.U. environment ministers.* ○ [+ how]
Psychologists have been examining how we make sense of events.

▶ COLLOCATIONS:
examined **by** *someone*
examine a **possibility/proposal/implication**
examine an **issue/effect/aspect**
examine *something* **critically/systematically**

▶ SYNONYMS: consider, investigate

ex|ami|na|tion /ɪɡˌzæmɪˈneɪʃən/ (examinations)

NOUN ○ [+ of] *The Navy is to carry out an examination of the wreck tomorrow.*
○ *He was later discharged after an examination at Westminster Hospital.*
○ *The proposal requires careful examination and consideration.*

▶ COLLOCATIONS:
an examination **of** *something*
conduct/undergo/perform an examination
a **forensic/physical/medical** examination
a **careful/internal/post-mortem** examination
a **detailed/close** examination
an examination **reveals/shows/finds** *something*

▶ SYNONYMS: inspection, consideration

---

ex|ceed /ɪkˈsiːd/ (exceeds, exceeding, exceeded)   `ACADEMIC WORD`

VERB If something **exceeds** a particular amount or number, it is greater or
larger than that amount or number. [FORMAL] ○ *Its research budget exceeds
$700 million a year.* ○ *The demand for places at some schools exceeds the supply.*
○ *His performance exceeded all expectations.*

▶ COLLOCATIONS:
exceed a **limit/expectation/target/supply**
far/greatly/easily exceed *something*

▶ SYNONYM: surpass

ex|cess /ɪkˈses/ (excesses)

1 NOUN An **excess of** something is a larger amount than is needed, allowed, or
usual. ○ *Large doses of vitamin C are not toxic, since the body will excrete any excess.*

▶ COLLOCATION: an excess **of** *something*

▸ **SYNONYMS:** surfeit, surplus
▸ **ANTONYM:** deficiency

2 PHRASE In excess of means more than a particular amount. [FORMAL]
○ *Avoid deposits in excess of £20,000 in any one account.* ○ *The energy value of dried fruits is considerably in excess of that of fresh items.*

ex|ces|sive /ɪkˈsesɪv/

ADJECTIVE If you describe the amount or level of something as **excessive**, you disapprove of it because it is more or higher than is necessary or reasonable. ○ *the alleged use of excessive force by police* ○ *The government says that local authority spending is excessive.*

▸ **COLLOCATIONS:**
an excessive **punishment/sentence/fine**
manifestly/grossly excessive
excessive **consumption/drinking/use/intake**
excessive **noise/speed/heat/force**

▸ **PHRASE:** excessive and disproportionate
▸ **SYNONYMS:** inordinate, undue, exorbitant
▸ **ANTONYM:** insufficient

ex|ces|sive|ly /ɪkˈsesɪvli/

ADVERB ○ *Managers are also accused of paying themselves excessively high salaries.* ○ *Some people will resort to smoking excessively, some turn to alcohol.*

▸ **COLLOCATIONS:**
excessively **generous/cautious/violent**
drink/exercise/worry excessively

---

ex|cerpt /ˈeksɜːpt/ (excerpts)   LITERATURE

NOUN An **excerpt** is a short piece of writing or music which is taken from a larger piece. ○ [+ *from*] *an excerpt from Tchaikovsky's Nutcracker* ○ [+ *from*] *He did excerpts from Macbeth and Midsummer Night's Dream.*

▸ **COLLOCATIONS:**
an excerpt **from** something
an excerpt from a **song/interview/broadcast**
read/play/publish an excerpt
audio/musical/brief excerpts
diary/book/film excerpts

▸ **SYNONYMS:** extract, part, section, selection

---

ex|change /ɪksˈtʃeɪndʒ/ (exchanges, exchanging, exchanged)

VERB If you **exchange** something, you replace it with a different thing, especially something that is better or more satisfactory. ○ *the chance to sell* back or exchange goods ○ [+ for] *If the car you have leased is clearly unsatisfactory, you can always exchange it for another.*

▶ **COLLOCATIONS:**
exchange something **for** something
exchange something for **cash/goods**

▶ **SYNONYMS:** change, trade

---

ex|clude /ɪksˈkluːd/ **(excludes, excluding, excluded)** `ACADEMIC WORD`

VERB If you **exclude** something that has some connection with what you are doing, you deliberately do not use it or consider it. ○ [+ from] *They eat only plant foods, and take care to exclude animal products from other areas of their lives.* ○ *In some schools, Christmas carols are being modified to exclude any reference to Christ.*

▶ **COLLOCATIONS:**
exclude something **from** something
deliberately/unfairly/temporarily exclude

▶ **SYNONYMS:** omit, reject

▶ **ANTONYM:** include

ex|clud|ing /ɪkˈskluːdɪŋ/

PREPOSITION You use **excluding** before mentioning a person or thing to show that you are not including them in your statement. ○ *The families questioned, excluding those on income support, have a net income of £200.20 a week.* ○ *Excluding water, half of the body's weight is protein.*

▶ **SYNONYMS:** except, without

▶ **ANTONYM:** including

ex|clu|sion /ɪkˈskluːʒən/ **(exclusions)**

NOUN The **exclusion of** something is the act of deliberately not using, allowing, or considering it. ○ [+ of] *It calls for the exclusion of all commercial lending institutions from the college loan program.* ○ *Certain exclusions and limitations apply.*

▶ **COLLOCATIONS:**
the exclusion **of** someone/something
exclusion **from** something
social exclusion
permanent/temporary/automatic exclusion
an exclusion **zone/order/clause/unit**

▶ **SYNONYM:** ban

▶ **ANTONYM:** inclusion

ex|ecu|tive /ɪɡ'zekjʊtɪv/ (executives)　　`BUSINESS` `POLITICS`

1 NOUN An **executive** is someone who is employed by a business at a senior level. Executives decide what the business should do, and ensure that it is done. ○ *an advertising executive* ○ *Her husband is a senior bank executive.*

▶ COLLOCATIONS:
　appoint an executive
　a **chief/senior/top** executive
　a **marketing/advertising/television/industry** executive

▶ SYNONYMS: director, official, manager

2 NOUN **The executive** is the part of the government of a country that is concerned with carrying out decisions or orders, as opposed to the part that makes laws or the part that deals with criminals. ○ *The government, the executive and the judiciary are supposed to be separate.*

▶ COLLOCATION: a **national/power-sharing** executive

▶ SYNONYMS: administration, government

---

ex|pand /ɪk'spænd/ (expands, expanding, expanded)　　`ACADEMIC WORD`

1 VERB If something **expands** or **is expanded**, it becomes larger. ○ *Engineers noticed that the pipes were not expanding as expected.* ○ *The money supply expanded by 14.6 per cent in the year to September.* ○ [V-ing] *a rapidly expanding universe*

2 VERB If something such as a business, organization, or service **expands**, or if you **expand** it, it becomes bigger and includes more people, goods, or activities. ○ *The popular ceramics industry expanded towards the middle of the 19th century.* ○ *Health officials are proposing to expand their services by organising counselling.*

▶ COLLOCATIONS:
　expanded **by** an amount
　an expanding **universe/economy/population**
　expand **capacity/coverage/production**
　expand the **scope/range** of something
　expand **rapidly/dramatically**

▶ SYNONYMS: increase, grow, enlarge, develop

▶ ANTONYMS: contract, shrink

expand on/upon

PHRASAL VERB If you **expand on** or **expand upon** something, you give more information or details about it when you write or talk about it. ○ *He used today's speech to expand on remarks he made last month.* ○ *a view that I will expand upon below*

▶ COLLOCATION: expand on a **theme/point/view**

▶ SYNONYMS: elaborate on, develop, enlarge on

ex|pan|sion /ɪk'spænʃən/

UNCOUNTABLE NOUN Expansion is the process of becoming greater in size, number, or amount. ○ [+ of] *the rapid expansion of private health insurance* ○ *a new period of economic expansion*

▶ COLLOCATIONS:
  the expansion **of** *something*
  rapid/further/future expansion
  economic/global/major expansion
  an expansion **plan/programme/project/team**

▶ SYNONYMS: growth, spread, increase, development

▶ ANTONYM: contraction

ex|pendi|ture /ɪk'spendɪtʃə/   BUSINESS ECONOMICS

UNCOUNTABLE NOUN Expenditure is the spending of money on something, or the money that is spent on something. [FORMAL] ○ *Policies of tax reduction must lead to reduced public expenditure.* ○ [+ on] *They should cut their expenditure on defence.*

▶ COLLOCATIONS:
  expenditure **on** something
  reduce/cut expenditure
  rising/falling/total expenditure
  advertising/development/health/public/government expenditure

▶ SYNONYMS: spending, costs

ex|ploit /ɪk'splɔɪt/   ACADEMIC WORD SOCIOLOGY
(exploits, exploiting, exploited)

1 VERB If you say that someone **is exploiting** you, you think that they are treating you unfairly by using your work or ideas and giving you very little in return. ○ *Critics claim he exploited black musicians for personal gain.* ○ *exploited workers*

▶ COLLOCATION: **ruthlessly/sexually/cruelly** exploit *someone*

2 VERB If you **exploit** something, you use it well, and achieve something or gain an advantage from it. ○ *Cary is hoping to exploit new opportunities in Europe.* ○ *So you feel that your skills have never been fully appreciated or exploited?*

▶ COLLOCATIONS:
  exploit a **loophole/opportunity/resource**
  commercially/successfully exploit *something*

▶ SYNONYM: use

ex|ploi|ta|tion /ˌeksplɔɪ'teɪʃən/

UNCOUNTABLE NOUN ○ *Extra payments should be made to protect the interests of the staff and prevent exploitation.*

▶ COLLOCATIONS:
the exploitation **of** someone/something
the exploitation of **resources/land/knowledge**
the exploitation of **children/women/animals**
prevent/combat exploitation
sexual/commercial exploitation
resource/oil/mineral exploitation

▶ SYNONYM: use

---

ex|port (exports, exporting, exported)   `ACADEMIC WORD` `BUSINESS`

> The verb is pronounced /ɪk'spɔːt/. The noun is pronounced /'ekspɔːt/.

1 VERB To **export** products or raw materials means to sell them to another country. ○ *The nation also exports beef.* ○ *[+ to] They expect the antibiotic products to be exported to Southeast Asia and Africa.* ○ *To earn foreign exchange we must export.*

▶ COLLOCATIONS:
export something **to** somewhere
export something **worldwide/overseas**
export **oil/goods/products**
illegally export something

▶ ANTONYM: import

2 NOUN Exports are goods which are sold to another country and sent there.
○ *He did this to promote American exports.* ○ *Ghana's main export is cocoa.*

▶ COLLOCATIONS:
exports **of** something
exports of **goods/products/commodities**
halt/boost/ban/increase exports
exports **rise/fall/grow**
cheap/expensive/illegal exports
total/net exports
oil/arms/agricultural/live exports
the export **market/trade**

▶ ANTONYM: import

exportation /ˌekspɔːrˈteɪʃən/

UNCOUNTABLE NOUN [mainly AM] ○ *an asymmetry between positive and negative exportation*

▶ COLLOCATION: **agricultural/industrial** exportation
▶ ANTONYM: importation

ex|pose /ɪkˈspəʊz/ (exposes, exposing, exposed) `ACADEMIC WORD`

1 VERB To **expose** something that is usually hidden means to uncover it so that it can be seen. ○ *Lowered sea levels exposed the shallow continental shelf beneath the Bering Sea.* ○ *a wall with exposed wiring*

▶ **COLLOCATIONS:**
  exposed **flesh/skin**
  an exposed **wall/surface**

▶ **SYNONYMS:** uncover, reveal, disclose

▶ **ANTONYMS:** cover, hide

2 VERB If someone **is exposed to** something dangerous or unpleasant, they are put in a situation in which it might affect them. ○ *[+ to] They had not been exposed to most diseases common to urban populations.* ○ *[+ to] people exposed to high levels of radiation*

▶ **COLLOCATIONS:**
  expose *someone* **to** *something*
  exposed to **sun/radiation/heat/X-rays**

▶ **SYNONYM:** subject

ex|po|sure /ɪkˈspəʊʒə/

UNCOUNTABLE NOUN **Exposure to** something dangerous means being in a situation where it might affect you. ○ *[+ to] Exposure to lead is known to damage the brains of young children.* ○ *[+ to] the potential exposure of people to nuclear waste*

▶ **COLLOCATIONS:**
  exposure **to** *something*
  sun/radiation/asbestos exposure
  risk/limit/reduce/increase/measure/cause exposure
  prolonged/repeated/excessive/constant exposure
  low-level/minimal/accidental exposure

▶ **SYNONYMS:** subjection, contact, experience

---

ex|press /ɪkˈspres/ (expresses, expressing, expressed) `LANGUAGE` `MATHS`

VERB When you **express** an idea or feeling, or **express yourself**, you show what you think or feel. ○ *He expressed grave concern at American attitudes.* ○ *He expresses himself easily in English.* ○ *[+ what] groping for some way to express what she felt*

▶ **COLLOCATIONS:**
  express a **feeling/view/opinion/idea**
  express **concern/disapproval/disappointment/regret**
  express **interest/doubt/hope**
  express *something* **clearly/openly/publicly/privately**

▶ **SYNONYMS:** communicate, convey

ex|pres|sion /ɪkˈspreʃən/ (expressions)

NOUN The **expression of** ideas or feelings is the showing of them through words, actions, or artistic activities. ○ [+ of] *Laughter is one of the most infectious expressions of emotion.* ○ *the rights of the individual to freedom of expression*

▶ **COLLOCATIONS:**
expression **of** *something*
an expression of **thanks/delight/grief/ideas/feelings/emotion**
a **facial** expression
a **blank/thoughtful/unreadable/pained** expression
artistic/creative/emotional/free expression

▶ **PHRASE:** freedom of expression

▶ **SYNONYMS:** communication, indication

ex|tend /ɪkˈstend/ (extends, extending, extended)

1 VERB If you **extend** something, you make it longer or bigger. ○ *This year they have introduced three new products to extend their range.* ○ *The building was extended in 1500.* ○ *an extended exhaust pipe*

▶ **SYNONYM:** lengthen

2 VERB If you **extend** something, you make it last longer than before or end at a later date. ○ [+ by] *They have extended the deadline by twenty-four hours.* ○ *an extended contract*

▶ **COLLOCATIONS:**
extend *something* **for/by** *a period*
extend a **deadline/ban/loan**
an extended **contract/welcome**
extend *something* **indefinitely**

▶ **SYNONYMS:** continue, stretch, lengthen

ex|ten|sion /ɪkˈstenʃən/

UNCOUNTABLE NOUN Extension is the process of making something bigger or making something continue for a longer period of time. ○ [+ to] *I was given a two-year extension to my contract* ○ *the space was large enough to build an extension*

▶ **COLLOCATIONS:**
an extension **of/to** *something*
an extension of a **ban/deadline/lease/benefit**
negotiate/approve/announce/offer an extension
build/open an extension
a **one-year/two-year** extension

ex|tent /ɪkˈstent/

1 NOUN If you are talking about how great, important, or serious a difficulty or situation is, you can refer to **the extent of** it. ○ [+ *of*] *The government itself has little information on the extent of industrial pollution.* ○ [+ *of*] *The full extent of the losses was disclosed yesterday.*

→ see note at **scale**

▶ **COLLOCATIONS:**
the extent **of** *something*
assess/determine/gauge the extent
reveal/realize/discover/appreciate the extent
the extent of the **damage/problem/injury**
the **full** extent

▶ **PHRASE:** the nature and extent of something

▶ **SYNONYMS:** magnitude, amount, degree, scale

2 PHRASE You use expressions such as **to a large extent**, **to some extent**, or **to a certain extent** in order to indicate that something is partly true, but not entirely true. ○ *It was and, to a large extent, still is a good show.* ○ *To some extent this was the truth.* ○ *To a certain extent it's easier for men to get work.* ○ *This also endangers American interests in other regions, although to a lesser extent.*

3 PHRASE You use expressions such as **to what extent**, **to that extent**, or **to the extent that** when you are discussing how true a statement is, or in what ways it is true. ○ *It's still not clear to what extent this criticism is originating from within the ruling party.* ○ *To that extent they helped bring about their own destruction.* ○ *We may not be able to do it to the extent that we would like.*

ex|te|ri|or /ɪkˈstɪəriə/ (exteriors)

1 NOUN The **exterior** of something is its outside surface. ○ [+ *of*] *Some of the cells on the exterior of the blastula are destined to become eyes or wings.* ○ [+ *of*] *The exterior of the building was elegant and graceful.*

▶ **COLLOCATIONS:**
the exterior **of** *something*
the exterior of a **house/building**
a **brick/stone/glass** exterior

▶ **SYNONYM:** outside

▶ **ANTONYM:** interior

2 ADJECTIVE You use **exterior** to refer to the outside parts of something or things that are outside something. ○ *The exterior walls were made of pre-formed concrete.* ○ *the oven's exterior surfaces*

▶ **COLLOCATIONS:**
an exterior **wall/staircase**
exterior **lighting/design/maintenance**

▶ **SYNONYMS:** outer, outside, external
▶ **ANTONYMS:** interior, inner

---

ex|ter|nal /ɪkˈstɜːnəl/ `ACADEMIC WORD`

ADJECTIVE External is used to indicate that something is on the outside of a surface or body, or that it exists, happens, or comes from outside. ○ *a much reduced heat loss through external walls* ○ *internal and external allergic reactions*

▶ **COLLOCATION:** external **factors/affairs/stimuli/influences**
▶ **PHRASE:** for external use
▶ **SYNONYM:** outside
▶ **ANTONYM:** internal

ex|ter|nal|ly /ɪkˈstɜːnəli/

ADVERB ○ *Vitamins can be applied externally to the skin.*

▶ **COLLOCATION:** **apply/use** *something* externally
▶ **ANTONYM:** internally

---

ex|tract /ˈekstrækt/ (extracts) `ACADEMIC WORD` `LITERATURE`

NOUN An **extract from** a book or piece of writing is a small part of it that is printed or published separately. ○ [+ *from*] *Read this extract from an information booklet about the work of an airline cabin crew.* ○ [+ *from*] *The orchestra played extracts from Beethoven and Brahms.*

▶ **COLLOCATIONS:**
  an extract **from** *something*
  an extract from a **book/letter/speech**
  edited/exclusive/brief extracts
▶ **SYNONYMS:** excerpt, passage

Ff

---

fac|ul|ty /ˈfækəlti/ **(faculties)**   EDUCATION ACADEMIC STUDY

NOUN A **faculty** is a group of related departments in some universities, or the people who work in them. [BRIT] ○ [+ of] *the Faculty of Social and Political Sciences.* ○ *the first staff of Edinburgh's new medical faculty*

▶ **COLLOCATIONS:**
the faculty **of** *something*
the **law/arts/science/engineering** faculty
a **university** faculty
join a faculty

▶ **RELATED WORD:** department

Fahr|en|heit /ˈfærənhaɪt/   SCIENCE GEOGRAPHY

ADJECTIVE Fahrenheit is a scale for measuring temperature, in which water freezes at 32 degrees and boils at 212 degrees. It is represented by the symbol °F. ○ *By mid-morning, the temperature was already above 100 degrees Fahrenheit.* ○ *choose from degrees centigrade or Fahrenheit*

● **Fahrenheit** is also a noun. ○ *He was asked for the boiling point of water in Fahrenheit.* ○ *television weather forecasts given in metric and Fahrenheit*

▶ **COLLOCATION:** *x* **degrees** Fahrenheit

▶ **RELATED WORDS:** centigrade, Celsius

---

fam|ine /ˈfæmɪn/   GEOGRAPHY SOCIOLOGY

UNCOUNTABLE NOUN Famine is a situation in which many people have little or no food, and may die. ○ *Thousands of refugees are trapped by war, drought and famine.* ○ *The civil war is obstructing distribution of famine relief by aid agencies.*

▶ **COLLOCATIONS:**
face famine
widespread famine
famine **relief**

▶ **RELATED WORD:** drought

---

fa|tal /ˈfeɪtəl/   MEDICINE

ADJECTIVE A **fatal** accident or illness causes someone's death. ○ *A hospital spokesman said she had suffered a fatal heart attack.* ○ *He had taken a massive overdose of pills which had proved fatal.*

▶ **COLLOCATIONS:**
a fatal **accident/crash/attack/shooting**
a fatal **disease/heart attack/injury/wound**
a fatal **dose/overdose**
potentially fatal
prove fatal

fa|tal|ly /ˈfeɪtəli/

ADVERB ○ *The dead soldier is reported to have been fatally wounded in the chest.* ○ *He was fatally shot two days later.*

▶ **COLLOCATION:** fatally **wounded/injured/shot/stabbed**

fa|tal|ity /fəˈtælɪti/ **(fatalities)**

NOUN A **fatality** is a death caused by an accident or by violence. [FORMAL]
○ *Road fatalities have declined more than 10 percent over the past 10 years.* ○ *Most fatalities occur in small mines that often lack safety equipment.*

▶ **COLLOCATIONS:**
traffic/road fatalities
cause a fatality

▶ **SYNONYM:** death

▶ **RELATED WORD:** casualty

fa|vour /ˈfeɪvə/ **(favours, favouring, favoured)**

1 VERB If you **favour** something, you prefer it to the other choices available.
[in AM, use **favor**] ○ *The French say they favour a transition to democracy.*
○ [+ v-ing] *Britain and the United States have strongly favoured retaining the sanctions.*

▶ **COLLOCATIONS:**
favoured **by** someone
strongly/heavily/clearly favour something
traditionally/increasingly favour something
favour a **candidate/approach/option**

▶ **ANTONYM:** oppose

2 PHRASE If you are **in favour of** something, you support it and think that it is a good thing. [in AM, use **favor**] ○ [+ of] *I wouldn't be in favour of income tax cuts.* ○ [+ of] *Yet this is a government which proclaims that it is all in favour of openness.* ○ *The vote passed with 111 in favour and 25 against.*

▶ **COLLOCATIONS:**
in favour **of** something
in favour of a **motion/resolution/proposal/action**
in favour of a **strike/marriage/ban/merger**

▶ **ANTONYM:** against

fea|sible /ˈfiːzəbəl/

ADJECTIVE If something is **feasible**, it can be done, made, or achieved.
○ [+ to-inf] *She questioned whether it was feasible to stimulate investment in these regions.* ○ *Supporters argue that the scheme is now technically and economically feasible.*

▶ **COLLOCATIONS:**
   perfectly feasible
   economically/financially/technically/politically feasible
▶ **SYNONYMS:** practicable, possible
▶ **ANTONYM:** unfeasible

fea|sibil|ity /ˌfiːzəˈbɪlɪti/

UNCOUNTABLE NOUN ○ [+ of] *The committee will study the feasibility of setting up a national computer network.*

▶ **COLLOCATIONS:**
   the feasibility **of** something
   study/examine/assess the feasibility of something
   a feasibility **study/report**

fea|ture /ˈfiːtʃə/ (features)   `ACADEMIC WORD`

NOUN A **feature of** something is an interesting or important part or characteristic of it. ○ [+ of] *The key feature of terrorists is their total disregard for the lives of innocent civilians.* ○ *Italian democracy's unique feature is that government has not alternated between two parties.* ○ *The ships have built-in safety features including specially-strengthened hulls.*

▶ **COLLOCATIONS:**
   a feature **of** something
   a **key/important/central** feature
   a **special/unique/striking/distinctive/distinguishing** feature
   a **safety/security/design** feature
▶ **SYNONYMS:** characteristic, quality

fed|er|al /ˈfedərəl/   `ACADEMIC WORD` `POLITICS`

1 ADJECTIVE A **federal** country or system of government is one in which the different states or provinces of the country have important powers to make their own laws and decisions. ○ *Five of the six provinces are to become autonomous regions in a new federal system of government.* ○ *Czechoslovakia would remain a federal state*

2 ADJECTIVE Federal also means belonging or relating to the national government of a federal country rather than to one of the states within it. ○ *The federal government controls just 6% of the education budget.* ○ *A federal judge ruled in her favour.*

▶ **COLLOCATIONS:**
a federal **system/state**
a federal **agency/authority/election**
a federal **court/judge/prosecutor/official**
federal **government/law/tax/funds/budget**

▶ **RELATED WORD:** provincial

fed|era|tion /ˌfedəˈreɪʃən/ (federations)

1 NOUN A **federation** is a federal country. ○ *the Russian Federation* ○ *in what remains of the Yugoslav federation*

2 NOUN A **federation** is a group of societies or other organizations which have joined together, usually because they share a common interest. ○ *the British Athletic Federation* ○ *[+ of] The organization emerged from a federation of six national agencies.*

▶ **COLLOCATION:** a federation **of** *something*

▶ **SYNONYM:** association

fee /fiː/ (fees)   `ACADEMIC WORD` `BUSINESS`

1 NOUN A **fee** is an amount of money that you pay to be allowed to do something. ○ *He hadn't paid his television licence fee.* ○ *[+ of] Expect to pay an entrance fee of 50-60 euros per head.*

2 NOUN A **fee** is the amount of money that a person or organization is paid for a particular job or service that they provide. ○ *Find out how much your surveyor's and solicitor's fees will be.* ○ *The legal fees amounted to almost £12 million.*

▶ **COLLOCATIONS:**
a fee **of** *£x*
charge/pay a fee
a **monthly/annual** fee
a **high/low/small/nominal/flat** fee
a **membership/entrance/licence** fee
legal/tuition/management/school/university fees

▶ **SYNONYM:** charge

fe|male /ˈfiːmeɪl/ (females)   `BIOLOGY` `SOCIOLOGY`

1 ADJECTIVE Someone who is **female** is a woman or a girl. ○ *In 1880, Melbourne University admitted female students for the first time.* ○ *Only 13 per cent of consultants are female.* ○ *Female athletes should take extra iron.*

2 ADJECTIVE **Female** matters and things relate to, belong to, or affect women rather than men. ○ *Female infertility is increasingly common.* ○ *Although she works in an engineering company she is in a traditional female role.*

3 NOUN You can refer to any creature that can lay eggs or produce babies from its body as a **female**. ○ *Each female will lay just one egg in April or May.*

● **Female** is also an adjective. ○ *the scent given off by the female aphid to attract the male*

▶ **COLLOCATIONS:**
female **sexuality/hormones**
a female **companion/colleague/friend/student**
a female **athlete/artist/singer**
predominantly/traditionally/exclusively female

▶ **ANTONYM:** male

> **USAGE: male** and **female**
>
> You use **male** and **female** as adjectives to talk about people and animals. ○ *male and female employees* ○ *The male and female birds are different colours.*
>
> You can also use **male** and **female** as nouns, but mostly in biology, especially to refer to animals. ○ *The adult female lays one egg on each fruit.*

---

field /fiːld/ (fields)

NOUN A particular **field** is a particular subject of study or type of activity. ○ [+ of] *Exciting artistic breakthroughs have recently occurred in the fields of painting, sculpture and architecture.* ○ *Each of the authors of the tapes is an expert in his field.*

▶ **COLLOCATIONS:**
the field **of** something
in a field
a **medical/scientific/academic** field
a specialist/expert in a field

▶ **SYNONYMS:** subject, area

---

fig|ure /ˈfɪgə, AM -gjər/ (figures) `ACADEMIC STUDY`

NOUN In a piece of writing, the diagrams which help to show or explain information are referred to as **figures**. ○ *If you look at a world map (see Figure 1) you can identify the major wine-producing regions.* ○ *Figure 1.15 shows which provinces lost populations between 1910 and 1920.*

→ see note at **bar chart**

---

fi|nite /ˈfaɪnaɪt/ `ACADEMIC WORD`

ADJECTIVE Something that is **finite** has a definite fixed size or extent. [FORMAL] ○ *Only a finite number of situations can arise.* ○ *Coal and oil are finite resources.*

▶ **COLLOCATION:** a finite **resource/number/period/amount/set**

▶ **SYNONYM:** limited

▶ **ANTONYM:** infinite

flex|ible /ˈfleksɪbəl/

1 ADJECTIVE A **flexible** object or material can be bent easily without breaking. ○ *brushes with long, flexible bristles* ○ *air is pumped through a flexible tube*

▸ **SYNONYM:** pliable

▸ **ANTONYMS:** inflexible, rigid

2 ADJECTIVE Something or someone that is **flexible** is able to change easily and adapt to different conditions and circumstances. ○ *more flexible arrangements to allow access to services after normal working hours* ○ *We encourage flexible working.*

▸ **COLLOCATIONS:**
   a flexible **approach/system/arrangement**
   flexible **working/working hours**
   a flexible **rate/market**

▸ **SYNONYM:** adaptable

▸ **ANTONYM:** inflexible

flexi|bil|ity /ˌfleksɪˈbɪlɪti/

UNCOUNTABLE NOUN ○ [+ *of*] *The flexibility of distance learning would be particularly suited to busy managers.* ○ [+ *of*] *The flexibility of the lens decreases with age.*

▸ **COLLOCATIONS:**
   the flexibility **of** something
   offer/provide/increase/show flexibility

▸ **SYNONYM:** adaptability

▸ **ANTONYM:** inflexibility

flow /fləʊ/ (flows, flowing, flowed)

1 VERB If a liquid, gas, or electrical current **flows** somewhere, it moves there steadily and continuously. ○ [+ *into*] *A stream flowed into the valley.* ○ [+ *into*] *The current flows into electric motors that drive the wheels.*

▸ **COLLOCATIONS:**
   flow **into** a place
   water/blood flows
   a **current** flows
   flow **freely**

● **Flow** is also a noun. ○ *It works only in the veins, where the blood flow is slower.* ○ [+ *of*] *It should be kept in a darkened room where there is a free flow of warm air.*

▸ **COLLOCATIONS:**
   a flow **of** something
   a **gas/air/water/lava** flow
   the **blood** flow
   a **steady/constant/strong/free** flow

2 VERB If a number of people or things **flow** from one place to another, they move there steadily in large groups, usually without stopping. ○ [+ *into*] *Large numbers of refugees continue to flow into the country.* ○ [+ *throughout*] *Troops patrol major roads to ensure that traffic flows freely throughout the country.*

▶ **COLLOCATION:** flow **into/throughout** *a place*

● **Flow** is also a noun. ○ [+ *of*] *She watched the steady flow of cars and buses along the street.*

▶ **COLLOCATIONS:**
a flow **of** *something*
a **steady/constant/free** flow

'flow chart (flow charts)   ACADEMIC STUDY

NOUN A **flow chart** or a **flow diagram** is a diagram which represents the sequence of actions in a particular process or activity. ○ [+ *of*] *a flow chart of the process* ○ *Design a flow chart to explain the registration process.*

→ see note at **bar chart**

---

fluc|tu|ate /ˈflʌktʃueɪt/   ACADEMIC WORD
(fluctuates, fluctuating, fluctuated)

VERB If something **fluctuates**, it changes a lot in an irregular way. ○ *The temperature fluctuates very little between daytime and night-time.* ○ *Share prices have fluctuated wildly in recent weeks.* ○ [V-ing] *the fluctuating price of oil*

▶ **COLLOCATIONS:**
a **price/rate/value** fluctuates
the **temperature/weight** fluctuates
fluctuate **wildly/significantly**

fluc|tua|tion /ˌflʌktʃuˈeɪʃən/ (fluctuations)

NOUN ○ [+ *in*] *Much of the seasonal fluctuation in death rates was caused by cold, the researchers concluded.* ○ [+ *in*] *daily fluctuations in core body temperature*

▶ **COLLOCATIONS:**
a fluctuation **in** *something*
a **currency/price/market** fluctuation
a **short-term/seasonal** fluctuation

> **EXTEND YOUR VOCABULARY**
>
> You can use **fluctuate/fluctuation** and **vary/variation** to describe something that changes frequently. If the level of something **fluctuates**, it goes up and down a lot over a period of time. ○ *Wheat prices fluctuated between £55 and £90 a ton.*
>
> If something **varies**, it changes or is different depending on the situation. ○ *The price varies according to your airport and time of arrival.*

flu|id /ˈfluːɪd/ (fluids)

SCIENCE

NOUN A **fluid** is a liquid. [FORMAL] ○ *The blood vessels may leak fluid, which distorts vision.* ○ *Make sure that you drink plenty of fluids.*

▶ COLLOCATIONS:
  a **bodily/body** fluid
  a **cleaning** fluid
▶ SYNONYM: liquid

fo|cus /ˈfəʊkəs/ (foci, focuses, focusing, focused)

ACADEMIC WORD

> The spellings **focusses**, **focussing**, **focussed** are also used. The plural of the noun can be either **foci** or **focuses**.

1 VERB If you **focus on** a particular topic or if your attention **is focused on** it, you concentrate on it and think about it, discuss it, or deal with it, rather than dealing with other topics. ○ [+ on] *The research effort has focused on tracing the effects of growing levels of five compounds.* ○ [+ on] *He is currently focusing on assessment and development.* ○ [+ on] *The company decided to focus exclusively on the home market.*

▶ COLLOCATIONS:
  focus **on** *something*
  focus **exclusively/solely/entirely** on *something*
  focus **mainly/heavily/largely** on *something*
▶ SYNONYM: concentrate

2 NOUN The focus of something is the main topic or main thing that it is concerned with. ○ [+ of] *The U.N.'s role in promoting peace is increasingly the focus of international attention.* ○ [+ of] *The ethnic problem in the country is crucial but it is not the primary focus of the negotiations.*

▶ COLLOCATIONS:
  the focus **of** *something*
  the **main/primary/central** focus

fol|low /ˈfɒləʊ/ (follows, following, followed)

1 VERB If it **follows** that a particular thing is the case, that thing is a logical result of something else being true or being the case. ○ [+ that] *If children acquire self-esteem as a consequence of doing well in school, it does not necessarily follow that raising their self-esteem will improve their academic achievement.* ○ [+ from] *It is easy to see the conclusions described in the text follow from this equation.*

▶ COLLOCATIONS:
  follow **from** *something*
  inevitably/automatically/not necessarily follow

2 **VERB** If you refer to the words that **follow** or **followed**, you are referring to the words that come next or came next in a piece of writing or speech. ○ *What follows is an eye-witness account.* ○ *There followed a list of places where Hans intended to visit.* ○ *General analysis is followed by five case studies.*

▶ **COLLOCATION:** followed **by** *something*

fol|low|ing /ˈfɒləʊɪŋ/

ADJECTIVE You use **following** to refer to something that you are about to mention. ○ *Write down the following information: name of product, type, date purchased and price.* ○ *The method of helping such patients is explained in the following chapters.*

● **The following** is also a pronoun. ○ *The following is a paraphrase of what was said.* ○ *One serving of any of the following would provide an adult's complete daily requirement of salt.*

form /fɔːm/ (forms, forming, formed)

1 **VERB** If something consists of particular things, people, or features, you can say that they **form** that thing. ○ *This idea formed the basis of his entire philosophy.* ○ *Cereals form the staple diet of an enormous number of people around the world.*

▶ **COLLOCATION:** form the **basis** of *something*

▶ **SYNONYM:** constitute

2 **VERB** If you **form** an organization, group, or company, you start it. ○ *Threadneedle is a company formed in 1994 with the merger of Allied Dunbar and Eagle Star.* ○ *[+ into] They formed themselves into teams.*

→ see note at **launch**

▶ **COLLOCATIONS:**
form **into** *something*
form a **government/coalition/committee**
form a **partnership/alliance/group/band**

▶ **SYNONYMS:** start, create

3 **VERB** When something natural **forms** or **is formed**, it begins to exist and develop. ○ *The stars must have formed 10 to 15 billion years ago.* ○ *Huge ice sheets were formed.*

▶ **COLLOCATIONS:**
a **planet/star/galaxy** forms
a **cell/clot** forms
cloud/ice forms

▶ **SYNONYM:** develop

for|ma|tion /fɔːˈmeɪʃən/ (formations)

1 **UNCOUNTABLE NOUN** **The formation of** something is the starting or creation of it. ○ *[+ of] the formation of a new government* ○ *[+ of] Lord Harewood* *announced the formation of English National Opera North*

▶ **COLLOCATIONS:**
the formation **of** *something*
the formation of a **government/alliance/coalition**
announce/encourage the formation of *something*

▶ **SYNONYM:** creation

2 NOUN The **formation** of something natural is the process in which it starts to exist and develop, and the shape that it has. ○ [+ *of*] *Salt interferes with the formation of ice crystals.* ○ *The cloud formations produce rain which falls on a vast territory.*

▶ **COLLOCATIONS:**
rock/diamond formation
star/planet/cloud formation
blood/bone/clot formation

---

for|mat /ˈfɔːmæt/ (formats) `ACADEMIC WORD`

NOUN The **format** of something is the way or order in which it is arranged and presented. ○ [+ *of*] *He explained the new format and policy of the paper.* ○ *music available in a digital format* ○ [+ *of*] *You all know the format of the show.* ○ *a large-format book*

▶ **COLLOCATIONS:**
the format **of** *something*
in a format
a **different/traditional/digital/electronic/online** format

▶ **SYNONYMS:** style, form

---

for|mer /ˈfɔːmə/

PRONOUN When two people, things, or groups have just been mentioned, you can refer to the first of them as **the former**. ○ *He writes about two series of works: the Caprichos and the Disparates. The former are a series of etchings done by Goya.* ○ *the wife may choose the former and the husband the latter*

▶ **ANTONYM:** latter

---

for|mu|la /ˈfɔːmjʊlə/ `ACADEMIC WORD` `MATHS` `CHEMISTRY`
(formulae or formulas)

1 NOUN A **formula** is a group of letters, numbers, or other symbols which represents a scientific or mathematical rule. ○ *He developed a mathematical formula describing the distances of the planets from the Sun.* ○ *using a standard scientific formula*

▶ **COLLOCATIONS:**
develop a formula
a **mathematical/scientific** formula

2 NOUN In science, the **formula** for a substance is a list of the amounts of various substances which make up that substance, or an indication of the atoms that it is composed of. ○ *Water's chemical formula is H2O.* ○ [+ *for*] *NO is the formula for nitric oxide*

▶ **COLLOCATIONS:**
the formula **for** *something*
the **chemical** formula

---

forth|com|ing /ˌfɔːˈθkʌmɪŋ/ `ACADEMIC WORD`

ADJECTIVE A **forthcoming** event is planned to happen soon. ○ *his opponents in the forthcoming elections* ○ *the forthcoming meeting, scheduled for January 19*

▶ **COLLOCATIONS:**
a forthcoming **election/meeting/event/marriage**
a forthcoming **album/book/tour/film**

▶ **SYNONYM:** impending

---

foun|da|tion /faʊnˈdeɪʃən/ (foundations) `ACADEMIC WORD`

1 NOUN The **foundation of** something such as a belief or way of life is the things on which it is based. ○ [+ *of*] *The issue strikes at the very foundation of our community.* ○ [+ *for*] *This laid the foundations for later modern economic growth.*

▶ **COLLOCATION:** the foundation **of/for** *something*

▶ **PHRASES:**
lay the foundations for something
shake the foundations of something
strike at the foundation of something

▶ **SYNONYM:** basis

2 NOUN A **foundation** is an organization which provides money for a special purpose such as research or charity. ○ [+ *for*] *the National Foundation for Educational Research* ○ *her response was to set about creating a charitable foundation*

▶ **COLLOCATIONS:**
a foundation **for** *something*
a **charitable** foundation

▶ **SYNONYMS:** organization, institute, society

---

frag|ment (fragments, fragmenting, fragmented)

> The noun is pronounced /ˈfrægmənt/. The verb is pronounced /frægˈment/.

1 NOUN A **fragment of** something is a small piece or part of it. ○ [+ *of*] *There were fragments of metal in my shoulder.* ○ [+ *of*] *She read everything, digesting every fragment of news.* ○ *glass fragments*

▶ **COLLOCATIONS:**
a fragment **of** *something*
a **small/tiny** fragment
a **bone/bullet/glass/metal** fragment
a fragment of **bone/glass/rock/metal**
a fragment of **information/conversation/evidence**
▶ **SYNONYM:** piece

2 VERB If something **fragments** or **is fragmented**, it breaks or separates into small pieces or parts. ○ *Fierce rivalries have traditionally fragmented the region.* ○ *[+ into] By the first century BC, Buddhism was in danger of fragmenting into small sects.*

▶ **COLLOCATIONS:**
fragment **into** *things*
highly fragmented

frag|men|ta|tion /ˌfrægmenˈteɪʃən/

UNCOUNTABLE NOUN ○ *[+ of] the extraordinary fragmentation of styles on the music scene* ○ *This is a time of social fragmentation, when communal and family bonds have eroded.*

▶ **COLLOCATION:** the fragmentation **of** *something*

frag|men|tary /ˈfrægməntəri, AM -teri/

ADJECTIVE Something that is **fragmentary** is made up of small or unconnected pieces. ○ *Any action on the basis of such fragmentary evidence would be foolish.* ○ *the fragmentary nature of our knowledge*

frame|work /ˈfreɪmwɜːk/ (frameworks) `ACADEMIC WORD`

NOUN A **framework** is a particular set of rules, ideas, or beliefs which you use in order to deal with problems or to decide what to do. ○ *[+ for] The purpose of the chapter is to provide a framework for thinking about why exchange rates change.* ○ *Doctors need a clear legal framework to be able to deal with difficult clinical decisions.*

▶ **COLLOCATIONS:**
within a framework
a framework **of/for** *something*
agree/develop/establish/set a framework
a **legal/regulatory/legislative/political** framework
a **conceptual/theoretical** framework

func|tion /ˈfʌŋkʃən/ (functions, functioning, functioned) `ACADEMIC WORD`

1 NOUN The **function** of something or someone is the useful thing that they do or are intended to do. ○ *This enzyme serves various functions.* ○ *[+ of] The* *main function of the merchant banks is to raise capital for industry.*

▶ COLLOCATIONS:
the function **of** *something/someone*
perform/serve a function
the **primary** function
a **basic/important/useful** function

▶ SYNONYMS: purpose, role

2 VERB If a machine or system **is functioning**, it is working or operating. ○ *The authorities say the prison is now functioning normally.* ○ *Conservation programs cannot function without local support.*

▶ COLLOCATIONS:
function **effectively/efficiently/smoothly**
barely function

▶ SYNONYMS: operate, work

func|tion|al /ˈfʌŋkʃənəl/

ADJECTIVE **Functional** means relating to the way in which something works or operates, or relating to how useful it is. ○ *Every new employee starts with a fully functional workspace and a full day of training in desktop tools.*

▶ SYNONYM: operational

---

fund /fʌnd/ (funds, funding, funded) ACADEMIC WORD ECONOMICS

1 PLURAL NOUN **Funds** are amounts of money that are available to be spent, especially money that is given to an organization or person for a particular purpose. ○ [+ for] *The concert will raise funds for research into Aids.* ○ *Funds are allocated according to regional needs.*

▶ COLLOCATIONS:
funds **for** *something*
raise/use/receive/provide/allocate/invest funds
public/federal/government/private funds

▶ SYNONYMS: money, finances

2 VERB When a person or organization **funds** something, they provide money for it. ○ *The Bush Foundation has funded a variety of faculty development programs.* ○ *The airport is being privately funded by a construction group.* ○ *a new privately funded scheme*

▶ COLLOCATIONS:
funded **by** *someone*
publically/privately/federally funded
largely/adequately/partly/jointly funded

▶ SYNONYM: finance

fund|ing /ˈfʌndɪŋ/

UNCOUNTABLE NOUN **Funding** is money which a government or organization provides for a particular purpose. ○ [+ for] *They hope for government funding for the scheme.* ○ *Many colleges have seen their funding cut.*

▶ **COLLOCATIONS:**
funding **for** *something*
seek/apply for/receive/secure funding
provide/increase/cut/boost funding
government/council/federal/public funding
research/education/arts funding
a funding **cut/gap/shortfall/crisis**

▶ **SYNONYMS:** money, finance

fun|da|men|tal /ˌfʌndəˈmentəl/ ACADEMIC WORD

ADJECTIVE You use **fundamental** to describe things, activities, and principles that are very important, basic, or essential. ○ *Our constitution embodies all the fundamental principles of democracy.* ○ *The fundamental problem lies in their inability to distinguish between reality and invention.* ○ *But on this question, the two leaders have very fundamental differences.*

▶ **COLLOCATIONS:**
a fundamental **principle/value/right**
a fundamental **change/shift/difference**
a fundamental **problem/question/issue/flaw**

▶ **SYNONYM:** basic

fun|da|men|tal|ly /ˌfʌndəˈmentəli/

ADVERB ○ *He disagreed fundamentally with the President's judgment.* ○ *Environmentalists say the treaty is fundamentally flawed.*

▶ **COLLOCATIONS:**
fundamentally **different/flawed/wrong/unfair**
fundamentally **change/alter/oppose** *something*
fundamentally **disagree**

▶ **SYNONYM:** profoundly

further|more /ˌfɜːðəˈmɔː/

ADVERB **Furthermore** is used to introduce a piece of information or opinion that adds to or supports the previous one. [FORMAL] ○ *Furthermore, they claim that any such interference is completely ineffective.* ○ *furthermore, even a well-timed therapy intervention may fail*

▶ **SYNONYMS:** moreover, in addition

Gg

gain /geɪn/ (gains, gaining, gained)

1 VERB If a person or place **gains** something such as an ability or quality, they gradually get more of it. ○ *It wasn't until the 1960s that her ideas first gained wider recognition.* ○ *[+ in] While it has lost its tranquility, the area has gained in liveliness.*

→ see note at **acquire**

▸ **COLLOCATIONS:**
gain **in** *something*
gain **experience/understanding**
gain **popularity/notoriety/approval/recognition**

▸ **SYNONYMS:** acquire, attain

2 VERB If you **gain** something, you obtain it, especially after a lot of hard work or effort. ○ *They realise that passing exams is no longer enough to gain a place at university.* ○ *Their efforts helped the hostages gain their freedom.*

▸ **COLLOCATIONS:**
gain **independence/freedom/entry/access**
gain a **place/position**

▸ **SYNONYMS:** obtain, earn

3 VERB If you **gain from** something such as an event or situation, you get some advantage or benefit from it. ○ *[+ from] The company didn't disclose how much it expects to gain from the two deals.* ○ *[+ from] It is sad that a major company should try to gain from other people's suffering.*

▸ **COLLOCATIONS:**
gain **from** *something*
gain from a **sale/trade/deal**
gain **financially/enormously/considerably**

▸ **SYNONYMS:** benefit, profit

▸ **ANTONYM:** lose

4 VERB To **gain** something such as weight or speed means to have an increase in that particular thing. ○ *Some people do gain weight after they stop smoking.* ○ *During this time, however, the stock market gained 15% per year.*

▸ **COLLOCATION:** gain **weight/speed/strength/value**

▸ **SYNONYM:** increase

▸ **ANTONYM:** lose

- **Gain** is also a noun. ○ [+ of] *News on new home sales is brighter, showing a gain of nearly 8% in June.* ○ *Excessive weight gain doesn't do you any good.*
  ▸ **COLLOCATION:** a gain **of** x
  ▸ **PHRASE:** weight gain
  ▸ **SYNONYMS:** increase, growth
  ▸ **ANTONYM:** loss

---

gath|er /'ɡæðə/ (gathers, gathering, gathered)

1 **VERB** If you **gather** things, you collect them together so that you can use them. ○ *The expedition gathered samples of animal and plant life.* ○ *Search teams spent weeks gathering thousands of pieces of wreckage.*

2 **VERB** If you **gather** information or evidence, you collect it, especially over a period of time and after a lot of hard work. ○ *The organization gathers information on the dangers of smoking.* ○ *The commission began to gather evidence for the forthcoming trial.* ○ [+ together] *The book gathers together all the short stories in a single volume.*

  ▸ **COLLOCATIONS:**
  gather *things* **together**
  gather **samples/information/evidence/data/material**
  ▸ **SYNONYM:** collect

---

gen|der /'dʒendə/ (genders) ACADEMIC WORD SOCIOLOGY

NOUN A person's **gender** is the fact that they are male or female. ○ *Women are sometimes denied opportunities solely because of their gender.* ○ *groups that are traditionally discriminated against on grounds of gender, colour, race, or age*

  ▸ **COLLOCATIONS:**
  the **opposite** gender
  gender **roles/stereotypes/differences**
  gender **equality/inequality**
  the gender **gap**
  ▸ **PHRASES:**
  race and gender
  age and gender
  class and gender
  ▸ **SYNONYM:** sex

---

gen|er|al|ize /'dʒenrəlaɪz/ (generalizes, generalizing, generalized)

VERB If you **generalize**, you say something that seems to be true in most situations or for most people, but that may not be completely true in all cases. [in BRIT, also use **generalise**] ○ *'In my day, children were a lot better behaved'.—'It's not true, you're generalizing'.* ○ [+ about] *It is still possible to generalize about regional styles.*

▶ COLLOCATION: generalize **about** *something*

▶ SYNONYMS: stereotype, hypothesize

gen|er|ali|za|tion /ˌdʒenrəlaɪˈzeɪʃən/ (generalizations)

NOUN [in BRIT, also use **generalisation**] ○ *He is making sweeping generalisations to get his point across.* ○ [+ *about*] *It's dangerous to make generalizations about education.*

▶ COLLOCATIONS:
a generalization **about** *something*
make generalizations
a **broad/abstract/simplistic/sweeping** generalization
a **negative/unfair** generalization

---

gen|er|ate /ˈdʒenəreɪt/ ACADEMIC WORD ENGINEERING SCIENCE
(generates, generating, generated)

1 VERB To **generate** something means to cause it to begin and develop. ○ *The Employment Minister said the reforms would generate new jobs.* ○ *the excitement generated by the changes in Eastern Europe*

▶ COLLOCATIONS:
generated **by** *something*
generate **excitement/publicity/controversy/enthusiasm**
generate **wealth/income/profit**

▶ SYNONYMS: create, cause

2 VERB To **generate** a form of energy or power means to produce it. ○ *The company, New England Electric, burns coal to generate power.*

▶ COLLOCATION: generate **electricity/energy/heat/power**

▶ SYNONYM: produce

gen|era|tion /ˌdʒenəˈreɪʃən/

UNCOUNTABLE NOUN Generation is the production of a form of energy or power from fuel or another source of power such as water. ○ *Japan has announced plans for a sharp rise in its nuclear power generation.*

▶ COLLOCATION: **power/heat/electricity** generation

▶ SYNONYM: production

---

ge|ol|ogy /dʒiˈɒlədʒi/ GEOGRAPHY

1 UNCOUNTABLE NOUN Geology is the study of the Earth's structure, surface, and origins. ○ *He was visiting professor of geology at the University of Jordan.*

2 UNCOUNTABLE NOUN The **geology** of an area is the structure of its land, together with the types of rocks and minerals that exist within it. ○ [+ *of*] *an expert on the geology of southeast Asia*

▶ COLLOCATIONS:
  the geology **of** *somewhere*
  the geology of the **area/region/island/earth**

geo|logi|cal /ˌdʒiːəˈlɒdʒɪkəl/

ADJECTIVE ○ *With geological maps you can find out all the proven sites of precious minerals.* ○ *a lengthy geological survey*

▶ COLLOCATIONS:
  a geological **survey/map/phenomenon**
  geological **features/characteristics**

ge|olo|gist /dʒiˈɒlədʒɪst/ (geologists)

NOUN A **geologist** is somebody who studies or is an expert in geology.
○ *Geologists have studied the way that heat flows from the earth.*

▶ COLLOCATIONS:
  a **mining/engineering/field** geologist
  a **distinguished/amateur/eminent** geologist

g

ge|om|etry /dʒiˈɒmɪtri/ MATHS

UNCOUNTABLE NOUN **Geometry** is the branch of mathematics concerned with the properties and relationships of lines, angles, curves, and shapes.
○ *the very ordered way in which mathematics and geometry describe nature*

germ /dʒɜːm/ (germs) MEDICINE BIOLOGY

NOUN A **germ** is a very small organism that causes disease. ○ *Chlorine is widely used to kill germs.* ○ *a germ that destroyed hundreds of millions of lives*

▶ COLLOCATIONS:
  germs **spread/multiply**
  germs **infect/attack** *something*
  something **kills/destroys/eliminates** germs
▶ SYNONYM: bacteria

ges|ture /ˈdʒestʃə/ (gestures)

NOUN A **gesture** is a movement that you make with a part of your body, especially your hands, to express emotion or information. ○ [+ *with*] *Sarah made a menacing gesture with her fist.* ○ *He throws his hands open in a gesture.*

▶ COLLOCATIONS:
  a gesture **with** *something*
  make a gesture
  a **hand/facial** gesture
  a **rude/obscene/threatening/dismissive/impatient** gesture

▶ **PHRASES:**
words and gestures
gestures and expressions
▶ **SYNONYMS:** movement, motion

---

globe /gləʊb/ (globes)   ACADEMIC WORD

1 NOUN You can refer to the world as **the globe** when you are emphasizing
how big it is or that something happens in many different parts of it.
○ *anticapitalism protests spanning the globe from Seattle to Genoa* ○ *70% of our
globe's surface is water.*

▶ **COLLOCATIONS:**
across/around the globe
traverse/travel/tour/span the globe
the globe's **surface/climate/population**
▶ **PHRASE:** every corner of the globe
▶ **SYNONYMS:** planet, earth, world

2 NOUN Any ball-shaped object can be referred to as a **globe**. ○ *The overhead
light was covered now with a white globe.*

▶ **COLLOCATIONS:**
a **crystal/glass/copper/bronze** globe
a **green/yellow/spherical/giant** globe
▶ **SYNONYM:** sphere

glob|al /ˈgləʊbəl/

ADJECTIVE You can use **global** to describe something that happens in all parts
of the world or affects all parts of the world. ○ *a global ban on nuclear testing*
○ *On a global scale, AIDS may well become the leading cause of infant death.*

▶ **COLLOCATIONS:**
a global **scale/reach**
a global **recession/downturn/recovery**
a global **brand/trend**
the global **economy/marketplace**
global **trade/growth/capitalism/poverty/terrorism**
increasingly global
▶ **PHRASE:** global warming
▶ **SYNONYMS:** worldwide, international
▶ **ANTONYM:** local

glob|al|ly /ˈgləʊbəli/

ADVERB ○ *a globally familiar trade name* ○ *Indian companies that compete globally*
▶ **COLLOCATIONS:**
export/trade/operate/compete globally

globally **significant/famous/successful/familiar**
▸ SYNONYMS: worldwide, internationally

glob|ali|za|tion /ˌgləʊbəlaɪˈzeɪʃən/

UNCOUNTABLE NOUN **Globalization** is the standardization or growth of something around the world, for example of a trade or industry. ○ [+ of] *The globalization of industry has affected food production in California.* ○ *a period of rapid economic globalization*

▸ COLLOCATIONS:
   the globalization **of** *something*
   the globalization of **economy/trade/industry**
   rapid/increasing globalization
   economic/corporate globalization

glos|sa|ry /ˈglɒsəri, AM ˈglɔːs-/ (glossaries) LANGUAGE ACADEMIC STUDY

NOUN A **glossary** of special, unusual, or technical words or expressions is an alphabetical list of them giving their meanings, for example at the end of a book on a particular subject. ○ [+ of] *a glossary of commonly used Japanese business terms*

▸ COLLOCATION: a glossary **of** *something*

goal /gəʊl/ (goals) ACADEMIC WORD

NOUN Something that is your **goal** is something that you hope to achieve, especially when much time and effort will be needed. ○ *Be realistic and set goals that are within reach.* ○ *Their goals are ambitious: to nearly double federal money for Down syndrome research.* ○ [+ of] *the Nationalist goal of independence*

→ see note at **aim**

▸ COLLOCATIONS:
   the goal **of** *something*
   set/accomplish/achieve/reach a goal
   the **ultimate/main/key/stated** goal
   an **achievable/ambitious/unrealistic** goal

▸ SYNONYMS: aim, objective, ambition

goods /gʊdz/ BUSINESS

PLURAL NOUN **Goods** are things that are made to be sold. ○ *Money can be exchanged for goods or services.* ○ *China is now producing high-quality goods at low cost.* ○ *a wide range of consumer goods*

▸ COLLOCATIONS:
   consumer/durable/manufactured/foreign goods
   electrical/household/sporting/luxury goods
   produce/manufacture/buy/sell/import/export goods

▶ **PHRASE:** goods and services
▶ **SYNONYMS:** merchandise, products

---

grade /greɪd/ (grades, grading, graded) `ACADEMIC WORD`

1 VERB If something **is graded**, its quality is judged, and it is often given a number or a name that indicates how good or bad it is. ○ *Dust masks are graded according to the protection they offer.* ○ *South Point College does not grade the students' work.*

▶ **COLLOCATIONS:**
a grading **system/structure**
grade an **exam/exercise/assignment**

▶ **SYNONYMS:** mark, categorize

2 NOUN Your **grade** in an examination or piece of written work is the mark you get, usually in the form of a letter or number, that indicates your level of achievement. ○ *Results show a 0.8 percentage point increase in candidates achieving a grade A.*

▶ **COLLOCATIONS:**
get/obtain/attain/achieve a grade
a **good/high/low** grade
A-Level/GCSE/university/exam grades
grade **A/B/C**

▶ **SYNONYMS:** mark, score

---

grav|ity /ˈɡrævɪti/ `PHYSICS`

UNCOUNTABLE NOUN Gravity is the force which causes things to drop to the ground. ○ *Arrows would continue to fly forward forever in a straight line were it not for gravity.*

▶ **COLLOCATIONS:**
the **planet's/earth's/moon's** gravity
gravity's **pull**

---

guar|an|tee /ˌɡærənˈtiː/ `ACADEMIC WORD`
(guarantees, guaranteeing, guaranteed)

1 VERB If one thing **guarantees** another, the first is certain to cause the second thing to happen. ○ *Surplus resources alone do not guarantee growth.* ○ [+ that] *one of the few ways to virtually guarantee that a fraudster cannot open an account in your name*

2 VERB If you **guarantee** something, you promise that it will definitely happen, or that you will do or provide it for someone. ○ *Most states guarantee the right to free and adequate education.* ○ *All students are guaranteed campus accommodation.*

▶ **COLLOCATIONS:**
  guarantee **freedom/security/rights/access**
  guarantee **safety/success/satisfaction**
  guarantee a **return/income**
  virtually/almost guarantee

▶ **SYNONYMS:** ensure, promise

3 NOUN A **guarantee** is a promise that something will definitely happen or that you will do or provide it. ○ [+ that] *The Editor can give no guarantee that they will fulfil their obligations.* ○ [+ of] *California's state Constitution includes a guarantee of privacy.*

▶ **COLLOCATIONS:**
  a guarantee **of** *something*
  a guarantee of **freedom/success/safety/quality**
  a **written/constitutional/cast-iron** guarantee
  seek/require a guarantee
  supply/offer/provide/obtain/secure a guarantee

▶ **SYNONYMS:** promise, pledge

---

guide|line /ˈgaɪdlaɪn/ (guidelines)   `ACADEMIC WORD`

NOUN Guidelines on something are rules or advice about how to do it.
  ○ [+ on] *The government should issue clear guidelines on the content of religious education.* ○ [+ for] *The accord also lays down guidelines for the conduct of American drug enforcement agents.*

▶ **COLLOCATIONS:**
  guidelines **on/for** *something*
  issue/establish/set/propose guidelines
  follow/violate/breach guidelines
  ethical/dietary/clinical/safety/sentencing guidelines
  strict/stringent/general/voluntary guidelines

▶ **SYNONYMS:** rule, procedure, recommendation, principle

Hh

hard|ship /ˈhɑːdʃɪp/ (hardships)

NOUN Hardship is a situation in which your life is difficult or unpleasant, often because you do not have enough money. ○ *Many people are suffering economic hardship.* ○ *The publicity surrounding the case had caused the family considerable hardship.*

▶ **COLLOCATIONS:**
  suffer/endure/face/flee/overcome hardship
  cause/inflict hardship
  economic/financial hardship
  extreme/severe/considerable/genuine/real hardship

▶ **SYNONYMS:** privation, suffering, adversity

harsh /hɑːʃ/ (harsher, harshest)

1 ADJECTIVE Harsh climates or conditions are very difficult for people, animals, and plants to live in. ○ *The climate is too harsh for grape growing.* ○ *the harsh desert environment* ○ *after the harsh experience of the war*

▶ **COLLOCATIONS:**
  a harsh **climate/winter/environment**
  a harsh **experience/regime**
  harsh **conditions**

▶ **SYNONYM:** severe

▶ **ANTONYM:** mild

2 ADJECTIVE Harsh actions or speech are unkind and show no understanding or sympathy. ○ *Immediate and harsh punishments could have a deterrent effect on others.* ○ *In 1994, a riot at Kingston prison brought about harsh criticism of the facility.*

▶ **COLLOCATIONS:**
  a harsh **punishment/sentence/penalty**
  harsh **criticism**
  unduly/unfairly/unnecessarily/overly harsh

▶ **SYNONYMS:** cruel, brutal, severe, stern

▶ **ANTONYMS:** kind, lenient

harsh|ness /ˈhɑːʃnəs/

UNCOUNTABLE NOUN ○ [+ *of*] *the harshness of their living conditions* ○ [+ *of*] *Police officers expressed surprise at the harshness of the seven year sentence.*

▶ **COLLOCATIONS:**
the harshness **of** *something*
the harshness of the **winter/climate/landscape**
the harshness of a **punishment/sentence**
unrelenting/unexpected/extraordinary harshness
▶ **SYNONYMS:** severity, cruelty
▶ **ANTONYMS:** mildness, leniency

---

hec|tare /ˈhekteə/ (hectares)

NOUN A **hectare** is a measurement of an area of land which is equal to 10,000 square metres, or 2.471 acres. ○ [+ *of*] *hundreds of hectares of farmland* ○ *a small strip of twelve hectares stretching from the road to the shore*
▶ **COLLOCATION:** *x* hectares **of** something

---

hence /hens/

ACADEMIC WORD

ADVERB You use **hence** to indicate that the statement you are about to make is a consequence of what you have just said. [FORMAL] ○ *The trade imbalance is likely to rise again in 1990. Hence a new set of policy actions will be required soon.* ○ *European music happens to use a scale of eight notes, hence the use of the term octave.*

> **EXTEND YOUR VOCABULARY**
>
> **Hence**, **thus** and **therefore** are used to introduce a consequence when you are talking about cause and effect. **Hence** and **thus** are more formal. ○ *They will be able to produce their own food and hence/thus free themselves from dependence on other nations.*
>
> **Therefore** emphasizes that something is the logical result of something else. ○ *Because more glucose is released during digestion of white bread it is therefore more fattening.*

---

he|redi|tary /hɪˈredɪtri/

BIOLOGY MEDICINE

ADJECTIVE A **hereditary** characteristic or illness is passed on to a child from its parents before it is born. ○ *Cystic fibrosis is the commonest fatal hereditary disease.* ○ *In men, hair loss is hereditary.*
▶ **COLLOCATIONS:**
a hereditary **disease**
a hereditary **trait/characteristic/factor**
▶ **SYNONYMS:** genetic, inherited

he|red|ity /hɪˈredɪti/

UNCOUNTABLE NOUN ○ *Heredity is not a factor in causing the cancer.* ○ *the view that heredity determines intelligence*

▶ **COLLOCATION:** heredity **determines/influences** *something*
▶ **PHRASE:** heredity and environment
▶ **SYNONYM:** genetics

---

high|light /ˈhaɪlaɪt/ (highlights, highlighting, highlighted) `ACADEMIC WORD`

VERB If someone or something **highlights** a point or problem, they emphasize it or make you think about it. ○ *This incident highlights the care needed when disposing of unwanted plants.* ○ *Once again, the 'Free Press' prefers not to highlight these facts.*

▶ **COLLOCATIONS:**
   highlight the **importance/need/danger/lack** of *something*
   a **report/survey/incident** highlights *something*
   clearly/dramatically highlighted
▶ **SYNONYMS:** emphasize, draw attention to, illustrate, expose

---

hori|zon|tal /ˈhɒrɪˌzɒntəl, AM ˈhɔːr-/

ADJECTIVE Something that is **horizontal** is flat and level with the ground, rather than at an angle to it. ○ *The board consists of vertical and horizontal lines.* ○ *The horizontal axis in both figures shows unexpected changes in exchange rates.*
→ see note at **axis**

● **Horizontal** is also a noun. ○ *Do not raise your left arm above the horizontal.*

▶ **COLLOCATIONS:**
   a horizontal **line/stripe/axis**
   virtually/completely/perfectly horizontal
▶ **RELATED WORDS:** vertical, diagonal

hori|zon|tal|ly /ˌhɒrɪˈzɒntəli, AM ˌhɔːr-/

ADVERB ○ [+ *across*] *a fence placed horizontally across the painting* ○ *The wings are designed to provide uplift when the plane is flying horizontally.*

▶ **COLLOCATIONS:**
   horizontally **across/along/between** *something*
   horizontally **over/under** *something*
   extended/suspended/spread/laid horizontally
▶ **RELATED WORDS:** vertically, diagonally

---

house|hold /ˈhaʊshəʊld/ (households)   `SOCIOLOGY`

NOUN A **household** is all the people in a family or group who live together in a house. ○ *a male-only household* ○ *Many poor households are experiencing real hardship.* ○ *The average household consists of three people.*

▶ **COLLOCATIONS:**
   a **single-parent/affluent/low-income** household

a **rural/average** household
household **income/spending/debt**
▶ PHRASE: the head of the household

humanities /hjuːˈmænɪtiz/ EDUCATION

PLURAL NOUN **The humanities** are the subjects such as history, philosophy, and literature which are concerned with human ideas and behaviour. ○ *students majoring in the humanities* ○ *Job seeking can be difficult for many humanities graduates.*
▶ COLLOCATION: a humanities **degree/graduate/student/professor**
▶ SYNONYM: arts
▶ RELATED WORD: sciences

hydro|gen /ˈhaɪdrədʒən/ SCIENCE

UNCOUNTABLE NOUN **Hydrogen** is a colourless gas that is the lightest and commonest element in the universe. ○ *a ball of liquid and gaseous hydrogen* ○ *Pure hydrogen is an explosive gas and difficult to store.*
▶ COLLOCATIONS:
  gaseous/liquid hydrogen
  neutral/atomic/pure hydrogen
  hydrogen **peroxide/fluoride/sulphide/chloride**

hy|giene /ˈhaɪdʒiːn/ MEDICINE

UNCOUNTABLE NOUN **Hygiene** is the practice of keeping yourself and your surroundings clean, especially in order to prevent illness or the spread of diseases. ○ *It was difficult to ensure hygiene when doctors were conducting numerous operations in quick succession.* ○ *a strict regime of cleanliness and personal hygiene*
▶ COLLOCATIONS:
  good/bad/poor/basic hygiene
  personal/oral/dental hygiene
  ensure/maintain hygiene
▶ SYNONYMS: cleanliness, sanitation

hy|gien|ic /haɪˈdʒiːnɪk, AM ˌhaɪˈdʒienɪk/

ADJECTIVE Something that is **hygienic** is clean and unlikely to cause illness. ○ *Young people are generally less scrupulous in following hygienic food practices.* ○ *Hospitals should be clean and hygienic.*
▶ COLLOCATIONS:
  hygienic **practices/conditions/habits**
  a hygienic **environment**

▶ **PHRASES:**
safe and hygienic
clean and hygienic
▶ **SYNONYMS:** clean, sanitary
▶ **ANTONYM:** unhygienic

---

hy|poth|esis /haɪˈpɒθɪsɪs/ `ACADEMIC STUDY` `ACADEMIC WORD`
(hypotheses)

NOUN A **hypothesis** is an idea which is suggested as a possible explanation for a particular situation or condition, but which has not yet been proved to be correct. [FORMAL] ○ *Work will now begin to test the hypothesis in rats.* ○ *Different hypotheses have been put forward to explain why these foods are more likely to cause problems.*

▶ **COLLOCATIONS:**
a **null/testable/scientific/statistical/reasonable** hypothesis
predict/propose/suggest/put forward a hypothesis
test/confirm/prove a hypothesis
▶ **SYNONYMS:** theory, proposal

hypo|theti|cal /ˌhaɪpəˈθetɪkəl/

ADJECTIVE If something is **hypothetical**, it is based on possible ideas or situations rather than actual ones. ○ *Candidates are required to describe what they would do in a variety of hypothetical situations.* ○ *a purely hypothetical question*

▶ **COLLOCATIONS:**
purely/entirely/strictly hypothetical
a hypothetical **situation/scenario/example/question/dilemma**
▶ **SYNONYM:** theoretical

hypo|theti|cal|ly /ˌhaɪpəˈθetɪkli/

ADVERB ○ *He was invariably willing to discuss the possibilities hypothetically.* ○ *It bases its figures on what it might, hypothetically, be earning on past investment.*

▶ **PHRASE:** hypothetically speaking
▶ **SYNONYM:** theoretically

Ii

ideal /aɪˈdiːəl/ (ideals)　POLITICS

NOUN An **ideal** is a principle, idea, or standard that seems very good and worth trying to achieve. ○ *The party has drifted too far from its socialist ideals.* ○ [+ *of*] *Republics embody the ideal of equality among citizens in political affairs.*

▶ COLLOCATIONS:
an ideal **of** *something*
an ideal of **perfection/beauty/equality/freedom/democracy**
a **lofty/noble/abstract** ideal
a **socialist/democratic/humanist** ideal
embody/espouse/uphold/cherish an ideal

▶ SYNONYMS: principle, belief, value

ideal|ism /aɪˈdiːəlɪzəm/

UNCOUNTABLE NOUN **Idealism** is the beliefs and behaviour of someone who has ideals and who tries to base their behaviour on these ideals. ○ [+ *of*] *She never lost her respect for the idealism of the 1960s.* ○ *This experience has tempered their idealism.*

▶ COLLOCATIONS:
the idealism **of** *someone/something*
youthful/romantic/misplaced idealism

▶ SYNONYM: optimism

▶ ANTONYMS: realism, pessimism, cynicism

ideal|is|tic /ˌaɪdiəˈlɪstɪk/

ADJECTIVE If you describe someone as **idealistic**, you mean that they have ideals, and base their behaviour on these ideals, even though this may be impractical. ○ *Idealistic young people died for the cause.* ○ *an over-simplistic and idealistic vision of family dynamics*

▶ COLLOCATION: an idealistic **notion/vision/view**

▶ SYNONYMS: optimistic, impractical

▶ ANTONYMS: realistic, pessimistic, cynical

iden|ti|cal /aɪˈdentɪkəl/　ACADEMIC WORD

ADJECTIVE Things that are **identical** are exactly the same. ○ [+ *to*] *The new buildings look identical to those built 200 years ago.* ○ *The two parties fought the last election on almost identical manifestos.*

▶ **COLLOCATIONS:**
identical **to/with** *something*
an identical **copy/score/twin**
identical **wording/circumstances**
functionally/genetically identical
look identical

▶ **SYNONYMS:** the same, indistinguishable

▶ **ANTONYM:** different

iden|ti|cal|ly /aɪˈdentɪkli/

ADVERB ○ *two separate but identically worded statements* ○ *Not all people respond identically to the same diet.*

▶ **COLLOCATION:** identically **dressed/worded**

▶ **ANTONYM:** differently

iden|ti|fy /aɪˈdentɪfaɪ/ (identifies, identifying, identified) ACADEMIC WORD

1 VERB If you can **identify** someone or something, you are able to recognize them or distinguish them from others. ○ *There are a number of distinguishing characteristics by which you can identify a Hollywood epic.*

▶ **COLLOCATIONS:**
postively identify *someone/something*
correctly/incorrectly identify *someone/something*

▶ **SYNONYMS:** recognize, distinguish

2 VERB If you **identify** something, you discover or notice its existence. ○ *Scientists claim to have identified natural substances with cancer-combating properties.* ○ [+ *as*] *It was not until the twentieth century that mosquitoes were identified as the carriers of malaria.*

▶ **COLLOCATIONS:**
identify *something* **as** *something*
identify a **cause/factor/need/gene/virus**

▶ **SYNONYM:** discover

iden|ti|fi|ca|tion /aɪˌdentɪfɪˈkeɪʃən/

UNCOUNTABLE NOUN The **identification** of something is the recognition that it exists, is important, or is true. ○ [+ *of*] *Early identification of a disease can prevent death and illness.* ○ [+ *of*] *the identification of training needs*

▶ **COLLOCATIONS:**
the identification **of** *something*
the identification of a **gene/protein/factor/need**

▶ **SYNONYM:** recognition

iden|tity /aɪˈdentɪti/ (identities)

NOUN Your **identity** is who you are. ○ *Abu is not his real name, but it's one he uses* *to disguise his identity.* ○ *the growing problem of identity theft* ○ [+ of] *The identities of the victims were announced.*

▶ COLLOCATIONS:
the identity **of** *someone*
the identity of a **victim/attacker/informant**
reveal/disclose/establish/confirm/verify *someone's* identity
steal/forge/protect *someone's* identity
mistaken/false/true identity
identity **theft/fraud**
an identity **card/thief**

---

i.e. /ˌaɪ ˈiː/ **i.e.** is used to introduce a word or sentence   ACADEMIC STUDY
which makes what you have just said clearer or gives details. ○ *strategic points – i.e. airports or military bases* ○ *concerns that the vitamin might be carcinogenic (i.e. cancer inducing)*

▶ SYNONYMS: that is, in other words

il|lit|er|ate /ɪˈlɪtərət/ (**illiterates**)   EDUCATION   LANGUAGE   SOCIOLOGY

ADJECTIVE Someone who is **illiterate** does not know how to read or write.
○ *seven out of ten prisoners are functionally illiterate* ○ *India's neglected and largely illiterate tribal populations*

▶ COLLOCATIONS:
functionally/practically illiterate
an illiterate **peasant/worker/adult/population**
▶ ANTONYM: literate

il|lus|trate /ˈɪləstreɪt/ (**illustrates, illustrating, illustrated**)   ACADEMIC WORD

1 VERB If you say that something **illustrates** a situation that you are drawing attention to, you mean that it shows that the situation exists. ○ *The example of the United States illustrates this point.* ○ [+ how] *The incident graphically illustrates how parlous their position is.* ○ [+ that] *The case also illustrates that some women are now trying to fight back.*

2 VERB If you use an example, story, or diagram to **illustrate** a point, you use it to show that what you are saying is true or to make your meaning clearer.
○ *To illustrate this point, Wolf gives an example from the car production sector in America.* ○ [+ with] *Throughout, she illustrates her analysis with excerpts from discussions.*

▶ COLLOCATIONS:
illustrate *something* **with/by** *something*
illustrate *something* by a **story/fact/example/case**
illustrate a **point/principle/difficulty**
illustrate the **importance/extent/complexity** of *something*
graphically/perfectly/vividly illustrate
▶ SYNONYMS: demonstrate, exemplify

illustration | 220

il|lus|tra|tion /ˌɪləˈstreɪʃən/

NOUN ○ *This can best be described by way of illustration.* ○ *[+ of] a perfect illustration of the way Britain absorbs and adapts external influences*

▶ **COLLOCATIONS:**
an illustration **of** *something*
an illustration of a **fact/effect/principle/difference**

▶ **PHRASE:** by way of illustration

▶ **SYNONYMS:** demonstration, example

---

im|mi|grate /ˈɪmɪɡreɪt/ ACADEMIC WORD SOCIAL SCIENCE
(immigrates, immigrating, immigrated)

VERB If someone **immigrates** to a particular country, they come to live or work in that country, after leaving the country where they were born. ○ *[+ to] a Russian-born professor who had immigrated to the United States* ○ *[+ from] He immigrated from Ulster in 1848.* ○ *10,000 people are expected to immigrate in the next two years.*

→ see note at **emigrate**

▶ **COLLOCATION:** immigrate **to/from** *somewhere*

▶ **RELATED WORDS:** migrate, emigrate

im|mi|gra|tion /ˌɪmɪˈɡreɪʃən/

UNCOUNTABLE NOUN **Immigration** is the coming of people into a country in order to live and work there. ○ *The government has decided to tighten its immigration policy.* ○ *[+ into] immigration into Europe* ○ *measures aimed at curbing illegal immigration*

→ see note at **emigrate**

▶ **COLLOCATIONS:**
immigration **into** *somewhere*
curb/restrict/combat/tackle/control immigration
mass/illegal immigration
an immigration **policy/law/official**
immigration **control**

▶ **RELATED WORDS:** migration, emigration

im|mi|grant /ˈɪmɪɡrənt/ **(immigrants)**

NOUN An **immigrant** is a person who has come to live in a country from some other country. ○ *industries that employ large numbers of illegal immigrants* ○ *Portugal, Spain and Italy all have large immigrant populations from Africa.*

→ see note at **emigrate**

▶ **COLLOCATIONS:**
a **skilled/illegal** immigrant
a **first-generation/second-generation** immigrant

deport/detain/smuggle immigrants
immigrants **arrive/settle/flee**
an immigrant **population/community/worker/visa**
▶ **ANTONYM:** emigrant
▶ **RELATED WORDS:** asylum seeker, refugee, migrant

---

im|pact (impacts, impacting, impacted)   `ACADEMIC WORD`

> The noun is pronounced /ˈɪmpækt/. The verb is pronounced /ɪmˈpækt/.

1 NOUN The **impact** that something has **on** a situation, process, or person is a sudden and powerful effect that it has on them. ○ [+ on] *the mining industry's devastating impact on the environment* ○ *an area where technology can make a real impact*

▶ **COLLOCATIONS:**
an impact **on** *something*
an impact on the **environment/economy**
an impact on **society/health/earnings/tourism**
a **historical/economic/environmental** impact
a **significant/important/major/profound** impact
a **lasting/immediate/negative/adverse/positive** impact
an impact **statement/assessment/study**

▶ **SYNONYMS:** effect, mark, impression

2 VERB To **impact on** a situation, process, or person means to affect them.
○ [+ on] *That would impact on inflation and competition.* ○ *the potential for women to impact the political process*

▶ **COLLOCATIONS:**
impact **on/upon** *something*
impact on/upon **growth/industry**
negatively/adversely/directly impact

▶ **SYNONYM:** affect

---

im|par|tial /ɪmˈpɑːʃəl/

ADJECTIVE Someone who is **impartial** is not directly involved in a particular situation, and is therefore able to give a fair opinion or decision about it.
○ *Citizens have the right to a speedy and public trial before an impartial jury.*
○ *Careers officers offer impartial advice to all pupils.*

▶ **COLLOCATIONS:**
impartial **advice**
an impartial **jury/tribunal/judge**
an impartial **analysis/investigation/manner**

▶ **SYNONYMS:** unbiased, neutral, objective, disinterested
▶ **ANTONYMS:** partial, biased

im|par|tial|ity /ˌɪmpɑːʃiˈælɪti/

UNCOUNTABLE NOUN ○ *a justice system lacking impartiality by democratic standards*

▶ **COLLOCATIONS:**
judicial/political impartiality
ensure/maintain impartiality

▶ **SYNONYMS:** neutrality, objectivity

▶ **ANTONYMS:** partiality, bias

im|par|tial|ly /ɪmˈpɑːʃəli/

ADVERB ○ *He has vowed to oversee the elections impartially.* ○ *an impartially conducted study*

▶ **SYNONYMS:** neutrally, objectively

▶ **ANTONYM:** partially

---

im|ple|ment /ˈɪmplɪmənt/ `ACADEMIC WORD`
(implements, implementing, implemented)

VERB If you **implement** something such as a plan, you ensure that what has been planned is done. ○ *The government promised to implement a new system to control financial loan institutions.* ○ *The report sets out strict inspection procedures to ensure that the recommendations are properly implemented.*

▶ **COLLOCATIONS:**
implement a **plan/policy/programme/change**
implement a **recommendation/directive**
successfully/poorly implement *something*

im|ple|men|ta|tion /ˌɪmplɪmənˈteɪʃən/

UNCOUNTABLE NOUN ○ [+ *of*] *Very little has been achieved in the implementation of the peace agreement.* ○ [+ *of*] *Full implementation of the ban was deferred until 2012.*

▶ **COLLOCATIONS:**
the implementation **of** *something*
the implementation of a **plan/policy/agreement**
oversee/monitor/delay/defer implementation
full/effective/successful implementation

---

im|pli|ca|tion /ˌɪmplɪˈkeɪʃən/ **(implications)** `ACADEMIC WORD`

NOUN The **implications of** something are the things that are likely to happen as a result. ○ [+ *of*] *the political implications of his decision* ○ [+ *for*] *The low level of investment has serious implications for future economic growth.*

▶ **COLLOCATIONS:**
the implications **of/for** *something*
far-reaching/profound/wide/serious implications
grasp/understand/consider the implications

▶ **SYNONYMS:** consequence, effect, ramifications

im|ply /ɪmˈplaɪ/ (implies, implying, implied) ACADEMIC WORD

VERB If an event or situation **implies** that something is the case, it makes you think it likely that it is the case. ○ [+ that] *Exports in June rose 1.5%, implying that the economy was stronger than many investors had realized.* ○ *A 'frontier-free' Europe implies a greatly increased market for all economic operators.*

▸ **COLLOCATION: not necessarily/clearly/strongly** imply *something*

▸ **SYNONYMS:** suggest, indicate, point to

im|port (imports, importing, imported) BUSINESS

The verb is pronounced /ɪmˈpɔːt/. The noun is pronounced /ˈɪmpɔːt/.

1 VERB To **import** products or raw materials means to buy them from another country for use in your own country. ○ *Britain spent nearly £5000 million more on importing food than selling abroad.* ○ [+ from] *imported goods from Mexico*

▸ **COLLOCATIONS:**
import *something* **from** *somewhere*
import **goods/products/oil/steel/beef**
import *x* **tonnes** of *something*

▸ **PHRASE:** importing and exporting

▸ **ANTONYM:** export

● **Import** is also a noun. ○ [+ of] *Germany, however, insists on restrictions on the import of Polish coal.* ○ *import duties on cars*

▸ **COLLOCATIONS:**
the import **of** *something*
import **tariffs/duty/restrictions**

▸ **ANTONYM:** export

2 NOUN Imports are products or raw materials bought from another country for use in your own country. ○ *farmers protesting about cheap imports* ○ *Exports fell 3 per cent while imports rose 1 per cent.*

▸ **COLLOCATIONS:**
cheap/expensive/illegal imports
beef/oil/steel imports
ban/restrict/allow imports
imports **rise/fall**

▸ **ANTONYM:** exports

im|por|ta|tion /ˌɪmpɔːˈteɪʃən/

UNCOUNTABLE NOUN ○ [+ of] *restrictions concerning the importation of birds*

▸ **COLLOCATIONS:**
the importation **of** *something*
the importation of **drugs/slaves/cattle**
legalize/allow/ban/prohibit importation

illegal/wholesale importation
▶ **ANTONYM:** exportation

im|pose /ɪmˈpəʊz/ (imposes, imposing, imposed) `ACADEMIC WORD`

VERB If you **impose** something **on** people, you use your authority to force them to accept it. ○ [+ on] *Britain imposed fines on airlines which bring in passengers without proper papers.* ○ *Many companies have imposed a pay freeze.*

▶ COLLOCATIONS:
impose something **on** someone/something
impose **restrictions/sanctions**
impose a **fine/tax/penalty/sentence/ban/limit**
a **judge/authority/government** imposes something
externally/unilaterally/centrally imposed

▶ SYNONYMS: dictate, enforce

im|po|si|tion /ˌɪmpəˈzɪʃən/

UNCOUNTABLE NOUN ○ [+ of] *the imposition of a ban on cycling in the city centre* ○ [+ of] *The key factor is that there is no imposition of locally unpopular development.*

▶ COLLOCATIONS:
the imposition **of** something
the imposition of **sanctions/tariffs/VAT**
the imposition of a **penalty/law**

▶ SYNONYM: enforcement

in|ac|cu|rate /ɪnˈækjʊrət/

ADJECTIVE If a statement or measurement is **inaccurate**, it is not accurate or correct. ○ *These figures are inaccurate and misleading.* ○ *The reports were based on inaccurate information.*

▶ COLLOCATIONS:
inaccurate **information/reporting**
an inaccurate **description/portrayal**
factually/historically/wildly/grossly inaccurate
figures/results are inaccurate
a **claim/report** is inaccurate

▶ SYNONYMS: wrong, incorrect
▶ ANTONYMS: accurate, correct

in|ac|cu|rate|ly /ɪnˈækjʊrətli/

ADVERB ○ *He claimed his remarks had been reported inaccurately.* ○ *Your story inaccurately cites a Waikato University study.*

▶ COLLOCATION: inaccurately **reported/described/portrayed**
▶ SYNONYMS: wrongly, incorrectly
▶ ANTONYMS: accurately, correctly

in|ac|cu|ra|cy /ɪnˈækjʊrəsi/ (inaccuracies)

NOUN The **inaccuracy** of a statement or measurement is the fact that it is not accurate or correct. ○ [+ of] *He was disturbed by the inaccuracy of the answers.* ○ *The report contains serious factual inaccuracies.*

▶ **COLLOCATIONS:**
the inaccuracy **of** something
factual/historical/glaring inaccuracy
contain/correct an inaccuracy

▶ **SYNONYMS:** incorrectness, mistakes

▶ **ANTONYM:** accuracy

> **ACADEMIC WRITING: Avoiding negatives**
>
> In formal, academic writing, you need to be as clear and accurate as possible. It is better to avoid negative constructions by using words like **inaccurate**, **irregular** and **unambiguous** that have a negative meaning. For example, the sentence: ○ *The allegations are based on inaccurate and incomplete data.* is clearer than: ○ *The allegations are based on data that are not accurate or complete.*

in|ad|equate /ɪnˈædɪkwət/

ADJECTIVE If something is **inadequate**, there is not enough of it or it is not good enough. ○ *Supplies of food and medicines are inadequate.* ○ *The problem goes far beyond inadequate staffing.*

▶ **COLLOCATIONS:**
inadequate to **deal with/meet** something
inadequate **funding/training/staffing/supervision**
an inadequate **supply/response**
woefully/grossly inadequate

▶ **SYNONYM:** deficient

▶ **ANTONYM:** adequate

in|ad|equate|ly /ɪnˈædɪkwətli/

ADVERB ○ *The projects were inadequately funded.* ○ *inadequately trained staff*

▶ **COLLOCATION:** inadequately **trained/funded/prepared/protected**

▶ **SYNONYM:** deficiently

▶ **ANTONYM:** adequately

in|con|sist|ent /ˌɪnkənˈsɪstənt/

1 ADJECTIVE If two statements are **inconsistent**, one cannot possibly be true if the other is true. ○ [+ with] *The evidence given in court was inconsistent with what he had previously told them.* ○ *The report is internally inconsistent and conflicts directly with previous reports by the Academy.*

2 ADJECTIVE If something is **inconsistent with** a set of ideas or values, it does not fit in well with them or match them. ○ [+ with] *This legislation is inconsistent with what they call Free Trade.* ○ [+ with] *The details of that meeting are by no means inconsistent with other evidence.*

▶ **COLLOCATIONS:**
inconsistent **with** *something*
inconsistent with a **principle/value/purpose/statement**
inconsistent with the **evidence**
internally/logically/fundamentally inconsistent

▶ **SYNONYMS:** contradictory, conflicting, incompatible

▶ **ANTONYM:** consistent

in|con|sist|en|cy /ɪnkən'sɪstənsi/ (inconsistencies)

NOUN If there are **inconsistencies** in two statements, one cannot be true if the other is true. ○ [+ in] *a series of inconsistencies in the data* ○ [+ of] *Hurd is aware of the complete inconsistency of his argument.* ○ [+ between] *the glaring inconsistency between the two statements*

▶ **COLLOCATIONS:**
the inconsistency **of/in** *something*
inconsistency **between** *things*
inconsistencies in **evidence/data**
glaring/apparent/internal inconsistencies

▶ **SYNONYM:** contradiction

▶ **ANTONYM:** consistency

in|dex /'ɪndeks/ (indexes) `ACADEMIC WORD` `ACADEMIC STUDY`

NOUN An **index** is an alphabetical list that is printed at the back of a book and tells you on which pages important topics are referred to. ○ *There's even a special subject index.*

→ see note at **appendix**

▶ **COLLOCATION:** an **alphabetical** index

▶ **RELATED WORD:** table of contents

in|di|cate /'ɪndɪkeɪt/ (indicates, indicating, indicated) `ACADEMIC WORD`

1 VERB If one thing **indicates** another, the first thing shows that the second is true or exists. ○ [+ that] *A survey of retired people has indicated that most are independent and enjoying life.* ○ [+ whether] *This indicates whether remedies are suitable for children.*

▶ **COLLOCATIONS:**
a **poll/study/survey/report** indicates *something*
research/findings/statistics indicate *something*
indicate the **extent/degree/presence/lack** of *something*

clearly/previously/otherwise indicated
▶ SYNONYMS: demonstrate, show

2 VERB If a technical instrument **indicates** something, it shows a measurement or reading. ○ *The needles that indicate your height are at the top right-hand corner.* ○ [+ that] *The temperature gauge indicated that it was boiling.*
▶ SYNONYM: show

in|di|ca|tion /ˌɪndɪˈkeɪʃən/ (indications)

NOUN An **indication** is a sign which suggests that something exists or is going to happen. ○ *All the indications are that we are going to receive reasonable support from abroad.* ○ [+ of] *These numbers give an indication of the extent of the disease.*
▶ COLLOCATIONS:
   an indication **of** something
   an indication of **strength/importance/progress**
   a **clear/strong/early/initial** indication
▶ SYNONYM: sign

in|di|ca|tor /ˈɪndɪkeɪtə/ (indicators)

NOUN An **indicator** is a measurement or value which gives you an idea of what something is like. ○ *vital economic indicators, such as inflation, growth and the trade gap* ○ [+ of] *The number of wells is a fair indicator of the demand for water.*
▶ COLLOCATIONS:
   an indicator **of** something
   an indicator **suggests/shows/points to** something
   a **key/reliable/broad/leading** indicator
   a **performance/stock/economic** indicator

in|di|rect /ˌɪndaɪˈrekt, -dɪr-/

ADJECTIVE An **indirect** result or effect is not caused immediately and obviously by a thing or person, but happens because of something else that they have done. ○ *Businesses are feeling the indirect effects from the recession that's going on elsewhere.* ○ *Millions could die of hunger as an indirect result of the war.*
▶ COLLOCATIONS:
   indirect **taxation/taxes/costs**
   an indirect **effect**
▶ ANTONYM: direct

in|di|rect|ly /ˌɪndaɪˈrektli, -dɪr-/

ADVERB ○ *Drugs are indirectly responsible for the violence.* ○ *The depletion of atmospheric ozone may indirectly affect our use of the coastal zone.*

▶ **COLLOCATIONS:**
indirectly **influenced/related/responsible**
indirectly **affect** *someone*
contribute/benefit indirectly

▶ **ANTONYM:** directly

---

in|dus|try /ˈɪndəstri/ (industries) `BUSINESS`

NOUN **Industry** is the work and processes involved in making products in factories. A particular **industry** consists of all the people and activities involved in a particular area of work. ○ *in countries where industry is developing rapidly* ○ *the motor vehicle and textile industries*

in|dus|trial /ɪnˈdʌstriəl/

1 ADJECTIVE You use **industrial** to describe things which relate to or are used in industry. ○ *industrial machinery and equipment* ○ *a link between industrial chemicals and cancer*

▶ **COLLOCATION:** industrial **machinery/products/production**

▶ **PHRASES:**
industrial action
an industrial estate
industrial relations

2 ADJECTIVE An **industrial** city or country is one in which industry is important or highly developed. ○ *ministers from leading western industrial countries*

▶ **COLLOCATION:** an industrial **area/city/country**

▶ **SYNONYMS:** industrialized, developed

---

in|evi|table /ɪnˈevɪtəbəl/ `ACADEMIC WORD`

ADJECTIVE If something is **inevitable**, it is certain to happen and cannot be prevented or avoided. ○ [+ *that*] *If the case succeeds, it is inevitable that other trials will follow.* ○ *The defeat had inevitable consequences for British policy.*

▶ **COLLOCATION:** an inevitable **consequence/result/conclusion**

▶ **SYNONYMS:** unavoidable, certain

▶ **ANTONYM:** avoidable

in|evi|tably /ɪnˈevɪtəbli/

ADVERB ○ *Technological changes will inevitably lead to unemployment.* ○ *Inevitably, the proposal is running into difficulties.*

▶ **COLLOCATION:** inevitably **result in/lead to/mean** *something*

▶ **SYNONYMS:** unavoidably, certainly

in|evi|tabil|ity /ɪnˌevɪtəˈbɪlɪti/ (inevitabilities)

NOUN ○ [+ *of*] *a statement which appeared to accept the inevitability of war*

► COLLOCATIONS:
the inevitability **of** something
the inevitability of **death/war**
accept/acknowledge the inevitability of something

---

in|fant /ˈɪnfənt/ (infants)   `BIOLOGY`

NOUN An **infant** is a baby or very young child. [FORMAL] ○ vaccinations of newborn infants ○ the infant mortality rate in Britain

► COLLOCATIONS:
a **newborn/premature** infant
infant **mortality/death**

► SYNONYMS: baby, child

in|fan|cy /ˈɪnfənsi/

UNCOUNTABLE NOUN Infancy is the period of your life when you are a very young child. ○ the development of the mind from infancy onwards ○ Only 50% of Afghan babies survive infancy.

► SYNONYM: childhood

---

in|fect /ɪnˈfekt/ (infects, infecting, infected)   `MEDICINE`

VERB To **infect** people, animals, or plants means to cause them to have a disease or illness. ○ A single mosquito can infect a large number of people. ○ objects used by an infected person ○ [+ with] people infected with HIV

► COLLOCATIONS:
infected **with** something
infected with a **virus**
infected with **flu/TB/bacteria**

in|fec|tion /ɪnˈfekʃən/ (infections)

1 UNCOUNTABLE NOUN Infection is the process of being infected with a disease or illness. ○ plants that are resistant to infection

2 NOUN An **infection** is a disease caused by germs or bacteria. ○ Ear infections are common in pre-school children. ○ Exactly which bacteria cause the infection is still unknown.

► COLLOCATIONS:
a **viral/bacterial/urinary/respiratory** infection
a **chest/ear/lung** infection
contract/transmit/spread an infection
prevent/combat/fight/treat/cure/detect an infection
an infection **recurs/develops**
infection **control/prevention**

► SYNONYMS: disease, illness, virus

in|fec|tious /ɪnˈfekʃəs/

ADJECTIVE ○ *infectious diseases such as measles* ○ *These viruses are highly infectious.*

▶ **COLLOCATIONS:**
an infectious **disease/agent**
highly infectious

▶ **SYNONYM:** contagious

in|fe|ri|or /ɪnˈfɪəriə/

ADJECTIVE Something that is **inferior** is not as good as something else.
○ *the inferior nutritional quality of foods which have been heavily processed* ○ [+ *to*]
If children were made to feel inferior to other children their confidence declined.

▶ **COLLOCATIONS:**
inferior **to** *something/someone*
inferior **quality/status**
an inferior **product**
vastly/intellectually inferior

▶ **SYNONYM:** worse
▶ **ANTONYMS:** superior, better

in|fi|nite /ˈɪnfɪnɪt/

ADJECTIVE Something that is **infinite** has no limit, end, or edge. ○ *an infinite number of atoms* ○ *Obviously, no company has infinite resources.*

▶ **COLLOCATION:** an infinite **universe/number/loop**
▶ **SYNONYMS:** boundless, limitless
▶ **ANTONYM:** finite

in|fin|ity /ɪnˈfɪnɪti/

UNCOUNTABLE NOUN Infinity is a number that is larger than any other number and can never be given an exact value. ○ *These permutations multiply towards infinity.* ○ [+ *of*] *There is always an infinity of numbers between any two numbers.*

in|fla|tion /ɪnˈfleɪʃən/   ECONOMICS

UNCOUNTABLE NOUN Inflation is a general increase in the prices of goods and services in a country. ○ *rising unemployment and high inflation* ○ *an inflation rate of only 2.2%*

▶ **COLLOCATIONS:**
control/reduce inflation
high/low/underlying/house/wage inflation
inflation **rises/falls**
inflation **runs at** *x* %
the inflation **rate/figures**

▶ **ANTONYM:** deflation

in|form /ɪnˈfɔːm/ (informs, informing, informed)

VERB If you **inform** someone **of** something, you tell them about it. ○ [+ of] *They would inform him of any progress they had made.* ○ [+ that] *contracts that inform customers that their details will be passed to a third party*

▶ COLLOCATIONS:
   inform *someone* **of/about** *something*
   inform *someone* of **developments/progress/findings**
   inform **parents/readers/patients/customers**
   inform the **public/police**
   reliably/fully/officially informed

▶ ANTONYM: conceal

EXTEND YOUR VOCABULARY

Tell is a common verb in everyday English to describe communication between two or more people. In more formal writing, you can use the verbs **inform** and **notify** to talk about passing on information in a formal or official context. You **notify** someone about a specific fact. You can **inform** someone about a fact or about a subject more generally. Remember that all these verbs are transitive and must be followed by an object - **tell/inform/notify** + *someone*. ○ *If a specific threat arises we would inform the public.*

Tell can be followed by two objects - **tell** *someone something.* ○ *He told friends and family the news yesterday.*

To use two objects (the person and the information) with **inform** or **notify** you use a preposition - **inform/notify** *someone* **of/about** *something.* ○ *Parents should be kept properly informed about their child's progress.* ○ *Teachers are told to notify police of drug-related incidents.*

---

infra|struc|ture /ˈɪnfrəstrʌktʃə/ (ACADEMIC WORD) (GEOGRAPHY)
(infrastructures)

NOUN The **infrastructure** of a country, society, or organization consists of the basic facilities such as transport, communications, power supplies, and buildings, which enable it to function. ○ *investment in infrastructure projects* ○ *a focus on improving existing infrastructure*

▶ COLLOCATIONS:
   the infrastructure **of** *something*
   have infrastructure **in place**
   build/rebuild/improve/destroy infrastructure
   existing/basic infrastructure
   transport/rail/telecommunications/security infrastructure
   infrastructure **improvement/spending/investment**

in|hab|it|ant /ɪnˈhæbɪtənt/ (inhabitants)   `GEOGRAPHY`

NOUN The **inhabitants** of a place are the people who live there. ○ [+ of] *the inhabitants of Glasgow* ○ *Jamaica's original inhabitants were the Arawak Indians.*

▶ **COLLOCATIONS:**
the inhabitants **of** *somewhere*
indigenous/native/original/local inhabitants

▶ **SYNONYMS:** resident, citizen

in|hab|it /ɪnˈhæbɪt/ (inhabits, inhabiting, inhabited)

VERB If a place or region **is inhabited** by a group of people or a species of animal, those people or animals live there. ○ *The valley is inhabited by the Dani tribe.* ○ *the people who inhabit these islands* ○ *a land primarily inhabited by nomads*

▶ **COLLOCATIONS:**
inhabited **by** *people*
inhabited by **tribes/creatures**
sparsely/densely/first inhabited
inhabit an **island/region/territory**

in|her|it /ɪnˈherɪt/ (inherits, inheriting, inherited)

1 VERB If you **inherit** money or property, you receive it from someone who has died. ○ *He has no son to inherit his land.* ○ [+ from] *paintings that he inherited from his father*

▶ **COLLOCATION:** inherit a **fortune/estate/legacy**

2 VERB If you **inherit** a characteristic or quality, you are born with it, because your parents or ancestors also had it. ○ [+ from] *We inherit many of our physical characteristics from our parents.* ○ *All sufferers from asthma have inherited a gene that makes them susceptible to the disease.* ○ *Stammering is probably an inherited defect.*

▶ **COLLOCATIONS:**
inherit *something* **from** *someone*
inherit a **trait/predisposition/characteristic/gene**
an inherited **defect/disorder**

ini|tial /ɪˈnɪʃəl/   `ACADEMIC WORD`

ADJECTIVE You use **initial** to describe something that happens at the beginning of a process. ○ *The initial reaction has been excellent.* ○ *The aim of this initial meeting is to clarify the issues.*

▶ **COLLOCATIONS:**
an initial **reaction/response/impression/diagnosis**
an initial **offering/purchase/investment/meeting**
the initial **stages/results/success**

▶ **SYNONYMS:** first, preliminary

▶ **ANTONYM:** last

ini|tial|ly /ɪˈnɪʃəli/

ADVERB Initially means soon after the beginning of a process or situation, rather than in the middle or at the end of it. ○ *Forecasters say the gales may not be as bad as they initially predicted.*

▶ **COLLOCATIONS:**
initially **refuse/deny/oppose/reject** *something*
initially **propose/plan/schedule/predict** *something*

▶ **SYNONYM:** originally

▶ **ANTONYM:** finally

---

in|no|va|tion /ˌɪnəˈveɪʃən/ (innovations) `ACADEMIC WORD`

1 NOUN An **innovation** is a new thing or a new method of doing something. ○ *The vegetarian burger was an innovation which was rapidly exported to Britain.* ○ *[+ of] the transformation wrought by the technological innovations of the industrial age*

2 UNCOUNTABLE NOUN Innovation is the introduction of new ideas, methods, or things. ○ *We must promote originality and encourage innovation.*

▶ **COLLOCATIONS:**
the innovations **of** *a period*
technological/technical/product innovation
foster/encourage/stifle innovation

▶ **SYNONYMS:** novelty, creativity

▶ **ANTONYM:** tradition

in|no|va|tive /ˈɪnəveɪtɪv/

ADJECTIVE ○ *products which are more innovative than those of their competitors* ○ *He was one of the most creative and innovative engineers of his generation.*

▶ **COLLOCATIONS:**
an innovative **design/approach/solution/idea**
an innovative **method/project/product/scheme**
technologically innovative

▶ **SYNONYMS:** new, original, state-of-the-art, creative

▶ **ANTONYM:** traditional

---

in|put /ˈɪnpʊt/ (inputs, inputting) `ACADEMIC WORD` `IT` `ENGINEERING`

The form **input** is used in the present tense and is also the past tense and past participle.

1 NOUN Input is information that is put into a computer. An **input** is a connection where information enters a computer or other device. ○ *an error in data input* ○ *an amplifier with an input socket*

▶ **COLLOCATIONS:**
an input **jack/socket/device**
stereo/audio/video/data input

▶ **ANTONYM:** output

2 VERB If you **input** information into a computer, you feed it in, for example by typing it on a keyboard. ○ [+ *onto*] *All this information had to be input onto the computer.*

▶ **COLLOCATIONS:**
input something **onto/into** something
input **data/information**

▶ **SYNONYMS:** type, enter

in|quiry /ɪnˈkwaɪəri/ (inquiries)

> The spelling **enquiry** is also used. **Inquiry** is sometimes pronounced /ˈɪŋkwɪri/ in American English.

1 NOUN An **inquiry** is a question which you ask in order to get some information. ○ *He made some inquiries and discovered she had gone to the Continent.* ○ *Having made further inquiries, we can confirm that a relationship did take place.*

▶ **COLLOCATIONS:**
make an inquiry
further inquiries

▶ **SYNONYM:** question

2 NOUN An **inquiry** is an official investigation. ○ *a crucial witness in the murder inquiry* ○ [+ *into*] *The Democratic Party has called for an independent inquiry into the incident.*

▶ **COLLOCATIONS:**
an inquiry **into** something
an inquiry into a **murder/death/affair/incident**
a **judicial/public/independent/police/murder/corruption** inquiry
conduct/hold/launch/order/adjourn/reopen an inquiry
an inquiry **concludes/reveals/investigates/hears** something

▶ **SYNONYM:** investigation

in|sert /ɪnˈsɜːt/ (inserts, inserting, inserted) `ACADEMIC WORD`

VERB If you **insert** an object **into** something, you put the object inside it. ○ [+ *into*] *tubes that are inserted into diseased arteries*

▶ **COLLOCATIONS:**
insert something **into** something
insert a **needle/pin/tube/catheter**
surgically/carefully/gently insert

in|sight /'ɪnsaɪt/ (insights) `ACADEMIC WORD`

NOUN If you gain **insight** or an **insight into** a complex situation or problem, you gain an accurate and deep understanding of it. ○ [+ into] *The project would give scientists new insights into what is happening to the Earth's atmosphere.*

▶ **COLLOCATIONS:**
insight **into** *something*
offer/give/provide/gain an insight
a **fascinating/valuable/fresh/unique/rare** insight

▶ **SYNONYMS:** awareness, understanding

▶ **ANTONYM:** ignorance

in|sig|nifi|cant /,ɪnsɪg'nɪfɪkənt/

ADJECTIVE Something that is **insignificant** is unimportant, especially because it is very small. ○ *The data were based on statistically insignificant samples.* ○ *In 1949 Bonn was a small, insignificant city.*

▶ **COLLOCATIONS:**
an insignificant **sum/amount/difference**
an insignificant **piece/detail/matter**
statistically/relatively/seemingly insignificant

▶ **SYNONYM:** unimportant

▶ **ANTONYM:** significant

in|spect /ɪn'spekt/ (inspects, inspecting, inspected) `ACADEMIC WORD`

1 VERB If you **inspect** something, you look at every part of it carefully in order to find out about it or check that it is all right. ○ *Safety engineers will periodically inspect the boiler and other machinery for structural defects.*

2 VERB When an official **inspects** a place or a group of people, they visit it and check it carefully, for example in order to find out whether regulations are being obeyed. ○ *Each hotel is inspected and, if it fulfils certain criteria, is recommended.* ○ *UN nuclear officials inspected four suspected nuclear weapons sites.*

▶ **COLLOCATIONS:**
inspect **damage**
inspect a **site/facility/property**
visually/carefully/periodically/regularly inspect *something*

▶ **SYNONYMS:** examine, check

in|spec|tion /ɪn'spekʃən/ (inspections)

NOUN ○ [+ of] *He had completed his inspection of the doors.* ○ [+ of] *Officers making a routine inspection of the vessel found fifty kilograms of the drug.* ○ *demands for weapons inspections*

▶ COLLOCATIONS:
an inspection **of** something
an inspection of a **site/plant/vehicle/facility**
resume/conduct/pass an inspection
a **weapons/arms/safety** inspection
a **routine/close** inspection
an inspection **team/regime/report**
an inspection **reveals** something
▶ SYNONYMS: examination, check, inquiry

---

in|stance /ˈɪnstəns/ (instances) ACADEMIC WORD

1 PHRASE You use **for instance** to introduce a particular event, situation, or person that is an example of what you are talking about. ○ *There are a number of improvements; for instance, both mouse buttons can now be used.* ○ *TB is an infinitely bigger problem than, for instance, AIDS.*
▶ SYNONYM: for example

2 NOUN An **instance** is a particular example or occurrence of something. ○ *The committee reported numerous instances where key information was not shared.* ○ [+ of] *an investigation into a serious instance of corruption*
▶ COLLOCATIONS:
an instance **of** something
a **rare/isolated/particular/specific/reported/recorded** instance
numerous/several instances
document/cite/record/report an instance
▶ SYNONYMS: example, case, occurrence

in|stinct /ˈɪnstɪŋkt/ (instincts) BIOLOGY

NOUN Instinct is the natural tendency that a person or animal has to behave or react in a particular way. ○ *A woman's maternal instincts are stimulated when there are children around.* ○ *He always knew what time it was, as if by instinct.*
▶ COLLOCATIONS:
a **basic/natural/gut/survival** instinct
a **killer/animal/maternal/competitive** instinct
▶ SYNONYMS: intuition, sense

in|stinc|tive /ɪnˈstɪŋktɪv/

ADJECTIVE An **instinctive** feeling, idea, or action is one that you have or do without thinking or reasoning. ○ *Ms Senatorova showed an instinctive feel for market economics.*
▶ COLLOCATION: an instinctive **feel/grasp/understanding/reaction**
▶ SYNONYMS: natural, intuitive

in|sti|tute /ˈɪnstɪtjuːt, AM -tuːt/ (institutes) `ACADEMIC WORD`

NOUN An **institute** is an organization set up to do a particular type of work, especially research or teaching. You can also use **institute** to refer to the building the organization occupies. ○ *the National Cancer Institute* ○ *an elite research institute devoted to computer software*

▶ **COLLOCATIONS:**
 found/establish an institute
 a **research/training** institute

▶ **SYNONYMS:** organization, foundation

in|sti|tu|tion /ˌɪnstɪˈtjuːʃən, AM -ˈtuː-/ (institutions) `ACADEMIC WORD`

NOUN An **institution** is a large important organization such as a university, church, or bank. ○ [+ *of*] *the Institution of Civil Engineers* ○ *Class size varies from one type of institution to another.* ○ *The Hong Kong Bank is Hong Kong's largest financial institution.*

▶ **COLLOCATIONS:**
 the institution **of** *something*
 a **financial/banking/lending** institution
 a **research/educational/academic/cultural/religious** institution

▶ **SYNONYMS:** organization, establishment

in|struc|tion /ɪnˈstrʌkʃən/ (instructions) `ACADEMIC WORD`

PLURAL NOUN Instructions are clear and detailed information on how to do something. ○ *Always read the instructions before you start taking the medicine.* ○ *an instruction manual for a camera*

▶ **COLLOCATIONS:**
 instructions **regarding** *something*
 strict/detailed/written/specific instructions
 step-by-step/simple instructions
 an instruction **manual/booklet**

▶ **SYNONYM:** directions

in|stru|ment /ˈɪnstrəmənt/ (instruments) `SCIENCE`

NOUN An **instrument** is a tool or device that is used to do a particular task, especially a scientific task. ○ [+ *for*] *instruments for cleaning and polishing teeth* ○ *The environment will be measured by about 60 scientific instruments.*

▶ **COLLOCATIONS:**
 an instrument **for** *something*
 a **scientific/surgical** instrument
 a **sensitive/blunt/sharp** instrument
 design/sterilize an instrument

▶ **SYNONYMS:** tool, device, mechanism

in|suf|fi|cient /ˌɪnsəˈfɪʃənt/

ADJECTIVE Something that is **insufficient** is not large enough in amount or degree for a particular purpose. [FORMAL] ○ *He decided there was insufficient evidence to justify criminal proceedings.* ○ *These efforts were insufficient to contain the crisis.*

▶ **COLLOCATIONS:**
insufficient **for** something
insufficient **evidence/funds**

▶ **SYNONYM:** inadequate

▶ **ANTONYMS:** sufficient, adequate

in|suf|fi|cient|ly /ˌɪnsəˈfɪʃəntli/

ADVERB ○ *Food that is insufficiently cooked can lead to food poisoning.* ○ *insufficiently trained medical staff*

▶ **SYNONYM:** inadequately

▶ **ANTONYMS:** sufficiently, adequately

in|sur|ance /ɪnˈʃʊərəns/ `BUSINESS`

UNCOUNTABLE NOUN Insurance is an arrangement in which you pay money to a company, and they pay money to you if something unpleasant happens to you, for example if your property is stolen or damaged, or if you get a serious illness. ○ *The insurance company paid out for the stolen jewellery and silver.* ○ [+ on] *We recommend that you take out travel insurance on all holidays.* ○ *regulation of the insurance industry*

▶ **COLLOCATIONS:**
insurance **on** something
an insurance **company/policy/premium/claim**
the insurance **industry**
health/medical/life/home/car/travel insurance
buy/purchase/take out/sell/carry insurance

▶ **SYNONYM:** cover

in|te|grate /ˈɪntɪɡreɪt/ (integrates, integrating, integrated) `ACADEMIC WORD`

1 VERB If someone **integrates** into a social group, or **is integrated** into it, they behave in such a way that they become part of the group or are accepted into it. ○ [+ into] *reforms to help immigrants integrate better into British society* ○ [+ with] *Integrating the kids with the community, finding them a role, is essential.*

▶ **COLLOCATIONS:**
integrate **into/with** something
integrate into **society**
integrate with a **community**

2 **VERB** If you **integrate** one thing **with** another, or one thing **integrates** **with** another, the two things become closely linked or form part of a whole idea or system. You can also say that two things **integrate**. ○ [+ *with*] *Integrating the pound with other European currencies could cause difficulties.* ○ [+ *into*] *Little attempt was made to integrate the parts into a coherent whole.*

▶ COLLOCATIONS:
integrate something **with/into** something
integrate a **component/application/system/database**
integrate **data/information/knowledge/efforts**

▶ SYNONYMS: fuse, incorporate, merge, assimilate, combine

▶ ANTONYMS: separate, divide

in|te|gra|tion /ˌɪntɪˈɡreɪʃən/

UNCOUNTABLE NOUN ○ [+ *of*] *the integration of disabled people into mainstream society* ○ *an aim to promote racial integration* ○ *closer European integration*

▶ COLLOCATIONS:
integration **of/with/into** something
racial/economic/European integration
close/further integration
facilitate/promote/achieve integration
an integration **process/issue**

▶ SYNONYMS: fusion, incorporation, assimilation

▶ ANTONYMS: separation, division

---

in|tend /ɪnˈtend/ (intends, intending, intended)

1 **VERB** If you **intend** to do something, you have decided or planned to do it. ○ [+ *to-inf*] *an opinion poll on how people intend to vote* ○ [+ *v-ing*] *I didn't intend coming to Germany to work.* ○ [+ *that*] *We had always intended that the new series would be live.*

▶ SYNONYMS: mean, plan

2 **VERB** If something **is intended** for a particular purpose, it has been planned to fulfil that purpose. If something **is intended** for a particular person, it has been planned to be used by that person or to affect them in some way. ○ [+ *for*] *This money is intended for the development of the tourist industry.* ○ [+ *to-inf*] *Columns are usually intended in architecture to add grandeur and status.* ○ [+ *as*] *Originally, Hatfield had been intended as a leisure complex.*

▶ COLLOCATIONS:
intended **for/as** something
originally/primarily intended

in|ten|tion /ɪnˈtenʃən/ (intentions)

NOUN An **intention** is an idea or plan of what you are going to do. ○ [+ *of*] *Beveridge announced his intention of standing for parliament.* ○ *The book achieved* *in the end the precise opposite of its stated intention.*

▶ COLLOCATIONS:
an intention **of doing** doing *something*
express/state/announce an intention
a **stated/expressed/original/good/true/noble** intention

▶ SYNONYMS: goal, objective, plan, purpose

in|ten|tion|al /ɪnˈtenʃənəl/

ADJECTIVE Something that is **intentional** is deliberate. ○ *Women who are the victims of intentional discrimination will be able to get compensation.*

▶ SYNONYMS: deliberate, planned
▶ ANTONYMS: accidental, unintentional

---

in|tense /ɪnˈtens/ `ACADEMIC WORD`

ADJECTIVE **Intense** is used to describe something that is very great or extreme in strength or degree. ○ *Ear infection can cause intense sudden pain.* ○ *His ideas stand up to intense intellectual scrutiny.*

▶ COLLOCATIONS:
intense **heat/cold/light/pain/flavour**
intense **pressure/competition/debate/criticism/scrutiny**

▶ SYNONYMS: acute, vivid, extreme
▶ ANTONYMS: mild, dull

in|tense|ly /ɪnˈtensli/

ADVERB ○ *The fast-food business is intensely competitive.* ○ *It was suddenly intensely silent.*

▶ COLLOCATIONS:
intensely **competitive/personal/private**
burn/suffer intensely
intensely **focused**

▶ SYNONYMS: acutely, vividly, extremely
▶ ANTONYM: mildly

in|ten|sity /ɪnˈtensɪti/

UNCOUNTABLE NOUN ○ *The attack was anticipated but its intensity came as a shock.* ○ [+ of] *the intensity of the mother's unforgiving anger*

▶ COLLOCATIONS:
the intensity **of** *something*
emotional/heightened/sheer/fierce intensity

▶ SYNONYMS: acuteness, vividness, extremity
▶ ANTONYM: mildness

in|ter|est /'ɪntrəst, -tərest/ (interests)   `ECONOMICS`

1 NOUN If something is in the **interests** of a particular person or group, it will benefit them in some way. ○ [+ of] *Did those directors act in the best interests of their club?* ○ *The media were required to act in the public interest.*

▶ COLLOCATIONS:
in the interests **of** *someone*
in the interests of **consumers/shareholders**
in the **public/national** interest
someone's **best** interests

2 NOUN If a person, country, or organization has an **interest in** a possible event or situation, they want that event or situation to happen because they are likely to benefit from it. ○ [+ in] *The West has an interest in promoting democratic forces in Eastern Europe.*

▶ COLLOCATIONS:
an interest **in** *something*
a **vested/particular/keen** interest

3 UNCOUNTABLE NOUN Interest is extra money that you receive if you have invested a sum of money. **Interest** is also the extra money that you pay if you have borrowed money or are buying something on credit. ○ *a current account which pays interest* ○ *This is an important step toward lower interest rates.*

▶ COLLOCATIONS:
pay/lose/accrue/earn interest
interest **rates/charges**

4 PHRASE If you do something **in the interests of** a particular result or situation, you do it in order to achieve that result or maintain that situation. ○ *a call for all businessmen to work together in the interests of national stability*

▶ COLLOCATION: in the interests of **fairness/justice/safety**

in|ter|est|ed /'ɪntrestɪd/

ADJECTIVE An **interested** party or group of people is affected by or involved in a particular event or situation. ○ *All the interested parties eventually agreed to the idea.*

▶ COLLOCATION: an interested **party/person/buyer**
▶ SYNONYM: involved
▶ ANTONYM: disinterested

inter|fere /ˌɪntə'fɪə/ (interferes, interfering, interfered)

1 VERB If you say that someone **interferes in** a situation, you mean they get involved in it although it does not concern them and their involvement is not wanted. ○ [+ in] *The U.N. cannot interfere in the internal affairs of any country.*

▶ COLLOCATIONS:
interfere **in** *something*

interfere in a **matter/process/affair**
the **right/ability** to interfere
▶ SYNONYM: intervene

2 VERB Something that **interferes with** a situation, activity, or process has a damaging effect on it. ○ [+ with] *Smoking and drinking interfere with your body's ability to process oxygen.*
▶ COLLOCATIONS:
interfere **with** *something*
interfere with **digestion/absorption/function**
▶ SYNONYMS: inhibit, obstruct

inter|fer|ence /ˌɪntəˈfɪərəns/

UNCOUNTABLE NOUN Interference by a person or group is their unwanted or unnecessary involvement in something. ○ [+ in] *The parliament described the decree as interference in the republic's internal affairs.* ○ [+ from] *Airlines will be able to set cheap fares without interference from the government.*
▶ COLLOCATIONS:
interference **in/with** *something*
interference **from** *someone*
interference in a **matter/process/affair**
unwarranted/undue/outside/political interference
▶ SYNONYM: intervention

in|te|ri|or /ɪnˈtɪəriə/ (interiors)

NOUN The **interior** of something is the inside part of it. ○ [+ of] *The interior of the house was furnished with heavy, old-fashioned pieces.* ○ *the boat's interior*
▶ COLLOCATIONS:
the interior **of** *something*
the interior of a **room/house/car/vehicle**
a **roomy/spacious/airy** interior
▶ SYNONYM: inside
▶ ANTONYM: exterior

inter|medi|ate /ˌɪntəˈmiːdiət/　ACADEMIC WORD

ADJECTIVE An **intermediate** stage, level, or position is one that occurs between two other stages, levels, or positions. ○ *a process commencing at the primitive stage and leading, through an intermediate stage, to modernity* ○ *hourly trains to Perugia, Assisi, and intermediate stations*
▶ COLLOCATION: an intermediate **stage**
▶ SYNONYM: middle
▶ ANTONYMS: initial, final

in|ter|nal /ɪnˈtɜːnəl/ ACADEMIC WORD

1 ADJECTIVE Internal is used to describe things that exist or happen inside a country or organization. ○ *The country stepped up internal security.* ○ *We now have a Europe without internal borders.* ○ *an internal mail box*

▶ **COLLOCATIONS:**
internal **affairs/security/politics**
an internal **inquiry/investigation/review/flight**

▶ **SYNONYM:** domestic

▶ **ANTONYMS:** external, foreign

2 ADJECTIVE Internal is used to describe things that exist or happen inside a particular person, object, or place. ○ *massive internal bleeding* ○ *disorders which affected the skin and internal organs alike*

▶ **COLLOCATIONS:**
an internal **organ**
internal **bleeding**

▶ **ANTONYM:** external

in|ter|nal|ly /ɪnˈtɜːnəli/

ADVERB ○ *Evening primrose oil is used on the skin as well as taken internally.* ○ *an internally consistent theory*

▶ **COLLOCATION:** internally **consistent/inconsistent/displaced**

▶ **ANTONYM:** externally

in|ter|pret /ɪnˈtɜːprɪt/ (interprets, interpreting, interpreted) ACADEMIC WORD

VERB If you **interpret** something in a particular way, you decide that this is its meaning or significance. ○ *[+ as] The whole speech might well be interpreted as a coded message to the Americans.* ○ *methods of gathering and interpreting data*

▶ **COLLOCATIONS:**
interpreted **as** *something*
interpret **data/results/meaning**
widely/correctly interpreted

▶ **SYNONYM:** understand

in|ter|pre|ta|tion /ɪnˌtɜːprɪˈteɪʃən/ (interpretations)

NOUN An **interpretation** of something is an opinion about what it means. ○ *The opposition put a different interpretation on the figures.* ○ *[+ of] a disagreement on the interpretation of scientific data*

▶ **COLLOCATIONS:**
an interpretation **of** *something*
an interpretation of **data**
an interpretation of a **law/rule/event**

a **literal/strict/subjective** interpretation
differing/conflicting/varying interpretations
offer/reject an interpretation
put an interpretation **on** *something*
▶ **PHRASE:** interpretation and analysis
▶ **SYNONYMS:** understanding, reading

---

in|ter|val /'ɪntəvəl/ (intervals)   `ACADEMIC WORD`

1 NOUN An **interval** between two events or dates is the period of time
between them. ○ [+ *of*] *The ferry service has restarted after an interval of 12 years.*
○ [+ *of*] *There was a long interval of silence.*
▶ **COLLOCATIONS:**
an interval **of** *something/time*
an interval **between** *things*
▶ **SYNONYM:** gap

2 PHRASE If something happens **at intervals**, it happens several times with
gaps or pauses in between. ○ *The subjects were monitored at intervals during
their adult life.*
▶ **SYNONYMS:** regularly, periodically

---

intro|duce /ˌɪntrə'djuːs, AM -'duːs/ (introduces, introducing, introduced)

VERB To **introduce** something means to cause it to enter a place or exist in a
system for the first time. ○ *The Government has introduced a number of other
money-saving moves.* ○ [+ *to*] *The word 'Pagoda' was introduced to Europe by the
17th-century Portuguese.*
▶ **COLLOCATIONS:**
introduce *something* **to/into** *a place*
introduce a **bill/scheme/system/concept**
introduce **legislation/measures**
▶ **SYNONYMS:** establish, launch
→ see note at **propose**

intro|duc|tion /ˌɪntrə'dʌkʃən/ (introductions)

1 NOUN The **introduction** of something is the process of bringing it into a
place or system for the first time. ○ [+ *of*] *He is best remembered for the
introduction of the moving assembly-line.* ○ [+ *of*] *the introduction of a privacy bill*
▶ **COLLOCATIONS:**
the introduction **of** *something*
the introduction of **legislation/technology**
the introduction of a **fee/scheme**
propose/oversee/delay the introduction
▶ **SYNONYMS:** establishment, launch

2 **NOUN** The **introduction to** a book, essay or talk is the part that comes at the beginning and tells you what the rest of the book, essay or talk is about. ○ [+ to] *Ellen Malos, in her introduction to 'The Politics of Housework', provides a summary of the debates.* ○ *An essay's introduction usually indicates what the topic and thesis are and why the topic is of some importance.*

▶ **COLLOCATIONS:**
  an introduction **to** *something*
  a **brief/concise** introduction
  write an introduction
▶ **SYNONYM:** preface
▶ **ANTONYM:** conclusion

---

in|va|lid /ɪnˈvælɪd/

1 **ADJECTIVE** If an action, procedure, or document is **invalid**, it cannot be accepted, because it breaks the law or some official rule. ○ *The trial was stopped and the results declared invalid.* ○ *He tried to leave for the Philippines on an invalid passport.*

2 **ADJECTIVE** An **invalid** argument or conclusion is wrong because it is based on a mistake. ○ *We think that those arguments are rendered invalid by the hard facts on the ground.* ○ *The paper lacked a coherent method and was statistically invalid.*

▶ **COLLOCATIONS:**
  an invalid **election/result/marriage/vote**
  an invalid **claim/argument**
  an invalid **passport/signature/ticket/contract**
  declare/deem/render *something* invalid
▶ **SYNONYMS:** null, false
▶ **ANTONYM:** valid

in|vali|date /ɪnˈvælɪdeɪt/ (invalidates, invalidating, invalidated)

1 **VERB** To **invalidate** something such as an argument, conclusion, or result means to prove that it is wrong or cause it to be wrong. ○ *Any form of physical activity will invalidate the results.* ○ *Some of the other criticisms were invalidated years ago.*

2 **VERB** If something **invalidates** something such as a law, contract, or election, it causes it to be considered illegal. ○ *An official decree invalidated the vote in the capital.* ○ *A contract signed now might be invalidated at some future date.*

▶ **COLLOCATION:** invalidate a **result/claim/vote/law**
▶ **SYNONYMS:** nullify, falsify
▶ **ANTONYM:** validate

---

in|vest /ɪnˈvest/ (invests, investing, invested) `ACADEMIC WORD` `BUSINESS`

1 VERB If you **invest in** something, or if you **invest** a sum of money, you use your money in a way that you hope will increase its value, for example by paying it into a bank, or buying shares or property. ○ [+ in] *He invested all our profits in gold shares.*

2 VERB When a government or organization **invests in** something, it gives or lends money for a purpose that it considers useful or profitable. ○ [+ in] *the British government's failure to invest in an integrated transport system* ○ *Why does Japan invest, on average, twice as much capital per worker per year than the United States?*

▶ COLLOCATIONS:
invest **in** *something*
invest in **stocks/bonds/securities/equities**
invest in **infrastructure/technology/equipment**
invest **money/capital/assets**
invest a **sum/amount**
primarily/principally/heavily/directly invest

in|vest|ment /ɪnˈvesmənt/ (investments)

1 UNCOUNTABLE NOUN **Investment** is the activity of investing money. ○ *The government must introduce tax incentives to encourage investment.*

2 NOUN An **investment** is an amount of money that you invest, or the thing that you invest it in. ○ [+ of] *an investment of twenty-eight million pounds* ○ [+ in] *Total foreign investment in America still constitutes only about 5% of U.S. assets.*

▶ COLLOCATIONS:
investment **in** *something/somewhere*
an investment **of** £x
investment in **stocks/bonds/infrastructure/technology**
attract/encourage/stimulate investment
foreign/private/direct/capital/property investment
an investment **bank/strategy/banker/adviser/dealer**
investment **banking/income**
▶ PHRASE: savings and investments

in|ves|tor /ɪnˈvestə/ (investors)

NOUN An **investor** is a person or organization that buys stocks or shares, or pays money into a bank in order to receive a profit. ○ [+ in] *The main investor in the project is the French bank Credit National.*

▶ COLLOCATIONS:
an investor **in** *something*
a **foreign/private/retail/individual** investor
▶ SYNONYMS: banker, lender

in|ves|ti|gate /ɪnˈvestɪgeɪt/ `ACADEMIC WORD`
(investigates, investigating, investigated)

VERB If you investigate something, you study or examine it carefully to find out the truth about it. ○ *Research in Oxford is now investigating a possible link between endometriosis and the immune system.* ○ *[+ how] Police are still investigating how the accident happened.*

▶ **COLLOCATIONS:**
investigate a **link/case/incident/complaint/allegation**
thoroughly/fully/properly investigate

▶ **SYNONYMS:** examine, explore, study, analyze

in|ves|ti|ga|tion /ɪnˌvestɪˈgeɪʃən/ **(investigations)**

NOUN ○ *[+ into] He ordered an investigation into the affair.* ○ *Brain functions are measurable and open to scientific investigation.*

▶ **COLLOCATIONS:**
an investigation **into** something
conduct/launch/undertake an investigation
a **criminal/police/murder/scientific/internal** investigation

▶ **SYNONYMS:** examination, study, analysis

ir|regu|lar /ɪˈregjʊlə/

1 ADJECTIVE If events or actions occur at **irregular** intervals, the periods of time between them are of different lengths. ○ *Cars passed at irregular intervals.* ○ *Antidepressants may cause an irregular heartbeat.* ○ *He worked irregular hours.*

▶ **COLLOCATIONS:**
an irregular **heartbeat/rhythm**
irregular **bleeding/breathing/hours/intervals**

▶ **SYNONYM:** variable
▶ **ANTONYM:** regular

2 ADJECTIVE Something that is **irregular** is not smooth or straight, or does not form a regular pattern. ○ *Irregular shapes were a feature of the design.*

▶ **SYNONYM:** uneven
▶ **ANTONYMS:** regular, even

ir|rel|evant /ɪˈrelɪvənt/ `ACADEMIC WORD`

ADJECTIVE If you describe something such as a fact or remark as **irrelevant**, you mean that it is not connected with what you are discussing or dealing with. ○ *[+ to] The government decided that their testimony would be irrelevant to the case.* ○ *essential facts buried in many irrelevant details*

▶ **COLLOCATIONS:**
irrelevant **to** *something*
an irrelevant **detail/distinction/opinion**
largely/totally/completely irrelevant
render/deem *something* irrelevant
▶ **SYNONYMS:** beside the point, unrelated, unimportant
▶ **ANTONYMS:** relevant, pertinent

---

iso|late /ˈaɪsəleɪt/ **(isolates, isolating, isolated)**　　　　　ACADEMIC WORD

1 VERB If you **isolate** something such as an idea or a problem, you separate it from others that it is connected with, so that you can concentrate on it or consider it on its own. ○ *attempts to isolate a single factor as the cause of the decline of Britain*

2 VERB To **isolate** a substance means to obtain it by separating it from other substances using scientific processes. ○ *We can use genetic engineering techniques to isolate the gene that is responsible.* ○ *[+ from] Researchers have isolated a new protein from the seeds of poppies.*

3 VERB To **isolate** a sick person or animal means to keep them apart from other people or animals, so that their illness does not spread. ○ *[+ from] Patients will be isolated from other people for between three days and one month after treatment.*

▶ **COLLOCATIONS:**
isolate *something/someone* **from** *something*
isolate *something/someone* from **the world/society**
isolate a **gene/virus/protein/cell**
▶ **SYNONYM:** separate
▶ **ANTONYM:** integrate

iso|la|tion /ˌaɪsəˈleɪʃən/

UNCOUNTABLE NOUN Isolation is when someone or something is separated from other people or things. ○ *[+ of] The epidemic finally stopped in mid-2003, due to stringent isolation of cases.*

iso|lat|ed /ˈaɪsəleɪtɪd/

ADJECTIVE An **isolated** example is an example of something that is not very common. ○ *They said the allegations related to an isolated case of cheating.*

▶ **COLLOCATION:** an isolated **incident/case/example**
▶ **SYNONYMS:** rare, single, unique
▶ **ANTONYM:** common

Jj

joint /dʒɔɪnt/

ADJECTIVE Joint means shared by or belonging to two or more people.
○ *a commercial joint venture between the BBC and Flextech* ○ *The two leaders issued a joint statement.*

▶ **COLLOCATIONS:**
a joint **venture/bid/agreement/decision**
a joint **statement/account**

▶ **SYNONYMS:** shared, collective

▶ **ANTONYM:** separate

joint|ly /ˈdʒɔɪntli/

ADVERB ○ *The Port Authority is an agency jointly run by New York and New Jersey.*
○ *federal and state governments which jointly fund public hospitals*

▶ **COLLOCATIONS:**
jointly **own/run/fund** *something*
jointly **develop/market/sponsor** *something*

▶ **SYNONYM:** together

▶ **ANTONYMS:** separately, singly

jour|nal /ˈdʒɜːnəl/ (journals) ACADEMIC WORD ACADEMIC STUDY

NOUN A **journal** is a magazine, especially one that deals with a specialized subject. ○ *All our results are published in scientific journals.*

▶ **COLLOCATIONS:**
a **scholarly/academic/respected/prestigious** journal
a **scientific/medical/literary** journal
a **peer-reviewed/online/quarterly** journal

jus|tice /ˈdʒʌstɪs/ LAW

1 UNCOUNTABLE NOUN Justice is fairness in the way that people are treated.
○ *He has a good overall sense of justice and fairness.* ○ *advocates for human rights and racial justice*

2 UNCOUNTABLE NOUN Justice is the legal system that a country uses in order to deal with people who break the law. ○ *Many in Toronto's black community* feel that the justice system does not treat them fairly. ○ A lawyer is part of the machinery of justice.

▶ **COLLOCATIONS:**
a **sense of** justice
obstruction of justice
seek/achieve/dispense/administer/deliver justice
pervert/obstruct/escape justice
racial/social justice
the justice **system**

▶ **SYNONYMS:** fairness, equality, law, legality

▶ **ANTONYMS:** injustice, unfairness

---

jus|ti|fy /ˈdʒʌstɪfaɪ/ (justifies, justifying, justified) `ACADEMIC WORD`

VERB To **justify** a decision, action, or idea means to show or prove that it is reasonable or necessary. ○ *No argument can justify a war.* ○ *Ministers agreed that this decision was fully justified by economic conditions.*

→ see note at **confirm**

▶ **COLLOCATIONS:**
justified **by** *something*
entirely/wholly/amply justified
morally/ethically/rationally/economically/scientifically justified
justify a **war/invasion/action/expense**

▶ **PHRASES:**
the end justifies the means
justify something on (the) grounds of something

▶ **SYNONYMS:** rationalize, explain, legitimize

jus|ti|fi|ca|tion /ˌdʒʌstɪfɪˈkeɪʃən/ (justifications)

NOUN A **justification for** something is an acceptable reason or explanation for it. ○ [+ for] *The only justification for a zoo is educational.* ○ *Most believed that the war lacked justification.*

▶ **COLLOCATIONS:**
justification **for** *something*
justification for a **war/invasion/action/murder**
provide/offer/find/lack justification
ample/sufficient/rational/moral/legal justification

▶ **SYNONYMS:** explanation, reason, excuse

Kk

key /kiː/ **(keys)**

NOUN The **key** on a map or diagram or in a technical book is a list of the symbols or abbreviations used and their meanings. ○ *You will find a key at the front of the book.*

→ see note at **axis**

▶ **SYNONYM:** legend

Ll

la|bel /ˈleɪbəl/ (labels, labelling, labelled) [ACADEMIC WORD] [ACADEMIC STUDY]
[in AM, use **labeling, labeled**]

VERB If you **label** a diagram, chart, picture etc, you write information saying what each part is or what each part represents. ○ *You could be asked to label diagrams.* ○ *There is a map, with key targets circled in red and clearly labelled.*

→ see note at **axis**

▶ COLLOCATION: **clearly** labelled

● **Label** is also a noun. ○ *The pattern is obvious as we look at all of the pictures and their labels in Figure 7.3.*

la|bour /ˈleɪbə/ [ACADEMIC WORD] [BUSINESS]

UNCOUNTABLE NOUN Labour is used to refer to the workers of a country or industry, considered as a group. [in AM, use **labor**] ○ *Latin America lacked skilled labour.* ○ *Immigrants arrived in the 1950s to deal with Britain's postwar labour shortages.*

▶ COLLOCATIONS:
skilled/semi-skilled/unskilled/cheap labour
the labour **market/force**
a labour **shortage/dispute**
labour **relations**

large|ly /ˈlɑːdʒli/

1 ADVERB You use **largely** to say that a statement is not completely true but is mostly true. ○ *The fund is largely financed through government borrowing.*

2 ADVERB Largely is used to introduce the main reason for a particular event or situation. ○ *Retail sales dipped 6/10ths of a percent last month, largely because Americans were buying fewer cars.* ○ [+ through] *The French empire had expanded, largely through military conquest.*

▶ COLLOCATION: largely **because of/through** something
▶ SYNONYMS: mainly, mostly
▶ RELATED WORD: partly

lat|ter /ˈlætə/

PRONOUN When two people, things, or groups have just been mentioned, you can refer to the second of them as **the latter**. ○ *At school, he enjoyed football* *and boxing; the latter remained a lifelong habit.* ○ *without hesitation they chose the latter*

▸ COLLOCATION: **choose/prefer** the latter

- **Latter** is also an adjective. ○ *Private share holdings exist in the UK, Italy and Portugal and plans are underway to increase the level of private investment in the latter two countries.* ○ *Adrienne heard nothing of the latter part of this speech.*

▸ COLLOCATION: the latter **stage/part/category**

▸ ANTONYM: former

> USAGE: **latter** or **later**?
>
> Be careful not to confuse these two words that look similar. You use **the latter** /ˈlætə/ (with two T's) to refer to the second or last of several things mentioned. ○ *Investors had the option of believing their own eyes, or taking Greenspan's word, and they opted for the latter.*
>
> You use **later** /ˈleɪtə/ (with one T) to talk about a time that comes after something else. ○ *He admitted later that he had been wrong.*

---

launch /lɔːntʃ/ (launches, launching, launched) SCIENCE BUSINESS

VERB If a company **launches** a new product, it makes it available to the public. ○ *Crabtree & Evelyn has just launched a new jam, Worcesterberry Preserve.* ○ *Marks & Spencer recently hired model Linda Evangelista to launch its new range.*

▸ COLLOCATION: launch a **product/model/brand/book/magazine/car**

▸ SYNONYM: unveil

- **Launch** is also a noun. ○ [+ of] *The company's spending has also risen following the launch of a new Sunday magazine.* ○ [+ of] *legal wrangling threatens to delay the launch of the product*

▸ COLLOCATIONS:
  the launch **of** something
  a **product/book** launch
  an **official** launch
  announce/delay/postpone a launch

> EXTEND YOUR VOCABULARY
>
> There are a range of words to talk about **starting** something. A company or an organization **launches** a new project or a new product.
> ○ *The charity has launched a new website for parents.*
>
> You **establish**, **form** or **found** a new organization or system.
> ○ *The current system was established in the early 1970s.* ○ *The seven airlines formed a consortium.* ○ *The company was founded in 1978 by the current managing director.*

law /lɔː/ (laws)   `SCIENCE`

1 NOUN A **law** is a natural process in which a particular event or thing always leads to a particular result. ○ [+ of] *The laws of nature are absolute.*

2 NOUN A **law** is a scientific rule that someone has invented to explain a particular natural process. ○ [+ of] *Newton's laws of motion* ○ [+ of] *the laws of physics*

▶ **COLLOCATIONS:**
the law **of** *something*
the law of **nature/gravity/motion**
the laws of **physics**

▶ **SYNONYM:** principle

lay|er /ˈleɪə/ (layers)   `ACADEMIC WORD`

NOUN A **layer** of a material or substance is a quantity or piece of it that covers a surface or that is between two other things. ○ [+ of] *The eyelids are protective layers of skin.* ○ [+ over] *holes appearing in the ozone layer over the polar regions*

▶ **COLLOCATIONS:**
a layer **of/over** *something*
a layer **over** *something*
a **thin/thick/protective** layer
the **top/bottom/upper/lower** layer
the **ozone** layer
form a layer

lead|ing /ˈliːdɪŋ/

ADJECTIVE The **leading** person or thing in a particular area is the one which is most important or successful. ○ *He's a leading member of Bristol's Sikh community.* ○ *Britain's future as a leading industrial nation depends on investment.*

▶ **COLLOCATIONS:**
a leading **figure/player/member**
a leading **politician/scientist/economist**
a leading **researcher/expert/authority**

▶ **SYNONYMS:** prominent, foremost

lec|ture /ˈlektʃə/   `ACADEMIC WORD` `EDUCATION` `ACADEMIC STUDY`
(lectures)

NOUN A **lecture** is a talk someone gives in order to teach people about a particular subject, usually at a university or college. ○ [+ by] *He attended a series of lectures by Professor Eric Robinson.* ○ [+ on] *He gave a three-hour lecture on Goethe.*

▶ **COLLOCATIONS:**
a lecture **by** *someone*
a lecture **on** *something*
give/deliver/attend a lecture
a lecture **tour/series/hall/theatre/room**
▶ **SYNONYM:** talk

lec|tur|er /ˈlektʃərə/ (lecturers)

NOUN A **lecturer** is a teacher at a university or college. ○ [+ *in*] *She's a lecturer in law at Southampton University.* ○ *there was an opening for a senior lecturer*
▶ **COLLOCATIONS:**
a lecturer **in** *something*
a **university/college** lecturer
a **senior/visiting/guest** lecturer
▶ **RELATED WORDS:** teacher, professor, tutor

left-wing /ˌleft ˈwɪŋ/ also left wing   POLITICS

ADJECTIVE **Left-wing** people have political ideas that are based on socialism.
○ *They said they would not be voting for him because he was too left-wing.*
○ *left-wing guerrillas*
▶ **COLLOCATIONS:**
a left-wing **group/party/government**
a left-wing **rebel/guerrilla/activist**
left-wing **politics**
▶ **ANTONYM:** right-wing

leg|is|late /ˈledʒɪsleɪt/   ACADEMIC WORD   LAW
(legislates, legislating, legislated)

VERB When a government or state **legislates**, it passes a new law. [FORMAL]
○ [+ *against*] *Most member countries have already legislated against excessive overtime.* ○ [+ *to-inf*] *You cannot legislate to change attitudes.*
▶ **COLLOCATION:** legislate **on/for/against** *something*

leg|is|la|tion /ˌledʒɪˈsleɪʃən/

UNCOUNTABLE NOUN **Legislation** consists of a law or laws passed by a government. [FORMAL] ○ [+ *to-inf*] *The government has introduced draft legislation to increase the maximum penalty for car theft.* ○ [+ *on*] *European legislation on copyright*
▶ **COLLOCATIONS:**
legislation **on** *something*
pass/introduce/enact/propose/approve legislation
change/amend/oppose/block/veto legislation
draft/emergency legislation

EXTEND YOUR VOCABULARY

In everyday English, we talk about **the law** to refer to legal issues in all kinds of contexts. ○ *Are these people breaking the law?* ○ *a law student*

In more formal writing, you talk about **legislation** to refer to the laws in specific areas and also the process of making laws. ○ *changes to employment legislation* ○ *The government introduced legislation restricting trade union rights.*

Legislation is an uncountable noun. You can talk about a **piece of legislation** to refer to a particular law. An **act** is a law that has been passed by a government. ○ *a highly complex piece of legislation* ○ *the 1995 disability discrimination act*

---

leg|is|la|tive /ˈledʒɪslətɪv, AM -leɪ-/

ADJECTIVE **Legislative** means involving or relating to the process of making and passing laws. [FORMAL] ○ *Today's hearing was just the first step in the legislative process.* ○ *the country's highest legislative body*

▶ **COLLOCATIONS:**
a legislative **body/assembly/council/committee**
legislative **change/power**
the legislative **process**

▶ **RELATED WORD:** legal

---

lia|ble /ˈlaɪəbəl/

1 PHRASE When something **is liable to** happen, it is very likely to happen. ○ *Only a small minority of the mentally ill are liable to harm themselves or others.* ○ *He is liable to change his mind quite rapidly.*

▶ **SYNONYM:** likely to

2 ADJECTIVE If people or things are **liable to** something unpleasant, they are likely to experience it or do it. ○ [+ to] *She will grow into a woman particularly liable to depression.* ○ [+ to] *This makes the muscles of the airways liable to constriction.*

▶ **SYNONYM:** prone

3 ADJECTIVE If you are **liable for** something such as a debt, you are legally responsible for it. ○ [+ for] *The airline's insurer is liable for damages to the victims' families.* ○ *As the killings took place outside British jurisdiction, the Ministry of Defence could not be held liable.*

▶ **COLLOCATIONS:**
liable **for** *something*
personally/legally liable
hold *someone* liable

▶ **SYNONYM:** legally responsible

lia|bil|ity /ˌlaɪəˈbɪlɪti/

UNCOUNTABLE NOUN ○ *He is claiming damages from London Underground, which has admitted liability but disputes the amount of his claim.* ○ *[+ for] This covers your legal liability for injury or damage which you may cause to others and their property.*

▶ **COLLOCATIONS:**
 liability **for** *something*
 accept/admit/deny liability
 legal/personal liability

▶ **SYNONYM:** responsibility

lib|er|al /ˈlɪbərəl/ (liberals)   `ACADEMIC WORD` `POLITICS`

1 ADJECTIVE Someone who has **liberal** views believes people should have a lot of freedom in deciding how to behave and think. ○ *She is known to have liberal views on divorce and contraception.* ○ *Traditional values were challenged in the 1960s by a more liberal attitude.*

▶ **COLLOCATIONS:**
 liberal **views/values**
 a liberal **attitude**

● **Liberal** is also a noun. ○ *a nation of free-thinking liberals*

2 ADJECTIVE A **liberal** system allows people or organizations a lot of political or economic freedom. ○ *a liberal democracy with a multiparty political system* ○ *They favour liberal free-market policies.*

▶ **COLLOCATION:** a liberal **democracy/society/state/policy**

li|cence /ˈlaɪsəns/ (licences)   `ACADEMIC WORD`

NOUN A **licence** is an official document which gives you permission to do, use, sell, or own something. [in AM, use **license**] ○ *Payne lost his driving licence a year ago for drink-driving.* ○ *[+ to-inf] It gained a licence to operate as a bank in 1981.*

▶ **COLLOCATIONS:**
 issue/grant/revoke/suspend a licence
 a **driving/fishing/gun** licence
 a **software/entertainment/gaming/liquor** licence
 a **television/radio/marriage** licence
 a **valid** licence
 a licence **application/fee/holder**

▶ **SYNONYM:** permit

li|cense /ˈlaɪsəns/ (licenses, licensing, licensed)

VERB To **license** a person or activity means to give official permission for the person to do something or for the activity to take place. ○ *This is a proposal* *that would require the state to license guns.* ○ [+ to-inf] *Under the agreement, the council can license a U.S. company to produce the drug.*

▶ **COLLOCATION:** license **technology/drugs/software**

> **USAGE: licence** or **license**?
>
> In British English, **licence** (with a C) is a noun and **license** (with an S) is a verb.
>
> In American English, **license** is both the noun and verb form.

life ex|pec|tan|cy /ˈlaɪf ɪkˌspektənsi/ [MEDICINE] [SOCIOLOGY]
(life expectancies)

NOUN The **life expectancy** of a person, animal, or plant is the length of time that they are normally likely to live. ○ *a dramatic increase in Western average life expectancy* ○ *They had longer life expectancies than their parents.*

▶ **COLLOCATIONS:**
the life expectancy **of** *something/someone*
the **average** life expectancy
a **long/short** life expectancy
the life expectancy **rate**

like|wise /ˈlaɪkwaɪz/ [ACADEMIC WORD]

ADVERB You use **likewise** when you are comparing two methods, states, or situations and saying that they are similar. ○ *All attempts by the Socialists to woo him back were spurned. Similar overtures from the right have likewise been rejected.* ○ *The V2 was not an ordinary weapon: it could only be used against cities. Likewise the atom bomb.*

▶ **SYNONYM:** similarly

lin|guis|tic /lɪŋˈgwɪstɪk/ **(linguistics)** [LANGUAGE]

1 ADJECTIVE Linguistic abilities or ideas relate to language or linguistics. ○ *They had the opportunity to test their linguistic skills on some Chinese visitors.* ○ *linguistic theory*

▶ **COLLOCATION:** linguistic **skills/ability/diversity**

2 UNCOUNTABLE NOUN Linguistics is the study of the way in which language works. ○ *Modern linguistics emerged as a distinct field in the nineteenth century.*

▶ **COLLOCATION:** **modern/historical/applied** linguistics

lin|guis|ti|cal|ly /lɪŋˈgwɪstɪkli/

ADVERB ○ *Somalia is an ethnically and linguistically homogeneous nation.* ○ *those from culturally and linguistically diverse backgrounds*

lin|guist /ˈlɪŋgwɪst/ (linguists)

NOUN A **linguist** is someone who studies or teaches linguistics. ○ *This son of a greenkeeper is a gifted linguist.* ○ *modern linguists have noted different strains*

lit|er|ate /ˈlɪtərət/ [EDUCATION] [LANGUAGE] [SOCIOLOGY]

ADJECTIVE Someone who is **literate** is able to read and write. ○ *Over one-quarter of the adult population are not fully literate.* ○ *He had left school barely literate and with little ambition or self-esteem.*
▶ **COLLOCATION: fully/barely** literate
▶ **ANTONYM:** illiterate
▶ **RELATED WORD:** numerate

lit|era|cy /ˈlɪtərəsi/

UNCOUNTABLE NOUN ○ *Many adults have some problems with literacy and numeracy.* ○ *The literacy rate there is the highest in Central America.*
▶ **COLLOCATIONS:**
 poor/basic literacy
 the literacy **rate**
▶ **PHRASE:** literacy and numeracy
▶ **RELATED WORD:** numeracy

log|ic /ˈlɒdʒɪk/ [ACADEMIC WORD]

UNCOUNTABLE NOUN Logic is a method of reasoning that involves a series of statements, each of which must be true if the statement before it is true. ○ *Apart from criminal investigation techniques, students learn forensic medicine, philosophy and logic.* ○ *to prove God's existence by means of deductive logic*

logi|cal /ˈlɒdʒɪkəl/

1 ADJECTIVE In a **logical** argument or method of reasoning, each step must be true if the step before it is true. ○ *Only when each logical step has been checked by other mathematicians will the proof be accepted.* ○ *while this is a fair and logical argument*
▶ **COLLOCATION:** a logical **step/argument**

2 ADJECTIVE The **logical** conclusion or result of a series of facts or events is the only one which can come from it, according to the rules of logic. ○ *If the climate gets drier, then the logical conclusion is that even more drought will occur.* ○ *a society that dismisses God as a logical impossibility*
▶ **COLLOCATION:** a logical **conclusion/result/extension/progression**

logi|cal|ly /ˈlɒdʒɪkli/

ADVERB ○ *From that it followed logically that he would not be meeting Hildegarde.* ○ *My professional training has taught me to look at things logically.*

long-term /ˈlɒŋ tɜːm, AM lɔːŋ/ (longer-term)

1 ADJECTIVE Something that is **long-term** has continued for a long time or will continue for a long time in the future. ○ *a new training scheme to help the long-term unemployed* ○ *a long-term solution to credit card fraud*

▶ **COLLOCATIONS:**
the long-term **effects/benefits/impact**
a long-term **plan/strategy/goal/problem/solution**
a long-term **relationship/commitment/investment**
someone's/something's long-term **future**
the long-term **unemployed**

▶ **ANTONYM:** short-term

2 NOUN When you talk about what happens in **the long term**, you are talking about what happens over a long period of time, either in the future or after a particular event. ○ *In the long term the company hopes to open offices in Moscow and other major cities.* ○ *Over the long term, such measures may only make the underlying situation worse.*

▶ **COLLOCATION: in/over** the long term

▶ **ANTONYM:** the short term

Mm

mag|net /'mægnɪt/ (magnets) PHYSICS

NOUN A **magnet** is a piece of iron or other material which attracts iron towards it. ○ *about a hundred times more powerful than a fridge magnet* ○ *superconductors are now used in power cables and to make powerful magnets*

▶ COLLOCATION: a **powerful/strong** magnet

mag|net|ic /mæg'netɪk/

ADJECTIVE If something metal is **magnetic**, it acts like a magnet. ○ *The moon exerts a magnetic pull on the Earth's water levels.* ○ *a material consisting of magnetic particles*

▶ COLLOCATIONS:
a magnetic **field/pull**
a magnetic **strip/compass**
magnetic **particles**

mag|ni|fy /'mægnɪfaɪ/ (magnifies, magnifying, magnified) SCIENCE

VERB To **magnify** an object means to make it appear larger than it really is, by means of a special lens or mirror. ○ *This version of the Digges telescope magnifies images 11 times.* ○ *A lens would magnify the picture so it would be like looking at a large TV screen.* ○ [V-ing] *magnifying lenses*

▶ COLLOCATIONS:
a magnifying **lens/glass**
magnify **images/pictures**
highly magnified

▶ SYNONYM: enlarge
▶ ANTONYM: reduce

mag|ni|fi|ca|tion /ˌmægnɪfɪ'keɪʃən/ (magnifications)

1 UNCOUNTABLE NOUN Magnification is the act or process of magnifying something. ○ *Pores are visible without magnification.* ○ [+ of] *the magnification of minute sounds through a computer*

▶ COLLOCATIONS:
magnification **of** *something*
magnification of **sound/light/images**

2 NOUN Magnification is the degree to which a lens, mirror, or other device can magnify an object, or the degree to which the object is magnified.

○ *The electron microscope uses a beam of electrons to produce images at high magnifications.* ○ *The magnification is 833,333 times the original size.*

▶ COLLOCATION: **low/high/maximum** magnification

---

main|stream /ˈmeɪnstriːm/ (mainstreams)

MEDIA

NOUN People, activities, or ideas that are part of the **mainstream** are regarded as the most typical, normal, and conventional because they belong to the same group or system as most others of their kind. ○ *people outside the economic mainstream* ○ [+ of] *This was the company's first step into the mainstream of scientific and commercial computing.* ○ *The show wanted to attract a mainstream audience.*

▶ COLLOCATIONS:
the mainstream **of** *something*
infiltrate/enter/join/penetrate the mainstream
the **scientific/literary/academic/political** mainstream
mainstream **politicians/republicans/feminists**
mainstream **sociology/cinema/politics**
a mainstream **audience**

▶ SYNONYMS: typical, average

---

main|tain /meɪnˈteɪn/

ACADEMIC WORD

(maintains, maintaining, maintained)

1 VERB If you **maintain** something, you continue to have it, and do not let it stop or grow weaker. ○ *The Department maintains close contacts with the chemical industry.* ○ *Such extrovert characters try to maintain relationships no matter how damaging these relationships may be.* ○ *emergency powers to try to maintain law and order*

2 VERB If you **maintain** something **at** a particular rate or level, you keep it at that rate or level. ○ [+ at] *The government was right to maintain interest rates at a high level.* ○ [+ at] *action is required to ensure standards are maintained at as high a level as possible*

▶ COLLOCATIONS:
maintain *something* **at** *a level*
maintain **standards/interest/levels/discipline/control/silence**
maintain **contacts/relationships**

▶ PHRASE: maintain law and order

> **EXTEND YOUR VOCABULARY**
>
> In everyday English, you use **keep** or **continue** to talk about something not stopping or staying the same. ○ *The teacher couldn't keep control of the class.* ○ *Oil consumption will continue at the same level.*

In more formal writing, you can use **maintain** or **sustain** to talk about keeping something the same. **Sustain** is often used to talk about keeping something at a high level, especially when this is difficult. ○ *The company encourages employees to maintain a healthy balance between their work and personal lives* ○ *Successive governments were unable to sustain economic growth.*

You use **retain** to talk about keeping something you already have and not losing it. ○ *The native peoples retain ownership and control of the land.*

main|te|nance /ˈmeɪntɪnəns/

UNCOUNTABLE NOUN If you ensure the **maintenance of** a state, process, or object, you make sure that they remain in a good or favourable condition. ○ [+ *of*] *the maintenance of peace and stability in Asia* ○ [+ *of*] *the importance of natural food to the maintenance of health*

▶ **COLLOCATIONS:**
the maintenance **of** *something*
the maintenance of **peace/standards/order/health**
the maintenance of the **equipment/building/facility**

▶ **SYNONYMS:** upkeep, continuation

ma|jor|ity /məˈdʒɒrɪti, AM -ˈdʒɔːr-/ [ACADEMIC WORD]

NOUN The **majority** of people or things in a group is more than half of them. ○ *Before the war a majority opposed invasion, yet 51% now think it was justified.* ○ [+ *of*] *The vast majority of our cheeses are made with pasteurised milk.*

▶ **COLLOCATIONS:**
the majority **of** *something*
the majority of **voters/people/citizens/members**
the majority of the **population/electorate**
a **vast/great/overwhelming/slim** majority
the majority **support/favour/endorse/reject/oppose** *something*

▶ **PHRASE:** in the majority
▶ **ANTONYM:** minority

male /meɪl/ (males)

1 **ADJECTIVE** Someone who is **male** is a man or a boy. ○ *Many women achievers appear to pose a threat to their male colleagues.* ○ *The London City Ballet has engaged two male dancers from the Bolshoi.* ○ *Most of the demonstrators were white and male.*

2 **ADJECTIVE** **Male** means relating, belonging, or affecting men rather than women. ○ *The rate of male unemployment in Britain is now the third worst in Europe.* ○ *a deep male voice*

3 NOUN You can refer to any creature that belongs to the sex that cannot lay eggs or have babies as a **male**. ○ *Males and females take turns brooding the eggs.*

● **Male** is also an adjective. ○ *After mating the male wasps tunnel through the sides of their nursery.*

▶ COLLOCATIONS:
a male **colleague/counterpart/friend/partner**
a male **dancer/athlete/model**
male **hormones/sexuality/dominance**
predominantly/exclusively male

▶ ANTONYM: female
→ see note at **female**

---

manu|fac|ture /ˌmænjʊˈfæktʃə/ `BUSINESS`
(manufactures, manufacturing, manufactured)

VERB To **manufacture** something means to make it in a factory, usually in large quantities. ○ *They manufacture the class of plastics known as thermoplastic materials.* ○ *The first three models are being manufactured at the factory in Ashton-under-Lyne.* ○ *The company imports foreign manufactured goods.*

▶ COLLOCATIONS:
manufacture **products/components**
manufacture **worldwide/overseas/abroad/locally**
synthetically/genetically/artificially manufactured
manufactured **goods**

▶ SYNONYM: produce

manu|fac|tur|ing /ˌmænjʊˈfæktʃərɪŋ/

UNCOUNTABLE NOUN ○ [+ *of*] *the manufacturing of a luxury type automobile*

▶ COLLOCATIONS:
the manufacturing **of** *something*
the manufacturing of **equipment/products/components**
a manufacturing **plant/facility**
the manufacturing **sector/industry**

manu|fac|tur|er /ˌmænjʊˈfæktʃərə/ **(manufacturers)**

NOUN A **manufacturer** is a business or company which makes goods in large quantities to sell. ○ *the world's largest doll manufacturer* ○ *major manufacturers and retailers of woodworking tools*

▶ COLLOCATIONS:
a **PC/hardware/equipment/clothing/automobile** manufacturer
a **Japanese/Italian/Swedish** manufacturer
a **major/rival** manufacturer
manufacturers **produce/supply/export** *something*

▶ SYNONYM: producer

mass /mæs/ (masses)

1 ADJECTIVE Mass is used to describe something which involves or affects a very large number of people. ○ *ideas on combating mass unemployment* ○ *weapons of mass destruction* ○ *the harm caused by mass tourism*

▶ COLLOCATIONS:
mass **destruction/migration/unemployment**
mass **protests/demonstrations**

2 NOUN A **mass of** a solid substance, a liquid, or a gas is an amount of it, especially a large amount which has no definite shape. ○ *before it cools and sets into a solid mass* ○ [+ of] *The fourteenth century cathedral was reduced to a mass of rubble.* ○ [+ of] *the strong temperature difference between the two masses of air*

▶ COLLOCATIONS:
a mass **of** something
a mass of **tissue/air/rubble**
a **solid/liquid** mass

3 NOUN In physics, the **mass** of an object is the amount of physical matter that it has. ○ *Astronomers know that Pluto and Triton have nearly the same size, mass, and density.* ○ [+ of] *the relative atomic mass of each atom within the molecule*

▶ COLLOCATION: the mass **of** something
▶ RELATED WORDS: density, weight

mas|ter's de|gree

/ˈmɑːstəz dɪgriː, ˈmæs-/ (master's degrees) also **Master's degree**

NOUN A **master's degree** is a university degree such as an MA or an MSc which is of a higher level than a first degree and usually takes one or two years to complete. **Masters** is also used in written and spoken English. ○ [+ in] *a Masters degree in Art Education* ○ [+ at] *She then took a master's degree at Oxford University.*

→ see note at **bachelor's degree**

▶ COLLOCATIONS:
a master's degree **in** something
a master's degree **at/from** somewhere
a master's degree in **business/psychology/journalism**
a master's degree at **university**
study for/take/obtain a master's degree
a master's degree **student/course**

ma|terial /məˈtɪəriəl/ (materials)

1 NOUN A **material** is a solid substance. ○ *electrons in a conducting material such as a metal* ○ *the design of new absorbent materials* ○ *recycling of all materials*

▶ **COLLOCATIONS:**
import/produce/recycle materials
a **raw/synthetic/toxic/recycled** material

▶ **SYNONYM:** substance

2 PLURAL NOUN Materials are the things that you need for a particular activity. ○ *The builders ran out of materials.* ○ *sewing materials*

▶ **COLLOCATION: sewing/building/art** materials

▶ **SYNONYM:** supplies

---

mat|ter /ˈmætə/ SCIENCE

1 UNCOUNTABLE NOUN Matter is the physical part of the universe consisting of solids, liquids, and gases. ○ *A proton is an elementary particle of matter.* ○ *He has spent his career studying how matter behaves at the fine edge between order and disorder.*

2 UNCOUNTABLE NOUN You use **matter** to refer to a particular type of substance. ○ *They feed mostly on decaying vegetable matter.* ○ *waste matter from industries*

▶ **COLLOCATION: waste/organic/vegetable** matter

▶ **SYNONYM:** substance

---

ma|ture /məˈtjʊə/ ACADEMIC WORD BIOLOGY
(matures, maturing, matured)

1 VERB When a child or young animal **matures**, it becomes an adult. ○ *Children are maturing earlier physically and are more exposed to, and targeted by, the media.* ○ *The eggs hatched and the chicks matured.*

▶ **COLLOCATION:** mature **physically/sexually**

▶ **SYNONYM:** develop

2 VERB When something **matures**, it reaches a state of complete development. ○ *When the trees matured they were cut in certain areas.* ○ *Their songwriting has matured.*

▶ **SYNONYM:** develop

3 VERB If someone **matures**, they become more fully developed in their personality and emotional behaviour. ○ *Many colleges actually recommend a year off before starting classes as a means to mature emotionally.* ○ *[+ as] You can see how he has matured as a person over the last 12 months.*

▶ **COLLOCATIONS:**
mature **as** *something*
mature as a **person/individual**
mature **intellectually/mentally/emotionally/spiritually**

▶ **SYNONYM:** grow up

maxi|mum /'mæksɪməm/ `ACADEMIC WORD`

1 **ADJECTIVE** You use **maximum** to describe an amount which is the largest that is possible, allowed, or required. ○ *The maximum sentence for supplying illegal drugs is life imprisonment.* ○ *China headed the table with maximum points.*

• **Maximum** is also a noun. ○ [+ of] *The law provides for a maximum of two years in prison.*

  ▶ **COLLOCATION:** a maximum **of** *an amount*
  ▶ **ANTONYM:** minimum

2 **ADJECTIVE** You use **maximum** to indicate how great an amount is. ○ *the maximum amount of information* ○ *It was achieved with minimum fuss and maximum efficiency.* ○ *a maximum security prison*

  ▶ **COLLOCATIONS:**
   maximum **efficiency/security/flexibility**
   the maximum **sentence/penalty/speed/amount/height/weight**
  ▶ **ANTONYM:** minimum

meas|ures /'meʒəz/ `POLITICS`

PLURAL NOUN When someone, usually a government or other authority, takes **measures** to do something, they carry out particular actions in order to achieve a particular result. [FORMAL] ○ [+ to-inf] *The government warned that police would take tougher measures to contain the trouble.* ○ [+ against] *He said stern measures would be taken against the killers.*

  ▶ **COLLOCATIONS:**
   measures **against** *someone/something*
   take/employ measures
   precautionary/preventative/practical measures
   health/safety/security measures
  ▶ **SYNONYM:** actions

mecha|nism /'mekənɪzəm/ `ACADEMIC WORD` `ENGINEERING`
(mechanisms)

NOUN In a machine or piece of equipment, a **mechanism** is a part, often consisting of a set of smaller parts, which performs a particular function. ○ *the locking mechanism* ○ *A bomb has been detonated by a special mechanism.*

  ▶ **COLLOCATIONS:**
   operate/trigger a mechanism
   a **locking/release/firing** mechanism
  ▶ **SYNONYM:** device

men|tal /ˈmentəl/ `ACADEMIC WORD` `MEDICINE`

1 **ADJECTIVE Mental** means relating to the process of thinking. ○ *the mental development of children* ○ *intensive mental effort*
  ▶ COLLOCATION: mental **development/effort/processes**

2 **ADJECTIVE Mental** means relating to the state or the health of a person's mind. ○ *The mental state that had created her psychosis was no longer present.* ○ *mental health problems*
  ▶ COLLOCATIONS:
  mental **health/illness/impairment**
  mental **anguish/distress**

men|tal|ly /ˈmentəli/

ADVERB ○ *the way the person functions physically, emotionally and mentally at work* ○ *an inmate who is mentally disturbed* ○ *the needs of the mentally ill*
  ▶ COLLOCATIONS:
  mentally **ill/handicapped/incompetent/alert**
  prepare/focus mentally
  mentally **tired/relaxed/prepared**
  ▶ PHRASES:
  mentally and physically
  mentally and emotionally

men|tion /ˈmenʃən/ **(mentions, mentioning, mentioned)**

VERB If you **mention** something, you say something about it, usually briefly. ○ *She did not mention her mother's absence.* ○ [+ *that*] *He mentioned that his father had been an attaché at the German Embassy in London.* ○ *For example, Sydney University's Professor of Medicine did not even mention insulin when lecturing on diabetes in 1923.*
  ▶ COLLOCATION: mention *something* **briefly/frequently/casually**

meth|od /ˈmeθəd/ **(methods)** `ACADEMIC WORD`

NOUN A **method** is a particular way of doing something. ○ [+ *of*] *The pill is the most efficient method of birth control.* ○ *new teaching methods* ○ [+ *of*] *Child psychologists have devised many ingenious methods of investigating this.*
  ▶ COLLOCATIONS:
  use/employ/adopt/devise/develop a method
  teaching/farming/cooking methods
  ▶ SYNONYMS: mode, manner

meth|od|ol|ogy /ˌmeθəˈdɒlədʒi/ **(methodologies)**

NOUN A **methodology** is a system of methods and principles for doing something, for example for teaching or for carrying out research. [FORMAL] ○ *Teaching methodologies vary according to the topic.* ○ *In their own work they may* *have favored the use of methodology different from mine.*

▶ **COLLOCATIONS:**
a **teaching/research/experimental** methodology
employ/devise/develop a methodology

micro|scope /ˈmaɪkrəskəʊp/ (microscopes) `SCIENCE`

NOUN A **microscope** is a scientific instrument which makes very small objects look bigger so that more detail can be seen. ○ *Dr. Maler can take thin sections of fish brain and use a microscope to study neurons at work.* ○ *They examined the remains under a powerful microscope.*

▶ **COLLOCATION:** a **powerful/conventional/atomic** microscope

micro|scop|ic /ˌmaɪkrəˈskɒpɪk/

1 ADJECTIVE Microscopic objects are extremely small, and usually can be seen only through a microscope. ○ *microscopic fibres of protein* ○ *Clouds of smoke contain microscopic particles that, when inhaled, penetrate deep into the lungs.*

▶ **COLLOCATION:** microscopic **particles/spores/fossils/parasites**

2 ADJECTIVE A **microscopic** examination is done using a microscope.
○ *Microscopic examination of a cell's chromosomes can reveal the sex of the fetus.*
○ *Finally, the cells were examined by microscopic autoradiography.*

▶ **ANTONYM:** macroscopic

min|er|al /ˈmɪnərəl/ (minerals) `SCIENCE` `GEOGRAPHY`

NOUN A **mineral** is a substance such as tin, salt, or sulphur that is formed naturally in rocks and in the earth. Minerals are also found in small quantities in food and drink. ○ *Warring factions obtained arms from international backers in exchange for money or precious minerals.* ○ *vitamin and mineral supplements*

▶ **COLLOCATIONS:**
precious/valuable/non-metallic minerals
essential/toxic minerals
mineral **supplements/deficiencies/deposits**
mineral **salt/water/calcium/zinc**

▶ **PHRASE:** vitamins and minerals

mini|mal /ˈmɪnɪməl/ `ACADEMIC WORD`

ADJECTIVE Something that is **minimal** is very small in quantity, value, or degree. ○ *The co-operation between the two is minimal.* ○ *One aim of these reforms is effective defence with minimal expenditure.*

▶ **COLLOCATION:** minimal **impact/effect/damage/risk/expenditure**
▶ **ANTONYM:** maximal

mini|mal|ly /ˈmɪnɪməli/

ADVERB ○ *He was paid, but only minimally.* ○ *minimally invasive techniques*

▶ **COLLOCATIONS:**
minimally **invasive/stressful/inconvenient**
minimally **satisfactory/acceptable**

mini|mum /ˈmɪnɪməm/ `ACADEMIC WORD`

ADJECTIVE You use **minimum** to describe an amount which is the smallest that is possible, allowed, or required. ○ *If found guilty, she faces a minimum sentence of ten years and 30 lashes.* ○ *a rise in the minimum wage*

● **Minimum** is also a noun. ○ [+ of] *This will take a minimum of one hour.* ○ *To provide welfare at a level greater than this bare minimum discourages self-reliance.*

▶ **COLLOCATIONS:**
a minimum **of** *something/an amount*
the minimum **amount/height/requirement/wage/sentence**
a **bare/absolute/required/stated** minimum

▶ **ANTONYM:** maximum

min|is|try /ˈmɪnɪstri/ (ministries) `ACADEMIC WORD` `POLITICS`

NOUN In Britain and some other countries, a **ministry** is a government department which deals with a particular thing or area of activity, for example trade, defence, or transport. ○ [+ of] *the Ministry of Justice* ○ *a spokesman for the Agriculture Ministry*

▶ **COLLOCATIONS:**
the ministry **of** *something*
the Ministry of **Agriculture/Education/Foreign affairs**
the **foreign** ministry

mi|nor|ity /mɪˈnɒrɪti, AM -ˈnɔːr-/ `ACADEMIC WORD` `SOCIOLOGY` (minorities)

1 NOUN If you talk about a **minority** of people or things in a larger group, you are referring to a number of them that forms less than half of the larger group, usually much less than half. ○ [+ of] *Nursery provision covers only a tiny minority of working mothers.* ○ *These children are only a small minority.* ○ *In the past conservatives have been in the minority.*

▶ **COLLOCATIONS:**
a minority **of** *people/things*
in a/the minority
the minority of the **population**
the minority of **voters/individuals/citizens**
a **small/tiny/sizeable/significant** minority

▶ **ANTONYM:** majority

2 NOUN A **minority** is a group of people of the same race, culture, or religion who live in a place where most of the people around them are of a different race, culture, or religion. ○ *the region's ethnic minorities* ○ *Students have called for greater numbers of women and minorities on the faculty.*

▶ COLLOCATIONS:
ethnic/racial/religious minorities
Christian/Muslim minorities
minority **rights**

---

mi|nus /ˈmaɪnəs/   MATHS

1 CONJUNCTION You use **minus** to show that one number or quantity is being subtracted from another. ○ *One minus one is zero.* ○ *They've been promised their full July salary minus the hardship payment.*

▶ SYNONYM: less
▶ ANTONYM: plus

2 ADJECTIVE **Minus** before a number or quantity means that the number or quantity is less than zero. ○ *The aircraft was subjected to temperatures of minus 65 degrees and plus 120 degrees.* ○ *What's the square root of minus 1?*

▶ COLLOCATION: minus **one/two/50/300**

---

mod|el /ˈmɒdəl/ (models, modelling, modelled)
[in AM, use **modeling**, **modeled**]

1 NOUN A **model** is a system that is being used and that people might want to copy in order to achieve similar results. [FORMAL] ○ [+ *of*] *We believe that this is a general model of managerial activity.* ○ [+ *of*] *the European model of social responsibility*

▶ COLLOCATIONS:
a model **of** *something*
a model of **efficiency/consistency/excellence**
introduce/adopt/follow a model

▶ SYNONYMS: system, example

2 NOUN A **model** of a system or process is a theoretical description that can help you understand how the system or process works, or how it might work. [FORMAL] ○ [+ *of*] *Darwin eventually put forward a model of biological evolution.*

▶ COLLOCATIONS:
a model **of** *something*
a model of the **universe**
a model of **evolution**
propose a model

▶ SYNONYM: theory

3 VERB If someone such as a scientist **models** a system or process, they make an accurate theoretical description of it in order to understand or explain how it works. [FORMAL] ○ *the mathematics needed to model a nonlinear system like an atmosphere* ○ *It is no surprise that we find such processes hard to model mathematically.*

mod|er|ate /ˈmɒdərət/

1 ADJECTIVE You use **moderate** to describe something that is neither large nor small in amount or degree. ○ *While a moderate amount of stress can be beneficial, too much stress can exhaust you.* ○ *Heavy drinkers die earlier than moderate drinkers.*

▶ COLLOCATIONS:
a moderate **amount/extent**
moderate **weather/heat/exercise/drinking**

▶ SYNONYM: reasonable

▶ ANTONYM: excessive

2 ADJECTIVE A **moderate** change in something is a change that is not great.
○ *Most drugs offer either no real improvement or, at best, only moderate improvements.*
○ *House prices are still quite moderate in relation to personal incomes.*

▶ COLLOCATION: a moderate **increase/growth/decline**

▶ SYNONYM: slight

mod|er|ate|ly /ˈmɒdərətli/

ADVERB ○ *Both are moderately large insects.* ○ *Share prices on the Tokyo Exchange declined moderately.*

▶ COLLOCATIONS:
drink/exercise/eat moderately
moderately **attractive/overweight/successful**
increase/rise/fall moderately

▶ SYNONYMS: reasonably, slightly

▶ ANTONYM: excessively

modi|fy /ˈmɒdɪfaɪ/ (modifies, modifying, modified)   `ACADEMIC WORD`

VERB If you **modify** something, you change it slightly, usually in order to improve it. ○ *The club members did agree to modify their recruitment policy.*
○ *The plane was a modified version of the C-130.*

→ see note at **adapt**

▶ COLLOCATIONS:
modify **food/crops/ingredients**
genetically/chemically modified
extensively/significantly modified

▶ SYNONYM: alter

modi|fi|ca|tion /ˌmɒdɪfɪˈkeɪʃən/ (modifications)

NOUN ○ *Relatively minor modifications were required.* ○ *behaviour modification techniques*

▶ **COLLOCATIONS:**
genetic/evolutionary/dietary/behaviour modification
a **minor/slight** modification

▶ **SYNONYMS:** alteration, change

---

moni|tor /ˈmɒnɪtə/ (monitors, monitoring, monitored) `ACADEMIC WORD`

1 VERB If you **monitor** something, you regularly check its development or progress, and sometimes comment on it. ○ *Officials had not been allowed to monitor the voting.* ○ *Senior managers can then use the budget as a control document to monitor progress against the agreed actions.*

▶ **COLLOCATIONS:**
closely/strictly/regularly/carefully monitored
monitor **progress/activity/effectiveness**
monitor the **situation**

▶ **SYNONYMS:** observe, oversee

2 NOUN A **monitor** is a machine that is used to check or record things, for example processes or substances inside a person's body. ○ *The heart monitor shows low levels of consciousness.* ○ *A blood glucose monitor at a local drug store costs around $25.*

▶ **COLLOCATION:** a **heart/heart-rate/glucose** monitor

---

mor|al /ˈmɒrəl, AM ˈmɔːr-/ `SOCIAL SCIENCE`

ADJECTIVE **Moral** means relating to beliefs about what is right or wrong.
○ *She describes her own moral dilemma in making the film.* ○ *matters of church doctrine and moral teaching* ○ *the moral issues involved in 'playing God'*

▶ **COLLOCATIONS:**
a moral **dilemma/code/compass**
moral **principles/judgements/obligations/responsibilities**

▶ **SYNONYM:** ethical

mor|al|ly /ˈmɒrəli, AM ˈmɔːr-/

ADVERB ○ *When, if ever, is it morally justifiable to allow a patient to die?* ○ *Is there really morally any difference between slaughtering a cow for food and a horse for food?*

▶ **COLLOCATION:** morally **justifiable/defensible/dubious/reprehensible**

▶ **SYNONYM:** ethically

---

more|over /mɔːˈrəʊvə/

ADVERB You use **moreover** to introduce a piece of information that adds to or supports the previous statement. [FORMAL] ○ *The young find everything so*

simple. The young, moreover, see it as their duty to be happy and do their best to be so.
○ *A new species, it was unique to Bali - moreover, it is this island's only endemic bird.*

▶ **SYNONYMS:** furthermore, in addition

---

mort|gage /'mɔːgɪdʒ/ (mortgages)　　ECONOMICS

NOUN A **mortgage** is a loan of money which you get from a bank or building society in order to buy a house. ○ *an increase in mortgage rates* ○ *the borrower was free to repay the mortgage at any time*

▶ **COLLOCATIONS:**
 repay/pay the mortgage
 mortgage **repayments/rates**

---

mo|ti|vate /'məʊtɪveɪt/　　ACADEMIC WORD
(motivates, motivating, motivated)

1 VERB If you **are motivated** by something, especially an emotion, it causes you to behave in a particular way. ○ *They are motivated by a need to achieve.* ○ *The crime was not politically motivated.*

▶ **COLLOCATIONS:**
 motivated **by** *something*
 motivated by **fear/money/greed/friendship/ideals**
 economically/politically/commercially motivated

2 VERB If someone **motivates** you to do something, they make you feel determined to do it. ○ [+ to-inf] *How do you motivate people to work hard and efficiently?* ○ *Never let it be said that the manager doesn't know how to motivate his players.*

▶ **COLLOCATION:** motivate **employees/learners/pupils**
▶ **SYNONYM:** inspire

mo|ti|va|tion /ˌməʊtɪ'veɪʃən/

UNCOUNTABLE NOUN Your **motivation** for doing something is what causes you to want to do it or is the act or process of someone making you feel determined to do something. ○ *His poor performance may be attributed to lack of motivation.* ○ *Gross's skill in motivation looked in doubt when his side began the second half badly.*

▶ **COLLOCATIONS:**
 a **lack** of motivation
 personal/political motivation
 lack/provide motivation
 staff/employee motivation

▶ **SYNONYMS:** inspiration, determination

move|ment /ˈmuːvmənt/ (movements)   SCIENCE POLITICS

NOUN A **movement** is a group of people who share the same beliefs, ideas, or aims. ○ *It's part of a broader Hindu nationalist movement.* ○ *the women's movement*
▶ COLLOCATIONS:
  a **separatist/union/independence/democracy** movement
  the **youth/peace/women's** movement

multi|na|tion|al /ˌmʌltiˈnæʃənəl/   BUSINESS
(multinationals) also **multi-national**

ADJECTIVE A **multinational** company has branches or owns companies in many different countries. ○ *The multinational company is increasingly becoming a world-wide phenomenon.* ○ *Not a single multinational firm operates in that country.*
● **Multinational** is also a noun. ○ *multinationals such as Ford and IBM* ○ *Large multinationals are also realising that they can become more efficient.*
▶ COLLOCATIONS:
  a multinational **corporation/company/firm**
  a **foreign-based/European/American** multinational
▶ SYNONYM: international

multi|ple /ˈmʌltɪpəl/

ADJECTIVE You use **multiple** to describe things that consist of many parts, involve many people, or have many uses. ○ *He died of multiple injuries.*
○ *The most common multiple births are twins, two babies born at the same time.*
▶ COLLOCATION: multiple **fractures/injuries/births/personality**

mu|tu|al /ˈmjuːtʃʊəl/   ACADEMIC WORD

ADJECTIVE You use **mutual** to describe a situation, feeling, or action that is experienced, felt, or done by both of two people mentioned. ○ *The East and the West can work together for their mutual benefit and progress.*
▶ COLLOCATIONS:
  mutual **trust/attraction/benefit**
  mutual **suspicion/dislike/hostility**
▶ SYNONYMS: shared, reciprocal

mu|tu|al|ly /ˈmjuːtʃʊəli/

ADVERB ○ *Attempts to reach a mutually agreed solution had been fruitless.*
○ *A meeting would take place at a mutually convenient time.*
▶ COLLOCATIONS:
  mutually **beneficial/advantageous**
  mutually **satisfactory/convenient**

Nn

name|ly /ˈneɪmli/

ADVERB You use **namely** to introduce detailed information about the subject you are discussing, or a particular aspect of it. ○ *One group of people seems to be forgotten, namely pensioners.* ○ *They were hardly aware of the challenge facing them, namely, to re-establish prosperity.*

▶ **SYNONYMS:** that is (to say), specifically

nar|row /ˈnærəʊ/ (narrower, narrowest, narrows, narrowing, narrowed)

1 ADJECTIVE Something that is **narrow** measures a very small distance from one side to the other, especially compared to its length or height. ○ *She had long, narrow feet.* ○ *the narrow strip of land joining the peninsula to the rest of the island*

▶ **COLLOCATIONS:**
a narrow **gap/street/strip/road/lane/corridor/passageway**
a narrow **channel/river/valley/opening**

▶ **SYNONYMS:** thin, slender

▶ **ANTONYMS:** wide, broad

2 VERB If something **narrows**, it becomes less wide. ○ *The wide track narrows before crossing another stream.* ○ *Narrowed blood vessels prevent blood from flowing to the heart.*

▶ **COLLOCATIONS:**
a **gap/gulf** narrows
a **valley/canyon/river** narrows
a narrowing **artery/airway**
narrow **significantly/considerably**

▶ **SYNONYMS:** constrict, contract

▶ **ANTONYMS:** open, widen

na|ture /ˈneɪtʃə/ (natures)

NOUN The **nature** of something is its basic quality or character. ○ [+ *of*] *the nature of the issues being investigated* ○ [+ *of*] *the ambitious nature of the programme* ○ *The protests had been non-political by nature.*

▶ **COLLOCATIONS:**
the nature **of** something
in/by nature

the nature of the **relationship/threat/crime**
the nature of **politics/reality/society**
the nature of the **regime/allegation/conflict**

---

ne|go|ti|ate /nɪˈgəʊʃieɪt/ (negotiates, negotiating, negotiated)

VERB If people **negotiate with** each other or **negotiate** an agreement, they talk about a problem or a situation such as a business arrangement in order to solve the problem or complete the arrangement. ○ [+ with] *It is not clear whether the president is willing to negotiate with the democrats.* ○ *The local government and the army negotiated a truce.* ○ [+ to-inf] *Three companies were negotiating to market the drug.*

▶ **COLLOCATIONS:**
negotiate **with** *someone*
negotiate **for** *something*
agree to/fail to/refuse to negotiate
a **government/company/union** negotiates
officials/mediators/representatives negotiate
negotiate a **settlement/deal/agreement/treaty/solution/contract**
the negotiating **table**
successfully/directly negotiate

▶ **SYNONYMS:** discuss, hold talks, settle

ne|go|tia|tion /nɪˌgəʊʃiˈeɪʃən/ (negotiations)

NOUN ○ *We have had meaningful negotiations and I believe we are very close to a deal.* ○ *After 10 years of negotiation, the Senate ratified the strategic arms reduction treaty.*

▶ **COLLOCATIONS:**
negotiation **between** *people*
under negotiation
conclude negotiations
negotiations **stall/fail/resume/restart/reopen**
government/peace/trade/political negotiations
intense/formal/direct/protracted negotiations
the **process of/basis for** negotiation

▶ **SYNONYMS:** bargaining, discussion, mediation, arbitration

ne|go|tia|tor /nɪˈgəʊʃieɪtə/ (negotiators)

NOUN **Negotiators** are people who take part in political or financial negotiations. ○ *the rebels' chief negotiator at the peace talks* ○ *The two American negotiators are calling for substantial cuts in external subsidies.*

▶ **COLLOCATIONS:**
a **peace/trade/arms** negotiator
a **chief/government/union** negotiator

▶ **SYNONYMS:** mediator, intermediary

neigh|bour|ing /ˈneɪbərɪŋ/

ADJECTIVE Neighbouring places or things are near other things of the same kind. [in AM, use **neighboring**] ○ *Rwanda is to hold talks with leaders of neighbouring countries next week.* ○ *Some Liberians sought refuge in the neighboring Ivory Coast.*

▶ COLLOCATION: a neighbouring **country/state/building**

▶ SYNONYMS: nearby, adjacent

nerve /nɜːv/ (nerves)   BIOLOGY

NOUN Nerves are long thin fibres that transmit messages between your brain and other parts of your body. ○ *spinal nerves* ○ *in cases where the nerve fibres are severed*

▶ COLLOCATIONS:
  the **optic/sciatic** nerve
  a **spinal/trapped/damaged** nerve
  nerve **fibres/endings/cells/impulses/tissue**
  nerve **damage**

net|work /ˈnetwɜːk/ (networks)   ACADEMIC WORD IT

1 NOUN A **network of** lines, roads, veins, or other long thin things is a large number of them which cross each other or meet at many points. ○ [+ *of*] *Strasbourg, with its rambling network of medieval streets* ○ [+ *of*] *a rich network of blood vessels and nerves*

▶ COLLOCATIONS:
  a network **of** *something*
  a network of **tunnels/rivers/canals/pipelines**

▶ SYNONYMS: web, grid

2 NOUN A **network of** people or institutions is a large number of them that have a connection with each other and work together as a system. ○ [+ *of*] *a network of local church people and other volunteers* ○ *He is keen to point out the benefits which the family network can provide.*

▶ COLLOCATIONS:
  a network **of** *people/things*
  a **terrorist/corporate/operator** network
  create/build/establish/expand a network

▶ SYNONYM: system

3 NOUN A particular **network** is a system of things which are connected and which operate together. ○ *a computer network with 154 terminals* ○ *Huge sections of the rail network are out of action.*

▶ COLLOCATIONS:
  install/operate a network

a **wireless/mobile/cable** network
a **television/computer/radio/phone** network
a **broadcasting/storage/communications** network
a **rail/railway/transport/distribution** network
a network **operator/provider/connection**
network **equipment/infrastructure/capacity**
▶ SYNONYM: system

---

neu|tral /ˈnjuːtrəl, AM ˈnuːt-/ `ACADEMIC WORD`

1 ADJECTIVE If a person or country adopts a **neutral** position or remains **neutral**, they do not support anyone in a disagreement, war, or contest. ○ *They'll meet on neutral territory.* ○ *[+ in] Those who had decided to remain neutral in the struggle now found themselves required to take sides.*

▶ COLLOCATIONS:
neutral **in** something
remain neutral
a neutral **stance/position/zone**
neutral **territory/ground**
politically neutral
▶ SYNONYMS: impartial, unbiased
▶ ANTONYM: biased

2 ADJECTIVE Neutral is used to describe something that is neither negative nor positive. ○ *Pure water is neutral with a pH of 7.* ○ *ICI is making a profit of £190m on the sale, which will have a neutral impact on its earnings.*

---

never|the|less /ˌnevəðəˈles/ `ACADEMIC WORD`

ADVERB You use **nevertheless** when saying something that contrasts with what has just been said. [FORMAL] ○ *Most marriages fail after between five and nine years. Nevertheless, people continue to get married.* ○ *There had been no indication of any loss of mental faculties. His whole life had nevertheless been clouded with a series of illnesses.*

▶ SYNONYMS: nonetheless, even so, still, yet

---

norm /nɔːm/ (norms) `ACADEMIC WORD` `SOCIOLOGY`

1 NOUN Norms are ways of behaving that are considered normal in a particular society. ○ *[+ of] the commonly accepted norms of democracy* ○ *[+ that] a social norm that says drunkenness is inappropriate behaviour*

▶ SYNONYMS: average, rule, value

2 NOUN A **norm** is an official standard or level that organizations are expected to reach. ○ *an agency which would establish European norms and co-ordinate national policies to halt pollution.*

▶ **COLLOCATIONS:**
a norm **of** *something*
the norms of **behaviour**
a **cultural/democratic/social/accepted** norm
accept/establish/meet the norms of *something*

▶ **SYNONYMS:** standard, rule

---

no|table /'nəʊtəbəl/

ADJECTIVE Someone or something that is **notable** is important or interesting.
○ [+ for] *The proposed new structure is notable not only for its height, but for its shape.* ○ *With a few notable exceptions, doctors are a pretty sensible lot.*

→ see note at **dramatic**

▶ **COLLOCATIONS:**
notable **for** *something*
a notable **exception/example/difference**
a notable **achievement/success/contribution**

▶ **SYNONYMS:** noteworthy, remarkable, marked, striking

▶ **ANTONYM:** unremarkable

no|tably /'nəʊtəbli/

ADVERB ○ [+ in] *It was a question of making sure certain needs were addressed, notably in the pensions area.* ○ *Old established friends are notably absent, so it's a good opportunity to make new contacts.*

▶ **COLLOCATIONS:**
notably **in** *something*
notably **absent/different/successful**

▶ **SYNONYMS:** particularly, strikingly

---

note /nəʊt/ (notes, noting, noted)

VERB If you **note** something, you mention it in order to draw people's attention to it. ○ [+ that] *The report notes that export and import volumes picked up in leading economies.* ○ *The yearbook also noted a sharp drop in reported cases of sexually transmitted disease.* ○ [+ how] *Note how the average level of job performance increases as the SR decreases.*

▶ **COLLOCATIONS:**
a **report/observer/analyst** notes *something*
note a **difference/increase/improvement/similarity**

▶ **PHRASES:**
please note
note with interest

▶ **SYNONYM:** observe

no|tion /ˈnəʊʃən/ (notions)   ACADEMIC WORD

NOUN A **notion** is an idea or belief about something. ○ [+ of] *We each have a notion of just what kind of person we'd like to be.* ○ [+ that] *I reject absolutely the notion that privatisation of our industry is now inevitable.*

→ see note at **concept**

▶ COLLOCATIONS:
a notion **of** *something*
the notion of **justice/equality/identity**
a **preconceived** notion
dismiss/reject/challenge a notion

▶ SYNONYMS: idea, concept

nu|clear /ˈnjuːkliə, AM ˈnuːk-/   ACADEMIC WORD   SCIENCE

1 ADJECTIVE Nuclear means relating to the nuclei of atoms, or to the energy released when these nuclei are split or combined. ○ *a nuclear power station* ○ *nuclear energy* ○ *nuclear physics*

▶ COLLOCATIONS:
a nuclear **power station/plant/facility**
nuclear **power/energy/waste/material**
nuclear **physics**

2 ADJECTIVE Nuclear means relating to weapons that explode by using the energy released when the nuclei of atoms are split or combined. ○ *They rejected a demand for the removal of all nuclear weapons from U.K. soil.* ○ *nuclear testing*

▶ COLLOCATION: a nuclear **weapon/test/programme**

▶ SYNONYM: atomic

nu|mer|al /ˈnjuːmərəl, AM ˈnuː-/ (numerals)   MATHS

NOUN Numerals are written symbols used to represent numbers. ○ *a flat, square wristwatch with classic Roman numerals* ○ *the numeral six*

▶ COLLOCATION: a **Roman** numeral

▶ SYNONYMS: number, digit

▶ RELATED WORD: letter

nu|mer|ous /ˈnjuːmərəs, AM ˈnuːm-/

ADJECTIVE If people or things are **numerous**, they exist or are present in large numbers. ○ *Sex crimes were just as numerous as they are today.* ○ *Numerous tests had been made, but no physical cause for her symptoms could be found.*

▶ COLLOCATIONS:
numerous **attempts/examples/occasions/times**
numerous **problems/studies**

n

EXTEND YOUR VOCABULARY

You use **a lot of**, **lots of** or **loads of** in informal and spoken English to describe a large number of something. ○ *I've been there loads of times*.

You use **many** in more formal writing, especially to talk about a large proportion of a group. ○ *Many experts believe that the system needs major modifications*.

You use **numerous** in formal writing to describe a large, but unknown number. ○ *There are numerous examples from other parts of the world*.
You can also use **innumerable** and **countless** to emphasize a number too large to count. ○ *It consists of innumerable tiny particles*.

---

nu|tri|tion /njuːˈtrɪʃən, AM ˈnuː-/ `MEDICINE`

UNCOUNTABLE NOUN Nutrition is the process of taking food into the body and absorbing the nutrients in those foods. ○ *There are alternative sources of nutrition to animal meat*.

▶ COLLOCATION: **good/poor/proper** nutrition
▶ SYNONYM: nourishment

nu|tri|tious /njuːˈtrɪʃəs, AM ˈnuː-/

ADJECTIVE Nutritious food contains substances which help your body to be healthy. ○ *It is always important to choose enjoyable, nutritious foods*. ○ *Some ready made meals are nutritious and very easy to prepare*.

▶ COLLOCATIONS:
nutritious **food**
a nutritious **meal/lunch**
highly nutritious
▶ SYNONYM: nourishing

nu|tri|tion|al /njuːˈtrɪʃənəl, AM ˈnuː-/

ADJECTIVE The **nutritional** content of food is all the substances that are in it which help you to remain healthy. ○ *Cooking vegetables reduces their nutritional value*.

▶ COLLOCATIONS:
nutritional **value/content/needs/factors/requirements**
a nutritional **supplement/deficiency**

Oo

ob|ject (objects, objecting, objected)

> The noun is pronounced /ˈɒbdʒɪkt/. The verb is pronounced /əbˈdʒekt/.

1 NOUN The **object** of what someone is doing is their aim or purpose. ○ [+ *of*] *The object of the exercise is to raise money for the charity.* ○ [+ *in*] *He made it his object in life to find the island.* ○ *My object was to publish a scholarly work on Peter Mourne.*

▶ **COLLOCATIONS:**
the object **of/in** *something*
the object of the **exercise**
someone's object in **life**

▶ **SYNONYMS:** purpose, aim, point

2 VERB If you **object** to something, you express your dislike or disapproval of it. ○ [+ *to*] *A lot of people will object to the book.* ○ [+ *that*] *Cullen objected that his small staff would be unable to handle the added work.* ○ *We objected strongly but were outvoted.*

▶ **COLLOCATIONS:**
object **to** *something*
object to the **idea/notion/use**
object **strongly**

▶ **SYNONYMS:** protest, argue

ob|jec|tion /əbˈdʒekʃən/ (objections)

NOUN If you make or raise an **objection to** something, you say that you do not like it or agree with it. ○ [+ *to*] *Some managers have recently raised objections to the PFA handling these negotiations.* ○ [+ *by*] *Despite objections by the White House, the Senate voted today to cut off aid.*

▶ **COLLOCATIONS:**
an objection **to** *something*
an objection **by** *someone*
raise/dismiss/overrule an objection
a **moral/religious** objection

▶ **SYNONYMS:** protest, opposition, complaint

▶ **ANTONYM:** approval

o

ob|jec|tive /əbˈdʒektɪv/ (objectives)

1 NOUN Your **objective** is what you are trying to achieve. ○ *Our main objective was the recovery of the child safe and well.* ○ *Our objective is to become the number-one digital corporation.*

→ see note at **aim**

▶ COLLOCATIONS:
the **primary/key** objective
achieve/set/meet an objective

▶ SYNONYMS: purpose, aim, goal

2 ADJECTIVE Objective information is based on facts. ○ *He had no objective evidence that anything extraordinary was happening.* ○ *It is futile to look for objective causes of drug addiction.*

▶ COLLOCATION: objective **evidence/truth/reality**

▶ SYNONYM: factual

▶ RELATED WORD: subjective

3 ADJECTIVE If someone is **objective,** they base their opinions on facts rather than on their personal feelings. ○ *I believe that a journalist should be completely objective.* ○ *I would really like to have your objective opinion on this.*

▶ COLLOCATIONS:
completely/supposedly/truly objective
an objective **opinion/account**

▶ SYNONYMS: impartial, unbiased, unprejudiced, open-minded

▶ ANTONYM: subjective

ob|jec|tive|ly /əbˈdʒektɪvli/

ADVERB Something that is done **objectively** is done according to facts rather than opinions or emotions. ○ *We simply want to inform people objectively about events.* ○ *Try to view situations more objectively, especially with regard to work.*

▶ COLLOCATION: **measure/assess/report/view** something objectively

▶ SYNONYM: impartially

▶ ANTONYM: subjectively

ob|jec|tiv|ity /ˌɒbdʒekˈtɪvɪti/

UNCOUNTABLE NOUN Objectivity is a lack of bias, personal opinion, or emotion. ○ *The poll, whose objectivity is open to question, gave the party a 39% share of the vote.* ○ *The psychiatrist must learn to maintain an unusual degree of objectivity.*

▶ COLLOCATIONS:
maintain/lack/lose objectivity
journalistic/scientific/professional objectivity

▶ SYNONYM: impartiality

▶ ANTONYM: subjectivity

ob|liga|tory /əˈblɪɡətri, AM -tɔːri/

ADJECTIVE If something is **obligatory**, you must do it because of a rule or a law. ○ *Most women will be offered an ultrasound scan during pregnancy, although it's not obligatory.* ○ *These rates do not include the charge for obligatory medical consultations.*

▶ **SYNONYMS:** compulsory, necessary
▶ **ANTONYMS:** optional, voluntary

ob|serve /əbˈzɜːv/ (observes, observing, observed)

VERB If you **observe** a person or thing, you watch them carefully, especially in order to learn something about them. ○ *Stern also studies and observes the behaviour of babies.* ○ [+ how] *I got a chance to observe how a detective actually works.*

▶ **COLLOCATIONS:**
  scientists/researchers observe *something*
  observe **behaviour**
  closely observe
▶ **SYNONYMS:** study, monitor

ob|ser|va|tion /ˌɒbzəˈveɪʃən/

UNCOUNTABLE NOUN Observation is the action or process of carefully watching someone or something. ○ [+ of] *careful observation of the movement of the planets* ○ *In hospital she'll be under observation all the time.*

▶ **COLLOCATIONS:**
  observation **of** *something*
  under observation
  observation of the **nature/behaviour** of *something*
  careful observation
  astronomical/scientific observation
▶ **SYNONYMS:** study, surveillance

ob|serv|er /əbˈzɜːvə/ (observers)

NOUN In scientific research, you can refer to someone who watches and studies something as an **observer**. ○ *He argues that truly objective science is impossible: the observer affects the system he or she observes.*

▶ **COLLOCATION:** a **scientific/independent/trained** observer

ob|tain /ɒbˈteɪn/ (obtains, obtaining, obtained) ACADEMIC WORD

VERB To **obtain** something means to get it or achieve it. [FORMAL] ○ *Evans was trying to obtain a false passport.* ○ *The perfect body has always been difficult to obtain.*

→ see note at **acquire**

▶ **COLLOCATIONS:**
obtain **help/approval/permission**
obtain **information/documents/financing**
obtain *something* **easily/fraudulently/illegally**

▶ **SYNONYMS:** get, acquire, achieve

---

oc|cu|pa|tion /ˌɒkjʊˈpeɪʃən/ (occupations) `ACADEMIC WORD` `BUSINESS`

NOUN Your **occupation** is your job or profession. ○ *I suppose I was looking for an occupation which was going to be an adventure.* ○ *Occupation: administrative assistant.*

▶ **SYNONYMS:** profession, work

oc|cu|pa|tion|al /ˌɒkjʊˈpeɪʃənəl/

ADJECTIVE **Occupational** means relating to a person's job or profession.
○ *Catching frequent colds is unfortunately an occupational hazard in this profession.*

▶ **COLLOCATIONS:**
an occupational **hazard/pension**
an occupational **therapist**
occupational **health**

▶ **SYNONYM:** job-related

---

oc|cu|py /ˈɒkjʊpaɪ/ (occupies, occupying, occupied) `ACADEMIC WORD`

1 VERB The people who **occupy** a building or a place are the people who live or work there. ○ *There were over 40 tenants, all occupying one wing of the hospital.* ○ *Land is, in most instances, purchased by those who occupy it.*

▶ **COLLOCATIONS:**
occupy **land**
occupy a **building/floor**

▶ **SYNONYM:** inhabit

2 VERB If someone or something **occupies** a particular place in a system, process, or plan, they have that place. ○ *We occupy a quality position in the market place.* ○ *Men still occupy more positions of power than women.*

▶ **COLLOCATION:** occupy a **position**

▶ **SYNONYM:** hold

3 VERB If something **occupies** a particular area or place, it fills or covers it, or exists there. ○ *Even quite small aircraft occupy a lot of space.* ○ *Bookshelves occupied most of the living room walls.*

▶ **COLLOCATIONS:**
occupy **space**
occupy a **wall/floor**

oc|cu|pant /ˈɒkjʊpənt/ (occupants)

NOUN The **occupants** of a building or room are the people who live or work there. ○ *Most of the occupants had left before the fire broke out.* ○ *The filing cabinets had all gone with the previous occupants.*
▶ **COLLOCATION**: a **previous/sole/original/future** occupant
▶ **SYNONYM**: occupier

oc|cur /əˈkɜː/ (occurs, occurring, occurred)　[ACADEMIC WORD]

1 VERB When something **occurs**, it happens. ○ [+ at] *If headaches only occur at night, lack of fresh air and oxygen is often the cause.* ○ [+ when] *The crash occurred when the crew shut down the wrong engine.*
▶ **COLLOCATIONS**:
occur **at** *a time*
changes/problems/incidents occur
accidents/deaths/diseases/injuries occur
naturally/normally occur

> **EXTEND YOUR VOCABULARY**
>
> In everyday English, you say often that something **happens** or **takes place**. ○ *The accident happened/took place in heavy rain.*
>
> In more formal writing, you can say that something **occurs**. ○ *The incident occurred on June 28.* ○ *Chemical changes occur at the two electrodes.*
>
> You can also say that some types of things **arise**.
>
> > a **problem/complication/difficulty** arises
> > a **question/issue/opportunity** arises

2 VERB When something **occurs** in a particular place, it exists or is present there. ○ *The cattle disease occurs more or less anywhere in Africa where the fly occurs.* ○ [+ on] *These snails do not occur on low-lying coral islands or atolls.*
▶ **COLLOCATIONS**:
occur **in/on** *somewhere*
frequently/naturally/normally occur
▶ **SYNONYM**: exist

oc|cur|rence /əˈkʌrəns, AM -ˈkɜːr-/ (occurrences)

NOUN An **occurrence** is something that happens. [FORMAL] ○ *Complaints seemed to be an everyday occurrence.* ○ [+ of] *There is no general agreed explanation for the occurrence of hallucinations.*
▶ **COLLOCATIONS**:
the occurrence **of** *something*
prevent/reduce/increase the occurrence of *something*
a **common/rare/daily/everyday** occurrence
▶ **SYNONYMS**: incident, happening, event, phenomenon

of|fence /əˈfens/ (offences) LAW

> The spelling **offense** is used in American English.

NOUN An **offence** is a crime that breaks a particular law and requires a particular punishment. ○ *Thirteen people have been charged with treason – an offence which can carry the death penalty.* ○ *[+ to-inf] In Britain the Consumer Protection Act makes it a criminal offence to sell goods that are unsafe.*

▶ COLLOCATIONS:
  commit/admit an offence
  a **criminal/serious/punishable** offence
  a **drug/sex/traffic** offence
▶ SYNONYM: crime

of|fend /əˈfend/ (offends, offending, offended)

VERB If someone **offends**, they commit a crime. [FORMAL] ○ *In Western countries girls are far less likely to offend than boys.* ○ *Victims wanted assurances their attackers would never offend again.*

▶ PHRASE: likely to offend
▶ SYNONYM: break the law

of|fend|er /əˈfendə/ (offenders)

NOUN An **offender** is a person who has committed a crime. ○ *The authorities often know that sex offenders will attack again when they are released.* ○ *an experimental scheme for young offenders*

▶ COLLOCATIONS:
  a **sex/dangerous/young/juvenile** offender
  a **registered/convicted** offender
  a **first-time/serial/repeat/persistent** offender
▶ PHRASE: young offender institution
▶ SYNONYM: criminal

on|going /ˌɒnˈgəʊɪŋ/ ACADEMIC WORD

ADJECTIVE An **ongoing** situation has been happening for quite a long time and seems likely to continue for some time in the future. ○ *There is an ongoing debate on the issue.* ○ *That research is ongoing.*

▶ COLLOCATIONS:
  an ongoing **debate/process/effort/war**
  an ongoing **investigation/dispute/discussion/debate**
  ongoing **research**
▶ SYNONYM: continuing

op|pose /əˈpəʊz/ (opposes, opposing, opposed)

VERB If you **oppose** someone or **oppose** their plans or ideas, you disagree with what they want to do and try to prevent them from doing it. ○ *Mr Taylor was not bitter towards those who had opposed him.* ○ *Many parents oppose bilingual education.*

▶ **COLLOCATIONS:**
oppose a **plan/move/view/idea/war/bill**
strongly oppose *something*

▶ **ANTONYM:** support

op|posed /əˈpəʊzd/

ADJECTIVE If you **are opposed to** something, you disagree with it or disapprove of it. ○ [+ to] *I am utterly opposed to any form of terrorism.* ○ [+ to] *We are strongly opposed to the presence of America in this region.*

▶ **COLLOCATIONS:**
opposed **to** *something*
opposed to **abortion/violence**

▶ **SYNONYM:** against

▶ **ANTONYM:** in favour of

op|pos|ing /əˈpəʊzɪŋ/

1 ADJECTIVE Opposing ideas or tendencies are totally different from each other. ○ *I have a friend who has the opposing view and felt that the war was immoral.*

2 ADJECTIVE Opposing groups of people disagree about something or are in competition with one another. ○ *The Georgian leader said that he still favoured dialogue between the opposing sides.* ○ *the opposing team*

▶ **COLLOCATIONS:**
an opposing **view**
an opposing **faction/camp/force/side/player**

op|po|si|tion /ˌɒpəˈzɪʃən/

1 UNCOUNTABLE NOUN Opposition is strong, angry, or violent disagreement and disapproval. ○ *The government is facing a new wave of opposition in the form of a student strike.* ○ [+ to] *Much of the opposition to this plan has come from the media.*

▶ **COLLOCATIONS:**
opposition **to** *something*
face opposition
strong/stiff/fierce/political/official opposition

▶ **SYNONYMS:** hostility, resistance

▶ **ANTONYM:** support

2 **UNCOUNTABLE NOUN** **The opposition** is the political parties or groups that are opposed to a government. ○ *The main opposition parties boycotted the election, saying it would not be conducted fairly.* ○ *the opposition refused to disarm its militia*

▶ **COLLOCATIONS:**
an opposition **party/group/politician/spokesman**
the opposition **boycotts/claims/demands** *something*
the opposition **accuses/attacks/criticizes** *someone*

---

op|tion /ˈɒpʃən/ (options) `ACADEMIC WORD`

1 **NOUN** An **option** is something that you can choose to do in preference to one or more alternatives. ○ *He's argued from the start that America and its allies are putting too much emphasis on the military option.* ○ *What other options do you have?*

▶ **COLLOCATIONS:**
the **preferred/viable** option
a **military/strategic** option

▶ **SYNONYMS:** alternative, choice

2 **NOUN** An **option** is one of a number of subjects which a student can choose to study as a part of his or her course. ○ *Several options are offered for the student's senior year.* ○ *You may choose options such as Conversation, Grammar, or Examination Preparation.*

op|tion|al /ˈɒpʃənəl/

ADJECTIVE If something is **optional**, you can choose whether or not you do it or have it. ○ *Finally, it becomes economic to offer the customer optional extras.* ○ *The violin part is more than an optional accompaniment.*

▶ **COLLOCATION:** an optional **extra**
▶ **ANTONYM:** compulsory

---

or|gan|ism /ˈɔːɡənɪzəm/ (organisms) `BIOLOGY`

NOUN An **organism** is an animal or plant, especially one that is so small that you cannot see it without using a microscope. ○ *Not all chemicals normally present in living organisms are harmless.* ○ *insect-borne organisms that cause sleeping sickness*

▶ **COLLOCATION:** a **living/live/marine** organism
▶ **SYNONYM:** creature

---

ori|gin /ˈɒrɪdʒɪn, AM ˈɔːr-/ (origins)

NOUN You can refer to the beginning, cause, or source of something as its **origin** or **origins**. ○ [+ *of*] *theories about the origin of life* ○ [+ *in*] *The disorder in* *military policy had its origins in Truman's first term.* ○ *Most of the thickeners are of plant origin.*

▶ **COLLOCATIONS:**
the origin **of** *something*
an origin **in** *something*
trace/explain the origin

▶ **PHRASE:** of unknown origin

▶ **SYNONYMS:** beginning, source

origi|nate /əˈrɪdʒɪneɪt/ (originates, originating, originated)

VERB When something **originates** or when someone **originates** it, it begins to happen or exist. [FORMAL] ○ [+ in] *The disease originated in Africa.* ○ [+ from] *All carbohydrates originate from plants.* ○ *No one has any idea who originated the story.*

→ see note at **commence**

▶ **COLLOCATIONS:**
originate **in/from** *something/somewhere*
originate in the **16th century/19th century**

▶ **SYNONYMS:** begin, start, invent, create

---

out|come /ˈaʊtkʌm/ (outcomes) `ACADEMIC WORD`

NOUN The **outcome** of an activity, process, or situation is the situation that exists at the end of it. ○ *Mr. Singh said he was pleased with the outcome.* ○ [+ of] *It's too early to know the outcome of her illness.* ○ *a successful outcome*

▶ **COLLOCATIONS:**
the outcome **of** *something*
await/predict/decide/affect/influence the outcome
the **likely** outcome
a **successful** outcome

▶ **SYNONYMS:** result, conclusion

---

out|look /ˈaʊtlʊk/ (outlooks)

NOUN The **outlook** for something is what people think will happen in relation to it. ○ *The economic outlook is one of rising unemployment.* ○ [+ for] *the uncertain outlook for the motor industry*

▶ **COLLOCATIONS:**
the outlook **for** *something*
the outlook for **growth/industry**
the **economic/short-term/long-term** outlook
a **bleak/gloomy/positive/optimistic/cautious/uncertain** outlook

▶ **SYNONYMS:** prospect, forecast

out|put /ˈaʊtpʊt/   `ACADEMIC WORD` `BUSINESS` `IT` `ENGINEERING`

1 UNCOUNTABLE NOUN Output is used to refer to something that a person or thing produces. ○ *Government statistics show the largest drop in industrial output for ten years.* ○ [+ of] *The gland enlarges in an attempt to increase the output of hormone.*

▶ **COLLOCATIONS:**
  the output **of** *something*
  boost/increase/reduce/cut output
  output **rises/falls**
  industrial/agricultural/economic/manufacturing/oil/power output
  total/annual output

▶ **ANTONYM:** input

2 UNCOUNTABLE NOUN The **output** of a computer or other device is the information or signals that it displays on a screen or prints on paper as a result of a particular program. ○ *You run the software, you look at the output, you make modifications.* ○ [+ from] *Screen copy is the output from a computer as seen on a screen.*

▶ **COLLOCATIONS:**
  the output **from** *something*
  digital/computer output
  an output **device**

▶ **ANTONYM:** input

out|weigh /ˌaʊtˈweɪ/ (outweighs, outweighing, outweighed)

VERB If one thing **outweighs** another, the first thing is of greater importance, benefit, or significance than the second thing. [FORMAL] ○ *The medical benefits of x-rays far outweigh the risk of having them.* ○ *The advantages of this deal largely outweigh the disadvantages.*

▶ **COLLOCATIONS:**
  outweigh the **benefits/risk/disadvantages/cost**
  the **advantages** outweigh *something*
  far outweigh *something*

▶ **SYNONYMS:** override, cancel out, balance out

oval /ˈəʊvəl/

ADJECTIVE Oval things have a shape that is like a circle but is wider in one direction than the other. ○ *the small oval framed picture of a little boy* ○ *For prescription eyewear, the shapes are mainly geometric, often rectangular, as well as oval and round.*

▶ **SYNONYM:** elliptical

over|come /ˌəʊvəˈkʌm/ (overcomes, overcoming, overcame)

VERB If you **overcome** a problem or a feeling, you successfully deal with it and control it. ○ *Molly had fought and overcome her fear of flying.* ○ *One way of helping children to overcome shyness is to boost their self-confidence.*

▶ **COLLOCATION:** overcome a **problem/difficulty/injury/deficit/obstacle**

▶ **SYNONYMS:** defeat, beat, conquer, survive

over|due /ˌəʊvəˈdjuː, AM -ˈduː/

1 ADJECTIVE If you say that a change or an event is **overdue**, you mean that you think it should have happened before now. ○ *This debate is long overdue.* ○ *Total revision of the law in this area is long overdue.*

▶ **COLLOCATIONS:**
an overdue **change/reform**
long overdue

▶ **SYNONYM:** belated

2 ADJECTIVE Overdue sums of money have not been paid, even though it is later than the date on which they should have been paid. ○ *Teachers have joined a strike aimed at forcing the government to pay overdue salaries and allowances.* ○ *Companies can claim up to £100 compensation for each overdue bill.*

▶ **COLLOCATION:** an overdue **payment/bill**

▶ **SYNONYM:** unpaid

over|lap /ˌəʊvəˈlæp/ (overlaps, overlapping, overlapped) `ACADEMIC WORD`

VERB If one idea or activity **overlaps** another, or **overlaps** with another, they involve some of the same subjects, people, or periods of time. ○ [+ with] *Christian holy week overlaps with the beginning of the Jewish holiday of Passover.* ○ *The needs of patients invariably overlap.* ○ [+ by] *Their life-spans overlapped by six years.*

▶ **COLLOCATIONS:**
overlap **with** something
overlap **by** an amount

▶ **SYNONYM:** coincide

over|seas /ˌəʊvəˈsiːz/ `ACADEMIC WORD` `GEOGRAPHY`

1 ADJECTIVE You use **overseas** to describe things that involve or are in foreign countries, usually across a sea or an ocean. ○ *He has returned to South Africa from his long overseas trip.* ○ *overseas trade figures*

▶ **COLLOCATIONS:**
an overseas **trip/travel/tour/market/operation**
overseas **aid**

▶ **SYNONYM:** foreign

▶ **RELATED WORD:** domestic

2 ADJECTIVE An **overseas** student or visitor comes from a foreign country, usually across a sea or an ocean. ○ *Every year nine million overseas visitors come to London.* ○ *firmly targeted at overseas buyers*

▶ COLLOCATION: an overseas **student/visitor/investor/buyer**

▶ SYNONYM: foreign

over|view /ˈəʊvəvjuː/ (overviews)

NOUN An **overview of** a situation is a general understanding or description of it as a whole. ○ [+ *of*] *The central section of the book is a historical overview of drug use.* ○ [+ *of*] *The purpose of this book is to provide an overview of the mammals of the world.*

▶ COLLOCATIONS:
an overview **of** *something*
an overview of a **subject/situation/process**
an overview of the **history/development** of *something*
provide/give/present/offer an overview
a **brief/comprehensive/detailed/general** overview

▶ SYNONYM: survey

Pp

---

pace /peɪs/ (paces)

NOUN The **pace** of something is the speed at which it happens or is done. ○ [+ of] *Many people are not satisfied with the pace of economic reform.* ○ *Interest rates would come down as the recovery gathered pace.*

▶ **COLLOCATIONS:**
the pace **of** *something*
the pace of **change/reform/growth/expansion**
gather pace
a **brisk/fast/record/slow** pace

▶ **SYNONYM:** speed

---

pan|el /ˈpænəl/ (panels) `ACADEMIC WORD`

1 NOUN A **panel** is a small group of people who are chosen to do something, for example to discuss something in public or to make a decision. ○ [+ of] *He assembled a panel of scholars to advise him.* ○ *The advisory panel disagreed with the decision.*

▶ **COLLOCATIONS:**
a panel **of** *people*
a panel of **experts/judges/scientists**
a **house/senate/congressional/review/advisory/independent** panel
a panel **investigates/reviews/judges** *something*
a panel **recommends/rules/concludes** that …

2 NOUN A **panel** is a flat rectangular piece of wood or other material that forms part of a larger object such as a door. ○ *the frosted glass panel set in the centre of the door* ○ *The craft relies on the solar panels for energy.*

▶ **COLLOCATIONS:**
a **solar/wooden/glass** panel
a **flat/removable/front/decorative** panel
assemble/install/attach a panel

---

par|al|lel /ˈpærəlel/ `ACADEMIC WORD`

ADJECTIVE If two lines, two objects, or two lines of movement are **parallel**, they are the same distance apart along their whole length. ○ *Sometimes the crystals join together in parallel lines.* ○ [+ with] *The Andes form a mountain range parallel with the coast.*

▶ COLLOCATIONS:
parallel **with/to** *something*
parallel **lines**

---

par|lia|ment /'pɑːləmənt/ **(parliaments)** also **Parliament**   `POLITICS`

NOUN The **parliament** of some countries, for example Britain, is the group of people who make or change its laws, and decide what policies the country should follow. ○ *Parliament today approved the policy, but it has not yet become law.* ○ *The new European parliament convenes in three weeks' time.*

▶ COLLOCATIONS:
dissolve/disband/elect a parliament
parliament **approves/ratifies/debates/passes** *something*
a **hung/minority** parliament
the **Russian/European** parliament

▶ PHRASES:
Houses of Parliament
Member of Parliament

▶ RELATED WORDS: Congress, Assembly

par|lia|men|ta|ry /ˌpɑːləˈmentəri/

ADJECTIVE Parliamentary is used to describe things that are connected with a parliament or with Members of Parliament. ○ *He used his influence to make sure she was not selected as a parliamentary candidate.* ○ *last month's parliamentary elections*

▶ COLLOCATIONS:
a parliamentary **candidate/committee/election/democracy**
parliamentary **privilege**

---

par|tial /'pɑːʃəl/

ADJECTIVE You use **partial** to refer to something that is not complete or whole. ○ *He managed to reach a partial agreement with both republics.* ○ *The government has introduced a partial ban on the use of cars in the city.*

▶ COLLOCATIONS:
partial **blindness/amnesia/paralysis**
a partial **agreement/solution/explanation**
partial **deregulation/nationalization/privatization**

▶ SYNONYM: incomplete

▶ ANTONYMS: complete, total

par|tial|ly /'pɑːʃəli/

ADVERB If something happens or exists **partially**, it happens or exists to some extent, but not completely. ○ *He was born with a rare genetic condition which has left him partially sighted.* ○ *partially hydrogenated oils*

▶ COLLOCATIONS:
partially **sighted/blind/deaf/paralyzed**
partially **responsible/attributable**
▶ SYNONYM: partly
▶ ANTONYM: completely

---

par|tici|pate /pɑːˈtɪsɪpeɪt/   `ACADEMIC WORD`
(participates, participating, participated)

VERB If you **participate in** an activity, you take part in it. ○ [+ in] *Hundreds of faithful Buddhists participated in the annual ceremony.* ○ [+ in] *Over half the population of this country participate in sport.* ○ [V-ing] *lower rates for participating corporations*

▶ COLLOCATIONS:
participate **in** *something*
participate in a **discussion/activity/debate/process**
participate **equally/willingly/effectively**
▶ SYNONYM: take part

par|tici|pa|tion /pɑːˌtɪsɪˈpeɪʃən/

UNCOUNTABLE NOUN ○ [+ in] *participation in religious activities* ○ [+ of] *a higher level of participation of women in the labour force*

▶ COLLOCATIONS:
participation **in** *something*
participation **of/by** *someone*
participation in a **discussion/activity/debate/process**
▶ SYNONYMS: involvement, inclusion
▶ ANTONYM: exclusion

par|tici|pant /pɑːˈtɪsɪpənt/ **(participants)**

NOUN The **participants** in an activity are the people who take part in it.
○ *40 of the course participants are offered employment with the company.*
○ *Conference participants agreed that Canada faces an urgent situation with respect to health-care provision.*

▶ COLLOCATIONS:
a participant **in** *something*
a participant in a **discussion/activity/debate/process**
a **willing/active/enthusiastic** participant
▶ ANTONYM: observer

---

part|ner|ship /ˈpɑːtnəʃɪp/ **(partnerships)**   `ACADEMIC WORD`

NOUN **Partnership** or a **partnership** is a relationship in which two or more people, organizations, or countries work together as partners. ○ [+ between] *the partnership between Germany's banks and its businesses* ○ [+ *between*] *a new partnership between universities and the private sector*

▶ COLLOCATIONS:
a partnership **between** *people*
a partnership **with** *someone*
in partnership
a **private/strategic/creative/successful/important** partnership
form/forge/create/strengthen a partnership

▶ SYNONYMS: relationship, association, collaboration

---

peak /piːk/ (peaks, peaking, peaked)

1 NOUN The **peak** of a process or an activity is the point at which it is at its strongest, most successful, or most fully developed. ○ [+ *of*] *The party's membership has fallen from a peak of fifty thousand.* ○ [+ *of*] *At the peak of the boom in 2000, revenues were $27.9 billion.* ○ *a flourishing career that was at its peak at the time of his death*

▶ COLLOCATIONS:
be **at** a peak
the peak **of** *something*
the peak of **perfection/excellence/fitness**
the peak of a **career/cycle**
reach/hit a peak

▶ PHRASE: peaks and troughs
▶ SYNONYMS: prime, high point
▶ ANTONYMS: low point, trough

2 VERB When something **peaks**, it reaches its highest value or its highest level. ○ [+ *at*] *Temperatures have peaked at over thirty degrees Celsius.* ○ *The crisis peaked in July 2008.* ○ *His career peaked during the 1990's.*

▶ COLLOCATIONS:
peak **at** *x*
inflation/output/temperature peaks
a **career/crisis** peaks

---

pen|al|ty /ˈpenəlti/ (penalties)   LAW

NOUN A **penalty** is a punishment that someone is given for doing something which is against a law or rule. ○ *One of those arrested could face the death penalty.* ○ *The maximum penalty is up to 7 years' imprisonment or an unlimited fine.*

▶ COLLOCATIONS:
the penalty **for** *something*
the **maximum/minimum/death** penalty
a **harsh/severe/tough** penalty
award/impose/face a penalty

▸ SYNONYM: punishment

▸ ANTONYM: reward

---

per|ceive /pə'siːv/ (perceives, perceiving, perceived) `ACADEMIC WORD`

VERB If you **perceive** someone or something **as** doing or being a particular thing, it is your opinion that they do this thing or that they are that thing. ○ [+ as] *Stress is widely perceived as contributing to coronary heart disease.* ○ [+ as] *Bioterrorism is perceived as a real threat in the United States.*

→ see note at **regard**

▸ COLLOCATIONS:

perceive *something/someone* **as** *something*

perceive *something* as a **threat/risk/challenge**

commonly/widely/generally/traditionally perceived

▸ SYNONYMS: believe, consider

per|cep|tion /pə'sepʃən/ (perceptions)

NOUN Your **perception of** something is the way that you think about it or the impression you have of it. ○ [+ of] *He is interested in how our perceptions of death affect the way we live.* ○ [+ among] *There was still a perception among the public that the city was unsafe.*

▸ COLLOCATIONS:

a perception **of** *something*

a perception **among** *people*

a **common/growing/general** perception

reinforce/heighten/foster/counter/alter/challenge a perception

▸ SYNONYMS: impression, understanding

per|cep|tible /pə'septɪbəl/

ADJECTIVE Something that is **perceptible** can only just be seen or noticed. ○ *a perceptible shift in US policy* ○ *There was no perceptible difference in temperature.*

▸ COLLOCATIONS:

a perceptible **shift/change/difference/improvement**

barely/scarcely/hardly perceptible

▸ SYNONYMS: discernible, noticeable

▸ ANTONYMS: indiscernible, imperceptible

per|cep|tibly /pə'septɪbli/

ADVERB ○ *After 1865 the growth of national craft unions quickened perceptibly.* ○ *America's attitude to European issues shifted perceptibly as a result of the end of the Cold War.*

▸ COLLOCATION: **alter/shift/tighten/widen** perceptibly

▸ SYNONYMS: discernibly, noticeably

▸ ANTONYM: imperceptibly

per cent /pə 'sent/ (per cent) also percent   `ACADEMIC WORD`

ADVERB If an amount is 10 **per cent** (10%) of a larger amount, it is equal to 10 hundredths of the larger amount. ○ [+ of] *20 to 40 per cent of the voters are undecided.* ○ *There has been a ten per cent increase in the number of new students.* ○ *The cholesterol level fell 45 per cent when colestipol was combined with niacin.*

▶ **COLLOCATIONS:**
   x per cent **of** *something*
   a *x* per cent **increase/decrease**
   fall/rise *x* per cent

per|cent|age /pə'sentɪdʒ/ (percentages)

NOUN A **percentage** is a fraction of an amount expressed as a particular number of hundredths of that amount. ○ [+ of] *Only a few vegetable-origin foods have such a high percentage of protein.* ○ [+ of] *A large percentage of the population speaks fluent English.*

▶ **COLLOCATIONS:**
   a percentage **of** *something*
   a percentage of the **population/workforce/household**
   a **large/high/sizeable/significant/small/tiny/low** percentage

▶ **SYNONYMS:** proportion, amount

> **USAGE: per cent** or **percentage**?
>
> You use **per cent** after a number to express an exact amount. ○ *10%/ten per cent of customers*
>
> You use **percentage** to talk more generally about a proportion of a group or amount. ○ *We found a higher percentage of women were being accepted.*

per|form /pə'fɔːm/ (performs, performing, performed)

1 VERB When you **perform** a task or action, especially a complicated one, you do it. ○ *A robot capable of performing the most complex brain surgery was unveiled by scientists yesterday.* ○ *Several grafts may be performed at one operation.*

2 VERB If something **performs** a particular function, it has that function. ○ *A complex engine has many separate components, each performing a different function.* ○ *Software can be run on a computer to enable it to perform various tasks.*

▶ **COLLOCATION:** perform a **task/action/act/function**
▶ **SYNONYMS:** carry out, undertake

3 VERB If someone or something **performs well**, they work well or achieve a good result. If they **perform badly**, they work badly or achieve a poor result. ○ *He had not performed well in his exams.* ○ *State-owned industries will always perform poorly.*

▶ COLLOCATIONS:
perform **well/strongly/admirably/consistently**
perform **badly/poorly/dismally**
▶ SYNONYM: work

per|for|mance /pə'fɔːməns/ (performances)

1 NOUN Someone's or something's **performance** is how successful they are
or how well they do something. ○ [+ of] *That study looked at the performance of
18 surgeons.* ○ *The job of the new director-general was to ensure that performance
targets were met.*

▶ COLLOCATIONS:
the performance **of** *someone/something*
good/strong/solid/poor/disappointing performance
financial/economic performance
improve/enhance/measure performance
performance **targets/indicators/criteria/standards**

2 NOUN The performance of a task is the fact or action of doing it. ○ [+ of] *He
devoted in excess of seventy hours a week to the performance of his duties.* ○ [+ of]
The people believe that the performance of this ritual is the will of the Great Spirit.

▶ COLLOCATIONS:
the performance **of** *something*
the performance of a **procedure/task/operation/duty**
the performance of a **ritual/ceremony/rite**

---

pe|rim|eter /pə'rɪmɪtə/ (perimeters)　　　MATHS

NOUN The **perimeter** of a shape or an area of land is the whole of its outer
edge or boundary. ○ [+ of] *Calculate the perimeter of squares and rectangles in
metres and centimetres.* ○ *Officers dressed in riot gear are surrounding the
perimeter fence.*

▶ COLLOCATIONS:
the perimeter **of** *something*
measure/calculate/mark a perimeter
a perimeter **fence/wall/gate**
patrol/guard/defend a perimeter
▶ SYNONYMS: boundary, edge

---

per|spec|tive /pə'spektɪv/ (perspectives)　　　ACADEMIC WORD

NOUN A particular **perspective** is a particular way of thinking about
something, especially one that is influenced by your beliefs or experiences.
○ [+ on] *two different perspectives on the nature of adolescent development* ○ [+ of]
*Most literature on the subject of immigrants in France has been written from the
perspective of the French themselves.* ○ *I would like to offer a historical perspective.*

▶ **COLLOCATIONS:**
a perspective **on** *something*
the perspective **of** *someone*
from the perspective of *someone/something*
a **historical/feminist/sociological** perspective
a **different/new/fresh** perspective

▶ **SYNONYMS:** viewpoint, position

---

phase /feɪz/ **(phases)**   `ACADEMIC WORD`

NOUN A **phase** is a particular stage in a process or in the gradual development of something. ○ [+ *of*] *This autumn, 6000 residents will participate in the first phase of the project.* ○ *The crisis is entering a crucial, critical phase.*

▶ **COLLOCATIONS:**
a phase **of** *something*
enter/commence/begin/undergo a phase
mark/herald/signal a phase
a **first/initial/early** phase
a **transitional/experimental/developmental** phase
a **crucial/critical/decisive** phase

▶ **SYNONYMS:** stage, period

PhD /ˌpiː eɪtʃ ˈdiː/ **(PhDs)** also **Ph.D.**   `EDUCATION` `ACADEMIC STUDY`

NOUN A **PhD** is a degree awarded to people who have done advanced research into a particular subject. **PhD** is an abbreviation for 'Doctor of Philosophy'. ○ [+ *in*] *He is more highly educated, with a PhD in Chemistry.* ○ *an unpublished PhD thesis*

▶ **COLLOCATIONS:**
a PhD **in** *something*
a PhD in **microbiology/linguistics**
a PhD **thesis/student/graduate**
research/pursue/undertake/complete/earn/gain a PhD

▶ **SYNONYM:** doctorate

---

phe|nom|enon /fɪˈnɒmɪnən, AM -nɑːn/ **(phenomena)**   `ACADEMIC WORD`

NOUN A **phenomenon** is something that is observed to happen or exist. [FORMAL] ○ *scientific explanations of natural phenomena* ○ *The drought-causing el Niño weather phenomenon may strike again this season.*

▶ **COLLOCATIONS:**
examine/observe/study/investigate a phenomenon
a **natural/supernatural/scientific** phenomenon
a **meteorological/cultural/global** phenomenon
a **widespread/familiar/common** phenomenon

phi|loso|phy /fɪˈlɒsəfi/ (philosophies) `ACADEMIC WORD`

UNCOUNTABLE NOUN **Philosophy** is the study or creation of theories about basic things such as the nature of existence, knowledge, and thought, or about how people should live. ○ *He studied philosophy and psychology at Cambridge.* ○ *traditional Chinese philosophy*

▸ COLLOCATION: **eastern/ancient/Greek** philosophy

phi|loso|pher /fɪˈlɒsəfə/ (philosophers)

NOUN A **philosopher** is a person who studies or writes about philosophy. ○ *the Greek philosopher Plato* ○ *However, many philosophers have argued that freedom is an illusion.*

pie chart /ˈpaɪ tʃɑːt/ (pie charts) `ACADEMIC WORD`

NOUN A **pie chart** is a circle divided into sections to show the relative proportions of a set of things. ○ *The pie chart above shows how much more Britain has saved in shares than bonds.* ○ *The pie chart indicates that one company has emerged as the dominant market share leader.*

→ see note at **bar chart**

▸ COLLOCATION: a pie chart **shows/indicates/displays** *something*

pio|neer /ˌpaɪəˈnɪə/ (pioneers, pioneering, pioneered) `HISTORY` `SCIENCE`

1 NOUN Someone who is referred to as a **pioneer** in a particular area of activity is one of the first people to be involved in it and develop it. ○ [+ *of/in*] *one of the leading pioneers of British photo journalism* ○ *an aeronautics pioneer*

▸ COLLOCATIONS:
a pioneer **in/of** *something*
a pioneer **pilot/photographer/researcher**
a **biotechnology/aviation** pioneer

▸ SYNONYMS: leader, innovator

2 VERB Someone who **pioneers** a new activity, invention, or process is one of the first people to do it. ○ *Professor Alec Jeffreys, who invented and pioneered DNA tests* ○ *the folk-tale writing style pioneered by Gabriel Garcia Marquez*

▸ COLLOCATIONS:
pioneered **by** *someone*
pioneer a **process/activity/invention/technique/method/approach**

▸ SYNONYM: develop

pio|neer|ing /ˌpaɪəˈnɪərɪŋ/

ADJECTIVE **Pioneering** work or a **pioneering** individual does something that has not been done before, for example by developing or using new methods or techniques. ○ *The school has won awards for its pioneering work with the community.* ○ *a pioneering Scottish surgeon and anatomist named John Hunter*

▶ **COLLOCATIONS:**
pioneering **work/surgery/research**
a pioneering **technique/concept/study**
a pioneering **surgeon/conservationist/geologist**
▶ **SYNONYMS:** leading, innovative

---

plant /plɑːnt, plænt/ (plants)   `BUSINESS` `ENGINEERING`

NOUN A **plant** is a factory or a place where power is produced. ○ *a regional sewage treatment plant* ○ *The plant provides forty per cent of the country's electricity.*

▶ **COLLOCATIONS:**
a **nuclear/hydroelectric/industrial** plant
a **manufacturing/recycling/chemical** plant
construct/build/upgrade a plant
▶ **SYNONYM:** factory

---

play|wright /ˈpleɪraɪt/ (playwrights)   `LITERATURE`

NOUN A **playwright** is a person who writes plays. ○ *Diniso is an award-winning playwright, director and actor.* ○ *The film is scripted by the playwright Wendy Wasserstein.*

▶ **COLLOCATIONS:**
a playwright **scripts/reworks/writes** *something*
a **prize-winning/award-winning** playwright
a **prolific/acclaimed/celebrated** playwright
▶ **SYNONYM:** dramatist

---

plot /plɒt/ (plots, plotting, plotted)   `LITERATURE`

1 NOUN The **plot** of a film, novel, or play is the connected series of events which make up the story. ○ *The special effects don't compensate for a basic lack of plot development.* ○ *an unexpected plot twist*

▶ **COLLOCATIONS:**
the plot **of** *something*
the plot of a **film/novel/play**
a plot **unfolds/twists/develops**
a **predictable/implausible/far-fetched** plot
a **complex/clever/elaborate** plot
a plot **synopsis/summary/twist**
plot **development**
▶ **SYNONYM:** storyline

2 VERB When someone **plots** something on a graph, they mark certain points on it and then join the points up. ○ *The graph needs to be plotted over several months for a pattern to emerge.* ○ *The graph above plots UK stock market returns against economic growth in the developed world.*

▶ COLLOCATIONS:
plot *something* **on/against** *something*
plot **points/values/numbers** on *something*
plot *something* on a **graph/chart**

---

plum|met /ˈplʌmɪt/ (plummets, plummeting, plummeted)

VERB If an amount, rate, or price **plummets**, it decreases quickly by a large amount. ○ *Temperatures plummeted as a cold front swept in from the North Pole.* ○ *[+ from/to/by] The shares have plummeted from 130p to 2.25p in the past year.*

→ see note at **dip**

▶ COLLOCATIONS:
plummet **to** *something*
plummet **from/by/to** *x*
weight/temperature plummets
stocks/shares/share prices plummet
someone's **popularity/confidence/self-esteem** plummets

▶ PHRASE: plummet to an all-time low

▶ SYNONYMS: plunge, drop, fall

▶ ANTONYMS: rise, soar

---

plus /plʌs/   ACADEMIC WORD   MATHS

1 **CONJUNCTION** You say **plus** to show that one number or quantity is being added to another. ○ *36 plus 5 squared is 61.* ○ *They will pay about $673 million plus interest.*

▶ COLLOCATIONS:
x plus *y* **is/equals** *z*
x plus **interest/VAT/tax**

▶ ANTONYM: minus

2 **ADJECTIVE Plus** before a number or quantity means that the number or quantity is greater than zero. ○ *The aircraft was subjected to temperatures of minus 65 degrees and plus 120 degrees.*

▶ ANTONYM: minus

---

pole /pəʊl/ (poles)   GEOGRAPHY

NOUN The earth's **poles** are the two opposite ends of its axis, its most northern and southern points. ○ *For six months of the year, there is hardly any light at the poles.* ○ *The satellite measures ice sheet thickness at the poles.*

▶ COLLOCATION: the **North/South** Pole

▶ RELATED WORDS: tropic, equator

po|lar /ˈpəʊlə/

ADJECTIVE Polar means near the North and South Poles. ○ *the rigours of life in the polar regions* ○ *Warmth melted some of the polar ice.* ○ *the ill-fated polar explorers*

▶ **COLLOCATIONS:**
polar **ice/exploration**
a polar **cap/region/expedition/explorer/adventurer**
▶ **RELATED WORD:** equatorial

---

poll /pəʊl/ **(polls, polling, polled)**   SOCIAL SCIENCE

1 NOUN A **poll** is a survey in which people are asked their opinions about something, usually in order to find out how popular something is or what people intend to do in the future. ○ *Polls show that the European treaty has gained support in Denmark.* ○ [+ *on*] *opinion polls on Venezuela's presidential election*

▶ **COLLOCATIONS:**
a poll **on** *something*
in the polls
a **straw/opinion/public/online** poll
a poll **shows/indicates/suggests/finds** *something*
conduct/carry out/publish a poll
▶ **SYNONYM:** survey

2 VERB If you **are polled on** something, you are asked what you think about it as part of a survey. ○ *More than 18,000 people were polled.* ○ [+ *on*] *Audiences were going to be polled on which of three pieces of contemporary music they liked best.*

▶ **COLLOCATIONS:**
poll *someone* **on** *something*
poll **consumers/households/voters/employers**
▶ **SYNONYM:** survey

---

por|tion /ˈpɔːʃən/ **(portions)**   ACADEMIC WORD

NOUN A **portion of** something is a part of it. ○ [+ *of*] *Damage was confined to a small portion of the castle.* ○ [+ *of*] *The protein portion of the enzyme is referred to as an apoprotein.* ○ [+ *of*] *the verbal and mathematics portions of the test*

▶ **COLLOCATIONS:**
a portion **of** *something*
a **large/major/sizable/small** portion
a **substantial/significant/considerable** portion
▶ **SYNONYM:** part

---

po|si|tion /pəˈzɪʃən/ **(positions)**

1 NOUN Your **position** in society is the role and the importance that you have in it. ○ [+ *of*] *the position of older people in society.* ○ [+ *of*] *the profoundly radical changes to the position of women brought about by the Divorce Act of 1857*
▶ **SYNONYMS:** standing, role

2 NOUN A **position** in a company or organization is a job. [FORMAL] ○ [+ *with*] *He left a career in teaching to take up a position with the Arts Council.* ○ *Hyundai* *said this week it is scaling back its U.S. operations by eliminating 50 positions.*

▶ COLLOCATIONS:
the position **of** *something/someone*
a position **in/with/as** *something*
a position in/with a **company/organization/firm**
a position as **chairman/president/director**
the position of **clerk/assistant/consultant**
occupy/accept/advertise/vacate a position

▶ SYNONYM: post

3 NOUN Your **position on** a particular matter is your attitude towards it or your opinion of it. [FORMAL] ○ [+ on] *He could be depended on to take a moderate position on most of the key issues.* ○ [+ on] *Mr Howard is afraid to state his true position on the republic, which is that he is opposed to it.*

▶ COLLOCATIONS:
a position **on** *something*
take/assume/adopt a position on *something*
a **moderate/clear/understandable** position

▶ SYNONYMS: stance, opinion, attitude

---

pos|sess /pəˈzes/ **(possesses, possessing, possessed)**

1 VERB If you **possess** something, you have it or own it. ○ *He was then arrested and charged with possessing an offensive weapon.* ○ *He is said to possess a fortune of more than two-and-a-half-thousand million dollars.*

▶ COLLOCATIONS:
illegally/unlawfully possess *something*
possess a **weapon**
possess **drugs/pornography**

▶ SYNONYMS: own, have

2 VERB If someone or something **possesses** a particular quality, ability, or feature, they have it. [FORMAL] ○ *individuals who are deemed to possess the qualities of sense, loyalty and discretion* ○ *This figure has long been held to possess miraculous power.*

▶ COLLOCATIONS:
possess a **quality/skill/talent**
possess **power/knowledge/strength**

┌───┐
EXTEND YOUR VOCABULARY

Have is a very common verb in everyday English and can be used in many contexts. ○ *She has a big house, lots of money and a great job.*

You can say that someone **owns** something or that it **belongs to** them if it is their property. ○ *All the directors own shares in the company.* ○ *The land belongs to a local farmer.*
└───┘

In more formal writing, and in legal contexts, you can say that someone **possesses** something. ○ *He was convicted of illegally possessing firearms.*

You can also say that someone **possesses** a quality or an ability.
○ *Candidates should possess good communication skills.*

pos|ses|sion /pə'zeʃən/ (possessions)

1 UNCOUNTABLE NOUN If you are **in possession of** something, you have it, because you have obtained it or because it belongs to you. [FORMAL] ○ [+ *of*] *Those documents are now in the possession of the Guardian.* ○ [+ *of*] *There is no legal remedy for her to gain possession of the house.* ○ *Religious pamphlets were found in their possession.*

▶ **COLLOCATIONS:**
   possession **of** *something*
   in *someone's* possession
   gain/lose/surrender/retain possession of *something*
   illegal/unlawful possession of *something*
   possession of a **weapon**
   possession of **drugs/pornography**

▶ **SYNONYM:** ownership

2 NOUN Your **possessions** are the things that you own or have with you at a particular time. ○ *People had lost their homes and all their possessions.* ○ *the acquisition of material possessions*

▶ **COLLOCATION:** **prized/treasured/material/personal** possessions

▶ **SYNONYM:** belongings

post|gradu|ate /ˌpəʊst'grædʒuət/ `EDUCATION` `ACADEMIC STUDY`
(postgraduates) also **post-graduate**

1 NOUN A **postgraduate** or a **postgraduate student** is a student with a first degree from a university who is studying or doing research at a more advanced level. **Postgrad** is also used in informal and spoken English. [in AM, use **graduate student**] ○ *In contrast to the undergraduates, the postgraduates who went abroad were chiefly engineers and physicists.* ○ *as a postgraduate studying International Relations at Oxford*

▶ **RELATED WORD:** undergraduate

2 ADJECTIVE Postgraduate study or research is done by a student who has a first degree and is studying or doing research at a more advanced level. [BRIT; in AM, use **graduate student**] ○ *postgraduate courses* ○ *Dr Hoffman did his postgraduate work at Leicester University.*

▶ **COLLOCATIONS:**
   a postgraduate **diploma/certificate/qualification**
   a postgraduate **student/course/thesis**

postgraduate **research/education/training/work**

▶ **RELATED WORD:** undergraduate

---

post|pone /pəʊs'pəʊn/ (postpones, postponing, postponed)

VERB If you **postpone** an event, you delay it or arrange for it to take place at a later time than was originally planned. ○ *The President is postponing the referendum, due to have been held in October, until August next year.* ○ *The visit has now been postponed indefinitely.*

▶ **COLLOCATIONS:**
postpone *something* **indefinitely/temporarily**
postpone *something* **until** *something*
postpone a **decision/event/election/visit**

▶ **SYNONYM:** delay

post|pone|ment /pəʊs'pəʊnmənt/ (postponements)

NOUN ○ *The postponement was due to a dispute over where the talks should be held.* ○ *[+ of] Mandela agreed to the postponement of undiluted one man one vote majority rule.*

▶ **COLLOCATIONS:**
the postponement **of** *something*
the postponement of a **meeting/election**
force/cause/request/announce a postponement

▶ **SYNONYM:** delay

---

po|ten|tial /pə'tenʃəl/ ACADEMIC WORD

ADJECTIVE You use **potential** to say that someone or something is capable of developing into the particular kind of person or thing mentioned. ○ *The firm has identified 60 potential customers at home and abroad.* ○ *We are aware of the potential problems and have taken every precaution.*

▶ **COLLOCATIONS:**
potential **growth/earnings/savings**
a potential **threat/conflict/danger**
a potential **customer/candidate/recruit**

▶ **SYNONYM:** possible

po|ten|tial|ly /pə'tenʃəli/

ADVERB ○ *Clearly this is a potentially dangerous situation.* ○ *Potentially this could damage the reputation of the whole industry.*

▶ **COLLOCATIONS:**
potentially **dangerous/lethal/fatal**
potentially **damage/contaminate/harm** *someone/something*

▶ **SYNONYM:** possibly

pow|er /paʊə/

SCIENCE PHYSICS ENGINEERING

(powers, powering, powered)

1 **UNCOUNTABLE NOUN** The **power** of something is the ability that it has to move or affect things. ○ *The Roadrunner had better power, better tyres, and better brakes.* ○ *massive computing power*

▶ **COLLOCATIONS:**
the power **of** something
computing/processing power

2 **UNCOUNTABLE NOUN** **Power** is energy, especially electricity, that is obtained in large quantities from a fuel source and used to operate lights, heating, and machinery. ○ *Nuclear power is cleaner than coal.* ○ *Solar power is an example of a renewable source of energy.* ○ *There is enough power to run up to four lights.*

▶ **COLLOCATIONS:**
power **from** something
power from a **source/generator/battery/plant**
nuclear/solar/electrical power
generate/restore power
a power **cable/plant/grid/supply/cut/outage**

▶ **SYNONYM:** energy

3 **VERB** The device or fuel that **powers** a machine provides the energy that the machine needs in order to work. ○ *The 'flywheel' battery could power an electric car for 600 miles on a single charge.* ○ *Vehicles can be powered by hydrogen and batteries.*

▶ **COLLOCATIONS:**
powered **by** something
powered by **steam/electricity/coal**
a **battery/engine/generator** powers something

▶ **SYNONYM:** operate

pow|er|ful /ˈpaʊəfʊl/

ADJECTIVE A **powerful** machine or substance is effective because it is very strong. ○ *powerful computer systems* ○ *Alcohol is also a powerful and fast-acting drug.*

▶ **COLLOCATIONS:**
a powerful **computer/weapon/engine**
powerful **drugs/medicine**

▶ **SYNONYMS:** strong, potent
▶ **ANTONYM:** weak

pow|er|ful|ly /ˈpaʊəfʊli/

ADVERB ○ *This drug is powerfully hallucinogenic.*

▶ **SYNONYM:** strongly
▶ **ANTONYM:** weakly

prac|tise /ˈpræktɪs/ (practises, practising, practised)

VERB When people **practise** something such as a custom, craft, or religion, they take part in the activities associated with it. [in AM, use **practice**]
○ *countries which practise multi-party politics* ○ *Acupuncture was practised in China as long ago as the third millennium BC.*

▶ **COLLOCATIONS:**
practise a **custom/craft/religion**
practise **yoga/meditation/acupuncture**
commonly/routinely/widely practised

prac|tice /ˈpræktɪs/ (practices)

NOUN You can refer to something that people do regularly as a **practice**.
○ *Some firms have cut workers' pay below the level set in their contract, a practice that is illegal in Germany.* ○ *The prime minister demanded a public inquiry into bank practices.*

▶ **COLLOCATIONS:**
the practice **of** *something*
the practice of **medicine/yoga/meditation**
a **corrupt/controversial/illegal/common/normal/accepted** practice

▶ **SYNONYMS:** custom, habit, procedure, system

> **USAGE: practise** or **practice**?
>
> In British English, **practise** (with an S) is the verb form and **practice** (with a C) is the noun form.
>
> In American English, **practice** is the verb and noun form.

pre|cise /prɪˈsaɪs/

ACADEMIC WORD

1 ADJECTIVE You use **precise** to emphasize that you are referring to an exact thing, rather than something vague. ○ *The precise location of the wreck was discovered in 1988.* ○ *He was not clear on the precise nature of his mission.* ○ *We will never know the precise details of his death.*

2 ADJECTIVE Something that is **precise** is exact and accurate in all its details. ○ *They speak very precise English.* ○ *His comments were precise and to the point.*

▶ **COLLOCATIONS:**
precise **details/figures/English**
the precise **moment/nature/location**
precise **information/instructions/measurements**
a precise **definition/description**

▶ **PHRASE:** precise and to the point

▶ **SYNONYMS:** exact, accurate

▶ **ANTONYMS:** imprecise, inexact, inaccurate, vague

pre|cise|ly /prɪˈsaɪsli/

1 ADVERB Precisely means accurately and exactly. ○ *Nobody knows precisely how many people are still living in the camp.* ○ *The meeting began at precisely 4.00 p.m.*

▶ COLLOCATIONS:
  at precisely *x o'clock*
  know/ascertain/calculate *something* precisely
  measure/specify/define *something* precisely

▶ PHRASE: precisely and accurately

▶ SYNONYMS: exactly, accurately

▶ ANTONYMS: imprecisely, inaccurately

2 ADVERB You can use **precisely** to emphasize that a reason or fact is the only important one there is, or that it is obvious. ○ *Children come to zoos precisely to see captive animals.* ○ *That is precisely the result the system is designed to produce.*

pre|ci|sion /prɪˈsɪʒən/

UNCOUNTABLE NOUN ○ *The interior is planned with military precision.*

▶ COLLOCATIONS:
  with precision
  military/surgical/geometric/absolute precision

▶ SYNONYMS: exactness, accuracy

▶ ANTONYMS: imprecision, inaccuracy

---

pre|dict /prɪˈdɪkt/ (predicts, predicting, predicted)　ACADEMIC WORD

VERB If you **predict** an event, you say that it will happen. ○ *Chinese seismologists have predicted earthquakes this year in Western China.* ○ [+ that] *Some analysts were predicting that online sales during the holiday season could top $10 billion.* ○ [+ when] *tests that accurately predict when you are most fertile*

▶ COLLOCATIONS:
  predict an **event/outcome**
  predict a **fall/drop/decline/rise/recovery/upturn**
  a **forecaster/economist/analyst** predicts *something*
  predict *something* **accurately/confidently/correctly**
  impossible/difficult/possible to predict
  widely/rightly/wrongly predicted

▶ SYNONYMS: forecast, foresee

pre|dic|tion /prɪˈdɪkʃən/ (predictions)

NOUN ○ [+ about] *He was unwilling to make a prediction about which books would sell in the coming year.* ○ *Weather prediction has never been a perfect science.*

▶ COLLOCATIONS:
  a prediction **about/of** *something*
  make/confirm/defy/dismiss a prediction

weather/climate/earthquake prediction
a **reliable/accurate** prediction
▶ SYNONYMS: forecast, prophesy

pre|dict|able /prɪˈdɪktəbəl/

ADJECTIVE ○ *This was a predictable reaction, given the bitter hostility between the two countries.* ○ *The result was entirely predictable.*
▶ COLLOCATIONS:
a predictable **reaction/outcome/consequence**
entirely/wholly/fairly predictable
▶ PHRASE: predictable and formulaic
▶ ANTONYM: unpredictable

---

pre|his|tor|ic /ˌpriːhɪˈstɒrɪk, AM -ˈtɔːr-/ HISTORY

ADJECTIVE **Prehistoric** people and things existed at a time before information was written down. ○ *the famous prehistoric cave paintings of Lascaux* ○ *Many of our prehistoric ancestors ate high-protein diets.*
▶ COLLOCATIONS:
a prehistoric **mammoth/fossil/painting/ancestor**
prehistoric **remains**

---

preju|dice /ˈpredʒʊdɪs/ (prejudices) SOCIOLOGY

NOUN **Prejudice** is an unreasonable dislike of a particular group of people or things, or a preference for one group of people or things over another.
○ *There was a deep-rooted racial prejudice long before the two countries went to war.*
○ [+ *against*] *There is widespread prejudice against workers over 45.*
▶ COLLOCATIONS:
without prejudice
prejudice **against** *someone*
racial/homophobic/anti-European prejudice
deep-seated/unwitting/ingrained prejudice
overcome/combat/challenge/reinforce/perpetuate prejudice

preju|diced /ˈpredʒʊdɪst/

ADJECTIVE ○ *Some landlords and landladies are racially prejudiced.* ○ *The law is also making prejudiced attitudes less acceptable.*
▶ COLLOCATIONS:
racially/deeply prejudiced
a prejudiced **attitude/assumption/belief**

preju|di|cial /ˌpredʒʊˈdɪʃəl/

ADJECTIVE If an action or situation is **prejudicial to** someone or something, it is harmful to them. [FORMAL] ○ [+ *to*] *You could face up to eight years in jail for* *spreading rumours considered prejudicial to security.* ○ *The judge agreed with the prosecution that such information would be too prejudicial for the jury to hear.*

▶ **COLLOCATIONS:**
prejudicial **to** *someone/something*
prejudicial **information/conduct/comments**
unfairly/blatantly/potentially prejudicial

▶ **SYNONYM:** harmful

▶ **ANTONYM:** harmless

---

pre|limi|nary /prɪ'lɪmɪnri, AM -neri/ `ACADEMIC WORD`

ADJECTIVE Preliminary activities or discussions take place at the beginning of an event, often as a form of preparation. ○ *Preliminary results show the Republican party with 11 percent of the vote.* ○ *Preliminary talks on the future of the bases began yesterday.*

▶ **COLLOCATIONS:**
a preliminary **report/hearing/agreement**
preliminary **results/talks/discussions**

▶ **SYNONYM:** initial

▶ **ANTONYM:** concluding

---

pres|ent /'prezənt/

1 ADJECTIVE If someone is **present at** an event, they are there. ○ [+ *at*] *The president was not present at the meeting.* ○ [+ *at*] *Nearly 85 per cent of men are present at the birth of their children.* ○ *The whole family was present.*

▶ **COLLOCATIONS:**
present **at** *something*
present at a **meeting/birth/ceremony**

2 ADJECTIVE If something, especially a substance or disease, is **present in** something else, it exists within that thing. ○ [+ *in*] *This special form of vitamin D is naturally present in breast milk.* ○ *If the gene is present, a human embryo will go on to develop as a male.*

▶ **COLLOCATIONS:**
present **in** *someone/something*
present in **saliva/tissue/fluid**
naturally/commonly/rarely present
a **molecule/enzyme/bacterium/gene** is present

▶ **ANTONYM:** absent

pres|ence /'prezəns/

1 UNCOUNTABLE NOUN Someone's **presence** in a place is the fact that they are there. ○ [+ *in*] *They argued that his presence in the village could only stir up trouble.* ○ [+ *at*] *Her Majesty later honoured the Headmaster with her presence at lunch.*

▶ **COLLOCATIONS:**
presence **in/at** *somewhere/something*
someone's presence at a **ceremony/dinner/conference/meeting**

▶ **ANTONYM:** absence

2 UNCOUNTABLE NOUN If you refer to the **presence** of a substance in another thing, you mean that it is in that thing. ○ [+ *of*] *The somewhat acid flavour is caused by the presence of lactic acid.* ○ [+ *of*] *the presence of a carcinogen in the water* ○ *Although the fluid presents no symptoms to the patient, its presence can be detected by a test.*

▶ **COLLOCATIONS:**
the presence **of** *something*
the presence of *something* **in** *something*
detect/indicate/confirm the presence of *something*

▶ **ANTONYM:** absence

---

pre|sent /prɪˈzent/ **(presents, presenting, presented)**

VERB When you **present** information, you give it to people in a formal way. ○ *We spend the time collating and presenting the information in a variety of chart forms.* ○ [+ *to*] *We presented three options to the unions for discussion.* ○ [+ *with*] *In effect, Parsons presents us with a beguilingly simple outline of social evolution.*

▶ **COLLOCATIONS:**
present *something* **to** *someone*
present *someone* **with** *something*
present **information/evidence/options**
present a **cheque/trophy/petition**
formally/annually/proudly present

▶ **SYNONYMS:** offer, provide, submit

pres|en|ta|tion /ˌprezənˈteɪʃən, AM ˌpriːzen-/ **(presentations)**

NOUN ○ [+ *of*] *in his first presentation of the theory to the Berlin Academy* ○ [+ *of*] *a fair presentation of the facts to a jury*

▶ **COLLOCATIONS:**
a presentation **of** *something*
a presentation of **data/information/facts**
a **multimedia/video/Powerpoint** presentation
a **formal/detailed/elaborate** presentation

---

pre|serve /prɪˈzɜːv/ **(preserves, preserving, preserved)**

1 VERB If you **preserve** a situation or condition, you make sure that it remains as it is, and does not change or end. ○ *We will do everything to preserve peace.* ○ *in order to preserve the integrity of the Gospel*

▶ **COLLOCATIONS:**
preserve the **integrity/unity** of *something*
preserve **peace/standards**

▶ **SYNONYMS:** maintain, protect

▶ **ANTONYM:** neglect

2 VERB If you **preserve** something, you take action to save it or protect it from damage or decay. ○ *the Government's aim of preserving biodiversity* ○ *The current administration has done little to preserve forest ecosystems.*

▶ **COLLOCATIONS:**
preserve a **building/house/habitat/ecosystem**
well/perfectly/beautifully preserved

▶ **SYNONYMS:** maintain, save, protect

▶ **ANTONYMS:** neglect, waste

pres|er|va|tion /ˌprezə'veɪʃən/

UNCOUNTABLE NOUN ○ [+ *of*] *the preservation of buildings of architectural or historic interest* ○ [+ *of*] *the preservation of the status quo*

▶ **COLLOCATIONS:**
the preservation **of** *something*
the preservation of a **species/forest**
historical/environmental/architectural preservation
ensure/promote/guarantee the preservation

▶ **SYNONYMS:** maintenance, protection

▶ **ANTONYM:** neglect

---

pres|sure /'preʃə/   `SCIENCE` `PHYSICS`

1 UNCOUNTABLE NOUN Pressure is force that you produce when you press hard on something. ○ *She kicked at the door with her foot, and the pressure was enough to open it.* ○ *The best way to treat such bleeding is to apply firm pressure.*

▶ **COLLOCATIONS:**
apply/exert/maintain/withstand/resist/relieve pressure
upward/downward/intense pressure

2 UNCOUNTABLE NOUN The **pressure** in a place or container is the force produced by the quantity of gas or liquid in that place or container. ○ *Warm air is now being drawn in from another high pressure area over the North Sea.*

▶ **COLLOCATIONS:**
high/low pressure
blood/air/atmospheric pressure
pressure **drops/rises/intensifies**
raise/lower the pressure

pre|sume /prɪˈzjuːm, AM -ˈzuːm/ `ACADEMIC WORD`
(presumes, presuming, presumed)

VERB If you **presume that** something is the case, you think that it is the case, although you are not certain. ○ *I presume you're here on business.* ○ *In Madagascar, nearly half of 176 indigenous palm species are endangered or presumed extinct.* ○ [+ to-inf] *areas that have been presumed to be safe* ○ [+ that] *It is presumed that the hormone melatonin is involved.*

▶ COLLOCATIONS:
presume **guilt/innocence**
presumed **dead/extinct/deceased/guilty/innocent/responsible**
wrongly/safely/widely/commonly presumed

▶ SYNONYM: assume

pre|sump|tion /prɪˈzʌmpʃən/ (presumptions)

NOUN A **presumption** is something that is accepted as true but is not certain to be true. ○ *the presumption that a defendant is innocent until proved guilty* ○ *stories that challenge presumptions and preconceptions*

▶ COLLOCATIONS:
the presumption **of** *something*
the presumption of **guilt/innocence/rationality**
a **widespread/general/initial** presumption
challenge/adopt/end a presumption

▶ SYNONYM: assumption

pri|ma|ry /ˈpraɪməri, AM -meri/ `ACADEMIC WORD`

1 ADJECTIVE You use **primary** to describe something that is very important. [FORMAL] ○ *His misunderstanding of language was the primary cause of his other problems.* ○ *The family continues to be the primary source of care and comfort for people as they grow older.*

▶ COLLOCATION: a primary **aim/concern/focus/reason/cause/source**

2 ADJECTIVE Primary is used to describe something that occurs first. ○ *It is not the primary tumour that kills, but secondary growths elsewhere in the body.*

▶ COLLOCATION: a primary **tumour/election/ballot/school**
▶ SYNONYMS: main, principal
▶ RELATED WORD: secondary

pri|mari|ly /ˈpraɪmərɪli, AM praɪˈmeərɪli/

ADVERB You use **primarily** to say what is mainly true in a particular situation. ○ *a book aimed primarily at high-energy physicists* ○ *Public order is primarily an urban problem.*

▶ COLLOCATIONS:
primarily **because of** *something*
primarily **aimed at/designed for** *someone*

primarily **focussed on/concerned with** something
▸ **SYNONYMS:** mainly, principally, chiefly

---

prime /praɪm/ ACADEMIC WORD

ADJECTIVE You use **prime** to describe something that is most important in a situation. ○ *Political stability, meanwhile, will be a prime concern.* ○ *It could be a prime target for guerrilla attack.* ○ *The prime objective of the organization is to increase profit.*

▸ **COLLOCATION:** a prime **concern/target/objective/candidate**
▸ **SYNONYMS:** main, principal

---

prin|ci|pal /ˈprɪnsɪpəl/ ACADEMIC WORD

ADJECTIVE **Principal** means first in order of importance. ○ *the country's principal source of foreign exchange earnings* ○ *Their principal concern is bound to be that of winning the next general election.*

▸ **COLLOCATIONS:**
a principal **concern/aim/objective/cause**
a principal **architect/dancer/conductor/speaker/adviser/analyst**
▸ **SYNONYMS:** main, chief

prin|ci|pal|ly /ˈprɪnsɪpəli/

ADVERB **Principally** means more than anything else. ○ *This is principally because the major export markets are slowing.* ○ *Embryonic development seems to be controlled principally by a very small number of master genes.*

▸ **COLLOCATION:** principally **because**
▸ **SYNONYMS:** mainly, chiefly

> **USAGE: principal** or **principle**?
>
> Be careful not to confuse these two words, they have the same pronunciation, but different spellings.
>
> **Principal** (ending -AL) is an adjective to describe the most important thing. ○ *the principal cause of the problem*
>
> **Principle** (ending -LE) is a noun meaning a basic law or rule. ○ *the basic principles of criminal justice*

---

prin|ci|ple /ˈprɪnsɪpəl/ **(principles)** ACADEMIC WORD

1 NOUN The **principles of** a particular theory or philosophy are its basic rules or laws. ○ [+ of] *a violation of the basic principles of Marxism* ○ *The doctrine was based on three fundamental principles.*

2 NOUN Scientific **principles** are general scientific laws which explain how something happens or works. ○ *These people lack all understanding of scientific principles.* ○ [+ of] *the principles of quantum theory*

▶ COLLOCATIONS:
the principles **of** something
scientific/universal/basic/fundamental/democratic principles
apply/uphold/accept principles
violate/undermine/abandon principles

▶ SYNONYMS: rule, law

3 PHRASE If you agree with something, or believe that something is possible, **in principle**, you agree in general terms to the idea of it, although you do not yet know if it will be possible. ○ *I agree with it in principle but I doubt if it will happen in practice.* ○ *Even assuming this to be in principle possible, it will not be achieved soon.*

▶ COLLOCATIONS:
agree/approve in principle
accept something in principle
possible in principle

▶ SYNONYM: in theory

▶ ANTONYM: in practice

→ see note at **principal**

---

pri|or /praɪə/ ACADEMIC WORD

1 ADJECTIVE You use **prior** to indicate that something has already happened, or must happen, before another event takes place. ○ *Prior knowledge of the program is not essential.* ○ *For the prior year, they reported net income of $1.1 million.*

▶ COLLOCATIONS:
prior **approval/permission/consent/agreement**
prior **knowledge/experience**
a prior **engagement/arrangement**
the prior **period/week/month/year**

▶ SYNONYM: previous

2 PHRASE If something happens **prior to** a particular time or event, it happens before that time or event. [FORMAL] ○ *Prior to his Japan trip, he went to New York.* ○ *This is the preliminary investigation prior to the official inquiry.*

▶ COLLOCATION: a **day/hour/week/month/year** prior to something

▶ SYNONYM: before

▶ ANTONYM: after

---

pri|or|ity /praɪˈɒrɪti, AM -ˈɔːr-/ (priorities) ACADEMIC WORD

NOUN If something is a **priority**, it is the most important thing you have to do or deal with, or must be done or dealt with before everything else you have to do. ○ *You may be surprised to find that your priorities change after having a baby.* ○ *The government's priority is to build more power plants.*

▶ **COLLOCATIONS:**
a priority **for** someone
a **first/top/high/low** priority
a **budget/funding/research/policy** priority
set/establish/identify/change a priority

▶ **PHRASES:**
give priority to sth
take/have priority over sth

pri|ori|tize /praɪ'ɒrɪtaɪz, AM -'ɔːr-/ (prioritizes, prioritizing, prioritized)

VERB If you **prioritize** something, you treat it as more important than other things. [in BRIT, also use **prioritise**] ○ *The government is prioritising the service sector, rather than investing in industry and production.* ○ *put emotion aside to prioritize spending*

pri|ori|ti|za|tion /praɪ,ɒrɪtaɪ'zeɪʃən, AM -,ɔːr-/

UNCOUNTABLE NOUN [in BRIT, also use **prioritisation**] ○ [+ *of*] *the government's prioritization of resource allocation* ○ *The plan does not suggest prioritization based on age.*

▶ **COLLOCATION:** the prioritization **of** something

pri|vate /'praɪvɪt/ `BUSINESS` `POLITICS`

ADJECTIVE Private industries and services are owned or controlled by an individual person or a commercial company, rather than by the state or an official organization. ○ *a joint venture with private industry* ○ *Bupa runs private hospitals in Britain.* ○ *Brazil says its constitution forbids the private ownership of energy assets.*

▶ **COLLOCATIONS:**
private **industry/ownership/insurance**
a private **investor/company/hospital/practice**

▶ **ANTONYM:** public

pri|vate|ly /'praɪvɪtli/

ADVERB ○ *No other European country had so few privately owned businesses.* ○ *She was privately educated at schools in Ireland and Paris.*

▶ **COLLOCATION:** privately **owned/run/held/funded/educated**

▶ **ANTONYM:** publicly

pri|vat|ize /'praɪvətaɪz/ (privatizes, privatizing, privatized)

VERB If a company, industry, or service that is owned by the state **is privatized**, the government sells it and makes it a private company. [in BRIT, also use **privatise**] ○ *The water boards are about to be privatized.* ○ *a pledge to privatise the rail and coal industries* ○ *the newly privatized FM radio stations*

▶ **COLLOCATIONS:**
privatize a **plan/company/industry/utility**
newly/partially/fully privatized
▶ **ANTONYM:** nationalize

pri|vati|za|tion /ˌpraɪvətaɪˈzeɪʃən/ (privatizations)

NOUN [in BRIT, also use **privatisation**] ○ [+ of] the privatisation of British Rail ○ fresh rules governing the conduct of future privatizations

▶ **COLLOCATIONS:**
the privatization **of** something
the privatization of **industry/property/enterprise**
a privatization **plan/program/process**
introduce/propose/advocate/scrap/reverse/oppose privatization
▶ **ANTONYM:** nationalization

---

prob|able /ˈprɒbəbəl/

ADJECTIVE If you say that something is **probable**, you mean that it is likely to be true or likely to happen. ○ It is probable that the medication will suppress the symptom without treating the condition. ○ A bomb was the incident's most probable cause.

▶ **COLLOCATIONS:**
a probable **cause/outcome/scenario**
highly/most probable
▶ **SYNONYM:** likely
▶ **ANTONYMS:** improbable, unlikely

prob|abil|ity /ˌprɒbəˈbɪlɪti/ (probabilities)

NOUN The **probability of** something happening is how likely it is to happen, sometimes expressed as a fraction or a percentage. ○ [+ of] Without a transfusion, the victim's probability of dying was 100%. ○ [+ of] The probabilities of crime or victimization are higher with some situations than with others.

▶ **COLLOCATIONS:**
the probability **of** something
calculate/compute/estimate/assess the probability
the **estimated/statistical/mathematical** probability
a **significant/reasonable/high/low/tiny** probability
▶ **SYNONYMS:** chance, likelihood, possibility
▶ **ANTONYM:** improbability

---

pro|cedure /prəˈsiːdʒə/ (procedures) `ACADEMIC WORD`

NOUN A **procedure** is a way of doing something, especially the usual or correct way. ○ A biopsy is usually a minor surgical procedure. ○ [+ in] Police insist that Michael did not follow the correct procedure in applying for a visa.

▸ **COLLOCATIONS:**
the procedure **for/in** something
a **standard/normal/simple/correct** procedure
a **surgical/medical/cosmetic** procedure
a **complaints/grievance/selection** procedure
perform/undergo/review/explain a procedure

▸ **SYNONYMS:** method, process

pro|cedur|al /prəˈsiːdʒərəl/

ADJECTIVE [FORMAL] ○ *A Spanish judge rejected the suit on procedural grounds.*
○ *The Paris talks will mainly be about procedural matters.*

▸ **COLLOCATION:** procedural **matters/issues/rules**

---

pro|duce /prəˈdjuːs, AM -ˈduːs/ (produces, producing, produced)

VERB To **produce** something means to cause it to happen. ○ *The drug is known to produce side-effects in women.* ○ *Talks aimed at producing a new world trade treaty have been under way for six years.*

▸ **COLLOCATION:** produce a **result/effect**

▸ **SYNONYMS:** cause, induce

---

pro|fes|sor /prəˈfesə/ (professors)　EDUCATION　ACADEMIC STUDY

1 **NOUN** A **professor** in a British university is the most senior teacher in a department. ○ *Ross is a university professor who specializes in defence issues.* ○ *In 1979, only 2% of British professors were female.*

2 **NOUN** A **professor** in an American or Canadian university or college is a teacher of the highest rank. ○ *Robert Dunn is a professor of economics at George Washington University.* ○ *Typically, the young college professor takes a job for a few years.*

▸ **COLLOCATIONS:**
a professor **of/in** something
a professor **at** somewhere
a **university/college/psychology** professor
a **distinguished/eminent** professor
a professor at a **university/college/centre/department**
a professor **specializes/lectures** in something

---

pro|file /ˈprəʊfaɪl/ (profiles)

NOUN A **profile** is a description of a person or group detailing their features or characteristics. ○ *Members can browse profiles online.* ○ *[+ of] Forensic scientists create a DNA profile of an individual from a sample of saliva or hair.*

▸ **COLLOCATIONS:**
a profile **of** something/someone

a **demographic/DNA/genetic/psychological** profile
fit/match/create/view a profile

▶ SYNONYM: description

---

pro|gram /ˈprəʊɡræm/ (programs, programming, programmed) [IT]

1 NOUN A **program** is a set of instructions that a computer follows in order to perform a particular task. ○ *The chances of an error occurring in a computer program increase with the size of the program.*

▶ COLLOCATIONS:
   a **computer/software** program
   design/develop/create/run a program

▶ SYNONYMS: software, code

2 VERB When you **program** a computer, you give it a set of instructions to make it able to perform a particular task. ○ [+ to-inf] *He programmed his computer to compare all the possible combinations.* ○ *a computer programmed to translate a story given to it in Chinese*

▶ COLLOCATIONS:
   program a **computer/machine/robot**
   digitally/remotely programmed

> USAGE: **program** or **programme**?
>
> In British English, a **programme** (ending -mme) is a series of events or actions, or something you watch on television. ○ *the training programme for new employees* ○ *a popular television programme*
>
> **Program** (ending -m) can be used as a noun or a verb to talk about computer software. ○ *a computer program to reformat the data* ○ *skilled engineers program computer-driven robots*
>
> In American English, **program** is the usual spelling for all of these meanings.

---

pro|gress /ˈprəʊɡres, AM ˈprɑː-/

UNCOUNTABLE NOUN **Progress** is a process of gradual improvement or development. ○ [+ in] *The medical community continues to make progress in the fight against cancer.* ○ *The two sides made little if any progress towards agreement.* ○ [+ of] *The Chancellor is reported to have been delighted with the progress of the first day's talks.*

▶ COLLOCATIONS:
   progress **in/towards/of** *something*
   little/great progress
   make progress

P

pro|gres|sion /prəˈgreʃən/ (progressions)

NOUN A **progression** is a gradual development from one state to another.
○ [+ of] *Both drugs slow the progression of HIV, but neither cures the disease.*
○ *a skills strategy which is aimed at improving career progression*

▸ **COLLOCATIONS:**
the progression **of** something
a **natural/logical/gradual** progression
career progression
halt/slow/prevent/accelerate progression

▸ **SYNONYM:** development

pro|gres|sive /prəˈgresɪv/

ADJECTIVE A **progressive** change happens gradually over a period of time.
○ *One prominent symptom of the disease is progressive loss of memory.* ○ *the progressive development of a common foreign and security policy*

▸ **COLLOCATIONS:**
a progressive **change/deterioration/disease**
a progressive **development/introduction/handover**

▸ **SYNONYM:** gradual
▸ **ANTONYM:** sudden

pro|gres|sive|ly /prəˈgresɪvli/

ADVERB ○ *Her symptoms became progressively worse.* ○ *The amount of grant the council received from the Government was progressively reduced.*

▸ **COLLOCATIONS:**
progressively **become/increase/reduce** something
progressively **worse/better**

▸ **SYNONYMS:** gradually, steadily
▸ **ANTONYM:** suddenly

---

pro|hib|it /prəˈhɪbɪt, AM prəʊ-/ `ACADEMIC WORD`
(prohibits, prohibiting, prohibited)

VERB If a law or someone in authority **prohibits** something, they forbid it or make it illegal. [FORMAL] ○ *a law that prohibits tobacco advertising in newspapers and magazines* ○ *Fishing is prohibited.* ○ [+ from] *Federal law prohibits foreign airlines from owning more than 25% of any U.S. airline.*

▸ **COLLOCATIONS:**
prohibited **from** doing something
the **constitution/law/government** prohibits something
prohibit **discrimination/smoking/drugs**
strictly/expressly/currently prohibited

▸ **SYNONYM:** forbid
▸ **ANTONYM:** permit

pro|hi|bi|tion /ˌprəʊɪˈbɪʃən/

UNCOUNTABLE NOUN ○ [+ *of*] *the prohibition of women on air combat missions*
○ [+ *of*] *the prohibition of alcohol*
▶ **COLLOCATION:** the prohibition **of** *something/someone*

---

proj|ect /prəˈdʒekt/ (projects, projecting, projected)

VERB If something **is projected**, it is planned or expected. ○ [+ *to-inf*] *The population is projected to more than double by 2025.* ○ *The government had been projecting a 5% consumer price increase for the entire year.* ○ *a projected deficit of $1.5 million*
▶ **COLLOCATIONS:**
  project a **decrease/deficit/shortfall/growth/increase/turnover**
  a **forecaster/economist/analyst** projects *something*
▶ **SYNONYMS:** forecast, expect, estimate

pro|jec|tion /prəˈdʒekʃən/ (projections)

NOUN A **projection** is an estimate of a future amount. ○ [+ *of*] *the company's projection of 11 million visitors for the first year* ○ *sales projections*
▶ **COLLOCATIONS:**
  a projection **of/for** *something*
  projections for **growth/inflation/profits**
  sales/economic/profit projections
▶ **SYNONYMS:** forecast, estimate

---

pro|mote /prəˈməʊt/ (promotes, promoting, promoted)   ACADEMIC WORD

1 VERB If people **promote** something, they help or encourage it to happen, increase, or spread. ○ *You don't have to sacrifice environmental protection to promote economic growth.*
▶ **COLLOCATIONS:**
  promote **awareness/growth/tourism**
  actively/vigorously/strongly promote *something*
▶ **SYNONYM:** encourage
▶ **ANTONYM:** discourage

2 VERB If a firm **promotes** a product, it tries to increase the sales or popularity of that product. ○ *He has announced a full British tour to promote his second solo album.* ○ [+ *as*] *a special St Lucia week where the island could be promoted as a tourist destination*
▶ **COLLOCATIONS:**
  promote *something* **as** *something*
  a **retailer/advert/billboard/website** promotes *something*
  promote a **product**

heavily/vigorously/aggressively promote *something*
▶ PHRASE: promote and market

pro|mo|tion /prəˈməʊʃən/

UNCOUNTABLE NOUN ○ [+ *of*] *The government has pledged to give the promotion of democracy higher priority.* ○ *disease prevention and health promotion*

▶ COLLOCATIONS:
the promotion **of** *something*
the promotion of **democracy/equality/diversity**
health/trade/tourism/product promotion

▶ PHRASES:
promotion and advertising
promotion and marketing

---

prop|er|ty /ˈprɒpəti/ (properties)   `SCIENCE`

NOUN The **properties** of a substance or object are the ways in which it behaves in particular conditions. ○ *A radio signal has both electrical and magnetic properties.* ○ [+ *of*] *the electromagnetic properties of electrons*

▶ COLLOCATIONS:
the properties **of** *something*
the properties of a **substance/liquid/object**
the properties of a **molecule/electron/atom**
magnetic/electrical/antibacterial properties

---

pro|por|tion /prəˈpɔːʃən/ (proportions)   `ACADEMIC WORD`

1 NOUN A **proportion of** a group or an amount is a part of it. [FORMAL] ○ [+ *of*] *A large proportion of the dolphins in that area will eventually die.* ○ [+ *of*] *A proportion of the rent is met by the city council.*

2 NOUN The **proportion of** one kind of person or thing in a group is the number of people or things of that kind compared to the total number of people or things in the group. ○ [+ *of*] *The proportion of women in the profession had risen to 17.3%.* ○ [+ *of*] *A growing proportion of the population is living alone.*

▶ COLLOCATIONS:
a proportion **of** *something*
a **large/high/substantial/significant/small/tiny** proportion
a proportion of the **population/workforce/electorate**
a proportion of the **rent/budget/income**

▶ SYNONYMS: amount, part, percentage

3 PHRASE If something is small or large **in proportion to** something else, it is small or large when compared with that thing. ○ *Children tend to have relatively larger heads than adults in proportion to the rest of their body.* ○ *Japan's* *contribution to the UN budget is much larger in proportion to its economy than that of almost any other country.*

▶ COLLOCATION: **small/large** in proportion to *something*
▶ SYNONYM: in relation to

---

pro|pose /prə'pəʊz/ **(proposes, proposing, proposed)**   `LITERATURE`

1 VERB If you **propose** something such as a plan or an idea, you suggest it for people to think about and decide upon. ○ *Britain is about to propose changes to some institutions.* ○ [+ that] *It was George who first proposed that we dry clothes in that locker.*

2 VERB If you **propose** a theory or an explanation, you state that it is possibly or probably true, because it fits in with the evidence that you have considered. [FORMAL] ○ *This highlights a problem faced by people proposing theories of ball lightning.* ○ [+ that] *Newton proposed that heavenly and terrestrial motion could be unified with the idea of gravity.*

▶ COLLOCATIONS:
  a **committee/government/theorist/scientist** proposes *something*
  propose **changes/talks/plans/reform**
  propose a **theory/explanation/solution**
  first/originally/initially proposed

> **EXTEND YOUR VOCABULARY**
>
> There are several verbs you can use to report new ideas or theories by other people. ○ *Ivan Sutherland first **proposed** what he called a 'virtual world' in 1965.* ○ *Many commenters **suggested** alternative approaches to achieving those goals.* ○ *A possible interpretation is **put forward** in later chapters.* ○ *This work is important because it **introduces** the concept of group interaction.*

pro|po|sal /prə'pəʊzəl/ **(proposals)**

NOUN A **proposal** is a plan or an idea, often a formal or written one, which is suggested for people to think about and decide upon. ○ [+ for] *The President is to put forward new proposals for resolving the country's constitutional crisis.* ○ *the government's proposals to abolish free health care*

▶ COLLOCATIONS:
  a proposal **for** *something*
  a **government/new/peace** proposal
  put forward/reject/compromise a proposal
▶ SYNONYMS: plan, idea

propo|si|tion /ˌprɒpə'zɪʃən/ **(propositions)**

NOUN A **proposition** is a statement or an idea which people can consider or discuss to decide whether it is true. [FORMAL] ○ *The proposition that democracies do not fight each other is based on a tiny historical sample.*

▶ **COLLOCATIONS:**
a **basic/realistic/feasible/doubtful** proposition
put forward/advance/accept a proposition
▶ **SYNONYMS:** statement, idea

prose /prəʊz/

UNCOUNTABLE NOUN Prose is ordinary written language, in contrast to poetry. ○ *Shute's prose is stark and chillingly unsentimental.* ○ *What he has to say is expressed in prose of exceptional lucidity and grace.*

▶ **COLLOCATIONS:**
lyrical/descriptive/poetic/graceful prose
craft/write/produce/publish prose
a **writer's/author's** prose
a prose **style**
▶ **PHRASE:** prose and poetry

pros|pect /ˈprɒspekt, AM ˈprɑː-/ (prospects)   ACADEMIC WORD

1 NOUN If there is a **prospect of** something happening, there is a possibility that it will happen. ○ [+ *of*] *The prospect of finding a job is slim at present.*
○ [+ *for*] *The prospects for peace in the country's eight-year civil war are becoming brighter.*

▶ **COLLOCATIONS:**
the prospect **of** *something*
the prospects **for** *something*
the prospect of **war/survival/recession/employment**
the prospects for **peace/recovery/growth/success**

2 NOUN A particular **prospect** is something that you expect or know is going to happen. ○ [+ *of*] *They now face the prospect of having to wear a cycling helmet by law.* ○ *Starting up a company may be a daunting prospect.*

▶ **COLLOCATIONS:**
the prospect **of** *something*
relish/welcome/savour/face/dread/contemplate the prospect
a **pleasant/promising/attractive/bleak/daunting/grim** prospect

pro|spec|tive /prəˈspektɪv, AM prɑː-/

1 ADJECTIVE You use **prospective** to describe someone who wants to be the thing mentioned or who is likely to be the thing mentioned. ○ *The story should act as a warning to other prospective buyers.* ○ *his prospective employers*

▶ **COLLOCATION:** a prospective **buyer/student/employer/customer**
▶ **SYNONYMS:** future, would-be

2 ADJECTIVE You use **prospective** to describe something that is likely to happen soon. ○ *the terms of the prospective deal* ○ *prospective economic growth*

▸ COLLOCATION: a prospective **deal/sale**

▸ SYNONYM: anticipated

---

pro|vide /prəˈvaɪd/ (provides, providing, provided)

VERB If you **provide** something that someone needs or wants, or if you **provide** them **with** it, you give it to them or make it available to them. ○ *They would not provide any details.* ○ [+ with] *The government was not in a position to provide them with food.*

▸ COLLOCATION: provide *someone* **with** *something*

▸ SYNONYM: give

pro|vi|sion /prəˈvɪʒən/

UNCOUNTABLE NOUN The **provision of** something is the act of giving it or making it available to people who need or want it. ○ [+ of] *The department is responsible for the provision of residential care services.* ○ [+ for] *nursery provision for children with special needs*

▸ COLLOCATIONS:
the provision **of** *something*
provision **for** *someone*
authorize/govern/restrict/forbid the provision of *something*
childcare/pension/broadband/welfare provision

---

psy|chol|ogy /saɪˈkɒlədʒi/ ACADEMIC WORD

UNCOUNTABLE NOUN **Psychology** is the scientific study of the human mind and the reasons for people's behaviour. ○ *Professor of Psychology at Bedford College* ○ *research in educational psychology*

▸ COLLOCATIONS:
educational/evolutionary psychology
clinical/cognitive psychology

psycho|logi|cal /ˌsaɪkəˈlɒdʒɪkəl/

ADJECTIVE **Psychological** means concerned with a person's mind and thoughts. ○ *John received constant physical and psychological abuse from his father.* ○ *Robyn's loss of memory is a psychological problem, rather than a physical one.*

▸ COLLOCATIONS:
psychological **abuse/trauma/distress**
a psychological **profile/insight/evaluation/disorder**

▸ PHRASE: psychological and physical

▸ SYNONYM: mental

psy|cholo|gist /saɪˈkɒlədʒɪst/ (psychologists)

NOUN A **psychologist** is a person who studies the human mind and tries to explain why people behave in the way that they do. ○ *Psychologists tested a group of six-year-olds with a video.*

▶ COLLOCATIONS:
   consult/employ/contact a psychologist
   a psychologist **studies/assesses/analyses** *something*
   a psychologist **interviews/evaluates/counsels** *someone*
   a **clinical/forensic/educational** psychologist

---

pub|lic /ˈpʌblɪk/ BUSINESS POLITICS

1 ADJECTIVE Public means relating to the government or state, or things that are done for the people by the state. ○ *The social services account for a substantial part of public spending.* ○ *the role of religion in shaping public policy*

2 ADJECTIVE Public buildings and services are provided for everyone to use. ○ *The new museum must be accessible by public transport.* ○ *a public health service*

▶ COLLOCATIONS:
   public **spending/policy/servants/services/buildings/transport**
   the public **sector**

▶ SYNONYMS: government, state

▶ ANTONYM: private

---

pub|lish /ˈpʌblɪʃ/ (publishes, publishing, published) ACADEMIC WORD MEDIA

VERB When a company **publishes** a book or magazine, it prints copies of it, which are sent to shops to be sold. If someone **publishes** a book or an article that they have written, they arrange to have it published. ○ *Dr Peters published the findings of his detailed studies last year.* ○ *The research was published online in the latest British Medical Journal.*

▶ COLLOCATIONS:
   publish *something* **on/in** *something*
   published **by** *someone*
   published in a **journal/newspaper/report/article**
   published **online/on a website/on the internet**
   publish a **book/report/article/paper**
   publish **findings/figures/research**

pub|li|ca|tion /ˌpʌblɪˈkeɪʃən/ (publications)

1 UNCOUNTABLE NOUN The **publication** of a book or magazine is the act of printing it and sending it to shops to be sold. ○ [+ *of*] *the publication of an article in a physics journal* ○ [+ *of*] *the online publication of the census*

▶ COLLOCATIONS:
   the publication **of** *something*
   the publication of a **book/report/journal/article**
   online/weekly/monthly publication
   prohibit/delay/ban/await/resume publication

2 NOUN A **publication** is a book or magazine that has been published. ○ *the ease of access to scientific publications on the internet* ○ *The magazine, which will be a quarterly publication, has received sponsorship from companies in the US.*

▶ **COLLOCATIONS:**
a publication **on** *something*
a publication on a **topic/subject**
a **weekly/monthly/quarterly** publication
a **digital/online/scientific/specialist** publication

---

pur|chase /ˈpɜːtʃɪs/ ACADEMIC WORD BUSINESS
(purchases, purchasing, purchased)

1 VERB When you **purchase** something, you buy it. [FORMAL] ○ *Nearly three out of every 10 new car buyers are purchasing their vehicles online.* ○ *[+ from] Most of those shares were purchased from brokers.*

→ see note at **acquire**

▶ **COLLOCATIONS:**
purchase *something* **from/through** *someone/somewhere*
a **customer/buyer/consumer** purchases *something*
purchase **shares/property/land**
purchase *something* **online**

▶ **ANTONYM:** sell

> **EXTEND YOUR VOCABULARY**
>
> You can use **purchase** as a more formal alternative to **buy** in academic writing. ○ *the cost of purchasing equipment*
>
> You can also use **acquire** when you talk about a business buying some types of things.
>
> a company acquires **assets/shares/property**

2 NOUN A **purchase** is something that you buy. [FORMAL] ○ *The latest data reveals that nine in every 10 internet users have made a purchase online.* ○ *Discounts are available for bulk purchases.*

▶ **COLLOCATIONS:**
make/complete/refund a purchase
online/bulk purchase

---

pur|sue /pəˈsjuː, -ˈsuː/ **(pursues, pursuing, pursued)** ACADEMIC WORD

1 VERB If you **pursue** an activity, interest, or plan, you carry it out or follow it. If you **pursue** a particular topic, you try to find out more about it by asking questions. [FORMAL] ○ *He said Japan would continue to pursue the policies laid down at the London summit.* ○ *If your original request is denied, don't be afraid to pursue the matter.*

▶ **COLLOCATIONS:**
 pursue a **policy/interest/career**
 pursue a **matter/question/claim**
▶ **SYNONYMS:** follow, follow up
▶ **ANTONYMS:** drop, abandon

2 VERB If you **pursue** a particular aim or result, you make efforts to achieve it, often over a long period of time. [FORMAL] ○ *The implication seems to be that it is impossible to pursue economic reform and democracy simultaneously.* ○ *Europe must pursue aggressively its programme of economic reform.*

▶ **COLLOCATIONS:**
 pursue a **result/aim/objective/agenda**
 pursue **reform/diplomacy/business**
 aggressively/actively/vigorously pursue *something*

pur|suit /pəˈsjuːt, AM -ˈsuːt/ (pursuits)

UNCOUNTABLE NOUN The **pursuit of** something is the process of trying to achieve it. The **pursuit of** an activity, interest, or plan consists of all the things that you do when you are carrying it out. ○ [+ *of*] *a young man whose relentless pursuit of excellence is conducted with single-minded determination* ○ [+ *of*] *The vigorous pursuit of policies is no guarantee of success.*

▶ **COLLOCATIONS:**
 the pursuit **of** *something*
 the pursuit of a **plan/activity/project**
 the pursuit of **truth/excellence/perfection/knowledge**
▶ **PHRASE:** in (the) pursuit of sth

put forward /pʊt ˈfɔːwəd/ (puts forward, putting forward)

PHRASAL VERB If you **put forward** a plan, proposal, or theory, you suggest that it should be considered for a particular purpose or job. ○ *He has put forward new peace proposals.* ○ *Various theories have been put forward to account for this apparent anomaly.*

→ see note at **propose**
▶ **COLLOCATION:** put forward a **plan/proposal/theory**
▶ **SYNONYM:** submit
▶ **ANTONYM:** withdraw

Qq

qual|ity /ˈkwɒlɪti/ (qualities)

1 UNCOUNTABLE NOUN The **quality** of something is how good or bad it is. ○ [+ of] *Patients reported a substantial improvement in their symptoms and their quality of life.* ○ *Other services vary dramatically in quality.* ○ *high-quality paper and plywood*

▶ **COLLOCATIONS:**
the quality **of** *something*
quality of **life/services/care/teaching**
improve/enhance/affect quality
poor/sound/high/superior quality
air/water/image quality
quality **control/assurance/standards**

▶ **PHRASE:** quality and quantity

▶ **SYNONYM:** standard

2 NOUN You can describe a particular characteristic of a person or thing as a **quality**. ○ *a childlike quality* ○ [+ of] *the pretentious quality of the poetry* ○ *Thyme tea can be used by adults for its antiseptic qualities.*

▶ **SYNONYM:** characteristic

quan|tity /ˈkwɒntɪti/ (quantities)

NOUN A **quantity** is an amount that you can measure or count. ○ [+ of] *a small quantity of water* ○ [+ of] *vast quantities of food* ○ *Cheap goods are available, but not in sufficient quantities to satisfy demand.*

▶ **COLLOCATIONS:**
a quantity **of** *something*
a quantity of **water/food/uranium/alcohol**
a **vast/sufficient/significant** quantity

▶ **SYNONYM:** amount

quan|ti|fy /ˈkwɒntɪfaɪ/ (quantifies, quantifying, quantified)

VERB If you try to **quantify** something, you try to calculate how much of it there is. ○ *It is difficult to quantify an exact figure as firms are reluctant to declare their losses.* ○ [+ how] *The study is the first to quantify how widespread the practice is.*

q

▶ **COLLOCATIONS:**
quantify the **amount/cost/effect** of *something*
difficult/hard/impossible to quantify
▶ **SYNONYMS:** measure, calculate

quan|ti|fi|able /ˈkwɒntɪfaɪəbəl/

ADJECTIVE Something that is **quantifiable** can be measured or counted in a
scientific way. ○ *A clearly quantifiable measure of quality is not necessary.*
▶ **SYNONYMS:** calculable, measurable
▶ **ANTONYM:** unquantifiable

---

ques|tion /ˈkwestʃən/ (questions, questioning, questioned)

1 VERB If you **question** something, you have or express doubts about
whether it is true, reasonable, or worthwhile. ○ *Scientists
began questioning the validity of the research because they could not reproduce the
experiments.* ○ *It never occurs to them to question the doctor's decisions.*
→ see note at **criticize**
▶ **COLLOCATIONS:**
question the **validity/legality** of *something*
question the **wisdom/motives/integrity** of *something/someone*
▶ **SYNONYMS:** challenge, doubt

2 NOUN A **question** about something is doubt or uncertainty about it.
○ [+ *about*] *There's no question about their success.* ○ *The paper says the President's
move has called into question the whole basis of democracy in the country.* ○ *The
relevance of these studies to the current situation is open to question.*
▶ **COLLOCATIONS:**
questions **about** *something*
in/beyond question
questions about **effectiveness/safety/viability**
raise questions
▶ **PHRASES:**
no question
call into question
open to question
▶ **SYNONYMS:** doubt, uncertainty

---

quote /kwəʊt/ (quotes, quoting, quoted) `ACADEMIC WORD` `ACADEMIC STUDY`

1 VERB If you **quote** someone as saying something, you repeat what they
have written or said. ○ [+ *as*] *He quoted Mr Polay as saying that peace
negotiations were already underway.* ○ *Mawby and Gill (1987) quote this passage
from the Home Office White Paper, 1964.* ○ [+ *from*] *O'Regan cites one
exception, quoting from a paper on cancer of the cervix.*

▶ **COLLOCATIONS:**
quoted **as** *saying something*
quote **from** *something*
quote from a **book/report**
quote a **passage/verse/source**

▶ **SYNONYMS:** cite, reference

▶ **RELATED WORD:** paraphrase

2 NOUN A **quote from** a book, poem, play, or speech is a passage or phrase from it. ○ [+ *from*] *The article starts with a quote from an unnamed member of the Cabinet.* ○ *The quote is attributed to the Athenean philosopher Socrates.*

▶ **COLLOCATIONS:**
a quote **from** *something/someone*
attribute a quote

▶ **SYNONYMS:** quotation, citation

▶ **RELATED WORD:** paraphrase

quo|ta|tion /kwəʊˈteɪʃən/ (quotations)

NOUN A **quotation** is a sentence or phrase taken from a book, poem, or play, which is repeated by someone else. ○ [+ *from*] *He illustrated his argument with quotations from Pasternak.*

▶ **COLLOCATIONS:**
a quotation **from** *something/someone*
a **biblical/indirect** quotation

▶ **SYNONYMS:** quote, citation

▶ **RELATED WORD:** paraphrase

USAGE: quote or quotation

You can use **quote** or **quotation** as a noun to talk about a sentence or phrase that you use from another source. **Quote** is slightly more informal and more common in spoken language and journalism.

Quotation is used in more formal, academic writing.

Quote is the only verb form.

Rr

race /reɪs/ (races)

NOUN A **race** is one of the major groups which human beings can be divided into according to their physical features, such as the colour of their skin.
  ○ *The College welcomes students of all races, faiths, and nationalities.*
  ○ *Discrimination by employers on the grounds of race and nationality was illegal.*

▶ COLLOCATIONS:
  mixed race
  race **relations/discrimination**
  a race **riot/row**

▶ SYNONYM: ethnicity

ra|cial /ˈreɪʃəl/

ADJECTIVE **Racial** describes things relating to people's race. ○ *the protection of national and racial minorities* ○ *the elimination of racial discrimination* ○ *It was his legal insights that led to racial integration in the United States.*

▶ COLLOCATIONS:
  racial **discrimination/tension/hatred/abuse**
  racial **integration/equality**
  a racial **minority/stereotype**

▶ SYNONYM: ethnic

rac|ist /ˈreɪsɪst/ (racists)

ADJECTIVE If you describe people, things, or behaviour as **racist**, you mean that they are influenced by the belief that some people are inferior because they belong to a particular race. ○ *You have to acknowledge that we live in a racist society.* ○ *This is an affluent area with no previous racist incidents.* ○ *his political and racist views*

▶ COLLOCATIONS:
  a racist **attack/taunt/chant/remark**
  a racist **society**
  institutionally/overtly/openly racist

● A **racist** is someone who is racist. ○ *He has a hard core of support among white racists.* ○ *the individuals who are most likely to become bullies, criminals or racists*

▶ COLLOCATIONS:
  a **white/violent/vicious** racist
  call/brand/label *someone* a racist

radi|cal /ˈrædɪkəl/ `ACADEMIC WORD`

ADJECTIVE **Radical** changes and differences are very important and great in degree. ○ *The country needs a period of calm without more surges of radical change.* ○ *The Football League has announced its proposals for a radical reform of the way football is run.*

▶ **COLLOCATIONS:**
a radical **departure/overhaul/change/reform**
truly/politically/genuinely radical

▶ **SYNONYM:** fundamental

radi|cal|ly /ˈrædɪkli/

ADVERB ○ *The power of the presidency may be radically reduced in certain circumstances.* ○ *two large groups of people with radically different beliefs and cultures* ○ *proposals for radically new models*

▶ **COLLOCATIONS:**
change/alter/overhaul something radically
radically **different/new**

▶ **SYNONYM:** fundamentally

ra|dius /ˈreɪdiəs/ (radii) `MATHS`

1 NOUN The **radius** around a particular point is the distance from it in any direction. ○ [+ *around*] *Nigel has searched for work in a ten-mile radius around his home.* ○ [+ *of*] *within a fifty-mile radius of the town* ○ *Fragments of twisted metal were scattered across a wide radius.*

▶ **COLLOCATIONS:**
a radius **of/around** something
in/within a radius of something
a **50-mile/ten-mile/1km** radius

▶ **SYNONYM:** circle

2 NOUN The **radius** of a circle is the distance from its centre to its outside edge. ○ [+ *of*] *He indicated a semicircle with a radius of about thirty miles.* ○ [+ *of*] *the radius of a circle is equal to one-half its diameter*

▶ **COLLOCATIONS:**
a radius **of** x
the radius of a **circle**

▶ **RELATED WORDS:** circumference, diameter

ran|dom /ˈrændəm/ `ACADEMIC WORD`

ADJECTIVE A **random** sample or method is one in which all the people or things involved have an equal chance of being chosen. ○ *The survey used a random sample of two thousand people across England and Wales.* ○ *The competitors will be subject to random drug testing.*

▶ **COLLOCATIONS:**
a random **sample/check/selection/test**
random **testing**
▶ **ANTONYM:** targeted

ran|dom|ly /ˈrændəmli/

ADVERB ○ *interviews with a randomly selected sample of thirty girls aged between 13 and 18* ○ *They were randomly allotted to one or other of two groups.*

▶ **COLLOCATIONS:** randomly **selected/chosen/picked**
randomly **assigned/allocated**

---

rap|id /ˈræpɪd/

1 ADJECTIVE A **rapid** change is one that happens very quickly. ○ *the country's rapid economic growth in the 1980's* ○ *the rapid decline in the birth rate in Western Europe*
→ see note at **dramatic**

▶ **COLLOCATIONS:**
a rapid **growth/rise/expansion/decline/change**
extremely/relatively/fairly rapid

2 ADJECTIVE A **rapid** movement is one that is very fast. ○ *He walked at a rapid pace.* ○ *The Tunnel will provide more rapid car transport than ferries.*

▶ **COLLOCATIONS:**
a rapid **pace/heartbeat**
rapid **breathing/transit**

rap|id|ly /ˈræpɪdli/

ADVERB ○ *countries with rapidly growing populations* ○ *'Operating profit is rising more rapidly,' he said.* ○ *He was moving rapidly around the room.*
→ see note at **dramatic**

▶ **COLLOCATIONS:**
grow/change/spread/expand/rise rapidly
breathe/pace rapidly
▶ **SYNONYMS:** quickly, swiftly
▶ **ANTONYM:** slowly

---

rate /reɪt/ (rates)

1 NOUN The **rate** at which something happens is the speed with which it happens. ○ *The rate at which hair grows can be agonisingly slow.* ○ *The world's tropical forests are disappearing at an even faster rate than experts had thought.*

▶ **COLLOCATIONS:**
a **fast/slow/alarming/normal** rate
growth/metabolic rate
▶ **SYNONYMS:** speed, pace

2 **NOUN** The **rate** at which something happens is the number of times it happens over a period of time. ○ [+ *of*] *New diet books appear at a rate of nearly one a week.* ○ *His heart rate was 30 beats per minute slower.* ○ *the highest divorce rate in Europe*

▶ **COLLOCATIONS:**
  a rate **of** *x*
  birth/mortality/death/divorce/survival/success rates
  someone's **heart** rate
  a rate **rises/falls**

3 **NOUN** The **rate** of taxation or interest is the amount of tax or interest that needs to be paid. It is expressed as a percentage of the amount that is earned, gained as profit, or borrowed. ○ *The government insisted that it would not be panicked into interest rate cuts.* ○ [+ *of*] *The card has a fixed annual rate of 9.9 % and no annual fee.*

▶ **COLLOCATIONS:**
  a rate **of** *x*
  fix/cut/raise/charge a rate
  a **fixed/variable/standard/base** rate
  a **mortgage/interest/tax/lending** rate
  a rate **increase/reduction**

▶ **SYNONYM:** percentage

---

ra|tio /ˈreɪʃiəʊ, AM -ʃəʊ/ (ratios)   ACADEMIC WORD

NOUN A **ratio** is a relationship between two things when it is expressed in numbers or amounts. For example, if there are ten boys and thirty girls in a room, the ratio of boys to girls is 1:3, or one to three. ○ [+ *of*] *In 1978 there were 884 students at a lecturer/student ratio of 1:15.* ○ [+ *of*] *The bottom chart shows the ratio of personal debt to personal income.* ○ *The adult to child ratio is 1 to 6.*

▶ **COLLOCATIONS:**
  a ratio **of** *something*
  a ratio of *x* **to** *y*
  calculate/adjust a ratio
  a **high/constant/low** ratio
  a **price-earnings/power-to-weight/pupil-teacher** ratio

▶ **SYNONYM:** proportion

---

ra|tion|al /ˈræʃənəl/   ACADEMIC WORD

ADJECTIVE **Rational** decisions and thoughts are based on reason rather than on emotion. ○ *He's asking you to look at both sides of the case and come to a rational decision.* ○ *Mary was able to short-circuit her stress response by keeping her thoughts calm and rational.*

> ▶ **COLLOCATIONS:**
> a rational **decision/argument/explanation/approach**
> rational **thought/analysis/debate**
> **perfectly** rational
> ▶ **PHRASE:** calm and rational
> ▶ **SYNONYMS:** sensible, logical
> ▶ **ANTONYM:** irrational

ra|tion|al|ly /ˈræʃənəli/

ADVERB ○ *It can be very hard to think rationally when you're feeling so vulnerable and alone.* ○ *Their ability to look rationally at problems will be a great asset.*

> ▶ **COLLOCATION:** **behave/act/think/respond** rationally
> ▶ **ANTONYM:** irrationally

---

re|act /riˈækt/ (reacts, reacting, reacted)　　ACADEMIC WORD

1 VERB When you **react to** something that has happened to you, you behave in a particular way because of it. ○ [+ to] *They reacted violently to the news.* ○ *It's natural to react with disbelief if your child is accused of bullying.*

→ see note at **respond**

> ▶ **COLLOCATIONS:**
> react **to/with** *something*
> react to **news/information/situation/announcement/decision**
> react with **fury/anger/horror/disbelief**
> **markets/investors/fans** react
> react **angrily/swiftly/strongly/positively**
> ▶ **SYNONYM:** respond

2 VERB When one chemical substance **reacts with** another, or when two chemical substances **react**, they combine chemically to form another substance. ○ [+ with] *Calcium reacts with water.* ○ *Under normal circumstances, these two gases react readily to produce carbon dioxide and water.*

> ▶ **COLLOCATIONS:**
> react **with** *something*
> react **readily/quickly/slowly/normally**

re|ac|tion /riˈækʃən/ (reactions)

1 NOUN Your **reaction** to something that has happened or something that you have experienced is what you feel, say, or do because of it. ○ [+ to] *Reaction to the visit is mixed.* ○ [+ of] *The initial reaction of most participants is fear.*

> ▶ **COLLOCATIONS:**
> a reaction **to** *something*
> the reaction **of** *someone*
> **provoke/trigger/cause/prompt** a reaction

a **positive/negative/mixed/adverse** reaction
an **emotional/angry** reaction
a **knee-jerk/initial/immediate/gut** reaction

▶ SYNONYM: response

2 NOUN A chemical **reaction** is a process in which two substances combine together chemically to form another substance. ○ [+ *between*] *Ozone is produced by the reaction between oxygen and ultra-violet light.* ○ *Catalysts are materials which greatly speed up chemical reactions.*

▶ COLLOCATIONS:
a reaction **between** *things*
a **chemical/chain** reaction
speed up/slow down/monitor/observe/cause a reaction

re|al|ity /ri'ælɪti/

1 UNCOUNTABLE NOUN You use **reality** to refer to real things or the real nature of things rather than imagined, invented, or theoretical ideas. ○ *Fiction and reality were increasingly blurred.* ○ *Psychiatrists become too caught up in their theories to deal adequately with reality.*

▶ COLLOCATIONS:
harsh/virtual/grim reality
political/economic/commercial reality
face/reflect/distort/understand reality

▶ SYNONYMS: fact, actuality

2 PHRASE You can use **in reality** to introduce a statement about the real nature of something, when it contrasts with something incorrect that has just been described. ○ *He came across as streetwise, but in reality he was not.* ○ *For convenience, we can classify these differences into three groups, although in reality they are innumerable.*

▶ SYNONYMS: in fact, actually, in truth

re|al|is|tic /ˌriːə'lɪstɪk/

ADJECTIVE If you are **realistic** about a situation, you recognize and accept its true nature and try to deal with it in a practical way. ○ [+ *about*] *Police have to be realistic about violent crime.* ○ *a realistic view of what we can afford*

▶ COLLOCATIONS:
realistic **about** *something*
a realistic **view/approach/assessment/option**
a realistic **expectation/goal/chance**

▶ ANTONYMS: unrealistic, impractical

re|al|is|ti|cal|ly /ˌriːə'lɪstɪkəli/

ADVERB ○ *As an adult, you can assess the situation realistically.* ○ *What results can you realistically expect?* ○ *the definition of what is realistically possible*

▶ COLLOCATIONS:
realistically **assess/hope/expect** *something*
realistically **possible/impossible**
▶ ANTONYM: unrealistically

---

rea|son /ˈriːzən/

UNCOUNTABLE NOUN The ability that people have to think and to make sensible judgments can be referred to as **reason**. ○ *a conflict between emotion and reason* ○ *Never underestimate their powers of reason and logic.* ○ *the man of madness and the man of reason*

▶ PHRASES:
the voice of reason
listen to reason
it stands to reason

rea|son|ing /ˈriːzənɪŋ/

UNCOUNTABLE NOUN Reasoning is the process by which you reach a conclusion after thinking about all the facts. ○ *[+ behind] the reasoning behind the decision* ○ *She was not really convinced by this line of reasoning.*

▶ COLLOCATIONS:
the reasoning **behind** *something*
understand/use/explain/follow the reasoning
moral/practical/logical/deductive reasoning
reasoning **ability/skill/power**
the reasoning **process**
▶ PHRASE: a line of reasoning
▶ SYNONYMS: thinking, logic

rea|son|able /ˈriːzənəbəl/

1 ADJECTIVE If you say that a decision or action is **reasonable**, you mean that it is fair and sensible. ○ *a perfectly reasonable decision* ○ *At the time, what he'd done had seemed reasonable.* ○ *reasonable grounds for complaint*

2 ADJECTIVE If you say that an expectation or explanation is **reasonable**, you mean that there are good reasons why it may be correct. ○ *It seems reasonable to expect rapid urban growth.* ○ *There must be some other reasonable answer.*

▶ COLLOCATIONS:
a reasonable **expectation/assumption/compromise/request**
reasonable **grounds/doubt**
sound/seem reasonable
perfectly reasonable
reasonable to **assume/expect**
▶ PHRASE: beyond a reasonable doubt
▶ SYNONYM: sensible
▶ ANTONYM: unreasonable

rea|son|ably /ˈriːzənəbli/

ADVERB ○ *You can reasonably expect your goods to arrive within six to eight weeks.* ○ *the panel says he acted reasonably based on the information he had access to*

▶ **COLLOCATIONS:**
reasonably **expect/believe/assume** something
act/behave/answer/ask reasonably

▶ **SYNONYM:** sensibly

▶ **ANTONYM:** unreasonably

rec|og|nize /ˈrekəgnaɪz/ (recognizes, recognizing, recognized)

1 VERB If someone says that they **recognize** something, they acknowledge that it exists or that it is true. [in BRIT, also use **recognise**] ○ [+ that] *We recognized that the situation was becoming increasingly dangerous.* ○ [+ that] *Well, of course I recognize that evil exists.*

▶ **SYNONYM:** acknowledge

2 VERB If people or organizations **recognize** something as valid, they officially accept it or approve of it. [in BRIT, also use **recognise**] ○ [+ as] *Most doctors appear to recognize homeopathy as a legitimate form of medicine.* ○ *a nationally recognized expert on psychology*

▶ **COLLOCATIONS:**
accept something **as** something
recognize the **importance/need/danger/reality/value**
a **court/award** recognizes someone/something
internationally/widely/officially recognized

▶ **SYNONYM:** accept

rec|og|ni|tion /ˌrekəgˈnɪʃən/

UNCOUNTABLE NOUN **Recognition of** something is an understanding and acceptance of it. ○ [+ of] *The CBI welcomed the Chancellor's recognition of the recession.* ○ [+ of] *This agreement was a formal recognition of an existing state of affairs.*

▶ **COLLOCATIONS:**
recognition **of** something
recognition of a **fact/need/qualification**
recognition of **independence/sovereignty**
formal/official/diplomatic/international recognition
belated/widespread recognition

re|cov|er /rɪˈkʌvə/ ACADEMIC WORD MEDICINE
(recovers, recovering, recovered)

1 VERB When you **recover from** an illness or an injury, you become well again. ○ [+ from] *He is recovering from a knee injury.* ○ *A policeman was recovering in hospital last night after being stabbed.* ○ *He is fully recovered from the virus.*

► **COLLOCATIONS:**
recover **from** *something*
recover from a **virus/infection/illness/injury/operation**
a **patient** recovers
a recovering **addict/alcoholic**
fully/completely/quickly recover
► **SYNONYM:** recuperate
► **ANTONYM:** relapse

2 VERB If something **recovers from** a period of weakness or difficulty, it improves or gets stronger again. ○ *The stock market index fell by 80% before it began to recover.* ○ [+ *from*] *He recovered from a 4-2 deficit to reach the quarter-finals.*

► **COLLOCATIONS:**
recover **from** *something*
recover from a **recession/slump/setback/downturn**
a **market/economy** recovers
► **SYNONYM:** rally

re|cov|ery /rɪˈkʌvəri/ (recoveries)

1 NOUN If a sick person makes a **recovery**, he or she becomes well again.
○ [+ *from*] *He made a remarkable recovery from a shin injury.* ○ *He had been given less than a one in 500 chance of recovery by his doctors.*

► **COLLOCATIONS:**
recovery **from** *something*
a **rapid/remarkable/miraculous/full/complete** recovery
a recovery **process/room/rate**

2 NOUN When there is a **recovery** in a country's economy, it improves.
○ *Interest-rate cuts have failed to bring about economic recovery.* ○ *In many sectors of the economy the recovery has started.*

► **COLLOCATIONS:**
recovery **from** *something*
predict/expect a recovery
economic recovery
a **slow/steady/sustainable/uncertain** recovery
a recovery **plan/programme**

---

re|duce /rɪˈdjuːs, AM -ˈduːs/ (reduces, reducing, reduced)

VERB If you **reduce** something, you make it smaller in size or amount, or less in degree. ○ *It reduces the risks of heart disease.* ○ *Consumption is being reduced by 25 per cent.* ○ *The reduced consumer demand is also affecting company profits.*

→ see note at **decline**

► **COLLOCATIONS:**
reduce *something* **by** *x*

reduce *something* by **half/a third**
reduce the **number/rate/level/size** of *something*
reduce **costs/debt/spending/taxes**
reduce **anxiety/pain/stress/violence**
reduce **waste/emissions**
dramatically/significantly/substantially reduce *something*
▶ SYNONYMS: decrease, lessen, lower
▶ ANTONYM: increase

re|duc|tion /rɪˈdʌkʃən/ (reductions)

NOUN ○ [+ of] *This morning's inflation figures show a reduction of 0.2 per cent from 5.8 per cent to 5.6.* ○ [+ in] *Many companies have announced dramatic reductions in staff.* ○ [+ of] *the reduction of inflation and interest rates*
▶ COLLOCATIONS:
a reduction **of** *x*
a reduction **in** *something*
the reduction **of** *something*
a reduction in **mortality/emissions/size/rates**
cost/deficit/tax/debt/poverty reduction
weight/noise/stress reduction
achieve/propose/announce/mean a reduction
a **significant/further/substantial/dramatic** reduction
▶ SYNONYMS: decrease, lowering
▶ ANTONYM: increase

re|fer /rɪˈfɜː/ (refers, referring, referred) `ACADEMIC STUDY`

VERB If you **refer to** a book or other source of information, you look at it in order to find something out and mention it in your own work. ○ [+ to] *Refer to Typical Sleep-Inducing Medicines in Figure 5.* ○ [+ to] *Concerning its origins we should like to refer to E. F. Schumacher, to the fieldwork of K. Hart and to the theoretical work of M. Lipton.*
▶ COLLOCATIONS:
refer **to** *something*
refer to a **work/article**
▶ SYNONYMS: allude to, mention, cite

ref|er|ence /ˈrefərəns/ (references)

NOUN A **reference** is a word, phrase, or idea which comes from something such as a book, poem, or play and which you use when making a point about something. ○ [+ from] *a reference from the Quran* ○ *historical references* ○ [+ to] *In Doyle's prison file there's a reference to a military intelligence report.*
→ see note at **appendix**

▶ **COLLOCATIONS:**
a reference **from/to** something
make/include/find a reference
quote/cite a reference
▶ **SYNONYMS:** quote, allusion

---

re|flect /rɪˈflekt/ (reflects, reflecting, reflected)

VERB If something **reflects** an attitude or situation, it shows that the attitude or situation exists or it shows what it is like. ○ *The Los Angeles riots reflected the bitterness between the black and Korean communities in the city.* ○ *Concern at the economic situation was reflected in the government's budget.*

▶ **COLLOCATIONS:**
a **view/concern/change/decision** reflects something
reflect a **fact/value/belief/interest**
clearly reflect something
▶ **SYNONYM:** show

re|flec|tion /rɪˈflekʃən/ (reflections)

NOUN If you say that something is a **reflection of** a particular person's attitude or **of** a situation, you mean that it is caused by that attitude or situation and therefore reveals something about it. ○ [+ of] *Inhibition in adulthood seems to be very clearly a reflection of a person's experiences as a child.*

▶ **COLLOCATIONS:**
a reflection **of** something
a reflection of a **fact/attitude/trend**
a **direct/clear/obvious** reflection of something
▶ **SYNONYM:** indication

---

re|form /rɪˈfɔːm/ (reforms, reforming, reformed)   POLITICS

1 NOUN Reform consists of changes and improvements to a law, social system, or institution. A **reform** is an instance of such a change or improvement. ○ *The party embarked on a programme of economic reform.* ○ [+ of] *He has urged reform of the welfare system.* ○ *The Socialists introduced fairly radical reforms.*

▶ **COLLOCATIONS:**
the reform **of** something
need/promise/demand reform
propose/implement/introduce a reform
economic/political/electoral/constitutional reform
welfare/tax/land/health/education reforms
a reform **programme/process/plan/bill**
▶ **SYNONYMS:** improvement, amendment, reorganization

2 VERB If someone **reforms** something such as a law, social system, or institution, they change or improve it. ○ *his plans to reform the country's economy* ○ *A reformed party would have to win the approval of the people.* ○ *proposals to reform the tax system*

▶ COLLOCATIONS:
reform the **economy/system/law**
radically/fundamentally/completely reform *something*

▶ SYNONYMS: improve, amend, reorganize

re|form|er /rɪˈfɔːmə/ (reformers)

NOUN A **reformer** is someone who tries to change and improve something such as a law or a social system. ○ *Charles Dickens, novelist and social reformer* ○ *Political reformers, in attacking the wrong issue, only made the situation worse.*

▶ COLLOCATIONS:
a **political/social/penal/radical** reformer
reformers **hope/argue/advocate/propose**

---

re|gard /rɪˈɡɑːd/ (regards, regarding, regarded)

1 VERB If you **regard** someone or something **as** being a particular thing or **as** having a particular quality, you believe that they are that thing or have that quality. ○ [+ *as*] *He was regarded as the most successful Chancellor of modern times.* ○ [+ *as*] *I regard creativity both as a gift and as a skill.*

▶ COLLOCATIONS:
regard *someone/something* **as** *something*
regard *someone* as a **contender/outsider**
regard *something* as a **classic**

> **EXTEND YOUR VOCABULARY**
>
> You use **think** and **believe** in many contexts to talk about your opinion of someone or something. Both verbs are followed by a clause, often starting with *that*. ○ *Many people think science is intimidating or just boring.* ○ *Some experts believe that Western diet could be a factor.*
>
> You use **regard** and **consider** in formal writing to say that you think about someone or something in a particular way. The two verbs are used in different constructions. ○ *The vast majority of people would regard these proposals as unreasonable.* ○ *Certain kinds of behavior are not considered socially acceptable.*
>
> You can also use **perceive** to talk about the opinions and beliefs of a group of people about someone or something. You often use **perceive** when you think that this belief or **perception** may be incorrect. ○ *Our real problem is that ageing is perceived to be a problem.*

r

2 **PHRASE** You can use **as regards** to indicate the subject that is being talked or written about. ○ *As regards the war, Haig believed in victory at any price.* ○ *A complete revolution of opinion has taken place as regards the formation of mountain chains.*

▶ **SYNONYMS:** concerning, regarding, relating to

3 **PHRASE** You can use **with regard to** or **in regard to** to indicate the subject that is being talked or written about. ○ *The department is reviewing its policy with regard to immunisation.* ○ *The prognosis is looking good, particularly in regard to her physical condition.*

▶ **SYNONYMS:** concerning, regarding

4 **PHRASE** You can use **in this regard** or **in that regard** to refer back to something that you have just said. ○ *In this regard nothing has changed.* ○ *I may have made a mistake in that regard.*

▶ **SYNONYMS:** on this/that point, in this/that respect

re|gard|ing /rɪˈgɑːdɪŋ/

PREPOSITION You can use **regarding** to indicate the subject that is being talked or written about. ○ *He refused to divulge any information regarding the man's whereabouts.* ○ *There are conflicting reports regarding the number of terrorists involved.*

▶ **SYNONYM:** concerning

---

reg|is|ter /ˈredʒɪstə/ (registers, registering, registered) `ACADEMIC WORD`

1 **VERB** If you **register** to do something, you put your name on an official list. ○ [+ to-inf] *Thousands lined up to register to vote.* ○ [+ for] *Many students register for these courses to widen skills for use in their current job.* ○ *registered voters*

▶ **COLLOCATIONS:**
register **for/with** *something*
register with a **dentist/authority/agency/embassy**
register for a **service/election**
a registered **voter/adviser/subscriber/nurse**
officially register

▶ **SYNONYMS:** enrol, enlist, sign up

2 **VERB** If you **register** something, you have it recorded on an official list. ○ *In order to register a car in Japan, the owner must have somewhere to park it.* ○ *They registered his birth.* ○ *a registered charity*

▶ **COLLOCATIONS:**
a registered **trademark/logo/firearm/charity**
register a **birth/complaint**
officially registered

▶ **SYNONYMS:** license, record

3 VERB When something **registers on** a scale or measuring instrument, it shows on the scale or instrument. You can also say that something **registers** a certain amount or level **on** a scale or measuring instrument. ○ [+ on] *It will only register on sophisticated X-ray equipment.* ○ *The earthquake registered 5.3 points on the Richter scale.* ○ *The scales registered a gain of 1.3 kilograms.*

▶ COLLOCATIONS:
register **on** *something*
register on a **radar/scale**
a **sensor** registers *something*
a **tremor/earthquake** registers *x*
register a **gain/increase/decline**
barely register

▶ SYNONYM: show

reg|is|tra|tion /ˌredʒɪˈstreɪʃən/

UNCOUNTABLE NOUN The **registration** of something such as a person's name or the details of an event is the recording of it in an official list. ○ [+ of] *They have campaigned strongly for compulsory registration of dogs.* ○ *With the high voter registration, many will be voting for the first time.* ○ *fill in the registration forms*

▶ COLLOCATIONS:
the registration **of** *something*
the registration of **dogs/guns/firearms/interest**
voter/vehicle/car registration
initial/compulsory/online registration
a registration **form/requirement/number/process/fee**

▶ SYNONYM: licensing

---

regu|late /ˈreɡjʊleɪt/   `ACADEMIC WORD` `BUSINESS`
(regulates, regulating, regulated)

VERB To **regulate** an activity or process means to control it, especially by means of rules. ○ *The powers of the European Commission to regulate competition are increasing.* ○ [V-ing] *As we get older the temperature-regulating mechanisms in the body tend to become a little less efficient.* ○ [V-ing] *regulating cholesterol levels*

▶ COLLOCATIONS:
regulate a **use/activity/industry**
a **law/state/government** regulates *something*

▶ SYNONYMS: control, manage

regu|lat|ed /ˈreɡjʊleɪtɪd/

ADJECTIVE ○ *a planned, state-regulated economy* ○ *It's a treatment that can carry risks, and in Britain it's strictly regulated.*

▶ COLLOCATIONS:
a regulated **company/industry/utility/economy**

strictly/tightly/heavily/highly/fully regulated
▶ SYNONYM: controlled
▶ ANTONYM: non-regulated

regu|la|tor /ˈregjʊleɪtə/ (regulators)

NOUN A **regulator** is a person or organization appointed by a government to regulate an area of activity such as banking or industry. ○ *Congress is being asked to investigate why it took so long for government regulators to shut the plant down.* ○ *An independent regulator will be appointed to ensure fair competition.*

▶ COLLOCATIONS:
ask/satisfy/concern/convince the regulator
a regulator **approves/investigates/blocks/orders** something
a **national/provincial/state/independent** regulator
a **financial/security/competition** regulator
a **rail/telecoms/energy** regulator

regu|la|tory /ˌregjʊˈleɪtəri/

ADJECTIVE ○ *the U.K.'s financial regulatory system* ○ *This new regulatory regime was designed to protect the public.*

▶ COLLOCATIONS:
a regulatory **system/regime/body/agency/authority**
a regulatory **requirement/framework**
regulatory **approval/reform**

---

re|ject /rɪˈdʒekt/ (rejects, rejecting, rejected)　　ACADEMIC WORD

VERB If you **reject** something such as a proposal, a request, or an offer, you do not accept it or you do not agree to it. ○ *Seventeen publishers rejected the manuscript before Jenks saw its potential.* ○ *reject the possibility of failure*

▶ COLLOCATIONS:
voters/shareholders reject something
a **board/parliament/union/committee** rejects something
a **judge/jury/court** rejects something
reject a **proposal/idea/offer/suggestion/claim/call**
flatly/firmly/unanimously/angrily reject something
reject something **outright**
▶ SYNONYMS: deny, turn down, decline
▶ ANTONYMS: accept, approve

re|jec|tion /rɪˈdʒekʃən/

UNCOUNTABLE NOUN ○ [+ of] *The rejection of such initiatives indicates that voters are unconcerned about the environment.* ○ *the chances of criticism and rejection*

▶ COLLOCATIONS:
the rejection **of** something

prevent/fear/avoid/face/risk rejection
overwhelming/repeated/initial rejection
▸ **PHRASE:** a letter of rejection
▸ **SYNONYM:** denial
▸ **ANTONYMS:** acceptance, approval

---

re|late /rɪˈleɪt/ (relates, relating, related)

1 VERB If something **relates to** a particular subject, it concerns that subject.
  ○ [+ to] *Other recommendations relate to the details of how such data is stored.*
  ○ [+ to] *It does not matter whether the problem you have relates to food, drink, smoking or just living.*

▸ **COLLOCATIONS:**
  relate **to** *something*
  a **document/issue/matter** relates to *something*
  a **rule/allegation/charge** relating to *something*
  information relating to *something*

▸ **SYNONYMS:** concern, involve

2 VERB The way that two things **relate**, or the way that one thing **relates to** another, is the sort of connection that exists between them. ○ *More studies will be required before we know what the functions of these genes are and whether they relate to each other.* ○ [+ to] *Cornell University offers a course that investigates how language relates to particular cultural codes.*

▸ **COLLOCATION:** relate **to** *something*
▸ **SYNONYM:** connect

re|lat|ed /rɪˈleɪtɪd/

ADJECTIVE If two or more things are **related**, there is a connection between them. ○ *The philosophical problems of chance and of free will are closely related.*
  ○ *equipment and accessories for diving and related activities*

▸ **COLLOCATIONS:**
  related **activities/information/matters/developments**
  closely/directly/inversely related

▸ **SYNONYM:** connected
▸ **ANTONYM:** unrelated

---

re|la|tion /rɪˈleɪʃən/ (relations)

1 NOUN Relations between people, groups, or countries are contacts between them and the way in which they behave towards each other.
  ○ [+ with] *Greece has established full diplomatic relations with Israel.* ○ [+ between] *Apparently relations between husband and wife had not improved.* ○ *The company has a track record of good employee relations.*

▶ **COLLOCATIONS:**
    relations **with** *someone*
    relations **between** *people*
    relations **improve/deteriorate/worsen**
    improve/establish/normalize/restore relations
    diplomatic/public/industrial/international relations
    race/gender/community relations
    normal/friendly/poor/close relations
▶ **SYNONYMS:** contact, link

USAGE: relations or **relationship**?

You use **relationship** to talk about the family and personal connections and friendships between individuals. ○ *She had a close relationship with her grandfather.*

You can use **relations** or **relationship** to talk about connections between groups of people and countries. You use **relations** particularly to refer to the way that two groups or countries communicate or deal with each other. ○ *the delicate diplomatic relations between the two countries*

You use **relationship** more to talk about the connection between two groups or countries that develops over time. ○ *Companies feel call centres can improve their relationship with customers.*

---

2 NOUN If you talk about the **relation of** one thing **to** another, you are talking about the ways in which they are connected. ○ [+ *of*] *It is a question of the relation of ethics to economics.* ○ [+ *between*] *a relation between youthful unemployment and drug-related offences.* ○ [+ *to*] *This theory bears no relation to reality.*

▶ **COLLOCATIONS:**
    the relation **of** *something* **to** *something*
    the relation **between** *things*
▶ **SYNONYMS:** concerning, regarding, with regard to, in respect of

3 PHRASE You can talk about something **in relation to** something else when you want to compare the size, condition, or position of the two things.
    ○ *The money he'd been ordered to pay was minimal in relation to his salary.*
    ○ *women's position in relation to men in the context of the family*

▶ **SYNONYM:** in comparison to

---

rela|tive /'relətɪv/

1 ADJECTIVE You use **relative** to say that something is true to a certain degree, especially when compared with other things of the same kind.
    ○ *The fighting resumed after a period of relative calm.* ○ *It is a cancer that can be cured with relative ease.*

2 ADJECTIVE You use **relative** when you are comparing the quality or size of two things. ○ *They chatted about the relative merits of London and Paris as places to live.* ○ *I reflected on the relative importance of education in 50 countries.*
▶ **COLLOCATIONS:**
relative **calm/obscurity/importance/safety**
relative **merits/advantages/strength**
▶ **SYNONYMS:** comparative, corresponding

3 PHRASE Relative to something means with reference to it or in comparison with it. ○ *House prices now look cheap relative to earnings.* ○ *The satellite remains in one spot relative to the earth's surface.*
▶ **SYNONYM:** in relation to

rela|tive|ly /ˈrelətɪvli/

ADVERB Relatively means to a certain degree, especially when compared with other things of the same kind. ○ *The sums needed are relatively small.* ○ *Such an explanation makes it relatively easy for a child to absorb metaphysical information.*
▶ **COLLOCATIONS:**
relatively **small/low/short/easy/simple**
relatively **easily/cheaply/recently/little**
▶ **SYNONYM:** comparatively

re|lease /rɪˈliːs/ (releases, releasing, released) ACADEMIC WORD

1 VERB If a person or animal **is released** from somewhere where they have been locked up or looked after, they are set free or allowed to go. ○ [+ *from*] *He was released from custody the next day.* ○ [+ *from*] *He is expected to be released from hospital today.* ○ *He was released on bail.*
▶ **COLLOCATIONS:**
released **from** *something*
released from **hospital/prison/jail/custody**
a **prisoner/detainee/patient** is released
police/kidnappers release *someone*
▶ **PHRASE:** released someone on bail
▶ **SYNONYMS:** set free, free, liberate
▶ **ANTONYM:** imprison

● **Release** is also a noun. ○ [+ *of*] *He called for the immediate release of all political prisoners.* ○ [+ *from*] *Serious complications have delayed his release from hospital.*
▶ **COLLOCATIONS:**
release **from** *something*
the release **of** *someone*
release from **hospital/prison/jail/custody**
the release of a **prisoner/hostage**

immediate/imminent/early release
call for/demand/secure *someone's* release

▶ SYNONYMS: liberation, discharge
▶ ANTONYM: imprisonment

2 VERB If someone in authority **releases** something such as a document or information, they make it available. ○ *They're not releasing any more details yet.* ○ *Figures released yesterday show retail sales were down in March.*

▶ COLLOCATIONS:
release a **document/transcript**
release **figures/details**
officially release *something*

▶ SYNONYMS: issue, publish, announce

● **Release** is also a noun. ○ [+ *of*] *Action had been taken to speed up the release of cheques.*

▶ COLLOCATIONS:
the release **of** *something*
the release of a **document/transcript**
the **official** release of *something*
a **press** release

▶ SYNONYMS: issue, publication, announcement

3 VERB If something **releases** gas, heat, or a substance, it causes it to leave its container or the substance that it was part of and enter the surrounding atmosphere or area. ○ *a weapon which releases toxic nerve gas* ○ *The contraction of muscles uses energy and releases heat.*

▶ COLLOCATIONS:
release **chemicals/toxins/adrenaline/hormones**
release *something* **accidentally/simultaneously**

▶ SYNONYM: discharge

● **Release** is also a noun. ○ [+ *of*] *Under the agreement, releases of cancer-causing chemicals will be cut by about 80 per cent.*

▶ COLLOCATIONS:
the release **of** *something*
the release of **chemicals/toxins/adrenaline/hormones**
the **accidental/simultaneous** release of *something*

▶ SYNONYM: discharge

---

rel|evant /ˈreləvənt/   ACADEMIC WORD

ADJECTIVE Something that is **relevant to** a situation or person is important or significant in that situation or to that person. ○ [+ *to*] *Is socialism still relevant to people's lives?* ○ *We have passed all relevant information on to the police.*

▶ **COLLOCATIONS:**
relevant **to** *someone/something*
directly/highly/especially relevant
relevant **information/experience**
a relevant **qualification/document/article**
the relevant **authorities**
▶ **SYNONYM:** pertinent
▶ **ANTONYM:** irrelevant

rel|evance /ˈreləvəns/

UNCOUNTABLE NOUN ○ [+ to] *Politicians' private lives have no relevance to their public roles.* ○ [+ to] *There are additional publications of special relevance to new graduates.*
▶ **COLLOCATIONS:**
relevance **to** *someone/something*
the relevance **of** *something*
question/determine the relevance of *something*
lack/have relevance
have **little** relevance
contemporary/social/practical relevance
particular/direct/immediate relevance
▶ **SYNONYM:** appropriateness
▶ **ANTONYM:** irrelevance

re|li|able /rɪˈlaɪəbəl/ `ACADEMIC WORD`

ADJECTIVE Information that is **reliable** or that is from a **reliable** source is very likely to be correct. ○ *There is no reliable information about civilian casualties.* ○ *It's very difficult to give a reliable estimate.* ○ *We have reliable sources.*
▶ **COLLOCATIONS:**
a reliable **statistic/prediction/indication/guide**
a reliable **source/informant/predictor/barometer**
reliable **intelligence/evidence/information**
▶ **SYNONYM:** trustworthy
▶ **ANTONYM:** unreliable

re|li|abil|ity /rɪˌlaɪəˈbɪlɪti/

UNCOUNTABLE NOUN ○ [+ of] *Both questioned the reliability of recent opinion polls.* ○ [+ of] *the reliability of her testimony* ○ [+ of] *Check the figures and set them beside other data to get some idea of their reliability.*
▶ **COLLOCATIONS:**
the reliability **of** *something*
the reliability of the **testimony/evidence/intelligence**
question/assure/assess/test the reliability of *something*

questionable/dubious/utter reliability
- ▶ SYNONYM: trustworthiness
- ▶ ANTONYM: unreliability

---

re|luc|tant /rɪˈlʌktənt/ `ACADEMIC WORD`

ADJECTIVE If you are **reluctant to** do something, you are unwilling to do it and hesitate before doing it, or do it slowly and without enthusiasm. ○ *Mr Spero was reluctant to ask for help.* ○ *The police are very reluctant to get involved in this sort of thing.*

- ▶ COLLOCATIONS:
  reluctant to **admit/discuss/accept** *something*
  reluctant to **talk/invest/comment/act**
  a reluctant **hero/ally/reader/witness**
  initially/increasingly/understandably reluctant
- ▶ SYNONYM: unwilling
- ▶ ANTONYM: willing

re|luc|tant|ly /rɪˈlʌktəntli/

ADVERB ○ *We have reluctantly agreed to let him go.* ○ *Rescuers reluctantly ended their search Thursday morning.*

- ▶ COLLOCATION: reluctantly **agree/accept/decide/admit**
- ▶ SYNONYMS: unwillingly, grudgingly
- ▶ ANTONYM: willingly

re|luc|tance /rɪˈlʌktəns/

UNCOUNTABLE NOUN ○ *Ministers have shown extreme reluctance to explain their position to the media.* ○ *British officials have indicated reluctance to quickly lift the ban.*

- ▶ COLLOCATIONS:
  show/express reluctance
  overcome/indicate/explain *someone's* reluctance
  growing/increasing reluctance
  initial/apparent/marked/understandable reluctance
- ▶ SYNONYM: unwillingness
- ▶ ANTONYM: willingness

---

rely /rɪˈlaɪ/ (relies, relying, relied) `ACADEMIC WORD`

VERB If you **rely on** someone or something, you need them and depend on them in order to live or work properly. ○ [+ *on/upon*] *They relied heavily on the advice of their professional advisers.* ○ [+ *on/upon*] *The Association relies on member subscriptions for most of its income.*

▶ **COLLOCATIONS:**
rely **on/upon** something/someone
rely on someone/something **for** something
manufacturers/employers/farmers rely on someone/something
rely **heavily** on someone/something
rely on **support/technology/donations/volunteers**

▶ **SYNONYM:** depend

re|li|ant /rɪ'laɪənt/

ADJECTIVE A person or thing that is **reliant on** something needs it and often cannot live or work without it. ○ [+ on/upon] These people are not wholly reliant on Western charity. ○ [+ on/upon] Lithuania is heavily reliant on Moscow for almost all its oil.

▶ **COLLOCATIONS:**
reliant **on/upon** something
reliant on **technology/tourism/aid/exports/oil**
heavily/less/increasingly/too reliant
become reliant on something

▶ **SYNONYM:** dependent
▶ **ANTONYM:** independent

re|li|ance /rɪ'laɪəns/

UNCOUNTABLE NOUN A person's or thing's **reliance on** something is the fact that they need it and often cannot live or work without it. ○ [+ on] the country's increasing reliance on foreign aid ○ [+ upon] The attack did signal a growing reliance upon political assassination in the Province.

▶ **COLLOCATIONS:**
reliance **on/upon** something
place/increase/reduce reliance on something
growing/continuing reliance
heavy/great/excessive/undue/total reliance

▶ **SYNONYM:** dependence

---

re|main /rɪ'meɪn/ (remains, remaining, remained)

VERB If someone or something **remains** in a particular state or condition, they stay in that state or condition and do not change. ○ The three men remained silent. ○ The government remained in control. ○ He remained a formidable opponent.

▶ **COLLOCATIONS:**
remain a **mystery/threat/secret/priority**
remain a **possibility/favourite**
remain **unchanged/silent/open/unclear**

▶ **SYNONYM:** continue

re|new|able /rɪ'njuːəbəl, AM -'nuː-/ `SCIENCE`

ADJECTIVE **Renewable** resources are natural ones such as wind, water, and sunlight which are always available. ○ *Wind turbines are devices which make use of renewable energy sources.* ○ *each winter's endlessly renewable supply of frozen water*

▸ **COLLOCATION:** a renewable **resource/fuel/source**

▸ **PHRASE:** a renewable energy source

▸ **ANTONYM:** non-renewable

re|port /rɪ'pɔːt/ (reports, reporting, reported)

VERB If you **report** something that has happened, you tell people about it. ○ [+ *that*] *Researchers reported that the incidence of the condition was rising significantly.* ○ *New cases are being reported more accurately.* ○ [+ *as*] *The foreign secretary is reported as saying that force will have to be used if diplomacy fails.*

▸ **COLLOCATIONS:**
report a **profit/loss**
a **newspaper/company/study/researcher/witness** reports

▸ **SYNONYMS:** relate, inform, communicate

rep|re|sent /ˌreprɪ'zent/ (represents, representing, represented)

1 VERB If you say that something **represents** a change, achievement, or victory, you mean that it is a change, achievement, or victory. [FORMAL or WRITTEN] ○ *These developments represented a major change in the established order.*

▸ **COLLOCATION:** represent a **difference/increase/shift/step**

2 VERB If a sign or symbol **represents** something, it is accepted as meaning that thing. ○ *a black dot in the middle of the circle is supposed to represent the source of the radiation*

▸ **SYNONYMS:** symbolize, signify

rep|re|senta|tive /ˌreprɪ'zentətɪv/

ADJECTIVE Someone who is typical of the group to which they belong can be described as **representative**. ○ [+ *of*] *He was in no way representative of dog-trainers in general.* ○ *fairly representative groups of adults*

▸ **COLLOCATIONS:**
representative **of** someone/something
representative of a **population/community**
a representative **sample/selection/range**
broadly representative

▸ **SYNONYMS:** typical, characteristic

▸ **ANTONYMS:** unrepresentative, atypical, uncharacteristic

re|pub|lic /rɪˈpʌblɪk/ (republics)　　ACADEMIC WORD　POLITICS

NOUN A **republic** is a country where power is held by the people or the representatives that they elect. Republics have presidents who are elected, rather than kings or queens. ○ *In 1918, Austria became a republic.* ○ *the Baltic republics* ○ [+ *of*] *the Republic of Ireland*

▶ **COLLOCATIONS:**
　the Republic **of** *x*
　a **breakaway/banana/separatist/island** republic

▶ **RELATED WORD:** monarchy

re|pub|li|can /rɪˈpʌblɪkən/

1 ADJECTIVE Republican means relating to a republic. In **republican** systems of government, power is held by the people or the representatives that they elect. ○ *the nations that had adopted the republican form of government*

▶ **COLLOCATION:** a republican **movement/leadership/parliament/cause**

2 ADJECTIVE In the United States, if someone is **Republican**, they belong to or support the Republican Party. ○ *Republican voters* ○ *Some families have been republican for generations.*

● A **Republican** is someone who supports or belongs to the Republican Party. ○ *What made you decide to become a Republican?*

▶ **COLLOCATION:** a **congressional/moderate/conservative** Republican
▶ **RELATED WORD:** Democrat

re|quest /rɪˈkwest/ (requests, requesting, requested)

1 VERB If you **request** something, you ask for it politely or formally. [FORMAL] ○ *The governor had requested a police presence to ensure external security.* ○ [+ *that*] *The Prime Minister requested that a State of Emergency be declared.*

▶ **COLLOCATIONS:**
　request **information/anonymity/permission**
　a **letter/customer** requests *something*
　formally/respectfully/specifically request *something*

▶ **SYNONYM:** ask for

2 NOUN If you make a **request**, you politely or formally ask someone to do something. ○ [+ *for*] *France had agreed to his request for political asylum.* ○ *Vietnam made an official request that the meeting be postponed.* ○ *a request, not a demand*

▶ **COLLOCATIONS:**
　a request **for** *something*
　a request for **information/assistance/help**
　receive/reject/refuse/deny/grant a request

▶ **SYNONYM:** appeal

re|quire /rɪˈkwaɪə/ (requires, requiring, required) `ACADEMIC WORD`

1 VERB If you **require** something or if something **is required**, you need it or it is necessary. [FORMAL] ○ *If you require further information, you should consult the registrar.* ○ [+ to-inf] *This isn't the kind of crisis that requires us to drop everything else.*

▶ **COLLOCATIONS:**
  require **surgery/treatment/attention**
  require **information/effort/investment**

▶ **SYNONYM:** need

2 VERB If a law or rule **requires** you **to** do something, you have to do it. [FORMAL] ○ [+ to-inf] *The rules also require employers to provide safety training.* ○ [+ that] *The law now requires that parents serve on the committees that plan and evaluate school programs.* ○ [+ of] *Then he'll know exactly what's required of him.*

▶ **COLLOCATIONS:**
  require *something* **of** *someone*
  the **law/rules/regulations** require *something*
  require *someone* to **pay/provide/attend/report**

▶ **SYNONYMS:** order, demand, oblige, instruct

re|quire|ment /rɪˈkwaɪəmənt/ (requirements)

1 NOUN A **requirement** is a quality or qualification that you must have in order to be allowed to do something or to be suitable for something. ○ *Its products met all legal requirements.* ○ [+ for] *Graduate status is the minimum requirement for entry to the teaching profession.*

▶ **COLLOCATIONS:**
  a requirement **for** *something*
  a requirement for **membership/entry**
  meet/satisfy/fulfil/impose/set a requirement
  the **minimum** requirement
  a **legal/statutory/essential** requirement
  entry/visa/registration/safety requirements

▶ **SYNONYMS:** condition, qualification, stipulation, specification

2 NOUN Your **requirements** are the things that you need. [FORMAL] ○ *Variations of this programme can be arranged to suit your requirements.* ○ [+ of] *a packaged food which provides 100 percent of your daily requirement of one vitamin*

▶ **COLLOCATIONS:**
  requirement **of** *something*
  daily/minimum/basic/essential requirements

▶ **SYNONYMS:** necessity, essential

re|serve /rɪˈzɜːv/ (reserves)

NOUN A **reserve** is a supply of something that is available for use when it is needed. ○ *The Gulf has 65 per cent of the world's oil reserves.* ○ [+ of] *Having a*

reserve of 24 hours' worth of water is the standard across Canada.

▶ COLLOCATIONS:
a reserve **of** *something*
reserves of **energy/oil/gas/strength/courage**
maintain/establish/deplete/replenish reserves
oil/gas/currency/gold reserves

▶ SYNONYMS: store, stock, supply

---

re|source /rɪˈzɔːs, AM ˈriːsɔːrs/ (resources)   `ACADEMIC WORD`

1 NOUN The **resources** of an organization or person are the materials, money, and other things that they have and can use in order to function properly. ○ *Some families don't have the resources to feed themselves properly.* ○ *There's a great shortage of resource materials in many schools.*

▶ COLLOCATIONS:
allocate/devote/commit/lack/stretch/limit resources
human/financial/limited resources
resource **management**

▶ SYNONYM: supplies

2 NOUN A country's **resources** are the things that it has and can use to increase its wealth, such as coal, oil, or land. ○ *resources like coal, tungsten, oil and copper* ○ *Today we are overpopulated, straining the earth's resources.*

▶ COLLOCATIONS:
natural/water/energy/mineral resources
the **world's/earth's** resources
a **country's/nation's** resources

▶ SYNONYMS: assets, materials

---

re|spect /rɪˈspekt/ (respects)

1 PHRASE You use expressions like **in this respect** and **in many respects** to indicate that what you are saying applies to the feature you have just mentioned or to many features of something. ○ *The children are not unintelligent – in fact, they seem quite normal in this respect.* ○ *In many respects Asian women see themselves as equal to their men.*

2 PHRASE You use **with respect to** to say what something relates to. In British English, you can also say **in respect of**. [FORMAL] ○ *Parents often have little choice with respect to the way their child is medically treated.* ○ *Where Dr Shapland feels the system is not working most effectively is in respect of professional training.*

▶ SYNONYMS: concerning, regarding, apropos of

---

re|spec|tive /rɪˈspektɪv/

ADJECTIVE Respective means relating or belonging separately to the individual people you are referring to. ○ *Steve and I were at very different stages*

in our respective careers. ○ *the respective roles of men and women*
▸ **COLLOCATION:** respective **class/division/category**
▸ **SYNONYMS:** own, particular, relevant, corresponding

re|spec|tive|ly /rɪˈspɛktɪvli/

ADVERB Respectively means in the same order as the items that you have just mentioned. ○ *Their sons, Ben and Jonathan, were three and six respectively.* ○ *Obesity and high blood pressure occurred in 16 per cent and 14 per cent of Australian adults, respectively.*
▸ **SYNONYM:** correspondingly

---

re|spond /rɪˈspɒnd/ (responds, responding, responded)   ACADEMIC WORD

VERB When you **respond** to something that is done or said, you react to it by doing or saying something yourself. ○ [+ to] *They are likely to respond positively to the President's request for aid.* ○ [+ with] *The army responded with gunfire and tear gas.*
▸ **COLLOCATIONS:**
respond **to/with** *something*
respond with **enthusiasm/generosity/applause/gunfire**
the **government/police/audience** responds
respond **quickly/positively/immediately/appropriately**

re|sponse /rɪˈspɒns/ (responses)

NOUN ○ [+ to/from] *There has been no response to his remarks from the government.* ○ *Your positive response will reinforce her actions.* ○ [+ to] *The meeting was called in response to a request from Venezuela.*
▸ **COLLOCATIONS:**
a response **to/from** *someone/something*
elicit a response
a **positive/overwhelming/delighted/surprising** response
a **swift/predictable/immediate/appropriate** response
▸ **PHRASES:**
a rapid response team
in response to something

EXTEND YOUR VOCABULARY

When you say or write something because someone has asked you a question, you **answer** or **reply**. You can also **reply to** a letter or message that someone has sent you. **Reply** is slightly more formal than **answer**. ○ *He answered their questions politely.* ○ *Due to the volume of inquiries, it may not be possible to reply individually to all users.*

You can use **respond** or **react** when you say or write something, or when you do something. **Respond** is more formal than **reply**. A **response** is always a direct result of a question or request. ○ *The company did not respond to requests for comment.* ○ *Moscow responded immediately by lifting the economic sanctions.*

A **reaction** can be caused by many different things, including events around you. ○ *Unions reacted with anger to the job losses.*

re|strict /rɪ'strɪkt/ (restricts, restricting, restricted) `ACADEMIC WORD`

1 VERB If you **restrict** something, you put a limit on it in order to reduce it or prevent it becoming too great. ○ *There is talk of raising the admission requirements to restrict the number of students on campus.* ○ [+ to] *The French, I believe, restrict Japanese imports to a maximum of 3 per cent of their market.*

2 VERB To **restrict** the movement or actions of someone or something means to prevent them from moving or acting freely. ○ *Villagers say the fence would restrict public access to the hills.* ○ *These dams restricted the flow of the river downstream.*

▶ **COLLOCATIONS:**
restrict something **to** something
restrict **access** to something
a **law/regulation** restricts something
restrict **imports/ freedom/movement/use**
severely restrict
▶ **SYNONYMS:** limit, restrain

re|stric|tion /rɪ'strɪkʃən/ (restrictions)

NOUN ○ [+ on] *Some restriction on funding was necessary.* ○ [+ of] *the justification for this restriction of individual liberty* ○ [+ on] *the lifting of restrictions on political parties*

▶ **COLLOCATIONS:**
a restriction **of/on** something
restrictions on **imports/trade**
impose/place/lift a restriction
necessary/tight/severe/legal restrictions
travel/investment/ownership/speed restrictions
▶ **SYNONYMS:** limitation, control
▶ **ANTONYM:** freedom

re|sult /rɪ'zʌlt/ (results, resulting, resulted)

1 VERB If something **results in** a particular situation or event, it causes that situation or event to happen. ○ [+ in] *Fifty per cent of road accidents result in head injuries.* ○ [+ in] *Continuous rain resulted in the land becoming submerged.*

▶ **COLLOCATIONS:**
result **in** something
result in **death/arrest**

result in a **loss/reduction/increase**

▶ **SYNONYMS:** cause, lead to

2 VERB If something **results from** a particular event or action, it is caused by that event or action. ○ [+ *from*] *Many hair problems result from what you eat.* ○ *Ignore the early warnings and illness could result.*

▶ **COLLOCATIONS:**
result **from** *something*
result from **use/exposure**
result from a **failure/lack**

▶ **SYNONYMS:** follow, develop, ensue

re|sult|ant /rɪˈzʌltənt/

ADJECTIVE Resultant means caused by the event just mentioned. [FORMAL] ○ *At least a quarter of a million people have died in the fighting and the resultant famines.*

▶ **COLLOCATION:** resultant **mess/confusion/chaos**

▶ **SYNONYMS:** consequent, ensuing

---

re|tail /ˈriːteɪl/   `BUSINESS`

UNCOUNTABLE NOUN Retail is the activity of selling goods direct to the public, usually in small quantities. ○ *retail stores* ○ *Retail sales grew just 3.8 percent last year.* ○ *The companies had come to sell - retail, wholesale or export.*

▶ **COLLOCATION:** retail **sales/prices/stores**

▶ **RELATED WORD:** wholesale

re|tail|er /ˈriːteɪlə/ (retailers)

NOUN A **retailer** is a person or business that sells goods to the public. ○ *Furniture and carpet retailers are among those reporting the sharpest annual decline in sales.* ○ *These can be purchased at many retailers and specialist medical suppliers.*

▶ **COLLOCATIONS:**
a **major/online/electrical/independent** retailer
a **clothing/discount/furniture/fashion** retailer

▶ **RELATED WORD:** wholesaler

---

re|tain /rɪˈteɪn/ (retains, retaining, retained)   `ACADEMIC WORD`

VERB To **retain** something means to continue to have that thing. [FORMAL] ○ *The interior of the shop still retains a nineteenth-century atmosphere.* ○ *Other countries retained their traditional and habitual ways of doing things.*

→ see note at **maintain**.

▶ **COLLOCATION:** retain **control/power/rights/links/moisture/heat**

▶ **SYNONYMS:** keep, maintain, preserve

▶ **ANTONYM:** lose

re|ten|tion /rɪˈtenʃən/

UNCOUNTABLE NOUN [FORMAL] ○ [+ of] *They supported the retention of a strong central government.* ○ *A deficiency in magnesium increases lead absorption and retention.*

▶ **COLLOCATIONS:**
the retention **of** something
the retention of **organs/staff/power**
cause/ensure the retention of something
improve/increase/reduce the retention of something
fluid/water/data/customer retention

▶ **PHRASE:** recruitment and retention

re|trieve /rɪˈtriːv/ (retrieves, retrieving, retrieved) 〔IT〕

VERB To **retrieve** information from a computer or from your memory means to get it back. ○ *Computers can instantly retrieve millions of information bits.* ○ *As the child gets older, so his or her strategies for storing and retrieving information improve.*

▶ **COLLOCATION:** retrieve **information/data**
▶ **PHRASE:** store and retrieve

re|triev|al /rɪˈtriːvəl/

UNCOUNTABLE NOUN ○ *electronic storage and retrieval systems* ○ [+ of] *the study of the organisation and retrieval of memories*

▶ **COLLOCATIONS:**
the retrieval **of** something
data/image/information retrieval

▶ **PHRASE:** storage and retrieval

re|veal /rɪˈviːl/ (reveals, revealing, revealed) 〔ACADEMIC WORD〕

VERB To **reveal** something means to make people aware of it. ○ *She has refused to reveal the whereabouts of her daughter.* ○ [+ that] *A survey of the British diet has revealed that a growing number of people are overweight.* ○ [+ how] *No test will reveal how much of the drug was taken.*

▶ **COLLOCATIONS:**
reveal a **secret/identity/plan**
reveal **details/information**
a **report/study/investigation/examination** reveals something
publicly/sensationally/exclusively reveal something

▶ **SYNONYMS:** disclose, divulge, uncover
▶ **ANTONYM:** hide

re|verse /rɪˈvɜːs/ (reverses, reversing, reversed)

`ACADEMIC WORD`

1 VERB When someone or something **reverses** a decision, policy, or trend, they change it to the opposite decision, policy, or trend. ○ *They have made it clear they will not reverse the decision to increase prices.* ○ *The rise, the first in 10 months, reversed the downward trend in Belgium's jobless rate.*

▶ **COLLOCATIONS:**
 reverse a **decision/policy/ruling**
 a **court** reverses *something*
 reverse a **situation/trend/decline**

▶ **SYNONYMS:** change, overrule, overturn

2 VERB If you **reverse** the order of a set of things, you arrange them in the opposite order, so that the first thing comes last. ○ *The normal word order is reversed in passive sentences.*

▶ **COLLOCATION:** reverse the **order/direction**

3 ADJECTIVE Reverse means opposite to what you expect or to what has just been described. ○ *The wrong attitude will have exactly the reverse effect.*

▶ **COLLOCATION:** the reverse **effect**

▶ **SYNONYM:** opposite

re|ver|sal /rɪˈvɜːsəl/ (reversals)

NOUN A **reversal of** a process, policy, or trend is a complete change in it. ○ [+ *of*] *The Financial Times says the move represents a complete reversal of previous U.S. policy.* ○ [+ *of*] *This marked a 7% increase on the previous year and the reversal of a steady five-year downward trend.*

▶ **COLLOCATIONS:**
 a reversal **of** *something*
 a reversal of a **policy/position/trend**
 mark/represent/cause/experience/suffer a reversal
 a reversal **occurs/comes**
 a **dramatic/complete/sudden/sharp** reversal

▶ **ANTONYM:** implementation

re|view /rɪˈvjuː/ (reviews, reviewing, reviewed)

1 NOUN A **review of** a situation or system is its formal examination by people in authority. This is usually done in order to see whether it can be improved or corrected. ○ [+ *of*] *The president ordered a review of U.S. economic aid to Jordan.* ○ *The White House quickly announced that the policy is under review.*

▶ **COLLOCATIONS:**
 under review
 a review **of** *something*
 a review of a **policy/decision/law**

conduct/launch/announce/order a review
come up for review
a **judicial/independent/comprehensive** review
a **spending/pay/defence** review
a review **panel/board/committee/body/process**

▶ SYNONYMS: revision, reassessment

2 NOUN A literature **review** is a summary of what has been written before on a subject. ○ *Literature reviews form a substantial part of any higher degree dissertation.*

3 VERB If you **review** a situation or system, you consider it carefully to see what is wrong with it or how it could be improved. ○ *The Prime Minister reviewed the situation with his Cabinet yesterday.* ○ *The next day we reviewed the previous day's work.*

▶ COLLOCATIONS:
review a **situation/proposal/case/document**
review *something's* **effectiveness/progress**
review the **evidence/legislation**
peer review

▶ SYNONYM: evaluation

---

re|vise /rɪˈvaɪz/ (revises, revising, revised)   `ACADEMIC WORD`

VERB If you **revise** something, you alter it to make it better or more accurate. ○ *He soon came to revise his opinion of the profession.* ○ *The United Nations has been forced to revise its estimates of population growth upwards.* ○ *[+ for] the work of revising articles for publication* ○ *The staff should work together to revise the school curriculum.*

▶ COLLOCATIONS:
revise *something* **for** *something*
a revised **version/edition/estimate/figure/offer**
revise a **forecast/plan/rule/proposal**
a **government/official/analyst** revises *something*
revise *something* **upward/downward**

▶ SYNONYMS: change, alter, amend

re|vi|sion /rɪˈvɪʒən/ (revisions)

NOUN ○ *The phase of writing that is actually most important is revision.* ○ *[+ of] A major addition to the earlier revisions of the questionnaire is the job requirement exercise.*

▶ COLLOCATIONS:
a revision **of** *something*
revision of **history/policy/rules/laws**

need/require/undergo revision
propose/undertake/approve a revision
minor/substantial/extensive/radical revision

▶ **SYNONYMS:** editing, correction, alteration

---

revo|lu|tion /ˌrevəˈluːʃən/ [ACADEMIC WORD] [HISTORY] [POLITICS]
(revolutions)

1 NOUN A **revolution** is a successful attempt by a large group of people to change the political system of their country by force. ○ *The period since the revolution has been one of political turmoil.* ○ *after the French Revolution* ○ *before the 1917 Revolution*

▶ **COLLOCATIONS:**
a revolution **begins/occurs/happens/fails**
a **quiet/peaceful/democratic/velvet** revolution
the **French/Russian** Revolution

▶ **SYNONYMS:** revolt, uprising

2 NOUN A **revolution** in a particular area of human activity is an important change in that area. ○ *[+ in] The nineteenth century witnessed a revolution in ship design and propulsion.* ○ *the industrial revolution*

▶ **COLLOCATIONS:**
a revolution **in** *something*
a revolution in **technology/communications/medicine/thinking**
undergo a revolution
a **cultural/industrial/digital/technological** revolution

▶ **SYNONYMS:** transformation, reformation

revo|lu|tion|ary /ˌrevəˈluːʃənri, AM -neri/

1 ADJECTIVE Revolutionary activities, organizations, or people have the aim of causing a political revolution. ○ *Do you know anything about the revolutionary movement?* ○ *the Cuban revolutionary leader, Jose Marti*

▶ **COLLOCATIONS:**
a revolutionary **movement/struggle/leader**
revolutionary **forces/change/upheaval**

▶ **SYNONYMS:** rebel, radical

2 ADJECTIVE Revolutionary ideas and developments involve great changes in the way that something is done or made. ○ *Invented in 1951, the rotary engine is a revolutionary concept in internal combustion.*

▶ **COLLOCATION:** a revolutionary **concept/invention/approach**

▶ **SYNONYMS:** innovative, radical, ground-breaking

revo|lu|tion|ize /ˌrevəˈluːʃənaɪz/
(revolutionizes, revolutionizing, revolutionized)

VERB When something **revolutionizes** an activity, it causes great changes in the way that it is done. [in BRIT, also use **revolutionise**] ○ *Over the past forty years plastics have revolutionised the way we live.* ○ *Automation revolutionized the olive industry in the early 1970s.*
- ▶ COLLOCATIONS:
  revolutionize a **field/treatment/industry**
  revolutionize **travel/communication**
- ▶ SYNONYM: transform

---

right-wing /ˈraɪt ˌwɪŋ/
`POLITICS`

ADJECTIVE A **right-wing** person or group has conservative or capitalist views. ○ *a right-wing government* ○ *Liberals say the paper is too right-wing.*
- ▶ COLLOCATIONS:
  a right-wing **extremist/politician/conspiracy/agenda**
  right-wing **politics**
- ▶ SYNONYMS: conservative, reactionary
- ▶ ANTONYM: left-wing

---

ro|tate /rəʊˈteɪt, AM ˈrəʊteɪt/ **(rotates, rotating, rotated)**

VERB When something **rotates** or when you **rotate** it, it turns with a circular movement. ○ *The Earth rotates round the sun.* ○ *Take each foot in both your hands and rotate it to loosen and relax the ankle.*
- ▶ COLLOCATIONS:
  the **Earth/sun** rotates
  something rotates a **blade/cylinder/disc**
  rotate **gently/constantly/rapidly/clockwise**
- ▶ SYNONYMS: revolve, turn, spin

ro|ta|tion /rəʊˈteɪʃən/ **(rotations)**

NOUN ○ [+ *of*] *the daily rotation of the earth upon its axis* ○ [+ *of*] *the point of rotation of the lever arms*
- ▶ COLLOCATIONS:
  the rotation **of** *something*
  a **daily/rapid/clockwise** rotation
- ▶ SYNONYMS: revolution, gyration, spinning

route /ruːt/ (routes)

ACADEMIC WORD

Pronounced /ruːt/ or /raʊt/ in American English.

NOUN A **route** is a way from one place to another. ○ [+ to] *the most direct route to the town centre* ○ *All escape routes were blocked by armed police.* ○ [+ from] *Tens of thousands lined the route from Dublin airport.*

▶ **COLLOCATIONS:**
  a route **to/from** *somewhere*
  take/follow/choose/travel a route
  establish/line/block a route
  a **main/direct/circuitous/alternative/scenic** route
  a **trade/escape/supply/bus** route
  a route **map/network**

rule /ruːl/ (rules, ruling, ruled)

LAW

VERB When someone in authority **rules** that something is true or should happen, they state that they have officially decided that it is true or should happen. [FORMAL] ○ [+ that] *The court ruled that laws passed by the assembly remained valid.* ○ [+ on] *The Israeli court has not yet ruled on the case.* ○ *A provincial magistrates' court last week ruled it unconstitutional.* ○ [+ against] *The committee ruled against all-night opening mainly on safety grounds.*

▶ **COLLOCATIONS:**
  rule **on/against/in favour of** *something*
  a **judge/court/panel/jury** rules
  rule **unanimously**
  rule on a **case/issue**

▶ **SYNONYMS:** pronounce, decide, judge

r

Ss

---

sam|ple /ˈsɑːmpəl, ˈsæm-/ (samples)

1 NOUN A **sample** of a substance is a small amount of it that is examined and analysed scientifically. ○ [+ of] *Samples of blood were taken for DNA testing.*
○ *a robotic mission that would collect rock and soil samples for more detailed analysis*

▶ **COLLOCATIONS:**
a sample **of** *something*
a sample of **blood/fluid/saliva**
a **urine/tissue/blood/soil** sample
take/collect/analyze/test a sample

▶ **SYNONYM:** specimen

2 NOUN A **sample** of people or things is a number of them chosen out of a larger group and then used in tests or used to provide information about the whole group. ○ [+ of] *We based our analysis on a random sample of more than 200 males.* ○ *The sample size used in the study was too small.*

▶ **COLLOCATIONS:**
a sample **of** *people*
a sample of **adults/voters**
a **random** sample
sample **size**

▶ **SYNONYM:** selection

---

sat|el|lite /ˈsætəlaɪt/ (satellites)　　SCIENCE

1 NOUN A **satellite** is an object which has been sent into space in order to collect information or to be part of a communications system. Satellites move continually round the Earth or around another planet. ○ *The rocket launched two communications satellites.* ○ *The signals are sent by satellite link.*

▶ **COLLOCATIONS:**
launch/deploy a satellite
a **communications** satellite
satellite **navigation/communication/tracking**

2 NOUN A **satellite** is a natural object in space that moves round a planet or star. ○ *the satellites of Jupiter*

▶ **COLLOCATION:** a satellite **orbits** *something*

▶ **SYNONYM:** moon

sat|is|fy /'sætɪsfaɪ/ (satisfies, satisfying, satisfied)

1 VERB To **satisfy** someone **that** something is true or has been done properly means to convince them by giving them more information or by showing them what has been done. ○ [+ that] *He has to satisfy the environmental lobby that real progress will be made to cut emissions.* ○ [+ that] *The statisticians were satisfied that the sample and the evidence were sufficient.*

▶ SYNONYMS: convince, persuade

2 VERB If you **satisfy** the requirements for something, you are good enough or have the right qualities to fulfil these requirements. ○ *The procedures should satisfy certain basic requirements.*

▶ COLLOCATIONS:
satisfy **requirements/objectives**
fully/reasonably/completely satisfy

▶ SYNONYMS: fulfil, meet

sat|is|fac|tory /ˌsætɪs'fæktəri/

ADJECTIVE Something that is **satisfactory** is acceptable to you or fulfils a particular need or purpose. ○ *The concept of instinct is not a satisfactory explanation of human behavior.* ○ *It seemed a very satisfactory arrangement.*

▶ COLLOCATIONS:
a satisfactory **conclusion/answer/outcome/solution**
a satisfactory **explanation/condition**
mutually/wholly/entirely satisfactory

▶ SYNONYMS: acceptable, adequate

▶ ANTONYMS: unsatisfactory, inadequate

scale /skeɪl/ (scales)

1 NOUN If you refer to the **scale** of something, you are referring to its size or extent, especially when it is very big. ○ [+ of] *However, he underestimates the scale of the problem.* ○ *The break-down of law and order could result in killing on a massive scale.*

▶ COLLOCATIONS:
the scale **of** *something*
the scale of a **problem/task/challenge/crisis/disaster**
a **grand/massive/vast/global** scale

▶ PHRASE: full-scale/large-scale/small-scale

> **EXTEND YOUR VOCABULARY**
>
> There are a number of words used in academic writing to talk about the size of something.
>
> You use **scale** and **extent** to talk about how large or serious something is. ○ *They didn't realize the scale/extent of the problem.*

> You use **range** and **scope** to refer to the number of things that
> something includes. ○ *They want to widen the range of goods available.*
> ○ *This limits the scope of the investigation.*

2 NOUN A **scale** is a set of levels or numbers which are used in a particular
system of measuring things or are used when comparing things. ○ *an
earthquake measuring five-point-five on the Richter scale* ○ *The higher up the social
scale they are, the more the men have to lose.*

▶ **COLLOCATIONS:**
the **Richter** scale
a **pay/salary/sliding** scale
the **social** scale

▶ **SYNONYM:** ranking

3 NOUN The **scale** of a map, plan, or model is the relationship between the
size of something in the map, plan, or model and its size in the real world.
○ [+ *of*] *The map, on a scale of 1:10,000, shows over 5,000 individual paths.*

▶ **COLLOCATIONS:**
a scale **of** *x*
a scale **model/drawing/replica**

---

scheme /skiːm/ (schemes) `ACADEMIC WORD`

NOUN A **scheme** is a plan or arrangement involving many people which is
made by a government or other organization. [mainly BRIT; in AM, use
program] ○ *schemes to help combat unemployment* ○ *a private pension scheme*

▶ **COLLOCATIONS:**
a **pension/compensation/insurance** scheme
a **housing/training/pilot** scheme
devise/launch/propose a scheme

▶ **SYNONYMS:** plan, system, programme

---

schol|ar|ship /ˈskɒləʃɪp/ (scholarships) `EDUCATION` `ACADEMIC STUDY`

NOUN If you get a **scholarship** to a school or university, your studies are paid
for by the school or university or by some other organization. ○ [+ *to*] *He got a
scholarship to the Pratt Institute of Art.* ○ *Scholarships are awarded on the basis of
academic achievement.* ○ *scholarships for women over 30*

▶ **COLLOCATIONS:**
a scholarship **to** *somewhere*
award/offer/win/receive a scholarship
a scholarship **holder/fund/programme**
a **college/university** scholarship

▶ **SYNONYMS:** bursary, grant, funding

scope /skəʊp/ ACADEMIC WORD

NOUN The **scope of** an activity, topic, or piece of work is the whole area which it deals with or includes. ○ [+ of] *Mr Dobson promised to widen the organisation's scope of activity.* ○ *the scope of a novel*

→ see note at **scale**

▶ COLLOCATIONS:
the scope **of** *something*
the scope of a **project/investigation/inquiry**
broaden/widen/expand/extend the scope of *something*

▶ SYNONYMS: scale, extent, range

screen /skriːn/ (screens, screening, screened) MEDICINE

VERB To **screen for** a disease means to examine people to make sure that they do not have it. ○ [+ for] *a quick saliva test that would screen for people at risk of tooth decay* ○ [+ for] *Men over 50 are routinely screened for prostate abnormalities.*

▶ COLLOCATIONS:
screen **for** *something*
screen for a **disease/abnormality/condition**
screen for **TB/diabetes/cancer**
screen a **patient/donor**
routinely/properly screen

▶ SYNONYMS: check, examine

screen|ing /ˈskriːnɪŋ/

NOUN ○ [+ for] *Britain has an enviable record on breast screening for cancer.* ○ *people participating in cancer screening programmes*

▶ COLLOCATIONS:
screening **for** *something*
a screening **programme/procedure/test**
cervical/breast/cancer screening
prenatal/antenatal screening

sec|ond|ary /ˈsekəndri, AM -deri/

ADJECTIVE If you describe something as **secondary**, you mean that it is less important than something else. ○ *The street erupted in a huge explosion, with secondary explosions in the adjoining buildings.* ○ *The actual damage to the brain cells is secondary to the damage caused to the blood supply.*

▶ COLLOCATIONS:
a secondary **objective/market/explosion**
seem/become secondary

▶ PHRASE: of secondary importance

▶ RELATED WORD: primary

sec|tor /'sektə/ (sectors)
ACADEMIC WORD | BUSINESS

NOUN A particular **sector** of a country's economy is the part connected with that specified type of industry. ○ *the nation's manufacturing sector* ○ *the service sector of the Hong Kong economy*

▶ **COLLOCATIONS:**
a sector **of** *something*
a sector of **industry/the economy**
the **private/public/voluntary** sector
the **manufacturing/technology/service/banking/retail** sector

se|cure /sɪ'kjʊə/
ACADEMIC WORD

ADJECTIVE A **secure** place is tightly locked or well protected, so that people cannot enter it or leave it. ○ *We shall make sure our home is as secure as possible from now on.* ○ *The building has secure undercover parking for 27 vehicles.*

▶ **COLLOCATIONS:**
secure **parking/accommodation**
a secure **unit/place/area/location**
make *something* secure

▶ **PHRASE:** safe and secure

▶ **SYNONYMS:** safe, guarded, protected

se|cure|ly /sɪ'kjʊəli/

ADVERB ○ *He locked the heavy door securely and kept the key in his pocket.* ○ *territory once securely under the control of the rebels*

▶ **COLLOCATION:** **fasten/store/lock/attach/fix** *something* securely

▶ **PHRASE:** safely and securely

▶ **SYNONYM:** safely

seek /siːk/ (seeks, seeking, sought)
ACADEMIC WORD

VERB If you **seek** something, you try to find it or obtain it. [FORMAL] ○ *Four people who sought refuge in the Italian embassy have left voluntarily.* ○ [+ for] *Candidates are urgently sought for the post of Conservative Party chairman.* ○ *Always seek professional legal advice before entering into any agreement.* ○ [+ from] *The couple have sought help from marriage guidance counsellors.*

▶ **COLLOCATIONS:**
seek *something* **from** *someone*
be sought **for** *something*
seek **help/advice/refuge/treatment**
seek **approval/permission/compensation**
actively/eagerly/urgently/desperately/unsuccessfully seek

▶ **SYNONYMS:** look for, pursue

S

seg|ment /ˈsegmənt/ (segments)

1 **NOUN** A **segment of** something is one part of it, considered separately from the rest. ○ [+ of] *the poorer segments of society* ○ [+ of] *the third segment of his journey*

▶ **COLLOCATIONS:**
a segment **of** *something*
a segment of **society**
a segment of the **population/public**

▶ **SYNONYMS:** section, part

2 **NOUN** A **segment** of a circle is one of the two parts into which it is divided when you draw a straight line through it. ○ *Divide the circle into segments like an orange.* ○ *The pie chart is divided into equal segments.*

▶ **COLLOCATIONS:**
a segment **of** *something*
a segment of a **circle/pie chart**

▶ **PHRASE:** divided into segments

3 **NOUN** A **segment** of a market is one part of it, considered separately from the rest. ○ [+ of] *Three-to-five day cruises are the fastest-growing segment of the market.* ○ *Women's tennis is the market leader in a growing market segment – women's sports.*

▶ **COLLOCATIONS:**
a segment **of** *something*
a segment of a **market/industry**
a **fast-growing/mid-sized/profitable** segment

▶ **SYNONYMS:** niche, sector

sel|dom /ˈseldəm/

ADVERB If something **seldom** happens, it happens only occasionally. ○ *They seldom speak.* ○ *Hypertension can be controlled but seldom cured.* ○ *The fines were seldom sufficient to force any permanent change.*

▶ **SYNONYMS:** rarely, hardly ever, infrequently

▶ **ANTONYMS:** often, frequently

se|lect /sɪˈlekt/ (selects, selecting, selected) `ACADEMIC WORD`

VERB If you **select** something, you choose it from a number of things of the same kind. ○ *Voters are selecting candidates for both U.S. Senate seats and for 52 congressional seats.* ○ *a randomly selected sample of school children*

▶ **COLLOCATIONS:**
select **for/from** *something*
select for **inclusion/testing/training**
select from a **list/shortlist/menu/range**
select a **candidate/delegate/winner/sample/option**

randomly/carefully/specially selected

▶ SYNONYMS: choose, pick out

se|lec|tion /sɪ'lekʃən/ (selections)

1 UNCOUNTABLE NOUN **Selection** is the act of selecting one or more people or things from a group. ○ *Darwin's principles of natural selection* ○ *Dr. Sullivan's selection to head the Department of Health was greeted with satisfaction.*

▶ COLLOCATIONS:
a **jury/team** selection
natural/Darwinian selection
a selection **process/panel/committee**

▶ SYNONYM: choice

2 NOUN A **selection of** people or things is a set of them that have been selected from a larger group. ○ [+ *of*] *a random selection of 1,300 Canadian exporters* ○ *selections from Dickens' A Christmas Carol*

▶ COLLOCATIONS:
a selection **of** *something*
a **huge/limited/random** selection

▶ SYNONYM: sample

---

semi|nar /'semɪnɑː/ (seminars) `EDUCATION` `ACADEMIC STUDY`

1 NOUN A **seminar** is a meeting where a group of people discuss a problem or topic. ○ *a series of half-day seminars to help businessmen get the best value from investing in information technology* ○ [+ *on*] *We conduct seminars on Immigration and Discrimination Law.*

2 NOUN A **seminar** is a class at a college or university in which the teacher and a small group of students discuss a topic. ○ *Students are asked to prepare material in advance of each weekly seminar.* ○ [+ *on*] *a seminar on a topic closely related to the course*

▶ COLLOCATIONS:
a seminar **on** *something*
attend/organize/conduct/hold a seminar
a seminar **room/topic/series/programme**
a **weekly/two-hour/three-day** seminar

▶ SYNONYMS: meeting, tutorial, workshop

---

sen|tence /'sentəns/ (sentences, sentencing, sentenced) `LAW`

1 NOUN In a law court, a **sentence** is the punishment that a person receives after they have been found guilty of a crime. ○ *They are already serving prison sentences for their part in the assassination.* ○ *He was given a four-year sentence.* ○ *The offences carry a maximum sentence of 10 years.* ○ *The court is expected to pass sentence later today.*

▶ COLLOCATIONS:
a sentence **for** something
a sentence for **rape/murder/manslaughter**
impose/receive/face/serve/carry a sentence
pass sentence
a **maximum/suspended/custodial/jail/prison/life** sentence
▶ PHRASE: the death sentence
▶ SYNONYM: punishment

2 VERB When a judge **sentences** someone, he or she states in court what their punishment will be. ○ [+ to] *A military court sentenced him to death in his absence.* ○ *He has admitted the charge and will be sentenced later.*

▶ COLLOCATIONS:
sentence *someone* **to** *something*
sentence *someone* to **death/imprisonment**
a **judge/court** sentences *someone*
sentence a **defendant/offender/prisoner**
▶ SYNONYM: convict

---

sepa|rate /ˈsepəreɪt/ (separates, separating, separated)

1 VERB If you **separate** people or things that are together, or if they **separate**, they move apart. ○ *Police moved in to separate the two groups.* ○ [+ from] *The front end of the car separated from the rest of the vehicle.* ○ [+ from] *a process in which small molecules are separated from larger ones*

2 VERB If you **separate** people or things that have been connected, or if one **separates from** another, the connection between them is ended. ○ [+ from] *They want to separate teaching from research.* ○ *It's very possible that we may see a movement to separate the two parts of the country.*

▶ COLLOCATIONS:
separate *something* **from** *something*
surgically/physically/forcibly/successfully separate
▶ SYNONYMS: disconnect, sever, split
▶ ANTONYMS: join, connect

sepa|ra|tion /ˌsepəˈreɪʃən/ (separations)

NOUN The **separation of** two or more things or groups is the fact that they are separate or become separate, and are not linked. ○ *Early spatial separations of groups of humans facilitated the development of physical variations.* ○ [+ between] *a 'Christian republic' in which there was a clear separation between church and state*

▶ COLLOCATIONS:
separation **of/between** *things*
separation **from** *something*

S

separation of **powers/races/sexes**
racial/physical/spatial/geographical separation

▶ **PHRASE:** separation of church and state
▶ **SYNONYMS:** disconnection, split, division
▶ **ANTONYMS:** connection, link

---

se|quence /ˈsiːkwəns/ (sequences)   `ACADEMIC WORD`

1 NOUN A **sequence of** events or things is a number of events or things that come one after another in a particular order. ○ [+ of] *the sequence of events which led to the murder* ○ [+ of] *A flow chart displays the chronological sequence of steps in a process.*

2 NOUN A particular **sequence** is a particular order in which things happen or are arranged. ○ *the colour sequence yellow, orange, purple, blue, green and white* ○ *The chronological sequence gives the book an element of structure.* ○ *a simple numerical sequence*

▶ **COLLOCATIONS:**
a sequence **of** things
a sequence of **events/letters/movements/steps**
a **chronological/logical/narrative/linear/numerical** sequence

▶ **SYNONYM:** series

se|quen|tial /sɪˈkwenʃəl/

ADJECTIVE Something that is **sequential** follows a fixed order. [FORMAL]
○ *the sequential story of the universe* ○ *In this way the children are introduced to sequential learning.*

▶ **COLLOCATIONS:**
sequential **reasoning/logic**
a sequential **narrative**

▶ **SYNONYMS:** consecutive, in order

---

se|vere /sɪˈvɪə/ (severer, severest)

1 ADJECTIVE You use **severe** to indicate that something bad or undesirable is great or intense. ○ *a business with severe cash flow problems* ○ *The majority of patients with multiple personality disorder experience severe depression.*

2 ADJECTIVE **Severe** punishments or criticisms are very strong or harsh. ○ *This was a dreadful crime and a severe sentence is necessary.* ○ *But perhaps the most severe criticisms have focused upon their military dimensions.*

▶ **COLLOCATIONS:**
severe **pain/depression/weather/flooding**
severe **consequences/symptoms/damage**
a severe **injury/illness/disability/shortage**
a severe **penalty/punishment/criticism/problem**

moderately/unusually/particularly/very severe

▸ **SYNONYMS:** extreme, intense, acute, tough

▸ **ANTONYMS:** mild, slight

se|vere|ly /sɪ'vɪəli/

ADVERB ○ *The U.N. wants to send food aid to 10 countries in Africa severely affected by the drought.* ○ *An aircraft overshot the runway and was severely damaged.*
○ *a campaign to try to change the law to punish dangerous drivers more severely*

▸ **COLLOCATIONS:**
severely **damaged/injured/weakened/disabled/ill**
severely **restricted/curtailed/disrupted**
severely **punished/reprimanded/criticized**

▸ **SYNONYMS:** extremely, intensely, acutely, harshly

▸ **ANTONYMS:** mildly, slightly

se|ver|ity /sɪverɪti/

UNCOUNTABLE NOUN ○ [+ *of*] *Several drugs are used to lessen the severity of the symptoms.* ○ [+ *of*] *a series of laws to increase the severity of punishment for illicit drug use*

▸ **COLLOCATIONS:**
the severity **of** something
the severity of a **sentence/punishment/illness/injury**
assess/determine/lessen/reduce the severity of something
great/extreme severity

▸ **SYNONYMS:** extremity, intensity, toughness, harshness

▸ **ANTONYM:** mildness

---

sex /seks/ (sexes)   ACADEMIC WORD   BIOLOGY   SOCIOLOGY

1 NOUN The two **sexes** are the two groups, male and female, into which people and animals are divided according to the function they have in producing young. ○ *an entertainment star who appeals to all ages and both sexes* ○ *differences between the sexes*

▸ **COLLOCATIONS:**
the **opposite/fair** sex
same-/single-sex

▸ **PHRASE:** the sexes

▸ **SYNONYM:** gender

2 UNCOUNTABLE NOUN **Sex** is the physical activity by which people can produce young. ○ *He was very open in his attitudes about sex.* ○ *Sex education in schools was made universal.* ○ *Most diabetics have a normal sex life.*

▸ **COLLOCATIONS:**
have sex

safe/unprotected/extramarital/under-age sex
sex **education/abuse**
a sex **offender/scandal/life**
▶ **PHRASES:**
sex and drugs
sex and violence
▶ **SYNONYMS:** sexual intercourse, copulation, lovemaking

sex|ual /ˈsekʃʊəl/

1 ADJECTIVE Sexual feelings or activities are connected with the act of sex or with people's desire for sex. ○ *Many marriage troubles spring from unsatisfactory sexual relationships.* ○ *incidents of domestic violence and sexual assault*
▶ **COLLOCATIONS:**
sexual **intercourse/activity/desire/orientation**
sexual **assault/abuse**
a sexual **relationship/partner/fantasy**

2 ADJECTIVE Sexual means relating to the differences between male and female people. ○ *Women's groups denounced sexual discrimination.*
▶ **COLLOCATION:** sexual **harassment/discrimination/politics**

---

sharp /ʃɑːp/ (sharper, sharpest)

ADJECTIVE A **sharp** change, movement, or feeling occurs suddenly, and is great in amount, force, or degree. ○ *There's been a sharp rise in the rate of inflation.* ○ *a new treatment for chronic, sharp pain associated with nerve injuries*
→ see note at **dramatic**
▶ **COLLOCATION:** a sharp **rise/increase/drop/decline/fall/pain/shock**
▶ **SYNONYMS:** dramatic, abrupt, intense
▶ **ANTONYM:** gradual

sharp|ly /ˈʃɑːpli/

ADVERB ○ *Unemployment among the over forties has risen sharply in recent years.* ○ *The latest survey shows buying plans for homes are sharply lower than in June.*
▶ **COLLOCATIONS:**
rise/fall/decline/drop sharply
sharply **lower/higher**
turn/swerve/veer/brake sharply
▶ **SYNONYMS:** dramatically, markedly

---

shift /ʃɪft/ (shifts, shifting, shifted)   ACADEMIC WORD

1 VERB If you **shift** something or if it **shifts**, it moves slightly. ○ *He shifted from foot to foot.* ○ [V-ing] *Firefighters have been hampered by high temperatures and shifting winds.*

▶ COLLOCATIONS:
shift **uncomfortably/restlessly/uneasily**
shift one's **weight/position**
▶ SYNONYM: move

2 VERB If someone's opinion, a situation, or a policy **shifts** or **is shifted**, it changes slightly. ○ *Attitudes to mental illness have shifted in recent years.* ○ *The emphasis should be shifted more towards Parliament.*
▶ COLLOCATION: shift the **focus/emphasis/balance**
▶ SYNONYMS: alter, change, adjust

• **Shift** is also a noun. ○ [+ in] *a shift in government policy* ○ *The migration towards technology as a service is a cultural shift.*
▶ COLLOCATIONS:
a shift **in** something
a shift in **focus/emphasis/power/priorities/attitudes**
a **sudden/major/cultural** shift
▶ SYNONYM: change

---

short|age /ˈʃɔːtɪdʒ/ (shortages)

NOUN If there is a **shortage of** something, there is not enough of it. ○ [+ of] *A shortage of funds is preventing the U.N. from monitoring relief.* ○ *Vietnam is suffering from a food shortage.*
▶ COLLOCATIONS:
a shortage **of** something
a shortage of **labour/housing/food/teachers/doctors**
a **food/labour/skills/housing/fuel** shortage
a **chronic/severe/acute/dire** shortage
ease/alleviate/address/face/experience a shortage
▶ SYNONYM: lack
▶ ANTONYMS: excess, abundance

---

sib|ling /ˈsɪblɪŋ/ (siblings)　　BIOLOGY　SOCIOLOGY

NOUN Your **siblings** are your brothers and sisters. [FORMAL] ○ *Some studies have found that children are more friendly to younger siblings of the same sex.* ○ *Sibling rivalry often causes parents anxieties.*
▶ COLLOCATIONS:
a **younger/elder** sibling
sibling **rivalry**

---

side-effect /ˈsaɪd ɪfekt/ (side-effects) also **side effect**　　MEDICINE

NOUN The **side-effects** of a drug are the effects, usually bad ones, that the drug has on you in addition to its function of curing illness or pain. ○ *The treatment*

*has a whole host of extremely unpleasant side-effects including weight gain, acne,
skin rashes and headaches.* ○ *Most patients suffer no side-effects.*

▶ COLLOCATIONS:
  experience/suffer/have side-effects
  serious/adverse/unpleasant/possible side-effects
  side-effects **include** *something*

▶ SYNONYM: reaction

---

sig|nal /ˈsɪɡnəl/ (signals)

`PHYSICS`

NOUN A **signal** is a series of radio waves, light waves, or changes in electrical
current which may carry information. ○ *high-frequency radio signals* ○ *a means
of transmitting television signals using microwave frequencies*

▶ COLLOCATIONS:
  send/transmit/emit/broadcast a signal
  receive/detect/decode a signal
  a **clear/strong/digital/analogue/radio/satellite** signal
  signal **processing**

---

sig|nifi|cant /sɪɡˈnɪfɪkənt/

`ACADEMIC WORD`

1 ADJECTIVE A **significant** amount or effect is large enough to be important
or affect a situation to a noticeable degree. ○ *A small but significant number of
11-year-olds are illiterate.* ○ *foods that offer a significant amount of protein* ○ *The
study is too small to show whether this trend is statistically significant.*
  → see note at **dramatic**

2 ADJECTIVE A **significant** fact, event, or thing is one that is important or
shows something. ○ *Time would appear to be the significant factor in this whole
drama.* ○ *a very significant piece of legislation*

▶ COLLOCATIONS:
  a significant **amount/proportion/difference/improvement**
  a significant **change/increase/effect/factor**
  a significant **number** of *people/things*
  seem/prove/become significant
  statistically significant

▶ SYNONYMS: important, large
▶ ANTONYMS: insignificant, minor

sig|nifi|cant|ly /sɪɡˈnɪfɪkəntli/

ADVERB ○ *The groups differed significantly in two areas.* ○ *America's airlines have
significantly higher productivity than European ones.* ○ *Significantly, the company
recently opened a huge store in Atlanta.*

▶ COLLOCATIONS:
  significantly **less/more/lower/higher/different**

significantly **reduced/altered/increased/changed**
differ/fluctuate/vary/increase/improve significantly
▶ **SYNONYM:** extremely
▶ **ANTONYM:** insignificantly

sig|nifi|cance /sɪgˈnɪfɪkəns/

UNCOUNTABLE NOUN The **significance** of something is the importance that it has, usually because it will have an effect on a situation or shows something about a situation. ○ [+ of] *Ideas about the social significance of religion have changed over time.* ○ *The difference did not achieve statistical significance.*

▶ **COLLOCATIONS:**
the significance **of** something
the significance of a **discovery/event/occasion/finding**
cultural/historical/political/religious significance
great/special/symbolic/statistical significance
attach significance to something
downplay/understand/appreciate the significance of something
assume/acquire significance
▶ **SYNONYM:** importance
▶ **ANTONYM:** insignificance

sim|pli|fy /ˈsɪmplɪfaɪ/ (simplifies, simplifying, simplified)

VERB If you **simplify** something, you make it easier to understand or you remove the things which make it complex. ○ *a plan to simplify the complex social security system* ○ *technology for simplifying trade procedures* ○ *a simplified version of the formula*

▶ **COLLOCATIONS:**
simplify a **procedure/process/diagram/task**
a simplified **version**
greatly/radically/vastly simplified
▶ **ANTONYM:** complicate

sim|pli|fi|ca|tion /ˌsɪmplɪfɪˈkeɪʃən/ (simplifications)

NOUN ○ *Like any such diagram, it is a simplification.* ○ [+ of] *Everyone favours the simplification of court procedures.*

▶ **COLLOCATIONS:**
the simplification **of** something
the simplification of a **procedure/structure/rule**
▶ **ANTONYM:** complication

simu|late /ˈsɪmjʊleɪt/ (simulates, simulating, simulated) `ACADEMIC WORD`

VERB If you **simulate** a set of conditions, you create them artificially, for example in order to conduct an experiment. ○ *The scientist developed one* model to simulate a full year of the globe's climate. ○ Cars are tested to see how much damage they suffer in simulated crashes.

▶ **COLLOCATION:** simulate **conditions/altitude/gravity**

▶ **SYNONYMS:** replicate, reproduce, model

simu|la|tion /ˌsɪmjʊˈleɪʃən/ (simulations)

NOUN Simulation is the process of simulating something or the result of simulating it. ○ [+ of] Training includes realistic simulation of casualty procedures. ○ [+ of] a simulation of the greenhouse effect

▶ **COLLOCATIONS:**
simulation **of** something
computer simulation
a simulation **model/tool**

sim|ul|ta|neous /ˌsɪmɵlˈteɪniəs, AM ˌsaɪm-/

ADJECTIVE Things which are **simultaneous** happen or exist at the same time. ○ the simultaneous release of the book and the album ○ The theatre will provide simultaneous translation in both English and Chinese.

▶ **COLLOCATION:** simultaneous **translation/attacks/actions**

▶ **SYNONYM:** concurrent

▶ **ANTONYM:** separate

sim|ul|ta|neous|ly /ˌsɪmɵlˈteɪniəsli, AM ˌsaɪm-/

ADVERB ○ The two guns fired almost simultaneously. ○ a spurt in economic growth that occurred simultaneously with extensive industrial investment

▶ **COLLOCATIONS:**
occur/happen/crash/explode simultaneously
broadcast/release/publish things simultaneously
almost simultaneously

soar /sɔː/ (soars, soaring, soared)

VERB If the amount, value, level, or volume of something **soars**, it quickly increases by a great deal. ○ Insurance claims are expected to soar. ○ Figures showed customer complaints had soared to record levels and profits were falling.

▶ **COLLOCATIONS:**
shares/stocks/prices/sales/ratings soar
unemployment/confidence/inflation soars

▶ **SYNONYM:** rise

▶ **ANTONYMS:** drop, fall, plummet

so|cial|ism /ˈsəʊʃəlɪzəm/ POLITICS

UNCOUNTABLE NOUN Socialism is a set of left-wing political principles whose general aim is to create a system in which everyone has an equal opportunity to benefit from a country's wealth. Under socialism, the country's main industries are usually owned by the state. ○ *In the classical exemplar of state socialism, the Soviet Union, private property was almost completely eliminated.*

▶ COLLOCATION: **state/democratic/Marxist** socialism

▶ SYNONYMS: communism, Marxism

▶ ANTONYM: capitalism

so|cial|ist /ˈsəʊʃəlɪst/ (socialists)

1 ADJECTIVE **Socialist** means based on socialism or relating to socialism. ○ *members of the ruling Socialist party* ○ *low-inflation policies practised by the socialist government*

▶ COLLOCATIONS:
a socialist **party/state/principle/revolution**
socialist **realism/ideology**

▶ SYNONYMS: communist, Marxist, left-wing

▶ ANTONYM: capitalist

2 NOUN A **socialist** is a person who believes in socialism or who is a member of a socialist party. ○ *The French electorate voted out the socialists.*

▶ COLLOCATIONS:
a **committed/democratic/radical/moderate/champagne** socialist
the **ruling/opposition** socialists

▶ SYNONYMS: communist, liberal

▶ ANTONYM: capitalist

so|ci|ol|ogy /ˌsəʊsiˈɒlədʒi/ [SOCIOLOGY]

UNCOUNTABLE NOUN **Sociology** is the study of society or of the way society is organized. ○ *a sociology professor at the University of North Carolina* ○ *a treatise on the sociology of religion*

▶ COLLOCATIONS:
the sociology **of** *something*
the sociology of **religion/science**
a sociology **professor/lecturer/department/student**

so|cio|logi|cal /ˌsəʊsiəˈlɒdʒɪkəl/

ADJECTIVE ○ *Psychological and sociological studies were emphasizing the importance of the family.* ○ *Viewed from a sociological perspective, the president's popularity might be a result of the changing nature of our attitude toward authority.*

▶ COLLOCATIONS:
a sociological **theory/analysis/study**
a sociological **perspective/explanation/understanding**

so|ci|olo|gist /ˌsəʊsiˈɒlədʒist/ (sociologists)

NOUN ○ By the 1950s some sociologists were confident that they had identified the key characteristics of capitalist society.

so|lar /ˈsəʊlə/

SCIENCE

1 ADJECTIVE Solar is used to describe things relating to the sun. ○ a total solar eclipse ○ Snow and ice reflect 80% to 90% of solar radiation back into space.

▶ **COLLOCATIONS:**
a solar **eclipse/storm**
solar **radiation**

▶ **PHRASE:** the solar system

2 ADJECTIVE Solar power is obtained from the sun's light and heat. ○ a government effort to promote solar power ○ A solar water heater reduces electricity consumption.

▶ **COLLOCATIONS:**
solar **power/energy**
a solar **panel/cell/heater**

sol|id /ˈsɒlɪd/ (solids)

1 ADJECTIVE A **solid** substance or object stays the same shape whether it is in a container or not. ○ the potential of greatly reducing our solid waste problem ○ weaning infants onto solid food

• **Solid** is also a noun. ○ Solids turn to liquids at certain temperatures.

2 ADJECTIVE A **solid** object or mass does not have a space inside it, or holes or gaps in it. ○ a tunnel carved through 50ft of solid rock ○ a solid wall of multicoloured trees ○ a solid mass of colour ○ The car park was absolutely packed solid with people.

▶ **COLLOCATIONS:** ·
solid **waste/food**
a solid **rock/wall**
packed/frozen solid

▶ **SYNONYMS:** hard, dense

▶ **ANTONYM:** liquid

so|lu|tion /səˈluːʃən/ (solutions)

CHEMISTRY

NOUN A **solution** is a liquid in which a solid substance has been dissolved. ○ a warm solution of liquid detergent ○ Vitamins in solution are more affected than those in solid foods.

▶ **COLLOCATIONS:**
a solution **of** something
a solution of **bleach/detergent/sugar**

some|what /ˈsʌmwɒt/
ACADEMIC WORD

ADVERB You use **somewhat** to indicate that something is the case to a limited extent or degree. [FORMAL] ○ *The results are somewhat surprising.* ○ *The outcome variables differed somewhat in the three groups.*

▸ **COLLOCATIONS:**
  somewhat **surprising/unusual/different/misleading**
  somewhat **more/less/differently**
  differ/vary/ease/subside somewhat

▸ **SYNONYM:** slightly

▸ **ANTONYM:** extremely

source /sɔːs/ (sources)
ACADEMIC WORD ACADEMIC STUDY

1 NOUN The **source of** something is the person, place, or thing which you get it from. ○ *Renewable sources of energy must be used where practical.* ○ *Tourism, which is a major source of income for the city, may be seriously affected.*

▸ **COLLOCATIONS:**
  a source **of** *something*
  a source of **information/inspiration**
  a source of **income/revenue/funding**
  a **heat/food/energy** source
  a **renewable/alternative/major/main** source

2 NOUN A **source** is a person or book that provides information for a news story or for a piece of research. ○ *Military sources say the boat was heading south at high speed.* ○ *Carson (1970) made extensive use of secondary data sources.*

▸ **COLLOCATIONS:**
  a source **of** *something*
  a **primary/secondary** source
  police/intelligence sources
  a **reliable/senior/unnamed/unidentified** source
  identify/locate/quote/cite a source
  sources **say/confirm/tell** *things*

3 NOUN The **source of** a difficulty is its cause. ○ [+ *of*] *Reactions to ointments are a common source of skin problems.*

▸ **COLLOCATIONS:**
  a source **of** *something*
  the source of a **problem**

▸ **SYNONYMS:** root, cause, origin

▸ **ANTONYMS:** result, effect

spe|cif|ic /spɪˈsɪfɪk/
ACADEMIC WORD

ADJECTIVE You use **specific** to refer to a particular fixed area, problem, or subject. ○ *Massage may help to increase blood flow to specific areas of the body.*

○ *There are several specific problems to be dealt with.* ○ *the specific needs of the individual*

▶ **COLLOCATIONS:**
a specific **area/location/target/group**
a specific **problem/need/issue/question/purpose**
▶ **SYNONYM:** particular
▶ **ANTONYM:** general

spe|cifi|cal|ly /spɪ'sɪfɪkli/

ADVERB ○ *the first nursing home designed specifically for people with AIDS* ○ *brain cells, or more specifically, neurons*

▶ **COLLOCATIONS:**
specifically **designed/targeted/aimed**
specifically **state/mention/exclude**
▶ **SYNONYM:** particularly
▶ **ANTONYM:** generally

speci|men /'spesɪmɪn/ (specimens)   `SCIENCE`

NOUN A **specimen** is a single plant or animal which is an example of a particular species or type and is examined by scientists. ○ *200,000 specimens of fungus are kept at the Komarov Botanical Institute.* ○ *North American fossil specimens*

▶ **COLLOCATIONS:**
a specimen **of** *something*
a **botanical/anatomical/fossil** specimen
a **rare/perfect/fine/exotic** specimen
collect/preserve specimens
▶ **SYNONYMS:** sample, example

sphere /sfɪə/ (spheres)

NOUN A **sphere** is an object that is completely round in shape like a ball.
○ *the volume of a hollow sphere*
▶ **COLLOCATION:** a **celestial/heavenly/microscopic/crystal** sphere
▶ **SYNONYM:** globe

spheri|cal /'sferɪkəl, AM 'sfɪr-/

ADJECTIVE [FORMAL] ○ *a spherical particle* ○ *Latitude was measured on the assumption the earth was perfectly spherical.*

▶ **COLLOCATIONS:**
a spherical **granule/particle/capsule/boulder**
spherical **trigonometry/geometry**
▶ **SYNONYMS:** globular, round

spi|ral /ˈspaɪərəl/ (spirals, spiralling, spiralled)
[in AM, use **spiraling**, **spiraled**]

1 NOUN A **spiral** is a shape which winds round and round, with each curve above or outside the previous one.

- **Spiral** is also an adjective. ○ *a spiral staircase* ○ *the Milky Way, a spiral galaxy with 100 billion stars*
  ▶ **COLLOCATION:** a spiral **staircase/stairway/ramp/galaxy**

2 VERB If something **spirals** or **is spiralled** somewhere, it grows or moves in a spiral curve. ○ *Vines spiralled upward toward the roof.* ○ *A joss stick spiralled smoke.*
  ▶ **COLLOCATION:** spiral **downward/upward**

spokes|person /ˈspəʊkspɜːsən/ (spokespersons or spokespeople)

NOUN A **spokesperson** is a person who speaks as the representative of a group or organization. ○ *A spokesperson for Amnesty, Norma Johnston, describes some cases.* ○ *A company spokesperson confirmed the dismissal.*

▶ **COLLOCATIONS:**
  a spokesperson **for** *something*
  a spokesperson for a **department/company/agency/group**
  a **police/official/military/departmental** spokesperson
  a spokesperson **says/confirms/denies** *things*
▶ **SYNONYMS:** speaker, representative

> **ACADEMIC WRITING: Gender neutral language**
>
> In modern usage, especially in formal contexts, it is considered better to use words for jobs and roles that do not specify whether it is a man or a woman. This shows that the person's gender is less important than their profession or position. For example **spokesperson** is preferred to **spokesman** or **spokeswoman**. Other gender neutral words include:
>
> **Salesperson** or **sales staff** instead of **salesman/saleswoman**
> **Chairperson** or **chair** instead of **chairman/chairwoman**
> **Police officer** instead of **policeman/policewoman**

spouse /spaʊs/ (spouses)   `SOCIOLOGY`

NOUN Someone's **spouse** is the person they are married to. ○ *Husbands and wives do not have to pay any inheritance tax when their spouse dies.*
  ▶ **SYNONYMS:** husband, wife, partner

square /skweə/ (squares, squaring, squared)   `MATHS`

1 VERB To **square** a number means to multiply it by itself. For example, **3 squared** is 3 × 3, or 9. **3 squared** is usually written as 3^2. ○ *Take the time in*

seconds, square it, and multiply by 5.12. ○ A squared plus B squared equals C squared.
▶ **RELATED WORD:** cube

2 NOUN The **square of** a number is the number produced when you multiply
that number by itself. For example, the square of 3 is 9. ○ the square of the
speed of light, an exceedingly large number
▶ **COLLOCATION:** the square **of** something/x
▶ **RELATED WORDS:** cube, square root

---

sta|ble /ˈsteɪbəl/ (stabler, stablest)   `ACADEMIC WORD`

ADJECTIVE If something is **stable**, it is not likely to change or come to an end
suddenly. ○ The price of oil should remain stable for the rest of the year. ○ a stable
marriage
▶ **COLLOCATIONS:**
  a stable **environment/condition/relationship/marriage**
  financially/politically/relatively/fairly stable
  remain/become stable
▶ **SYNONYM:** steady
▶ **ANTONYM:** unstable

sta|bil|ity /stəˈbɪlɪti/

UNCOUNTABLE NOUN ○ It was a time of political stability and progress.
○ U. N. peacekeepers were dispatched to ensure stability in the border region.
▶ **COLLOCATIONS:**
  stability **of/in** something
  the stability of a **region/area/country**
  restore/maintain/ensure/threaten stability
  long-term/relative/regional stability
  political/social/economic/financial stability
▶ **PHRASE:** peace and stability
▶ **ANTONYM:** instability

sta|bi|lize /ˈsteɪbɪlaɪz/ (stabilizes, stabilizing, stabilized)

VERB If something **stabilizes**, or **is stabilized**, it becomes stable. [in BRIT,
also use **stabilise**] ○ Although her illness is serious, her condition is beginning to
stabilize. ○ Officials hope the move will stabilize exchange rates.
▶ **COLLOCATIONS:**
  stabilize a **country/situation**
  a **condition/market/economy** stabilizes
▶ **SYNONYM:** steady
▶ **ANTONYM:** destabilize

stand|ard /ˈstændəd/ (standards)

1 NOUN A **standard** is a level of quality or achievement, especially a level that is thought to be acceptable. ○ [+ of] *improvements in the general standard of living* ○ *There will be new national standards for hospital cleanliness.*

2 NOUN A **standard** is something that you use in order to judge the quality of something else. ○ *systems that were by later standards absurdly primitive*

▶ **COLLOCATIONS:**
  a standard **of** *something*
  a standard of **excellence/living/conduct/behaviour**
  set/raise/maintain/meet a standard
  industry/safety/living standards
  a **high/minimum/strict/national/professional** standard
  the standard **required**

▶ **SYNONYMS:** guideline, level

3 ADJECTIVE You use **standard** to describe things which are usual and normal. ○ *It was standard practice for untrained clerks to advise in serious cases such as murder.* ○ *the standard format for a scientific paper*

▶ **COLLOCATIONS:**
  a standard **model/feature/format/rate/size**
  standard **equipment/practice/procedure**

▶ **PHRASE:** standard English

▶ **SYNONYMS:** normal, regular, usual

▶ **ANTONYMS:** non-standard, abnormal, unusual, irregular

stand|point /ˈstændpɔɪnt/ (standpoints)

NOUN From a particular **standpoint** means looking at an event, situation, or idea in a particular way. ○ *He believes that from a military standpoint, the situation is under control.* ○ *From a marketing standpoint, store cards have a definite appeal.*

▶ **COLLOCATIONS:**
  a **legal/moral/ethical/practical/statistical** standpoint
  a **business/marketing/consumer/health** standpoint

▶ **SYNONYMS:** point of view, perspective

state /steɪt/ (states, stating, stated)

VERB If you **state** something, you say or write it in a formal or definite way. ○ *The table clearly states the amount of fat found in commonly used foods.* ○ [+ that] *The police report stated that he was arrested for allegedly assaulting his wife.* ○ *Buyers who do not apply within the stated period can lose their deposits.*

▶ **COLLOCATIONS:**
  state a **fact/reason/preference**

state **clearly/explicitly/categorically/unequivocally**
state **repeatedly/incorrectly/publicly**
a **letter/document/report/rule/article** states *something*
▶ SYNONYMS: declare, relate

state|ment /'steɪtmənt/ (statements)

NOUN A **statement** is something that you say or write which gives information in a formal or definite way. ○ *'Things are moving ahead.' – I found that statement vague and unclear.* ○ *The 350-page report was based on statements from witnesses to the events.*

▶ COLLOCATIONS:
make/issue/release a statement
a **brief/formal/written/official/public** statement

---

sta|tis|tics /stə'tɪstɪks/   ACADEMIC WORD

1 PLURAL NOUN **Statistics** are facts which are obtained from analysing information expressed in numbers, for example information about the number of times that something happens. ○ *Official statistics show real wages declining by 24%.* ○ *There are no reliable statistics for the number of deaths in the battle.*

▶ COLLOCATIONS:
official/economic/national statistics
statistics **show/indicate/reveal/suggest** *things*
compile/collect/release/publish statistics

▶ SYNONYMS: figures, numbers

2 UNCOUNTABLE NOUN **Statistics** is a branch of mathematics concerned with the study of information that is expressed in numbers. ○ *a professor of Mathematical Statistics*

sta|tis|ti|cal /stə'tɪstɪkəl/

ADJECTIVE ○ *The report contains a great deal of statistical information.* ○ *Other controls accounting for measurement noise confirmed the statistical significance of the relationship.*

▶ COLLOCATIONS:
statistical **analysis/data/evidence/figures/information**
statistical **significance/probability/correlation**
a statistical **method/technique**

▶ SYNONYM: numerical

sta|tis|ti|cal|ly /stə'tɪstɪkli/

ADVERB ○ *The results are not statistically significant.* ○ *Statistically, ninety-eight percent of all acute sunstroke cases are fatal.*

▶ COLLOCATIONS:
statistically **significant/insignificant**
statistically **valid/meaningful/proven**
statistically **speaking**
analyze/prove *something* statistically

stat|is|ti|cian /ˌstætɪˈstɪʃən/ (statisticians)

NOUN A **statistician** is a person who studies statistics or who works using statistics. ○ *Government statisticians published figures that showed a 0.9 per cent fall in the volume of goods sold in December.*

▶ COLLOCATION: a **government/department/official/chief** statistician
▶ SYNONYMS: analyst, economist

sta|tus /ˈsteɪtəs/   `ACADEMIC WORD`

1 **UNCOUNTABLE NOUN** Your **status** is your social or professional position. ○ *People of higher status tend more to use certain drugs.* ○ *women and men of wealth and status* ○ *Metal daggers and horses may have been status symbols of an invading elite.*

2 **UNCOUNTABLE NOUN** **Status** is the importance and respect that someone has among the public or a particular group. ○ *Nurses are undervalued, and they never enjoy the same status as doctors.*

3 **UNCOUNTABLE NOUN** The **status** of something is the importance that people give it. ○ *Those things that can be assessed by external tests are being given unduly high status.*

▶ COLLOCATIONS:
the status **of** *something*
high/low/equal/elevated status
social/socioeconomic/official status
attain/enjoy/gain/grant/confer status
a **status** symbol
▶ PHRASE: wealth and status
▶ SYNONYMS: importance, prestige, standing, rank, station

steady /ˈstedi/ (steadier, steadiest)

ADJECTIVE A **steady** situation continues or develops gradually without any interruptions and is not likely to change quickly. ○ *Despite the steady progress of building work, the campaign against it is still going strong.* ○ *The improvement in standards has been steady and persistent.* ○ *a steady stream of traffic*

▶ COLLOCATIONS:
steady **progress/decline/improvement/growth**
a steady **supply/stream/trickle/rise/increase**
▶ SYNONYMS: regular, even

steadi|ly /ˈstedɪli/

ADVERB ○ *Overseas student numbers in Britain have been rising steadily for a decade.* ○ *The company has steadily been losing market share to Boeing and Airbus.*

▸ **COLLOCATIONS:**
  climb/rise/grow/increase/improve steadily
  decrease/decline/fall/breathe/rain steadily

▸ **SYNONYM:** evenly

▸ **ANTONYM:** unevenly

---

steep /stiːp/ (steeper, steepest)

1 ADJECTIVE A **steep** slope rises at a very sharp angle and is difficult to go up. ○ *San Francisco is built on 40 hills and some are very steep.* ○ *a narrow, steep-sided valley*

2 ADJECTIVE A **steep** increase or decrease in something is a very big increase or decrease. ○ *Consumers are rebelling at steep price increases.* ○ *Many smaller emerging Asian economies are suffering their steepest economic declines for half a century.*

→ see note at **dramatic**

▸ **COLLOCATIONS:**
  a steep **hill/slope/descent/gradient**
  a steep **rise/increase/fall/decline/curve**

▸ **SYNONYMS:** sharp, sheer

▸ **ANTONYMS:** gradual, gentle

steep|ly /ˈstiːpli/

ADVERB ○ *The road climbs steeply, with good views of Orvieto through the trees.* ○ *steeply terraced valleys* ○ *Unemployment is rising steeply.*

▸ **COLLOCATION: rise/climb/slope/drop/fall** steeply

---

ste|reo|type /ˈsteriətaɪp/   `SOCIOLOGY`
(stereotypes, stereotyping, stereotyped)

1 NOUN A **stereotype** is a fixed general image or set of characteristics that a lot of people believe represent a particular type of person or thing. ○ *Such a crass observation does nothing but reinforce negative racial stereotypes.* ○ *the cultural stereotypes of women in contemporary society*

▸ **COLLOCATIONS:**
  a stereotype **of/about** *someone*
  a **racial/black/negative/sexual/gender** stereotype
  perpetuate/reinforce/fit/challenge a stereotype

▸ **PHRASE:** stereotype and prejudice

2 VERB If someone **is stereotyped** as something, people form a fixed general idea or image of them, so that it is assumed that they will behave in a particular way. ○ [+ *as*] *Psychiatric patients are often stereotyped as dangerous.* ○ *Their image in the media is stereotyped and distorted.*

▶ COLLOCATIONS:
be stereotyped **as** something
unfairly/viciously stereotyped

▶ SYNONYMS: label, typecast

ste|reo|typi|cal /ˌsteriəʊˈtɪpɪkəl/

ADJECTIVE ○ *Dara challenges our stereotypical ideas about gender and femininity.* ○ *People have a very stereotypical image of scientists as guys in white coats.*

▶ COLLOCATION: a stereotypical **image/view/role**

stimu|late /ˈstɪmjʊleɪt/ (stimulates, stimulating, stimulated)

1 VERB To **stimulate** something means to encourage it to begin or develop further. ○ *America's priority is rightly to stimulate its economy.* ○ *The Russian health service has stimulated public interest in home cures.*

▶ COLLOCATIONS:
stimulate the **economy**
stimulate **growth/demand/production**

▶ SYNONYM: encourage

2 VERB If something **stimulates** a part of a person's body, it causes it to move or start working. ○ *Exercise stimulates the digestive and excretory systems.* ○ [+ *to-inf*] *The body is stimulated to build up resistance.*

▶ COLLOCATIONS:
stimulate **circulation/nerves/glands**
stimulate the **appetite**

stimu|la|tion /ˌstɪmjʊˈleɪʃən/

UNCOUNTABLE NOUN ○ *an economy in need of stimulation* ○ *physical stimulation* ○ [+ *of*] *the chemical stimulation of drugs*

▶ COLLOCATIONS:
stimulation **of** something
provide/need/require stimulation
physical/sexual/nerve/brain stimulation

stimu|lus /ˈstɪmjʊləs/ (stimuli)

NOUN A **stimulus** is something that encourages activity in people or things. ○ *Interest rates could fall soon and be a stimulus to the U.S. economy.* ○ *It is through our nervous system that we adapt ourselves to our environment and to all external stimuli.*

▶ COLLOCATIONS:
a **conditioned/sensory/external/short-term** stimulus
a **fiscal/monetary/economic** stimulus
a stimulus **package/plan**

straight|forward /ˌstreɪt'fɔːwəd/ ACADEMIC WORD

ADJECTIVE If you describe something as **straightforward**, you approve of it
because it is easy to do or understand. ○ *Cost accounting is a
relatively straightforward process.* ○ *The question seemed straightforward enough.*
○ *simple straightforward language*

▶ **COLLOCATIONS:**
  fairly/relatively/pretty straightforward
  a straightforward **narrative/task/explanation/answer**
▶ **SYNONYMS:** uncomplicated, clear
▶ **ANTONYM:** complicated

strain /streɪn/ (strains, straining, strained)

1 NOUN If **strain** is put **on** an organization or system, it has to do more than it
is able to do. ○ *The prison service is already under considerable strain.* ○ [+ on] *The
vast expansion in secondary education is putting an enormous strain on the system.*

▶ **COLLOCATIONS:**
  under strain
  a strain **on** *something*
  put/place strain on *something*
  strain on a **relationship/system/budget/economy**
  slight/severe/enormous/considerable strain
▶ **SYNONYM:** pressure

2 VERB To **strain** something means to make it do more than it is able to do.
  ○ *The volume of scheduled flights is straining the air traffic control system.*
  ○ *Resources will be further strained by new demands for housing.*

▶ **COLLOCATIONS:**
  strain **relations/resources**
  severely/somewhat/further strained
  a strained **relationship**
▶ **SYNONYM:** stretch

strat|egy /'strætədʒi/ (strategies) ACADEMIC WORD

NOUN A **strategy** is a general plan or set of plans intended to achieve
something, especially over a long period. ○ *Next week, health ministers gather
in Amsterdam to agree a strategy for controlling malaria.* ○ *a customer-led
marketing strategy*

▶ **COLLOCATIONS:**
  a strategy **for** *something*
  devise/adopt/pursue/implement/develop a strategy
  a **long-term/overall/national** strategy
  a **marketing/pricing/investment/growth/economic** strategy
▶ **SYNONYMS:** policy, plan

stra|tegic /strə'tiːdʒɪk/

ADJECTIVE **Strategic** means relating to the most important, general aspects of something such as a military operation or political policy, especially when these are decided in advance. ○ *the new strategic thinking which NATO leaders produced at the recent London summit* ○ *The island is of strategic importance to France.*

▶ COLLOCATIONS:
strategic **planning/thinking/marketing/importance**
a strategic **plan/point/position/site**

▶ SYNONYMS: important, critical, key

---

strength /streŋθ/

UNCOUNTABLE NOUN The **strength** of something is how strong it is. ○ [+ of] *She has always been encouraged to swim to build up the strength of her muscles.* ○ *America values its economic leadership, and the political and military strength that goes with it.*

strength|en /'streŋθən/ (strengthens, strengthening, strengthened)

VERB To **strengthen** something means to make it stronger. If something **strengthens**, it becomes stronger. ○ *The dollar strengthened against most other currencies.* ○ *Community leaders want to strengthen controls at external frontiers.* ○ *Yoga can be used to strengthen the immune system.*

▶ COLLOCATIONS:
strengthen **ties/unity/co-operation/democracy/resolve**
strengthen a **relationship/bond/argument**
strengthen the **economy**
strengthen **muscles/bones**
the **economy/dollar/pound/yen** strengthens
greatly/immeasurably/further strengthen

▶ SYNONYMS: reinforce, enhance, fortify
▶ ANTONYM: weaken

---

stress /stres/ (stresses, stressing, stressed)   ACADEMIC WORD

1 VERB If you **stress** a point in a discussion, you put extra emphasis on it because you think it is important. ○ [+ that] *The spokesman stressed that the measures did not amount to an overall ban.* ○ *They also stress the need for improved employment opportunities, better transport and health care.*

▶ COLLOCATIONS:
stress the **importance/significance/urgency** of *something*
stress the **need** for *something*
repeatedly stress

▶ SYNONYM: emphasize

- **Stress** is also a noun. ○ [+ on] *Japanese car makers are laying ever more stress on European sales.*

  ▶ COLLOCATIONS:
  a stress **on** *something*
  lay/place stress on *something*

  ▶ SYNONYM: emphasis

2 UNCOUNTABLE NOUN If you feel under **stress**, you feel worried and tense because of difficulties in your life. ○ *Individuals develop colds, backache, or eczema when they are under stress.* ○ *a wide range of stress-related problems* ○ *Relaxation exercises can relieve stress.*

  ▶ COLLOCATIONS:
  under stress
  cope with/deal with/handle stress
  cause/experience/relieve/reduce stress
  emotional/mental/psychological/work-related stress
  chronic/severe/extreme stress
  stress **related**

  ▶ PHRASES:
  stress and anxiety
  post-traumatic stress disorder

  ▶ SYNONYMS: anxiety, worry, strain

3 NOUN **Stresses** are strong physical pressures applied to an object.
  ○ *Earthquakes happen when stresses in rock are suddenly released as the rocks fracture.*

---

strug|gle /ˈstrʌɡəl/ (struggles, struggling, struggled)

1 VERB If you **struggle to** do something, you try hard to do it, even though other people or things may be making it difficult for you to succeed. ○ *They had to struggle against all kinds of adversity.* ○ [+ to-inf] *Those who have lost their jobs struggle to pay their supermarket bills.*

  ▶ COLLOCATIONS:
  struggle **against** *something*
  struggle to **cope/survive/recover**
  struggle to **overcome/maintain/keep/find** *something*

  ▶ PHRASE: struggle against the odds

  ▶ SYNONYMS: battle, fight

2 NOUN A **struggle** is a long and difficult attempt to achieve something such as freedom or political rights. ○ [+ for] *India's struggle for independence* ○ *IT directors now face an uphill struggle to win back respect from their business peers.*

  ▶ COLLOCATIONS:
  a struggle **for/against** *something*

a struggle **with** *someone/something*
a struggle for **survival/independence/freedom/democracy**
a struggle against **terrorism/apartheid**
a struggle with **cancer/illness/addiction**
a **constant/ongoing/uphill/bitter/long** struggle
a **power/class/freedom/political** struggle

▶ SYNONYM: battle

---

style /staɪl/ (styles)   [ACADEMIC WORD]

1 NOUN The **style** of something is the general way in which it is done or presented, which often shows the attitudes of the people involved.
○ *Our children's different needs and learning styles created many problems.*
○ [+ *of*] *Belmont Park is a broad sweeping track which will suit the European style of running.*

2 NOUN In the arts, a particular **style** is characteristic of a particular period or group of people. ○ [+ *of*] *six scenes in the style of a classical Greek tragedy* ○ *a mixture of musical styles*

▶ COLLOCATIONS:
a style **of** *something*
a style of **life/music/writing/management/leadership**
a **leadership/management/teaching** style
a **prose/architectural/musical** style
a **particular/distinctive/contrasting** style

▶ SYNONYMS: method, technique

---

sub|ject /'sʌbdʒɪkt/ (subjects)

1 NOUN Someone or something that is the **subject of** criticism, study, or an investigation is being criticized, studied, or investigated. ○ [+ *of*] *Some of the positions Mr. Meredith has adopted have made him the subject of criticism.* ○ [+ *of*] *the argument that only observable behaviour is a proper subject of psychological investigation*

▶ COLLOCATIONS:
a subject **of** *something*
a subject of **criticism/investigation/inquiry**
a subject of **speculation/controversy/debate**

2 NOUN In an experiment or piece of research, the **subject** is the person or animal that is being tested or studied. [FORMAL] ○ *'White noise' was played into the subject's ears through headphones.* ○ *Subjects in the study were asked to follow a modified diet.*

▶ COLLOCATION: subjects **participate/report/experience/respond**
▶ SYNONYM: participant

sub|jec|tive /səb'dʒektɪv/

ADJECTIVE Something that is **subjective** is based on personal opinions and feelings rather than on facts. ○ *We know that taste in art is a subjective matter.* ○ *The way they interpreted their past was highly subjective.*

▶ **COLLOCATIONS:**
   inherently/highly/purely subjective
   a subjective **judgement/interpretation/evaluation/experience**

▶ **ANTONYM:** objective

sub|jec|tive|ly /səb'dʒektɪvli/

ADVERB ○ *Our preliminary results suggest that people do subjectively find the speech clearer.*

▶ **COLLOCATION:** subjectively **experienced/defined**

▶ **ANTONYM:** objectively

sub|jec|tiv|ity /ˌsʌbdʒək'tɪvɪti/

UNCOUNTABLE NOUN ○ *They accused her of flippancy and subjectivity in her reporting of events in their country.*

▶ **ANTONYM:** objectivity

sub|mit /səb'mɪt/ (submits, submitting, submitted)   ACADEMIC WORD

VERB If you **submit** a proposal, report, or request **to** someone, you formally send it to them so that they can consider it or decide about it. ○ *[+ to] They submitted their reports to the Chancellor yesterday.* ○ *Head teachers yesterday submitted a claim for a 9 per cent pay rise.*

▶ **COLLOCATIONS:**
   submit *something* **to** *someone*
   submit a **proposal/bid/request/application/claim**
   submit a **report/document/sample**
   submit *one's* **resignation**

▶ **SYNONYMS:** present, hand in

sub|mis|sion /səb'mɪʃən/ (submissions)

NOUN ○ *Diploma and certificate courses do not normally require the submission of a dissertation.* ○ *A written submission has to be prepared.*

▶ **COLLOCATIONS:**
   the submission **of** *something*
   the submission of a **dissertation/report/proposal**
   make/lodge/receive a submission
   a **written/oral** submission

---

sub|se|quent /ˈsʌbsɪkwənt/

ADJECTIVE You use **subsequent** to describe something that happened or existed after the time or event that has just been referred to. [FORMAL]
○ *the increase of population in subsequent years* ○ *Those concerns were overshadowed by subsequent events.*

▶ **COLLOCATIONS:**
  a subsequent **year/event/period/generation**
  a subsequent **investigation/inquiry/purchase**
▶ **SYNONYMS:** following, next
▶ **ANTONYM:** previous

sub|se|quent|ly /ˈsʌbsɪkwəntli/

ADVERB ○ *She subsequently became the Faculty's President.* ○ *Kermes were then believed to be berries, but were subsequently discovered to be scale insects.*

▶ **COLLOCATION:** subsequently **discover/withdraw/arrest/release**
▶ **SYNONYM:** later
▶ **ANTONYM:** previously

---

sub|si|dy /ˈsʌbsɪdi/ (subsidies)

NOUN A **subsidy** is money that is paid by a government or other authority in order to help an industry or business, or to pay for a public service.
○ *European farmers are planning a massive demonstration against farm subsidy cuts.* ○ *They've also slashed state subsidies to utilities and transportation.*

▶ **COLLOCATIONS:**
  a **farm/agricultural/export** subsidy
  a **state/public/government/federal** subsidy
  provide/receive/cut/reduce/eliminate a subsidy
  subsidy **cuts**
▶ **SYNONYMS:** grant, aid

sub|si|dize /ˈsʌbsɪdaɪz/ (subsidizes, subsidizing, subsidized)

VERB If a government or other authority **subsidizes** something, they pay part of the cost of it. [in BRIT, also use **subsidise**] ○ *Around the world, governments have subsidized the housing of middle and upper-income groups.* ○ *pensions that are subsidised by the government*

▶ **COLLOCATIONS:**
  the **government** subsidizes *something*
  heavily/unfairly subsidized
▶ **SYNONYM:** support

---

sub|stan|tial /səbˈstænʃəl/

ADJECTIVE **Substantial** means large in amount or degree. [FORMAL]
○ *A substantial number of studies have shown that there is a lower mortality rate in*

people with high blood pressure. ○ *a very substantial improvement*

▶ COLLOCATIONS:
a substantial **number/amount/sum/portion/proportion**
a substantial **increase/improvement/gain**
substantial **damage**

▶ SYNONYMS: significant, considerable

▶ ANTONYMS: insubstantial, small

sub|stan|tial|ly /səbˈstænʃəli/

ADVERB If something changes **substantially** or is **substantially** different, it changes a lot or is very different. [FORMAL] ○ *The percentage of girls in engineering has increased substantially.* ○ *The price was substantially higher than had been expected.*

▶ COLLOCATIONS:
increase/reduce/differ/contribute substantially
substantially **different/higher/more/less**

▶ SYNONYMS: significantly, considerably

▶ ANTONYM: slightly

---

sub|sti|tute /ˈsʌbstɪtjuːt, AM -tuːt/   `ACADEMIC WORD`
(substitutes, substituting, substituted)

1 VERB If you **substitute** one thing **for** another, or if one thing **substitutes for** another, it takes the place or performs the function of the other thing. ○ [+ for] *They were substituting violence for dialogue.* ○ *He substituted different isotopes into the model and charted the changes.*

▶ COLLOCATION: substitute *something* **for** *something*

▶ SYNONYMS: change, replace

2 NOUN A **substitute** is something that you have or use instead of something else. ○ [+ for] *the increased use of nuclear energy as a substitute for fossil fuels* ○ *tests on humans to find a blood substitute made from animal blood*

▶ COLLOCATIONS:
a substitute **for** *something*
use/find/become a substitute
a **blood/sugar/milk** substitute
a **poor/suitable/adequate** substitute

▶ SYNONYMS: replacement, equivalent

sub|sti|tu|tion /ˌsʌbstɪˈtjuːʃən, AM -ˈtuː-/ (substitutions)

NOUN ○ [+ of] *safety concerns over the substitution of ingredients* ○ *the nature and pace of technology substitution*

▶ COLLOCATIONS:
the substitution **of** *something*

crop/import/technology substitution
make a substitution

---

sub|tle /ˈsʌtəl/ (subtler, subtlest)

1 ADJECTIVE Something that is **subtle** is not immediately obvious or
noticeable. ○ *the slow and subtle changes that take place in all living things*
○ *Intolerance can take subtler forms too.* ○ *There is a subtle distinction between a
withdrawal and a retreat.*

2 ADJECTIVE Subtle smells, tastes, sounds, or colours are pleasantly complex
and delicate. ○ *subtle shades of brown* ○ *delightfully subtle scents*

▶ COLLOCATIONS:
a subtle **change/difference/distinction**
a subtle **nuance/shade/flavour/hint**
▶ SYNONYM: delicate
▶ ANTONYM: obvious

sub|tly /ˈsʌtli/

ADVERB ○ *The truth is subtly different.* ○ *These substances could subtly alter neural
connections*

▶ COLLOCATIONS:
subtly **different/shaded/nuanced**
change/alter subtly

sub|tle|ty /ˈsʌtəlti/ (subtleties)

1 NOUN Subtleties are very small details or differences which are not
obvious. ○ [+ *of*] *His fascination with the subtleties of human behaviour makes him
a good storyteller.*

▶ COLLOCATIONS:
the subtleties **of** *something*
grasp/appreciate/understand the subtleties
▶ SYNONYM: detail

2 UNCOUNTABLE NOUN Subtlety is the quality of being not immediately
obvious or noticeable, and therefore difficult to describe. ○ *African dance is
vigorous, but full of subtlety.* ○ [+ *of*] *Many of the resulting wines lack the subtlety of
the original model.*

▶ COLLOCATION: the subtlety **of** *something*
▶ SYNONYM: nuance

---

suf|fi|cient /səˈfɪʃənt/   ACADEMIC WORD

ADJECTIVE If something is **sufficient for** a particular purpose, there is enough of it
for the purpose. ○ [+ to-inf] *One metre of fabric is sufficient to cover the exterior of
an 18-in-diameter hatbox.* ○ *There was not sufficient evidence to secure a conviction.*

▶ COLLOCATIONS:
sufficient **for** *something*
sufficient to **cover/justify/warrant** *something*
sufficient **evidence/resources/funding**
a sufficient **quantity/number/reason**

▶ SYNONYM: enough

▶ ANTONYM: insufficient

suf|fi|cient|ly /sə'fɪʃəntli/

ADVERB ○ *300,000 years after the Big Bang, the Universe had cooled sufficiently for protons and electrons to combine into neutral hydrogen atoms.* ○ *The holes were sufficiently large to serve as nests.*

▶ COLLOCATIONS:
recover/heal/mature/cool sufficiently
sufficiently **large/flexible/robust**

▶ ANTONYM: insufficiently

sug|gest /sə'dʒest, AM səg'dʒ-/ (suggests, suggesting, suggested)

VERB If one thing **suggests** another, it implies it or makes you think that it might be the case. ○ [+ *that*] *Earlier reports suggested that a meeting would take place on Sunday.* ○ *Its hairy body suggests a mammal.* ○ *The scientific evidence suggests otherwise.*

→ see note at **propose**

▶ COLLOCATIONS:
evidence/research suggests
data/findings suggest *something*
a **poll/study/report/study** suggests *something*
strongly/tentatively suggest
suggest **otherwise**

▶ SYNONYMS: indicate, imply

sum /sʌm/ (sums, summing, summed) ACADEMIC WORD BUSINESS MATHS

1 NOUN A **sum of** money is an amount of money. ○ [+ *of*] *Large sums of money were lost.* ○ [+ *of*] *Even the relatively modest sum of £50,000 now seems beyond his reach.*

▶ COLLOCATIONS:
a sum **of** *x*
a sum of **money/cash**
a **large/huge/vast** sum
invest/pay a sum

▶ SYNONYM: amount

2 NOUN In mathematics, **the sum of** two numbers is the number that is obtained when they are added together. ○ [+ *of*] *The sum of all the angles of a triangle is 180 degrees.*

▶ COLLOCATION: the sum **of** *something*

sum up

1 PHRASAL VERB If you **sum** something **up**, you describe it as briefly as possible. ○ *Let us first sum up the principal points made in this introductory chapter.* ○ *Negley Farson summed the situation up for all of BEA.*

2 PHRASAL VERB If you **sum up** after a speech or at the end of a piece of writing, you briefly state the main points again. ○ *To sum up: We welcome the statement of the Government and appreciate its willingness to work cooperatively with us.*

▶ COLLOCATIONS:
sum up a **mood/feeling/situation**
sum up **succinctly/briefly/neatly**

▶ SYNONYMS: summarize, conclude

---

sum|mary /ˈsʌməri/ (summaries) `ACADEMIC STUDY` `ACADEMIC WORD`

NOUN A **summary of** something is a short account of it, which gives the main points but not the details. ○ [+ *of*] *What follows is a brief summary of the process.* ○ *In summary, it is my opinion that this complete treatment process was very successful.*

▶ COLLOCATIONS:
a summary **of** *something*
a **brief/written/executive** summary

▶ PHRASE: in summary

▶ SYNONYMS: résumé, abstract, précis

sum|ma|rize /ˈsʌməraɪz/ (summarizes, summarizing, summarized)

VERB If you **summarize** something, you give a summary of it. [in BRIT, also use **summarise**] ○ *Table 3.1 summarizes the information given above.* ○ *Basically, the article can be summarized in three sentences.*

▶ COLLOCATIONS:
summarize **information/findings/data/results**
summarize a **discussion/argument**
succinctly/briefly summarize

▶ SYNONYMS: sum up, outline

---

sup|plement /ˈsʌplɪmənt/ `ACADEMIC WORD`
(supplements, supplementing, supplemented)

VERB If you **supplement** something, you add something to it in order to improve it. ○ *people doing extra jobs outside their regular jobs to supplement their* incomes ○ [+ with] *I suggest supplementing your diet with vitamins E and A.*

▶ COLLOCATIONS:

supplement *something* **with** *something*

supplement a **diet/income**

▶ SYNONYMS: augment, enhance, enrich

● **Supplement** is also a noun. ○ [+ to] *Business sponsorship must be a supplement to, not a substitute for, public funding.*

▶ COLLOCATION: a supplement **to** *something*

▶ SYNONYM: addition

sup|plemen|ta|ry /ˌsʌplɪˈmentri, AM -teri/

ADJECTIVE **Supplementary** things are added to something in order to improve it. ○ *the question of whether or not we need to take supplementary vitamins* ○ *Provide them with additional background or with supplementary information.*

▶ COLLOCATIONS:

supplementary **food/vitamins/oxygen/information**

a supplementary **question/fee/grant/budget**

▶ SYNONYMS: extra, additional

---

sup|ply /səˈplaɪ/ (supplies, supplying, supplied) `BUSINESS` `ECONOMICS`

1 VERB If you **supply** someone with something that they want or need, you give them a quantity of it. ○ *an agreement not to produce or supply chemical weapons* ○ [+ with] *a pipeline which will supply the major Greek cities with Russian natural gas* ○ [+ to] *the blood vessels supplying oxygen to the brain*

▶ COLLOCATIONS:

supply *someone/something* **with** *something*

supply *something* **to** *something/someone*

a **company/firm/institution** supplies *things*

supply **food/arms/oxygen/electricity/equipment/data/information**

supply a **product**

2 NOUN A **supply of** something is an amount of it which someone has or which is available for them to use. ○ [+ of] *The brain requires a constant supply of oxygen.* ○ *Most urban water supplies in the United States now contain fluoride in varying amounts.*

▶ COLLOCATIONS:

a supply **of** *something*

a supply of **oxygen/electricity/fuel**

a **plentiful/abundant/adequate/limited** supply

water/gas/electricity/oxygen/medical supplies

3 UNCOUNTABLE NOUN **Supply** is the quantity of goods and services that can be made available for people to buy. ○ *Prices change according to supply and demand.*

▶ **PHRASE:** supply and demand

▶ **ANTONYM:** demand

---

sup|port /sə'pɔːt/ (supports, supporting, supported)

VERB If a fact **supports** a statement or a theory, it helps to show that it is true or correct. ○ *The Freudian theory about daughters falling in love with their father has little evidence to support it.* ○ *This observation is supported by the archaeological evidence.*

→ see note at **confirm**

▶ **COLLOCATIONS:**
support a **view/notion/idea/theory**
evidence/data/findings support *something*

▶ **SYNONYMS:** substantiate, back up

● **Support** is also an uncountable noun. ○ *[+ for] History offers some support for this view.* ○ *The study did not lend support to the hypothesis.*

▶ **COLLOCATIONS:**
support **for** *something*
offer/lend support

▶ **SYNONYM:** evidence

---

sur|face /'sɜːfɪs/ (surfaces)

NOUN The **surface** of something is the flat top part of it or the outside of it. ○ *Ozone forms a protective layer between 12 and 30 miles above the Earth's surface.* ○ *tiny little waves on the surface of the water* ○ *Its total surface area was seven thousand square feet.*

▶ **COLLOCATIONS:**
the surface **of** *something*
on the surface
the **earth's/moon's** surface
a **smooth/slippery/flat** surface
a surface **area/temperature/layer**

---

sur|gery /'sɜːdʒəri/ MEDICINE

UNCOUNTABLE NOUN **Surgery** is medical treatment in which someone's body is cut open so that a doctor can repair, remove, or replace a diseased or damaged part. ○ *His father has just recovered from heart surgery.* ○ *Mr Clark underwent five hours of emergency surgery.* ○ *the decision to perform this surgery*

▶ **COLLOCATIONS:**
have/undergo/need/require/perform surgery
heart/knee/shoulder surgery
cosmetic/plastic/emergency/keyhole/laser surgery

sur|geon /'sɜːdʒən/ (surgeons)

NOUN A **surgeon** is a doctor who is specially trained to perform surgery. ○ *a heart surgeon* ○ *Two surgeons performed the keyhole surgery.* ○ *the plastic surgeon who specialized in this type of injury*

▶ COLLOCATIONS:
a **heart/brain/plastic/orthopaedic** surgeon
a surgeon **inserts/implants/removes/cuts** something

sur|gi|cal /'sɜːdʒɪkəl/

1 ADJECTIVE Surgical equipment and clothing is used in surgery. ○ *an array of surgical instruments* ○ *a pair of surgical gloves*

2 ADJECTIVE Surgical treatment involves surgery. ○ *A biopsy is usually a minor surgical procedure.* ○ *surgical removal of a tumor*

▶ COLLOCATIONS:
surgical **instruments/gloves**
surgical **treatment/intervention/removal**
a surgical **procedure/technique/mask**

▶ SYNONYM: medical

sur|gi|cal|ly /'sɜːdʒɪkli/

ADVERB ○ *In very severe cases, bunions may be surgically removed.*

▶ COLLOCATION: surgically **removed/repaired**
▶ SYNONYM: medically

---

sur|round|ings /sə'raʊndɪŋz/

PLURAL NOUN When you are describing the place where you are at the moment, or the place where you live, you can refer to it as your **surroundings**. ○ *The child's need to interact with immediate surroundings is critical to language development.* ○ *Schumacher adapted effortlessly to his new surroundings.*

▶ COLLOCATION: **natural/immediate/beautiful/familiar** surroundings
▶ SYNONYMS: environment, location, setting

---

sur|vey (surveys, surveying, surveyed) ACADEMIC WORD

> The noun is pronounced /'sɜːveɪ/. The verb is pronounced /sə'veɪ/, and can also be pronounced /'sɜːveɪ/.

1 NOUN If you carry out a **survey**, you try to find out detailed information about a lot of different people or things, usually by asking people a series of questions. ○ *The council conducted a survey of the uses to which farm buildings are put.* ○ *According to the survey, overall world trade has also slackened.*

> **COLLOCATIONS:**
> **according to** a survey
> **conduct/carry out** a survey
> a **recent/national/comprehensive/consumer/opinion** survey
> a survey **shows/finds/reveals/suggests** *things*

> **SYNONYMS:** analysis, study

2 VERB If you **survey** a number of people, companies, or organizations, you try to find out information about their opinions or behaviour, usually by asking them a series of questions. ○ *Business Development Advisers surveyed 211 companies for the report.* ○ *Only 18 percent of those surveyed opposed the idea.*

> **COLLOCATION:** survey **people/members/companies/voters**

---

sus|pect /ˈsʌspekt/ (suspects) `LAW`

NOUN A **suspect** is a person who the police or authorities think may be guilty of a crime. ○ *Police have arrested a suspect in a series of killings and sexual assaults in the city.*

> **COLLOCATIONS:**
> **arrest/detain/identify** a suspect
> a **prime/key/terrorist/crime/murder** suspect

---

sus|tain /səˈsteɪn/ (sustains, sustaining, sustained) `ACADEMIC WORD`

VERB If you **sustain** something, you continue it or maintain it for a period of time. ○ *Euphoria cannot be sustained indefinitely.* ○ *a period of sustained economic growth throughout 1995*

→ see note at **maintain**

> **COLLOCATIONS:**
> sustained **growth**
> a sustained **attack**
> **indefinitely/artificially** sustained

> **SYNONYMS:** maintain, continue

sus|tain|able /səˈsteɪnəbəl/

1 ADJECTIVE You use **sustainable** to describe the use of natural resources when this use is kept at a steady level that is not likely to damage the environment. ○ *the management, conservation and sustainable development of forests* ○ *Try to buy wood that you know has come from a sustainable source.*

> **COLLOCATIONS:**
> sustainable **agriculture/fishery/forestry**
> a sustainable **forest/future/source**
> **ecologically/environmentally** sustainable

> **SYNONYMS:** environmentally friendly, ecological
> **ANTONYM:** unsustainable

2 ADJECTIVE A **sustainable** plan, method, or system is designed to continue at the same rate or level of activity without any problems. ○ *the creation of an efficient and sustainable transport system* ○ *a sustainable recovery in consumer spending*

▸ **COLLOCATIONS:**
sustainable **recovery/growth/development**
a sustainable **policy**

▸ **ANTONYM:** unsustainable

sus|tain|abil|ity /sə,steɪnə'bɪlɪti/

UNCOUNTABLE NOUN ○ *the growing concern about environmental sustainability* ○ *[+ of] doubts about the sustainability of the current economic expansion*

▸ **COLLOCATIONS:**
the sustainability **of** *something*
ecological/environmental/long-term sustainability

---

sym|bol /'sɪmbəl/ (symbols)

`ACADEMIC WORD`

1 NOUN Something that is a **symbol of** a society or an aspect of life seems to represent it because it is very typical of it. ○ *To them, the monarchy is the special symbol of nationhood.*

2 NOUN A **symbol of** something such as an idea is a shape or design that is used to represent it. ○ *Later in this same passage Yeats resumes his argument for the Rose as an Irish symbol.*

3 NOUN A **symbol for** an item in a calculation or scientific formula is a number, letter, or shape that represents that item. ○ *mathematical symbols and operations*

▸ **COLLOCATIONS:**
a symbol **of/for** *something*
a symbol of **strength/resistance/hope/unity/freedom**
a **potent/powerful/visible/religious/status/sex** symbol
a symbol **denotes/indicates** *something*

▸ **SYNONYMS:** sign, representation

sym|bol|ic /sɪm'bɒlɪk/

1 ADJECTIVE If you describe an event, action, or procedure as **symbolic**, you mean that it represents an important change, although it has little practical effect. ○ *the symbolic importance of the trip* ○ *The move today was largely symbolic.*

2 ADJECTIVE Something that is **symbolic of** a person or thing is regarded or used as a symbol of them. ○ *[+ of] Yellow clothes are worn as symbolic of spring.*

▸ **COLLOCATIONS:**
symbolic **of** *something*
symbolic **importance/significance/meaning/value**

a symbolic **gesture/act**
largely/highly/purely symbolic
▸ **SYNONYMS:** representative, iconic, metaphorical
▸ **ANTONYM:** literal

sym|bol|ize /ˈsɪmbəlaɪz/ (symbolizes, symbolizing, symbolized)

VERB If one thing **symbolizes** another, it is used or regarded as a symbol of it. [in BRIT, also use **symbolise**] ○ *The fall of the Berlin Wall symbolised the end of the Cold War between East and West.*
▸ **COLLOCATION:** symbolize **unity/oppression/hope**
▸ **SYNONYMS:** represent, signify

sys|tem|at|ic /ˌsɪstəˈmætɪk/

ADJECTIVE Something that is done in a **systematic** way is done according to a fixed plan, in a thorough and efficient way. ○ *A systematic review was carried out.* ○ *They had not found any evidence of a systematic attempt to rig the ballot.*
▸ **COLLOCATION:** a systematic **way/attempt/approach/review**
▸ **SYNONYMS:** orderly, methodical
▸ **ANTONYM:** unsystematic

sys|tem|ati|cal|ly /ˌsɪstəˈmætɪkli/

ADVERB ○ *The army has systematically violated human rights.* ○ *Both Canadian linguistic cultures continue to differ systematically from the American.*
▸ **COLLOCATIONS:**
systematically **destroy/dismantle/violate** *something*
systematically **murder/abuse/torture** *people*
▸ **SYNONYM:** methodically
▸ **ANTONYM:** unsystematically

S

Tt

tar|get /'tɑːgɪt/

ACADEMIC WORD

(targets, targeting or **targetting, targeted** or **targetted)**

1 NOUN A **target** is a result that you are trying to achieve. ○ *The budgets should be based on company objectives, and set realistic targets.* ○ *an exports target of $5 billion a year*

▶ COLLOCATIONS:
a target **of** *x*
set/achieve/meet/reach/miss/exceed a target
a **realistic/tough/ambitious** target
a **government** target
a **performance/growth/sales/profit/financial** target
a target **rate/weight/time**

▶ SYNONYMS: objective, goal

2 VERB To **target** a particular person or thing means to decide to attack or criticize them. ○ *He targets the economy as the root cause of the deteriorating law and order situation.* ○ *Supermarkets have attached security tags to small, valuable items targeted by thieves.*

▶ COLLOCATIONS:
targeted **by** *someone*
targeted by **vandals/thieves/fraudsters/terrorists**
target **foreigners/militants/drinkers**
specifically/aggressively/unfairly target

▶ SYNONYMS: attack, blame, criticize

● **Target** is also a noun. ○ *[+ of] In the past they have been the target of racist abuse.* ○ *[+ for] The professor has been a frequent target for animal rights extremists.*

▶ COLLOCATIONS:
the target **of** *something*
a target **for** *someone*
a **soft/easy/legitimate/potential/possible** target
the **main/prime** target
a target of **attack/criticism/abuse/violence**

3 VERB If you **target** a particular group of people, you try to appeal to those people or affect them. ○ *The campaign will target American insurance companies.* ○ *The company has targeted adults as its primary customers.*

t

▸ COLLOCATIONS:
  targeted **at** *someone*
  targeted at **consumers/voters/investors/teenagers**
  primarily/mainly/actively target *someone*

▸ SYNONYMS: aim at, focus on

● **Target** is also a noun. ○ *a prime target group for marketing strategies*

  ▸ COLLOCATIONS:
  a target **for** *someone/something*
  a **main/prime** target
  a target **group/market/audience**

---

tele|com|mu|ni|ca|tions /ˌtelɪkəmjuːnɪˈkeɪʃənz/   IT

UNCOUNTABLE NOUN Telecommunications is the technology of sending signals and messages over long distances using electronic equipment, for example by radio and telephone. ○ *The rate of technological advance in the electronics and telecommunications industries has been astounding.*

▸ COLLOCATIONS:
  wireless telecommunications
  a telecommunications **company/firm/giant/group**
  the telecommunications **industry/sector/market**
  a telecommunications **service/network/system**
  telecommunications **equipment**

---

tense /tens/ (tenser, tensest)   ACADEMIC WORD

1 ADJECTIVE A **tense** situation or period of time is one that makes people anxious, because they do not know what is going to happen next. ○ *This gesture of goodwill did little to improve the tense atmosphere at the talks.* ○ *There were a few tense moments before the presentation.*

  ▸ COLLOCATIONS:
  a tense **situation/atmosphere/relationship/moment**
  tense **negotiations**

▸ SYNONYMS: strained, anxious

2 ADJECTIVE If muscles, ropes, etc are **tense**, they are stretched firm and tight.
  ○ *Tense muscles tear easily.*

▸ SYNONYMS: taut, tight
▸ ANTONYMS: loose, relaxed

● **Tense** is also a verb. ○ *Stand with your feet apart and tense your muscles.*
  ○ *It involves tensing and relaxing muscle groups, starting with your feet.*

▸ SYNONYMS: tauten, tighten
▸ ANTONYMS: loosen, relax

ten|sion /ˈtenʃən/

1 **UNCOUNTABLE NOUN** **Tension** is the feeling that is produced in a situation when people are anxious and do not trust each other, and when there is a possibility of sudden violence or conflict. ○ [+ *between*] *The tension between the two countries is likely to remain.* ○ *years of political tension and conflict*

▶ **COLLOCATIONS:**
tension **between** *things*
create/cause/increase/raise/heighten tension
ease/reduce/defuse tension
racial/political/religious/ethnic/social tension
growing/rising/increasing/escalating/mounting tension

▶ **PHRASE:** tension is high

▶ **SYNONYM:** anxiety

2 **UNCOUNTABLE NOUN** The **tension** in something such as a rope or wire is the extent to which it is stretched tight. ○ *The reassuring tension of the rope moved with him, neither too tight nor too loose.* ○ *the tension created when tightening the wire*

▶ **SYNONYM:** tightness

▶ **ANTONYM:** slack

term /tɜːm/

PHRASE If you talk about something **in terms of** something or **in** particular **terms**, you are specifying which aspect of it you are discussing or from what point of view you are considering it. ○ [+ *of*] *Our goods compete in terms of product quality, reliability and above all variety.* ○ *Paris has played a dominant role in France, not just in political terms but also in economic power.*

ter|mi|nol|ogy /ˌtɜːmɪˈnɒlədʒi/ `ACADEMIC STUDY` `LANGUAGE`

UNCOUNTABLE NOUN The **terminology** of a subject is the set of special words and expressions used in connection with it. ○ *In medical terminology a gallop rhythm means that the heart is failing because the cardiac muscle is badly damaged and dilated.*

▶ **COLLOCATION:** **medical/technical/legal/business** terminology

▶ **SYNONYMS:** jargon, vocabulary

ter|ri|tory /ˈterətri, AM -tɔːri/ `GEOGRAPHY` `BIOLOGY`

1 **UNCOUNTABLE NOUN** **Territory** is land which is controlled by a particular country or ruler. ○ *The government denies that any of its territory is under rebel control.* ○ *India and Pakistan have fought wars over the disputed territory of Kashmir.* ○ *Russian territory*

▶ **COLLOCATIONS:**
enter/seize/conquer/occupy/control territory

occupied/disputed/neutral territory

▶ SYNONYM: land

2 UNCOUNTABLE NOUN An animal's **territory** is an area which it regards as its own and which it defends when other animals try to enter it. ○ *The territory of a cat only remains fixed for as long as the cat dominates the area.*

ter|ri|to|rial /ˌterɪ'tɔːriəl/

1 ADJECTIVE Territorial means concerned with the ownership of a particular area of land or water. ○ *It is the only republic which has no territorial disputes with the others.* ○ *Both Chile and Argentina feel very strongly about their territorial claims to Antarctica.*

▶ COLLOCATIONS:
a territorial **dispute/claim/boundary/limit**
territorial **waters/integrity**

2 ADJECTIVE If you describe an animal or its behaviour as **territorial**, you mean that it has an area which it regards as its own, and which it defends when other animals try to enter it. ○ *Two cats in one house will also exhibit territorial behaviour.*

▶ COLLOCATION: **fiercely/highly** territorial

---

ter|ror|ist /'terərɪst/ (terrorists)   POLITICS

NOUN A **terrorist** is a person who uses violence, especially murder and bombing, in order to achieve political aims. ○ *One American was killed and three were wounded in terrorist attacks.* ○ *the September 11 terrorist atrocities in the US*

▶ COLLOCATIONS:
a terrorist **attack/act/bombing/incident/threat/target/plot**
terrorist **activity/violence**
a terrorist **organization/network/group**
a **suspected/alleged** terrorist

ter|ror|ism /'terərɪzəm/

UNCOUNTABLE NOUN Terrorism is the use of violence, especially murder and bombing, in order to achieve political aims or to force a government to do something. ○ *We will fight terrorism and the terrorists who carried out this explosion.* ○ *He is currently facing terrorism charges in Virginia.*

▶ COLLOCATIONS:
international/global/cross-border terrorism
fight/combat/tackle/defeat terrorism
condemn/support terrorism
a terrorism **charge/expert/suspect/threat**

---

text /tekst/ (texts)   ACADEMIC STUDY   ACADEMIC WORD   LANGUAGE

NOUN A **text** is a book or other piece of writing, especially one connected with science or learning. ○ *Her text is believed to be the oldest surviving manuscript by a female physician.* ○ *a tool that can translate English text into spoken Mandarin*

▶ **COLLOCATIONS:**
 a **sacred/biblical/religious/legal/medical** text
 translate/edit/write/study/interpret a text
▶ **SYNONYM:** book

tex|tu|al /'tekstʃʊəl/

ADJECTIVE **Textual** means relating to written texts, especially literary texts.
○ *close textual analysis of Shakespeare*

▶ **COLLOCATION:** textual **analysis/interpretation/criticism**
▶ **SYNONYM:** literary

the|ol|ogy /θiˈɒlədʒi/

UNCOUNTABLE NOUN **Theology** is the study of the nature of God and of religion and religious beliefs. ○ *He began studying theology with a view to becoming a priest.* ○ *a Christian theology course*

▶ **COLLOCATION:** **Christian/Islamic** theology

theo|logi|cal /ˌθiːəˈlɒdʒɪkəl/

ADJECTIVE ○ *Critics of the Pope said he focused too much power in the hands of the Vatican and smothered theological debate.*

▶ **COLLOCATIONS:**
 a theological **question/issue/point**
 theological **debate/argument/study/training**

theo|lo|gian /ˌθiːəˈləʊdʒən/ (theologians)

NOUN A **theologian** is someone who studies the nature of God, religion, and religious beliefs. ○ *the philosopher and theologian John Henry Newman*

▶ **COLLOCATION:** a **Christian/Catholic/Protestant/Jewish** theologian
▶ **PHRASES:**
 a theologian and philosopher
 a theologian and historian

theo|ry /'θɪəri/ (theories)   ACADEMIC WORD

1 NOUN A **theory** is a formal idea or set of ideas that is intended to explain something. ○ [+ *of*] *Einstein formulated the Theory of Relativity in 1905.*

▶ **COLLOCATIONS:**
 a theory **of** *something*
 the theory of **evolution/relativity**
 develop/propose/formulate/test/prove/apply a theory
 a **scientific/evolutionary** theory
▶ **SYNONYMS:** principle, law, rule

2 PHRASE You use **in theory** to say that although something is supposed to be true or to happen in the way stated, it may not in fact be true or happen in that way. ○ *A school dental service exists in theory, but in practice, there are few dentists to work in it.* ○ *In theory, the technology is straightforward.*

▶ SYNONYM: theoretically
▶ RELATED WORD: in practice

theo|reti|cal /ˌθiːəˈretɪkəl/

1 ADJECTIVE A **theoretical** study or explanation is based on or uses the ideas and abstract principles that relate to a particular subject, rather than the practical aspects or uses of it. ○ *theoretical physics* ○ *There is no theoretical model to explain the impact of inflation on growth.*

▶ COLLOCATIONS:
a theoretical **analysis/framework**
a theoretical **model/argument/study**
▶ ANTONYM: practical

2 ADJECTIVE If you describe a situation as a **theoretical** one, you mean that although it is supposed to be true or to exist in the way stated, it may not in fact be true or exist in that way. ○ *This is certainly a theoretical risk but in practice there is seldom a problem.* ○ *These fears are purely theoretical.*

▶ COLLOCATIONS:
a theoretical **risk/possibility**
purely/largely theoretical

---

there|fore /ˈðeəfɔː/

ADVERB You use **therefore** to introduce a logical result or conclusion. ○ *Muscle cells need lots of fuel and therefore burn lots of calories.* ○ *We expect to continue to gain new customers and therefore also market share.*

→ see note at **hence**
▶ SYNONYM: thus

---

the|sis /ˈθiːsɪs/ (theses) `ACADEMIC WORD` `EDUCATION` `ACADEMIC STUDY`

1 NOUN A **thesis** is an idea or theory that is expressed as a statement and is discussed in a logical way. ○ *This thesis does not stand up to close inspection.* ○ *One of the arguments used to support the thesis is that students who rely on their parents for money feel great pressure to get good grades.*

2 NOUN A **thesis** is a long piece of writing based on your own ideas and research that you do as part of a university degree, especially a higher degree such as a PhD. ○ [+ on] *He was awarded his PhD for a thesis on industrial robots.*

▶ COLLOCATIONS:
a thesis **on** something
write/support/develop/submit a thesis

the **central/main** thesis
a **doctoral/PhD** thesis
▸ SYNONYMS: dissertation, argument, theory

> **ACADEMIC WRITING: A thesis-led essay**
>
> In a **thesis-led** piece of writing, you state your **thesis** at the beginning. That is, you explain your position or point of view in your introduction. Then you provide arguments and evidence to support your **thesis**.
>
> In an **argument-led** essay, you set out the different **arguments** or points of view and you do not give your own position until the end, in your conclusion.

Third World /ˈθɜːd ˌwɜːld/ `POLITICS` `GEOGRAPHY`

NOUN Some countries in Africa, Asia, and South America are sometimes referred to all together as **the Third World**, especially those parts that are poor, do not have much power, and are not considered to be highly developed. ○ *studies of malnourished mothers in the Third World* ○ *He urged Britons to campaign on the streets to help end Third World poverty.*

▸ COLLOCATIONS:
in the Third World
a Third World **country/nation/economy**
Third World **governments/leaders/development/debt/poverty**
▸ SYNONYM: developing countries
▸ RELATED WORD: First World

thus /ðʌs/

ADVERB You use **thus** to show that what you are about to mention is the result or consequence of something else that you have just mentioned. [FORMAL] ○ *Even in a highly skilled workforce some people will be more capable and thus better paid than others.* ○ *women's access to the basic means of production and thus to political power*
→ see note at **hence**
▸ SYNONYMS: therefore, hence

tol|er|ate /ˈtɒləreɪt/ (tolerates, tolerating, tolerated)

VERB If you **tolerate** a situation or person, you accept them although you do not particularly like them. ○ *It is vital that councils do not tolerate substandard care.* ○ *The Army does not tolerate inappropriate behaviour.*

▸ COLLOCATIONS:
tolerate **behaviour/racism/corruption/dissent**
grudgingly/barely/never tolerate *something*
▸ SYNONYMS: accept, condone

tol|er|ant /ˈtɒlərənt/

1 **ADJECTIVE** If you describe someone as **tolerant**, you approve of the fact that they allow other people to say and do as they like, even if they do not agree with or like it. ○ [+ of] *They need to be tolerant of different points of view.* ○ *Other changes include more tolerant attitudes to unmarried couples having children.*

▸ **COLLOCATIONS:**
   tolerant **of** *something*
   a tolerant **society/country/attitude**
   racially tolerant

▸ **SYNONYM:** accepting

▸ **ANTONYM:** intolerant

2 **ADJECTIVE** If a plant, animal, or machine is **tolerant of** particular conditions or types of treatment, it is able to bear them without being damaged or hurt. ○ [+ of] *plants which are more tolerant of dry conditions.*

▸ **COLLOCATION:** tolerant **of** *something*

tol|er|ance /ˈtɒlərəns/

UNCOUNTABLE NOUN ○ [+ of] *his tolerance and understanding of diverse human nature* ○ *a unique culture, of which religious tolerance was an important part*

▸ **COLLOCATIONS:**
   tolerance **of** *something*
   show tolerance
   religious/racial/political tolerance

▸ **SYNONYM:** acceptance

▸ **ANTONYM:** intolerance

---

tox|ic /ˈtɒksɪk/ `SCIENCE` `MEDICINE`

ADJECTIVE A **toxic** substance is poisonous. ○ *the cost of cleaning up toxic waste* ○ [+ to] *These products are not toxic to humans.*

▸ **COLLOCATIONS:**
   toxic **to** *someone/something*
   highly/potentially toxic
   a toxic **chemical/substance/metal/effect**
   toxic **waste/fumes/material/gas/emissions**

▸ **SYNONYMS:** poisonous, dangerous

▸ **ANTONYMS:** non-toxic, safe

---

trade /treɪd/ (trades, trading, traded) `BUSINESS`

1 **UNCOUNTABLE NOUN** **Trade** is the activity of buying, selling, or exchanging goods or services between people, companies, or countries. ○ *The ministry had direct control over every aspect of foreign trade.* ○ [+ with] *Texas has a long history of trade with Mexico.*

▶ **COLLOCATIONS:**
trade **with** *someone/something*
trade **between** *people/things*
international/global/foreign/world trade
free/fair/illegal/illicit trade
the **drug/sex/slave/arms** trade
a trade **agreement/embargo/war/deficit/surplus**
trade **talks/negotiations/sanctions**
▶ **SYNONYMS:** commerce, business

2 VERB When people, firms, or countries **trade**, they buy, sell, or exchange goods or services between themselves. ○ [+ *with*] *They had years of experience of trading with the West.* ○ [+ *in*] *He has been trading in antique furniture for 25 years.*
▶ **COLLOCATIONS:**
trade **in** *something*
trade **with** *someone*
▶ **SYNONYM:** do business

---

trait /treɪt, treɪ/ **(traits)**

NOUN A **trait** is a particular characteristic, quality, or tendency that someone or something has. ○ *The study found that some alcoholics had clear personality traits showing up early in childhood.* ○ *Do we inherit traits such as agility and sporting excellence, and musical or artistic ability?*
▶ **COLLOCATIONS:**
inherit/share a trait
a **personality/character/human/family** trait
a **physical/psychological/behavioural/cultural/genetic** trait
▶ **SYNONYMS:** characteristic, attribute, quality

---

trans|fer **(transfers, transferring, transferred)** `ACADEMIC WORD`

The verb is pronounced /træns'fɜː/. The noun is pronounced /'trænsfɜː/.

1 VERB If you **transfer** something or someone **from** one place **to** another, or they **transfer from** one place **to** another, they go from the first place to the second. ○ [+ *from/to*] *He wants to transfer some money to the account of his daughter.* ○ [+ *from/to*] *The person can transfer from wheelchair to seat with relative ease.*
▶ **COLLOCATION:** transfer **from/to** *something*
▶ **SYNONYM:** move

● **Transfer** is also a noun. ○ [+ *of*] *Arrange for the transfer of medical records to your new doctor.* ○ *The bank reserves the right to reverse any transfers or payments.*

▶ **COLLOCATIONS:**
the transfer **of** *something*
make/complete a transfer

2 VERB If something **is transferred**, or **transfers**, **from** one person or group of people **to** another, the second person or group gets it instead of the first. ○ [+ *to*] *The chances of the disease being transferred to humans is extremely remote.* ○ [+ *from/to*] *On 1 December the presidency of the Security Council automatically transfers from the U.S. to Yemen.*

▶ **COLLOCATIONS:**
transfer **from/to** *something*
transfer **automatically/directly**

▶ **SYNONYM:** pass

● **Transfer** is also a noun. ○ [+ *of*] *the transfer of power from the old to the new regimes*

▶ **COLLOCATION:** the transfer **of** *something*

---

trans|form /trænsˈfɔːm/
(transforms, transforming, transformed)

1 VERB To **transform** something **into** something else means to change or convert it into that thing. ○ [+ *into*] *Your metabolic rate is the speed at which your body transforms food into energy.* ○ [+ *from/into*] *Delegates also discussed transforming them from a guerrilla force into a regular army.*

2 VERB To **transform** something or someone means to change them completely and suddenly so that they are much better or more attractive. ○ *The spread of the internet and mobile telephony have transformed society.* ○ [+ *into*] *Yeltsin was committed to completely transforming Russia into a market economy.*

▶ **COLLOCATIONS:**
transform *something* **from/into** *something*
completely/magically/dramatically transform
transform **society**
transform a **country/business/area**
transform the **economy/landscape/country/world**

▶ **SYNONYMS:** change, convert

trans|for|ma|tion /ˌtrænsfəˈmeɪʃən/

NOUN ○ *one of the most astonishing economic transformations seen since the second world war* ○ *After 1959, the Spanish economy underwent a profound transformation.*

▶ **COLLOCATIONS:**
the transformation **of** *something*
undergo/see/make a transformation
a transformation **occurs/takes place**
a **radical/dramatic/profound/complete** transformation

a **social/economic/personal/political/cultural** transformation
▶ SYNONYM: change

---

trans|par|ent /træns'pærənt, AM -'per-/

1 ADJECTIVE If an object or substance is **transparent**, you can see through it.
○ *a sheet of transparent coloured plastic* ○ *a transparent plastic tube*
▶ SYNONYMS: see-through, clear
▶ ANTONYM: opaque

2 ADJECTIVE If a situation, system, or activity is **transparent**, it is easily understood or recognized. ○ *We are now striving hard to establish a transparent parliamentary democracy.* ○ *The company has to make its accounts as transparent as possible.*
▶ COLLOCATIONS:
make *something* transparent
a transparent **process/system**
completely transparent
▶ SYNONYMS: open, clear

trans|par|ent|ly /træns'pærəntli, AM -'per-/

ADVERB ○ *The system was clearly not functioning smoothly or transparently.*
○ *Government activities must be conducted openly, transparently and effectively.*
▶ SYNONYM: openly

trans|par|en|cy /træns'pærənsi, AM -'per-/

1 UNCOUNTABLE NOUN Transparency is the quality that an object or substance has when you can see through it. ○ [+ *of*] *Cataracts is a condition that affects the transparency of the lenses.*
▶ COLLOCATION: the transparency **of** *something*

2 UNCOUNTABLE NOUN The **transparency** of a process, situation, or statement is its quality of being easily understood or recognized, for example because there are no secrets connected with it, or because it is expressed in a clear way. ○ [+ *in*] *openness and transparency in the Government's economic decision-making*
▶ COLLOCATIONS:
transparency **in** *something*
increase/improve/ensure transparency
greater/full transparency
▶ PHRASES:
transparency and accountability
openness and transparency
▶ SYNONYM: clarity

trend /trend/ (trends) `ACADEMIC WORD`

NOUN A **trend** is a change or development towards something new or different. ○ *This is a growing trend.* ○ [+ *towards*] *There has been a trend towards part-time employment.* ○ *the downward trend in gasoline prices*

▶ COLLOCATIONS:
a trend **towards** something
buck/defy/reverse/reflect/continue a trend
a **growing/emerging/new/recent** trend
the **latest/current** trend
a **general/underlying/overall/global/international** trend
a **social/economic/cultural** trend
a **downward/upward/disturbing/worrying** trend

▶ SYNONYMS: tendency, movement

tri|al /traɪəl/ (trials) `SCIENCE` `MEDICINE`

NOUN A **trial** is an experiment in which you test something by using it or doing it for a period of time to see how well it works. If something is **on trial**, it is being tested in this way. ○ *They have been treated with this drug in clinical trials.* ○ *The robots have been on trial for the past year.*

▶ COLLOCATIONS:
be **on** trial
a **clinical** trial
carry out/conduct/undertake/undergo a trial

▶ SYNONYM: test

trig|ger /ˈtrɪgə/ (triggers, triggering, triggered) `ACADEMIC WORD`

1 VERB If something **triggers** an event or situation, it causes it to begin to happen or exist. ○ *the incident which triggered the outbreak of the First World War* ○ *The current recession was triggered by a slump in consumer spending.*

▶ COLLOCATIONS:
trigger a **response/reaction/change**
trigger a **crisis/attack/war/debate**
trigger a **tsunami/landslide/avalanche**

▶ SYNONYM: spark

2 NOUN If something acts as a **trigger for** another thing such as an illness, event, or situation, the first thing causes the second thing to begin to happen or exist. ○ [+ *for*] *Stress may act as a trigger for these illnesses.*

▶ COLLOCATION: a trigger **for** something

trop|ics /ˈtrɒpɪks/ `GEOGRAPHY`

PLURAL NOUN **The tropics** are the parts of the world that lie between two lines of latitude, the tropic of Cancer, 23 ½° north of the equator, and the tropic of Capricorn, 23 ½° south of the equator.

▶ **RELATED WORD:** equator

tropi|cal /'trɒpɪkəl/

ADJECTIVE Tropical means belonging to or typical of the tropics. ○ *By far the most serious tropical disease is malaria.* ○ *a plan to preserve the world's tropical forests*

▶ COLLOCATIONS:

a tropical **disease/storm/cyclone/climate**
a tropical **country/paradise/island/forest/rainforest/jungle**
tropical **fruit/fish/plant**

---

tu|tor /'tjuːtə, AM 'tuːt-/ (tutors)   EDUCATION   ACADEMIC STUDY

NOUN A **tutor** is a teacher at a British university or college. In some American universities or colleges, a **tutor** is a teacher of the lowest rank. ○ [+ *in*] *He is course tutor in archaeology at the University of Southampton.* ○ *Liam surprised his tutors by twice failing a second year exam.*

▶ COLLOCATIONS:

a tutor **in** *something*
a **course** tutor
a tutor **group**

▶ SYNONYMS: teacher, lecturer

tu|to|rial /tjuː'tɔːrɪəl, AM 'tuːt-/ (tutorials)

NOUN In a university or college, a **tutorial** is a regular meeting between a tutor and one or several students, for discussion of a subject that is being studied. ○ *The methods of study include lectures, tutorials, case studies and practical sessions.* ○ *Students attend weekly tutorials.*

▶ COLLOCATION: **give/attend** a tutorial

tui|tion /tjʊ'ɪʃən, AM tʊ-/

UNCOUNTABLE NOUN If you are given **tuition** in a particular subject, you are taught about that subject. ○ [+ *in*] *The courses will give you tuition in all types of outdoor photography.* ○ *You need to pay your tuition fees and to support yourself financially.*

▶ COLLOCATIONS:

tuition **in** something
give/provide/offer/receive tuition
private/personal/one-to-one/individual tuition
college/university tuition
tuition **fees**

▶ SYNONYMS: teaching, instruction

Uu

ul|ti|mate /ˈʌltɪmət/

1 **ADJECTIVE** You use **ultimate** to describe the final result or aim of a long series of events. ○ *He said it is still not possible to predict the ultimate outcome.* ○ *The ultimate aim is to expand the network further.*

▶ **COLLOCATIONS:**
the ultimate **aim/goal/objective**
the ultimate **fate/outcome/result/destination**

▶ **SYNONYMS:** eventual, final

2 **ADJECTIVE** You use **ultimate** to describe the most important or powerful thing of a particular kind. ○ *the ultimate power of the central government* ○ *Of course, the ultimate authority remained the presidency.*

▶ **COLLOCATIONS:**
the ultimate **control/power/authority**
the ultimate **challenge/responsibility**

▶ **SYNONYMS:** most important, highest

ul|ti|mate|ly /ˈʌltɪmətli/

1 **ADVERB** **Ultimately** means finally, after a long and often complicated series of events. ○ *Whatever the scientists ultimately conclude, all of their data will immediately be disputed.* ○ *It was a tough but ultimately worthwhile struggle.*

▶ **COLLOCATION:** ultimately **decide/conclude/succeed**

▶ **SYNONYMS:** eventually, in the end

2 **ADVERB** You use **ultimately** to indicate that what you are saying is the most important point in a discussion. ○ *Ultimately, Bismarck's revisionism scarcely affected or damaged British interests at all.*

un|am|bigu|ous /ˌʌnæmˈbɪɡjuəs/

ADJECTIVE If you describe a message or comment as **unambiguous**, you mean that it is clear and cannot be understood wrongly. ○ *It was an election result that sent the party an unambiguous message.* ○ *The instructions were clear and unambiguous.*

▶ **COLLOCATION:** an unambiguous **message/statement**

▶ **PHRASE:** clear and unambiguous

▶ **ANTONYM:** ambiguous

un|am|bigu|ous|ly /ˌʌnæmˈbɪɡjʊəsli/

ADVERB ○ *He has failed to dissociate himself clearly and unambiguously from the attack.*
- ▶ **COLLOCATION: state/declare/answer/demonstrate** unambiguously
- ▶ **PHRASE:** clearly and unambiguously
- ▶ **ANTONYM:** ambiguously

under|go /ˌʌndəˈɡəʊ/   `ACADEMIC WORD`
(undergoes, undergoing, underwent, undergone)

VERB If a person or thing **undergoes** something necessary or unpleasant, it happens to them. ○ *New recruits have been undergoing training in recent weeks.* ○ *When cement powder is mixed with water it undergoes a chemical change and sets hard.*
- ▶ **COLLOCATIONS:**
  undergo an **operation**
  undergo **surgery/treatment/therapy/training**
  undergo **refurbishment/restoration/repairs**
  undergo a **change/transformation/facelift/reaction**
  undergo a **review/assessment/evaluation/test/check**

under|gradu|ate /ˌʌndəˈɡrædʒʊət/   `EDUCATION` `ACADEMIC STUDY`
(undergraduates)

NOUN An **undergraduate** is a student at a university or college who is studying for his or her first degree. **Undergrad** is also used in informal and spoken English. ○ *Economics undergraduates are probably the brightest in the university.* ○ *undergraduate degree programmes*
- ▶ **COLLOCATIONS:**
  a **history/engineering/science** undergraduate
  an undergraduate **degree/course/programme/student**
  undergraduate **study/education**
- ▶ **RELATED WORDS:** postgraduate, graduate

under|line /ˌʌndəˈlaɪn/ **(underlines, underlining, underlined)**

VERB If one thing, for example an action or an event, **underlines** another, it draws attention to it and emphasizes its importance. ○ *The report underlined his concern that standards were at risk.* ○ [+ *how*] *The incident underlines how easily things can go wrong.*
- ▶ **COLLOCATION:** underline a **need/problem/difficulty/danger/concern**
- ▶ **PHRASES:**
  underline the importance of *something*
  underline the fact that ...
- ▶ **SYNONYMS:** underscore, emphasize, highlight

u

under|ly|ing /ˌʌndəˈlaɪɪŋ/

ACADEMIC WORD

ADJECTIVE The **underlying** features of an object, event, or situation are not obvious, and it may be difficult to discover or reveal them. ○ *To stop a problem you have to understand its underlying causes.* ○ *I think that the underlying problem is education, unemployment and bad housing.*

▶ **COLLOCATIONS:**
an underlying **cause/reason/problem/issue**
an underlying **principle/assumption/theme/philosophy**
an underlying **trend**

▶ **SYNONYMS:** basic, fundamental

under|take /ˌʌndəˈteɪk/

ACADEMIC WORD

(undertakes, undertaking, undertook, undertaken)

VERB When you **undertake** a task or job, you start doing it and accept responsibility for it. ○ *She undertook the arduous task of monitoring the elections.* ○ *Students are encouraged to undertake research in areas in which the department has particular expertise.*

▶ **COLLOCATIONS:**
undertake **work/research/training/exercise**
undertake a **study/project/activity/task/tour**
undertake a **review/analysis/investigation/survey**

▶ **SYNONYMS:** do, carry out

under|tak|ing /ˈʌndəteɪkɪŋ/ (undertakings)

NOUN An **undertaking** is a task or job, especially a large or difficult one. ○ *Organizing the show has been a massive undertaking.* ○ *the nineteenth century's most ambitious scientific undertaking*

▶ **COLLOCATION:** a **major/massive/huge/ambitious** undertaking

▶ **SYNONYMS:** job, task

un|doubt|ed /ʌnˈdaʊtɪd/

ADJECTIVE You can use **undoubted** to emphasize that something exists or is true. ○ *The event was an undoubted success.* ○ *a man of undoubted parliamentary skills* ○ *his undoubted intellectual ability*

▶ **COLLOCATIONS:**
an undoubted **success/star**
undoubted **ability/talent/skill/potential**

▶ **SYNONYMS:** definite, undisputed

▶ **ANTONYM:** doubtful

un|doubt|ed|ly /ʌnˈdaʊtɪdli/

ADVERB ○ *Undoubtedly, political and economic factors have played their part.* ○ *These sort of statistics are undoubtedly alarming.* ○ *It is undoubtedly true that*

harder times are on the way.

▶ **SYNONYMS:** without doubt, certainly

---

un|ion /'juːnjən/ (unions) `BUSINESS`

NOUN A **union** is a workers' organization which represents its members and which aims to improve things such as their working conditions and pay. ○ *Women in all types of employment can benefit from joining a union.* ○ *Union officials criticized management tactics.*

▶ **COLLOCATIONS:**
   join a union
   a union **represents** *someone*
   a union **leader/member/official/representative/activist**
   union **membership**

▶ **SYNONYM:** trade union

---

unique /juːˈniːk/ `ACADEMIC WORD`

1 ADJECTIVE Something that is **unique** is the only one of its kind. ○ *Each person's signature is unique.* ○ *The area has its own unique language, Catalan.*

▶ **COLLOCATIONS:**
   a unique **opportunity/experience/position/situation/event**
   a unique **characteristic/insight/style/feature**

2 ADJECTIVE If something is **unique to** one thing, person, group, or place, it concerns or belongs only to that thing, person, group, or place. ○ [+ *to*] *No one knows for sure why adolescence is unique to humans.* ○ [+ *to*] *This interesting and charming creature is unique to Borneo.*

▶ **COLLOCATION:** unique **to** *someone/something*

unique|ly /juːˈniːkli/

ADVERB ○ *Because of the extreme cold, the Antarctic is a uniquely fragile environment.* ○ *The problem is not uniquely American.*

---

unit /'juːnɪt/ (units)

1 NOUN If you consider something as a **unit**, you consider it as a single, complete thing. ○ *Agriculture was based in the past on the family as a unit.*

2 NOUN A **unit** of measurement is a fixed standard quantity, length, or weight that is used for measuring things. The litre, the centimetre, and the ounce are all units. ○ *The curie became a unit of measurement of radioactivity.* ○ *the imperial units of measurement* ○ *a unit of radiation measurement*

▶ **PHRASE:** a unit of measurement

---

uni|ver|sal /ˌjuːnɪˈvɜːsəl/

1 ADJECTIVE Something that is **universal** relates to everyone in the world or everyone in a particular group or society. ○ *The insurance industry has produced* its own proposals for universal health care. ○ The desire to look attractive is universal.

▶ COLLOCATIONS:
universal **childcare/health care/suffrage/literacy**
a universal **language/truth**
universal **appeal**

2 ADJECTIVE Something that is **universal** affects or relates to every part of the world or the universe. ○ universal diseases ○ the law of universal gravitation

▶ SYNONYM: worldwide

uni|ver|sal|ly /juːnɪˈvɜːsəli/

1 ADVERB If something is **universally** believed or accepted, it is believed or accepted by everyone with no disagreement. ○ a universally accepted point of view ○ The scale of the problem is now universally recognised.

▶ COLLOCATIONS:
universally **accepted/recognised**
universally **acknowledged/condemned**

2 ADVERB If something is **universally** true, it is true everywhere in the world or in all situations. ○ The disadvantage is that it is not universally available.

▶ COLLOCATION: universally **available/accessible/popular**

---

un|sta|ble /ˌʌnˈsteɪbəl/

ADJECTIVE You can describe something as **unstable** if it is likely to change suddenly, especially if this creates difficulty or danger. ○ After the fall of the Prime Minster in 1801 there was a decade of unstable government. ○ The situation is unstable and potentially dangerous.

▶ COLLOCATIONS:
an unstable **situation/government/regime/region/country**
very/highly/increasingly/politically unstable

▶ SYNONYMS: fragile, volatile, unsettled

▶ ANTONYM: stable

> **USAGE:** Noun form
>
> The noun form of **unstable** is **instability**. ○ postwar economic and political instability

---

ur|ban /ˈɜːbən/ GEOGRAPHY

ADJECTIVE **Urban** means belonging to, or relating to, a town or city. ○ She lived well away from the urban sprawl of London. ○ By 2020 most people in Asia will be living in urban areas.

▶ COLLOCATIONS:
an urban **area/environment/landscape**

4 | **utilization**

urban **space/sprawl/design/development/planning**
urban **regeneration/renaissance/renewal/life**
an urban **community/population**
▶ ANTONYM: rural

ur|ban|ized /'ɜːbənaɪzd/

ADJECTIVE An **urbanized** country or area has many buildings and a lot of industry and business [in BRIT, also use **urbanised**]. ○ Zambia is black Africa's most urbanised country. ○ All the nice areas in Florida are becoming more and more urbanized.

▶ COLLOCATIONS:
become urbanized
an urbanized **area/region**
highly/increasingly urbanized

ur|bani|za|tion /ˌɜːbənaɪˈzeɪʃən/

UNCOUNTABLE NOUN **Urbanization** is the process of creating towns in country areas. [in BRIT, also use **urbanisation**] ○ Rapid urbanization is one of the gravest challenges facing governments and communities alike.

▶ COLLOCATION: **rapid/increasing** urbanization
▶ PHRASE: industrialization and urbanization

---

uti|lize /'juːtɪlaɪz/ (utilizes, utilizing, utilized)   ACADEMIC WORD

VERB If you **utilize** something, you use it. [FORMAL; in BRIT, also use **utilise**] ○ Sound engineers utilize a range of techniques to enhance the quality of the recordings. ○ Minerals can be absorbed and utilized by the body in a variety of different forms.

▶ COLLOCATIONS:
utilize a **strategy/technique/method/approach/service/resource**
utilize **technology/energy/power**
fully/effectively utilize something
▶ SYNONYMS: use, employ

uti|li|za|tion /ˌjuːtɪlaɪˈzeɪʃən/

UNCOUNTABLE NOUN [in BRIT, also use **utilisation**] ○ [+ of] the utilisation of human resources ○ [+ of] the economic utilization of atomic energy

▶ COLLOCATIONS:
the utilization **of** something
full/maximum/effective/inefficient utilization
maximize/improve/increase utilization
impair/prevent utilization
▶ SYNONYMS: use, employment

Vv

vague /veɪɡ/ (vaguer, vaguest)

ADJECTIVE If something written or spoken is **vague**, it does not explain or express things clearly. ○ *Marx was intentionally vague about the structure and functioning of the socialist economy.* ○ *Police have only a vague description of the vehicle.*

▶ COLLOCATIONS:
vague **information/wording**
a vague **reference/description/term**
deliberately/intentionally vague

▶ SYNONYMS: imprecise, unclear, ambiguous

▶ ANTONYMS: precise, clear

val|id /'vælɪd/   ACADEMIC WORD

1 ADJECTIVE A **valid** argument, comment, or idea is based on sensible reasoning. ○ *They put forward many valid reasons for not exporting.* ○ *Some of these arguments are valid.* ○ *This is a perfectly valid approach, but it has its drawbacks.*

▶ COLLOCATIONS:
a valid **reason/point/argument/claim**
a valid **comment/question/comparison/criticism**
perfectly/equally/entirely valid

▶ SYNONYMS: legitimate, sound, solid, reasonable

2 ADJECTIVE If something such as a number is **valid**, it is within an acceptable range of values or restrictions. ○ *software that generates valid numbers* ○ *a valid password* ○ *a statistically valid sample*

▶ ANTONYM: invalid

va|lid|ity /və'lɪdɪti/

UNCOUNTABLE NOUN The **validity of** an argument, a piece of information or a result is whether it is based on sensible reasoning or methods and can be believed or trusted. ○ *This argument has lost much of its validity.* ○ *Many scientists are questioning the validity of the claims of the study.*

▶ COLLOCATIONS:
the validity **of** *something*
question/challenge/doubt the validity of *something*
check/test/assess/determine the validity of *something*

demonstrate/accept/confirm the validity of *something*
▶ SYNONYMS: worth, legitimacy, strength

---

value /ˈvæljuː/ (values, valuing, valued)

1 UNCOUNTABLE NOUN The **value** of something such as a quality, attitude, or method is its importance or usefulness. If you place a particular **value** on something, that is the importance or usefulness you think it has. ○ *Further studies will be needed to see if these therapies have any value.* ○ *Current sales figures tell us something of value about what is really going on.*
▶ COLLOCATIONS:
   place/put a value on *something*
   artistic/actual/real/true/great value
   a value **judgement**
▶ PHRASE: of (no) value
▶ SYNONYM: worth

2 VERB If you **value** something or someone, you think that they are important and you appreciate them. ○ *a culture in the workplace which values learning and development* ○ *Authority is rooted in a patriarchal system; males are highly valued.*
▶ COLLOCATIONS:
   value a **contribution/input/opinion**
   value **freedom/diversity/friendship/support/life**
   value a **skill/opportunity/experience**
   value *something/someone* **greatly/highly**
▶ SYNONYMS: admire, approve of

3 PLURAL NOUN The **values** of a person or group are the moral principles and beliefs that they think are important. ○ *The countries of South Asia also share many common values.* ○ *The Health Secretary called for a return to traditional family values.*
▶ COLLOCATIONS:
   share/reflect values
   modern/traditional/moral/cultural/social/family values
▶ SYNONYMS: beliefs, morals

4 NOUN A **value** is a particular number or amount. ○ *Normal values lie between 1.0 and 3.0mg per 100ml blood serum.* ○ *These calculations were based on average values for velocity and acceleration.*
▶ SYNONYMS: number, amount, figure

---

va|pour /ˈveɪpə/ (vapours)   SCIENCE   GEOGRAPHY

NOUN **Vapour** consists of tiny drops of water or other liquids in the air, which appear as mist. [in AM, use **vapor**] ○ *Cold air can hold very little water vapour compared with warm air.* ○ *the vapour trail of a jet across the sky*
▶ SYNONYMS: mist, fog

va|por|ize /ˈveɪpəraɪz/ (vaporizes, vaporizing, vaporized)

VERB If a liquid or solid **vaporizes** or if you **vaporize** it, it changes into vapour or gas. [in BRIT, also use **vaporise**] ○ *The benzene vaporized and formed a huge cloud of gas.*

▶ **SYNONYM:** evaporate

vary /ˈveəri/ (varies, varying, varied) ACADEMIC WORD

1 VERB If things **vary**, they are different from each other in size, amount, or degree. ○ *Assessment practices vary in different schools or colleges.* ○ [+ from] *The text varies from the earlier versions.* ○ [V-ing] *Different writers will prepare to varying degrees.*

2 VERB If something **varies** or if you **vary** it, it becomes different or changed. ○ *The cost of the alcohol duty varies according to the amount of wine in the bottle.* ○ *Company officials should make sure that security routines are varied.*

→ see note at **fluctuate**

▶ **COLLOCATIONS:**
vary **from** *something*
vary from *something* **to** *something*
vary from **region to region/person to person**
vary **considerably/enormously/greatly/widely**
opinions/prices/estimates/practices vary
varying **degrees/sizes/lengths/amounts**

▶ **SYNONYMS:** differ, change

vari|ation /ˌveəriˈeɪʃən/ (variations)

NOUN A **variation** is a change or slight difference in a level, amount, or quantity. ○ [+ in] *The survey found a wide variation in the prices charged for canteen food.* ○ *Scotland's employment rate shows significant regional variations.*

▶ **COLLOCATIONS:**
variation **in** *something*
seasonal/genetic/regional variation
wide/considerable/slight variation
show variation

▶ **SYNONYMS:** difference, diversity
▶ **ANTONYM:** similarity

vari|able /ˈveəriəbəl/ (variables)

NOUN A **variable** is a factor that can change in quality, quantity, or size, which you have to take into account in a situation. ○ *Decisions could be made on the basis of price, delivery dates, after-sales service or any other variable.* ○ *Other variables in making forecasts for the industry include the weather and the general economic climate.*

▶ COLLOCATIONS:
  a **dependent/independent** variable
  demographic/socioeconomic/extraneous variables
  manipulate/measure/identify/examine variables
  variables **determine/influence/cause** something
▶ SYNONYM: factor

ver|dict /ˈvɜːdɪkt/ (verdicts) LAW

NOUN In a court of law, the **verdict** is the decision that is given by the jury or judge at the end of a trial. ○ *The jury returned a unanimous guilty verdict.* ○ *Three judges will deliver their verdict in October.*

▶ COLLOCATIONS:
  reach/return/deliver/announce/appeal/overturn a verdict
  a **guilty/not-guilty/open** verdict
  a **final/unanimous/majority** verdict
  a **jury/court** verdict
▶ SYNONYMS: decision, decree, ruling

veri|fy /ˈverɪfaɪ/ (verifies, verifying, verified)

VERB If you **verify** something, you check that it is true by careful examination or investigation. ○ *continued testing to verify the accuracy of the method* ○ *[+ that] A clerk simply verifies that the payment and invoice amount match.*

→ see note at **confirm**

▶ COLLOCATIONS:
  verify a **claim/figure**
  verify the **accuracy/authenticity/identity** of something/someone
  independently/immediately/easily verify
▶ SYNONYMS: check, confirm

veri|fi|ca|tion /ˌverɪfɪˈkeɪʃən/

UNCOUNTABLE NOUN ○ *[+ of] All charges against her are dropped pending the verification of her story.* ○ *the agency's verification procedures*

▶ COLLOCATIONS:
  verification **of** something
  independent/accurate verification
  a verification **procedure/process/system**
▶ SYNONYM: confirmation

ver|sa|tile /ˈvɜːsətaɪl, AM -təl/

ADJECTIVE A tool, machine, or material that is **versatile** can be used for many different purposes. ○ *Never before has computing been so versatile.* ○ *The most versatile domesticated plant is the coconut palm.*

▶ SYNONYMS: adaptable, flexible

ver|sa|til|ity /ˌvɜːsəˈtɪlɪti/

UNCOUNTABLE NOUN ○ [+ of] *the versatility of the software*

▸ COLLOCATIONS:
the versatility **of** something
offer/provide versatility
great versatility

▸ SYNONYMS: adaptability, flexibility

---

verse /vɜːs/   `ARTS` `LITERATURE`

UNCOUNTABLE NOUN **Verse** is writing arranged in lines which have rhythm and which often rhyme at the end. ○ *a slim volume of verse* ○ *Shakespearian blank verse*

▸ COLLOCATIONS:
blank/rhymed/rhyming verse
write/compose/recite verse

▸ SYNONYM: poetry

▸ RELATED WORD: prose

---

ver|sion /ˈvɜːʃən, -ʒən/ (versions)   `ACADEMIC WORD`

NOUN A **version of** something is a particular form of it in which some details are different from earlier or later forms. ○ [+ of] *an updated version of his book* ○ [+ of] *the film version of Tess of the d'Urbervilles*

▸ COLLOCATIONS:
a version **of** something
a **new/updated/modern/revised/edited** version
a **handheld/film/stage** version
the **original** version
release/launch/produce a version

---

ver|sus /ˈvɜːsəs/

PREPOSITION You use **versus** to indicate that two figures, ideas, or choices are opposed. The abbreviation **vs.** is used in written notes. ○ *Only 18.8% of the class of 1982 had some kind of diploma four years after high school, versus 45% of the class of 1972.* ○ *bottle-feeding versus breastfeeding*

▸ SYNONYMS: as opposed to, compared with

---

ver|ti|cal /ˈvɜːtɪkəl/

ADJECTIVE Something that is **vertical** stands or points straight up. ○ *The price variable is shown on the vertical axis, with quantity demanded on the horizontal axis.* ○ *The gadget can be attached to any vertical or near vertical surface.*

→ see note at **axis**

▶ **COLLOCATIONS:**
a vertical **axis/cliff/drop/shaft**
almost/nearly vertical

▶ **RELATED WORDS:** horizontal, diagonal

ver|ti|cal|ly /ˈvɜːtɪkli/

ADVERB ○ *Cut each bulb in half vertically.* ○ *Discs should be stored vertically.*

▶ **COLLOCATIONS:**
stack/align/store/hang/arrange *something* vertically
rise/ascend/descend/dive vertically

▶ **SYNONYM:** upwards

▶ **RELATED WORD:** horizontally

via /vaɪə, ˈviːə/ `ACADEMIC WORD`

1 PREPOSITION If someone or something goes somewhere **via** a particular place, they go through that place on the way to their destination. ○ *In vertebrates food passes into the stomach from the mouth via the oesophagus.* ○ *Mr Baker will return home via Britain and France.*

2 PREPOSITION If you do something **via** a particular means or person, you do it by making use of that means or person. ○ *The technology to allow relief workers to contact the outside world via satellite already exists.* ○ *Translators can now work from home, via electronic mail systems.*

▶ **COLLOCATIONS:**
via **satellite/email/text message**
via the **internet/telephone**

▶ **SYNONYMS:** by way of, through

view|point /ˈvjuːpɔɪnt/ (viewpoints)

NOUN Someone's **viewpoint** is the way that they think about things in general, or the way they think about a particular thing. ○ *The novel is shown from the girl's viewpoint.* ○ *to reconcile diverse viewpoints about an issue*

▶ **COLLOCATIONS:**
differing/conflicting/diverse viewpoints
a **moral/alternative/objective** viewpoint
express/represent/share/oppose a viewpoint

▶ **SYNONYMS:** point of view, stance

vir|tual /ˈvɜːtʃʊəl/ `ACADEMIC WORD`

1 ADJECTIVE You can use **virtual** to indicate that something is so nearly true that for most purposes it can be regarded as true. ○ *the virtual disappearance of marriage as an institution among poor black people* ○ *conditions of virtual slavery*

▶ COLLOCATIONS:
a virtual **certainty/impossibility**
a virtual **prisoner/standstill/monopoly**
the virtual **disappearance/elimination** of *something*

▶ SYNONYM: near

2 ADJECTIVE Virtual objects and activities are generated by a computer to simulate real objects and activities. ○ *software that generates virtual environments of war zones* ○ *a virtual shopping centre*

▶ COLLOCATIONS:
virtual **reality**
a virtual **environment/world/community/tour/network**

▶ SYNONYMS: computerized, online

vir|tu|al|ly /ˈvɜːtʃʊəli/

ADVERB You can use **virtually** to indicate that something is so nearly true that for most purposes it can be regarded as true. ○ *Virtually all of the symptoms of schizophrenia may be classified as psychotic.* ○ *It would have been virtually impossible to research all the information.*

▶ COLLOCATIONS:
virtually **impossible/unknown/unlimited/all**
virtually **identical/unchanged/indistinguishable**
virtually **assure/guarantee**

▶ SYNONYMS: almost, nearly, essentially

vi|rus /ˈvaɪərəs/ (viruses)   MEDICINE IT

1 NOUN A **virus** is a kind of germ that can cause disease. ○ *There are many different strains of flu virus.* ○ *HIV, the virus believed to cause AIDS*

▶ COLLOCATIONS:
have/contract/catch a virus
transmit/spread/carry a virus
a **flu/influenza/polio/stomach/respiratory** virus
a **deadly/infectious** virus
a virus **spreads/mutates**
a virus **causes/infects** *something*

▶ SYNONYMS: illness, disease, infection

▶ RELATED WORD: bacterium

2 NOUN In computer technology, a **virus** is a program that introduces itself into a system, altering or destroying the information stored in the system. ○ *By the time a virus is detected it will almost certainly have infected other disks.*

▶ COLLOCATIONS:
create/spread/detect/remove a virus

a **computer** virus
a virus **causes/infects/attacks** something

vi|ral /ˈvaɪərəl/

ADJECTIVE A **viral** disease or infection is caused by a virus. ○ *a 65-year-old patient suffering from severe viral pneumonia*

▶ **COLLOCATIONS:**
a viral **infection/illness/outbreak**
viral **pneumonia/meningitis**

▶ **RELATED WORD:** bacterial

---

vis|ible /ˈvɪzɪbəl/ `ACADEMIC WORD`

1 ADJECTIVE If something is **visible**, it can be seen. ○ *The warning lights were clearly visible.* ○ [+ to] *They found a bacterium visible to the human eye.*

2 ADJECTIVE You use **visible** to describe something or someone that people notice or recognize. ○ *The most visible sign of the intensity of the crisis is unemployment.* ○ *The cabinet is a highly visible symbol of the executive branch of the United States government.*

▶ **COLLOCATIONS:**
visible **to/from** something
barely/plainly/clearly/highly/very visible
less/more/still visible
a visible **sign/symbol/reminder/presence/manifestation**
make something visible

▶ **SYNONYMS:** clear, evident, noticeable
▶ **ANTONYMS:** invisible, hidden
▶ **RELATED WORDS:** audible, tangible

vis|ibly /ˈvɪzɪbli/

ADVERB ○ *Persons dying from cancer or other degenerative disorders grow thin and visibly waste away.* ○ *They emerged visibly distressed and weeping.*

▶ **COLLOCATION:** visibly **distressed/upset/angry/shaken**
▶ **SYNONYMS:** evidently, noticeably

---

vi|sion /ˈvɪʒən/ `ACADEMIC WORD` `MEDICINE` `BIOLOGY`

1 UNCOUNTABLE NOUN Your **vision** is your ability to see clearly with your eyes. ○ *It causes blindness or serious loss of vision.*

2 UNCOUNTABLE NOUN Your **vision** is everything that you can see from a particular place or position. ○ *Your total field of vision is more than 220°.* ○ *I saw other indistinct shapes that stayed out of vision.*

▶ **COLLOCATIONS:**
clear/blurred/20-20 vision
peripheral/double/tunnel/X-ray/night vision
loss of vision
impair/obstruct/obscure vision
▶ **PHRASE:** one's field of vision
▶ **SYNONYMS:** sight, eyesight, view
▶ **ANTONYM:** blindness

---

vis|ual /ˈvɪʒʊəl/

ACADEMIC WORD

ADJECTIVE Visual means relating to sight, or to things that you can see.
  ○ *the graphic visual depiction of violence* ○ *music, film, dance, and the visual arts*
  ○ *people with visual impairment*
  ▶ **COLLOCATIONS:**
  visual **arts/information/imagery**
  visual **perception/acuity/impairment**
  a visual **memory/cue**

visu|al|ly /ˈvɪʒʊəli/

ADVERB ○ *visually impaired boys and girls* ○ *These creatures are visually spectacular.*
  ▶ **COLLOCATIONS:**
  visually **impaired**
  visually **arresting/stunning/striking/appealing**

---

vi|tal /ˈvaɪtəl/

ADJECTIVE If you say that something is **vital**, you mean that it is necessary or
very important. ○ [+ to] *The port is vital to supply relief to millions of drought
victims.* ○ *It is vital that records are kept.*
  ▶ **COLLOCATIONS:**
  vital **to/for** *something*
  vital **information**
  a vital **role/service/contribution**
  a vital **part/component/element/ingredient/link/organ**
  strategically/politically/economically/absolutely vital
  ▶ **PHRASE:** of vital importance
  ▶ **SYNONYMS:** crucial, essential
  ▶ **ANTONYMS:** unimportant, inessential

vi|tal|ly /ˈvaɪtəli/

ADVERB ○ *Public attitudes are vitally important to governmental effectiveness.*
  ▶ **SYNONYMS:** extremely, utterly

volt /vəʊlt/ (volts) ENGINEERING PHYSICS

NOUN A **volt** is a unit used to measure the force of an electric current. The abbreviation **V** is often used in written notes. ○ *The power lines were carrying about 15,000 volts of electricity.* ○ *a 24 volt battery*

▶ **RELATED WORD:** watt

volt|age /'vəʊltɪdʒ/ (voltages)

NOUN The **voltage** of an electrical current is its force measured in volts. ○ *The systems are getting smaller and using lower voltages.* ○ *high-voltage power lines*

▶ **COLLOCATIONS:**
apply/generate/measure/use voltage
high/low voltage

▶ **SYNONYMS:** electricity, current

vol|ume /'vɒljuːm/ (volumes) ACADEMIC WORD

1 NOUN The **volume of** something is the amount of it that there is. ○ [+ *of*] *Senior officials will be discussing how the volume of sales might be reduced.* ○ [+ *of*] *the sheer volume of traffic and accidents*

▶ **COLLOCATIONS:**
the volume **of** *something*
the volume of **traffic/shares/data**
export/sales/traffic volume
the **average/total/estimated** volume
the **sheer/huge/high** volume
increase/reduce volume

▶ **SYNONYM:** amount

2 NOUN The **volume** of an object is the amount of space that it contains or occupies. ○ *When egg whites are beaten they can rise to seven or eight times their original volume.*

▶ **SYNONYM:** capacity
▶ **RELATED WORD:** area

3 NOUN A **volume** is one book or journal in a series of books or journals. The abbreviation **vol.** is used in written notes and bibliographies. ○ [+ *of*] *the first volume of his autobiography* ○ [+ *of*] *The article appeared in volume 41 of the journal Communication Education.*

→ see note at **edit**
▶ **COLLOCATION:** a volume **of** *something*

vol|un|tary /ˈvɒləntri, AM -teri/ ·ACADEMIC WORD·

1 ADJECTIVE Voluntary actions or activities are done because someone chooses to do them and not because they have been forced to do them. ○ *The scheme, due to begin next month, will be voluntary.*

▸ **COLLOCATIONS:**
voluntary **redundancy/retirement/euthanasia**
a voluntary **contribution/action/programme/test/course**

▸ **SYNONYM:** optional

▸ **ANTONYMS:** compulsory, mandatory

2 ADJECTIVE Voluntary work is done by people who are not paid for it, but who do it because they want to do it. ○ *charities and voluntary organizations* ○ *He'd been working at the local hostel for the homeless on a voluntary basis.*

▸ **COLLOCATIONS:**
a voluntary **organization/group**
voluntary **work**
the voluntary **sector**

▸ **PHRASE:** on a voluntary basis

▸ **SYNONYM:** charitable

▸ **ANTONYM:** paid

vol|un|tar|ily /ˈvɒləntrəli, AM -terɪli/

ADVERB ○ *The company wanted staff to leave voluntarily.*

▸ **COLLOCATIONS:**
resign/leave/surrender voluntarily
voluntarily **withdraw/recall** *something*

vol|un|teer /ˌvɒlənˈtɪə/ (volunteers, volunteering, volunteered)

1 NOUN A **volunteer** is someone who does work without being paid for it, because they want to do it. ○ *Volunteers are needed to help visit elderly people's homes.*

▸ **COLLOCATIONS:**
recruit/need/seek volunteers
a **trained/unpaid/dedicated/community** volunteer
a volunteer **firefighter/helper/organization**
volunteer **work**

2 VERB If you **volunteer to** do something, you offer to do it without being forced to do it. ○ [+ to-inf] *the number of men volunteering to become sperm donors* ○ [+ for] *The majority of people will volunteer for early retirement if the financial terms are acceptable.* ○ [+ as] *She volunteered as a nurse in a soldiers' rest-home.*

▶ **COLLOCATIONS:**
volunteer **for/as** *something*
volunteer for a **task/job/assignment**
volunteer to **help/join** *something*
volunteer *one's* **services**

vul|ner|able /ˈvʌlnərəbəl/

1 ADJECTIVE Someone who is **vulnerable** is weak and without protection, with the result that they are easily hurt physically or emotionally. ○ *Old people are particularly vulnerable members of our society.*

2 ADJECTIVE If someone or something is **vulnerable to** something, they have some weakness or disadvantage which makes them more likely to be harmed or affected by that thing. ○ [+ to] *People with high blood pressure are especially vulnerable to diabetes.*

▶ **COLLOCATIONS:**
vulnerable **to** *something*
vulnerable to **attack/damage/fire**
vulnerable **children/women/people**
a vulnerable **position**
especially/highly/increasingly vulnerable
become/remain vulnerable

▶ **SYNONYMS:** weak, prone, susceptible, exposed
▶ **ANTONYMS:** protected, strong

vul|ner|abil|ity /ˌvʌlnərəˈbɪlɪti/ **(vulnerabilities)**

NOUN ○ *hackers attempting to exploit vulnerabilities in Microsoft products* ○ [+ to] *Taking long-term courses of certain medicines may increase vulnerability to infection.*

▶ **COLLOCATIONS:**
vulnerability **to** *something*
security/genetic/emotional vulnerability
exploit vulnerability

▶ **SYNONYMS:** weakness, susceptibility, exposure
▶ **ANTONYM:** strength

v

Ww

wave /weɪv/ (waves)

1 NOUN A **wave** is a sudden increase in heat or energy that spreads out from an earthquake or explosion. ○ [+ of] *The shock waves of the earthquake were felt in Teheran.* ○ *the seismic waves generated by natural earthquakes*

▸ **COLLOCATIONS:**
a wave **of/from** *something*
a wave of/from an **earthquake/explosion**
a **shock/seismic/blast** wave

2 NOUN Waves are the form in which things such as sound, light, and radio signals travel. ○ *Sound waves, light waves, and radio waves have a certain frequency, or number of waves per second.* ○ *the wave amplitude of light*

▸ **COLLOCATIONS:**
a **sound/radio/light/high-frequency** wave
wave **amplitude/frequency**
emit/send/detect a wave

wel|fare /ˈwelfeə/

1 UNCOUNTABLE NOUN The **welfare** of a person or group is their health, comfort, and happiness. ○ *For reasons of animal welfare, farmers can no longer keep pigs confined in stalls.* ○ [+ of] *He was the head of a charity for the welfare of children.*

▸ **COLLOCATIONS:**
the welfare **of** *someone/something*
the welfare of **animals/children**
animal/child/social/public welfare
endanger/promote welfare
▸ **PHRASE:** health and welfare
▸ **SYNONYM:** well-being

2 ADJECTIVE Welfare services are provided to help with people's living conditions and financial problems. ○ *Child welfare services are well established and comprehensive.* ○ *He has urged complete reform of the welfare system.*

▸ **COLLOCATIONS:**
a welfare **state/system/service/programme**
welfare **benefits/reform**
▸ **SYNONYM:** social

where|as /weərˈæz/ ACADEMIC WORD

CONJUNCTION You use **whereas** to introduce a comment which contrasts with what is said in the main clause. ○ *Pensions are linked to inflation, whereas they should be linked to the cost of living.* ○ *Whereas the population of working age increased by 1 million between 1981 and 1986, today it is barely growing.*
▶ **SYNONYM:** while

while /waɪl/

1 CONJUNCTION You use **while** to introduce a clause which contrasts with the other part of the sentence. ○ *The first two services are free, while the third costs £35.00.* ○ *While chronic anger increases the risk of heart disease in men, for women it is anxiety that poses this risk.*
▶ **SYNONYM:** whereas

2 CONJUNCTION You use **while** in a clause to say that although something is the case, it does not affect the truth of the other part of the sentence. ○ *While the numbers of such developments are relatively small, the potential market is large.* ○ *While details may vary, the essence remains the same.*
▶ **SYNONYM:** although

whilst /waɪlst/

CONJUNCTION **Whilst** means the same as **while**. It is used mainly in British English in formal and literary contexts. ○ *Whilst droughts are not uncommon in many parts of the country, the coastal region remains humid throughout the year.* ○ *Whilst every care has been taken to ensure accuracy, the publishers cannot accept legal responsibility for any problems that arise.*
▶ **SYNONYMS:** whereas, although

wide|spread /ˈwaɪdspred/ ACADEMIC WORD

ADJECTIVE Something that is **widespread** exists or happens over a large area, or to a great extent. ○ *There is widespread support for the new proposals.* ○ *Food shortages are widespread.*
▶ **COLLOCATIONS:**
  widespread **condemnation/criticism/opposition**
  widespread **support/acceptance/agreement**
  widespread **concern/fear/interest/use**
  a widespread **belief/feeling/view/problem**
  widespread **looting/flooding/fraud/damage**
▶ **SYNONYM:** extensive
▶ **ANTONYM:** limited

W

with|draw /wɪð'drɔː/

(withdraws, withdrawing, withdrew, withdrawn)

1 VERB If you **withdraw** something, you remove it or take it away. [FORMAL] ○ *The university rarely withdraws offers of admission.* ○ *government plans to withdraw financial support*

2 VERB If you **withdraw from** an activity or organization, you stop taking part in it. ○ [+ from] *The African National Congress threatened to withdraw from the talks.* ○ [+ from] *The team has withdrawn from the tournament due to high cost of travel.*

▶ COLLOCATIONS:
withdraw *something* **from** *something*
withdraw from a **treaty/tournament/race**
withdraw from **participation/talks**
withdraw **support/funding**
withdraw a **request/offer**
hastily/gradually/temporarily withdraw

▶ SYNONYM: remove

with|draw|al /wɪð'drɔːəl/ (withdrawals)

1 NOUN The **withdrawal of** something is the act or process of removing it, or ending it. [FORMAL] ○ [+ of] *If you experience any unusual symptoms after withdrawal of the treatment then contact your doctor.*

2 UNCOUNTABLE NOUN Someone's **withdrawal from** an activity or an organization is their decision to stop taking part in it. ○ *his withdrawal from government in 1946*

▶ COLLOCATIONS:
withdrawal **of** *something*
withdrawal of **support**

▶ SYNONYM: removal

---

work|force /'wɜːkfɔːs/ (workforces) `BUSINESS`

1 NOUN The **workforce** is the total number of people in a country or region who are physically able to do a job and are available for work. ○ *a country where half the workforce is unemployed* ○ *large numbers of women entering the workforce*

2 NOUN The **workforce** is the total number of people who are employed by a particular company. ○ *an employer of a very large workforce* ○ *SkyWest confirmed they had made 6 per cent of their workforce redundant.* ○ *44 % of the workforce is female.*

w

▶ **COLLOCATIONS:**
  x% **of** the workforce
  a **skilled/total/ageing/large** workforce
  enter/join/re-enter/train the workforce
▶ **SYNONYMS:** staff, personnel

---

work|place /ˈwɜːkpleɪs/ **(workplaces)** also **work place**   `BUSINESS`

NOUN Your **workplace** is the place where you work. ○ *the difficulties facing women in the workplace* ○ *Workplace canteens are offering healthier foods than ever before.*

▶ **COLLOCATIONS:**
  in the workplace
  workplace **safety/agreements**
  a workplace **crèche/nursery/canteen**
  a **modern/family-friendly/safe** workplace

W

XYZ

zone /zəʊn/ (zones)

NOUN A **zone** is an area that has particular features or characteristics. ○ *Many people have stayed behind in the potential war zone.* ○ *The area has been declared a disaster zone.* ○ *travellers flying across several time zones*

▶ **COLLOCATIONS:**
  a **war/disaster/danger** zone
  a **time** zone
  a **no-fly/no-go/exclusion** zone
  a **demilitarized/neutral/military/industrial** zone
  a **coastal** zone
  declare/enforce/establish/create/enter/patrol a zone

▶ **SYNONYMS:** area, region, section, territory